Acquisitions and Corporate Strategy

Corporate restructuring (acquisitions, alliances, and divestment) is a visible form of corporate strategy. For example, firm investments in buying and selling assets exceed the gross domestic product of the majority of nations. Most research in this area examines acquisitions, but informing practice is limited by examining acquisitions in isolation or using a narrow focus. For example, a lingering problem is that average acquisition performance is consistently around zero, suggesting a need to identify practically relevant relationships.

In addressing this need, research on three fundamental questions is covered: (1) How do acquisitions relate to other corporate strategy options? (2) What helps to predict acquisition performance? and (3) What are persistent acquisition research issues? The first question is intended to overcome a research limitation that acquisitions are often examined independent of other corporate strategies, including internal development, alliances, and divestment. The second question addresses novel relationships associated with the primary focus of acquisition research in examining what drives acquisition performance. The third question reflects on the underlying complexity of the phenomenon that makes it a challenge to identify what drives acquisition performance. Overall, the intent of presenting ideas on these fundamental questions is to illustrate promising areas for future research.

This book presents the latest state of knowledge on the topic and will be of interest to researchers, academics, and advanced students in the fields of strategic management, international business, and organizational studies.

David R. King is the Higdon Professor of Management at Florida State University, USA.

Routledge Research in Strategic Management

This series explores, develops and critiques the numerous models and frameworks designed to assist in strategic decision making in internal and external environments. It publishes scholarly research in all methodologies and perspectives that comprise the discipline, and welcomes diverse multi-disciplinary research methods, including qualitative and quantitative studies, and conceptual and computational models. It also welcomes the practical application of the strategic management process to a business world inspired by new economic paradigms.

1. **Strategic Analysis: Processes and Tools**
   Andrea Beretta Zanoni

2. **Strategic Management and the Circular Economy**
   Marcello Tonelli and Nicoló Cristoni

3. **Strategic and Innovative Pricing: Price Models for a Digital Economy**
   Mathias Cöster, Einar Iveroth, Nils-Göran Olve, Carl-Johan Petri and Alf Westelius

4. **Competitive International Strategy: Key Implementation Issues**
   Edited by Anders Pehrsson

5. **Ambidextrous Strategy: Antecedents, Strategic Choices, and Performance**
   Agnieszka Zakrzewska-Bielawska

6. **Strategic Management During a Pandemic**
   Edited by Vikas Kumar and Gaurav Gupta

7. **Acquisitions and Corporate Strategy: Alliances, Performance, and Divestment**
   Edited by David R. King

Acquisitions and Corporate Strategy
Alliances, Performance, and Divestment

Edited by David R. King

NEW YORK AND LONDON

First published 2022
by Routledge
605 Third Avenue, New York, NY 10158

and by Routledge
4 Park Square, Milton Park, Abingdon, Oxon, OX14 4RN

Routledge is an imprint of the Taylor & Francis Group, an informa business

© 2022 selection and editorial matter, David R. King; individual chapters, the contributors

The right of David R. King to be identified as the author of the editorial material, and of the authors for their individual chapters, has been asserted in accordance with sections 77 and 78 of the Copyright, Designs and Patents Act 1988.

All rights reserved. No part of this book may be reprinted or reproduced or utilised in any form or by any electronic, mechanical, or other means, now known or hereafter invented, including photocopying and recording, or in any information storage or retrieval system, without permission in writing from the publishers.

Trademark notice: Product or corporate names may be trademarks or registered trademarks, and are used only for identification and explanation without intent to infringe.

Library of Congress Cataloging-in-Publication Data
A catalog record for this title has been requested

ISBN: 978-1-032-03636-6 (hbk)
ISBN: 978-1-032-03637-3 (pbk)
ISBN: 978-1-003-18830-8 (ebk)

DOI: 10.4324/9781003188308

Typeset in Sabon
by Newgen Publishing UK

Contents

Acknowledgments	vii
List of illustrations	viii
About the contributors	x

Reflection on corporate restructuring research 1
DAVID R. KING

SECTION I
**How do acquisitions relate to other corporate
strategy options?** 9
DAVID R. KING

1 Alliances as precursors to an acquisition 13
ELIO SHIJAKU, DAVID R. KING, AND AINHOA URTASUN

2 Review of divestment research 26
SINA AMIRI, DAVID R. KING, AND SAMUEL M. DEMARIE

3 What follows what? Sequences and combinations of
acquisitions and divestitures 48
OLEKSANDRA KOCHURA, NICOLA MIRC, AND
DENIS LACOSTE

4 Cross-border acquisition and greenfield investment:
Substitutes or complements? 76
NAN ZHANG AND JOSEPH A. CLOUGHERTY

vi *Contents*

SECTION II
What helps to predict acquisition performance?   103
DAVID R. KING

5 Merging dynamic capabilities and acquisition process
research: Toward an integrative theoretical framework   107
SVANTE SCHRIBER

6 Capability transfer: Improved performance from
acquiring polluting targets   128
PANKAJ C. PATEL AND DAVID R. KING

7 Cross-border acquisition performance insights from
predictive modeling   157
CAMILLA JENSEN, PETER ZÁMBORSKÝ, AND DAVID R. KING

SECTION III
What are persistent acquisition research issues?   177
DAVID R. KING

8 A reconceptualization: The mis(measurement) of
acquisition performance ten years later   179
OLIMPIA MEGLIO

9 Improving acquisition research methods: Addressing
endogeneity   202
GONZALO MOLINA-SIEIRO

10 Cultural dynamics in acquisitions   225
SATU TEERIKANGAS AND MELANIE HASSETT

Predictions for corporate restructuring research   251
DAVID R. KING

Index   257

Acknowledgments

A book combining expertise on topics related to corporate restructuring inevitably involves a community effort. This includes people not directly involved as prior research offers inspiration for additional inquiry. As a result, any acknowledgment of those influencing this book is inherently incomplete. Still, I would like to thank the publisher for taking on the project. Additionally, I would like to thank specific contributions by a few people beyond contributing chapters. Specifically, Olimpia Meglio helped serve as editor for Chapter 2. Additionally, Florian Bauer, Olimpia Meglio, Gonzalo Molina-Sieiro, and Svante Schriber served as reviewers of chapters. All chapters were edited, but Chapters 2, 4, and 5 were also blind reviewed.

Illustrations

Figures

1.1	Precursors influencing acquisition activity	14
2.1	Overview of divestment research	28
5.1	Framework combining acquisition process and dynamic capabilities influence on firm adaptation	111
6.1	Conceptual framework on influence of green capabilities	131
7.1	Representative decision tree resulting from predictive modeling	164
7.2	Variable importance plot for categorical T-statistic predictive model	164
9.1	Collider variables that introduce bias as a control	205
9.2	Collider bias from an endogenous control	205
9.3	Excluding confounder variables introduces bias	206
9.4	Instrumental variable estimation	214
9.5	Exclusion restriction violation	216
9.6	Exogeneity assumption violation	217
10.1	Factors affecting cultural change following acquisitions	235
10.2	Working across national cultures in acquisitions	238

Tables

I.1	Focus of research by acquisition phase	2
1.1	Variable means, standard deviation, and correlations	19
1.2	Results for predicting alliances and acquisitions	20
3.1	Different potential perspectives to study corporate restructuring sequences	51
3.2	Four scenarios of acquisition and divestiture sequence	55
4.1	Descriptive statistics and pairwise correlations	87
4.2	Tobit estimation results for two regression equations	91
II.1	Measures of acquisition performance	104
6.1	Control variables	142
6.2	Results of analysis	144
7.1	Constructs underlying study variables	160

7.2	Transforming the effect size (T-stat for cultural distance) into a categorical variable	161
7.3	Linear prediction modeling results with CBA performance using Z-scores	162
10.1	Synthesis of the levels of analysis in the study of cultural challenges in acquisitions	239

About the contributors

Sina Amiri is an assistant professor of Management at the J. Whitney Bunting College of Business, Georgia College and State University. His primary research interests are corporate divestiture and strategic restructuring. Sina earned a PhD in Strategic Management from Iowa State University.

Joseph A. Clougherty, PhD University of Southern California, is Professor of Business Administration at the University of Illinois at Urbana-Champaign. Much of his research considers the antecedents and consequences of acquisition activity while employing an interdisciplinary approach (combining management, industrial organization, and political economy) that is international in scope.

Samuel M. DeMarie is an associate professor of Management at the Ivy College of Business, Iowa State University. Sam's research interests are business strategy, large-scale change initiatives, and leadership. Sam earned a PhD in Strategic Management from Arizona State University.

Melanie Hassett is a lecturer in International Business at Sheffield University Management School in the UK, and a Senior Fellow at Turku School of Economics, University of Turku, Finland. Her areas of expertise include internationalization strategies, cross-border acquisitions, and research methods. Her current research focuses on emotions and the sociocultural dynamics in cross-border mergers and acquisitions, as well as time in international business research.

Camilla Jensen has a background in cultural studies and a PhD in Economics from SDU, Denmark. She is an associate professor in Economics at Roskilde University, Denmark and a Senior Research Fellow in International Trade at the UK Trade Policy Observatory at the University of Sussex Business School in Brighton. Her research is in international trade, focusing on multinational firms, technology transfer, and trade.

David R. King received his PhD from Indiana University, and he is the Higdon Professor of Management at Florida State University. His primary research interest is acquisition activity and performance.

About the contributors xi

Oleksandra Kochura is currently a PhD candidate at TBS Education and the University of Toulouse Capitole. Her doctoral research interests lie in the corporate divestiture process and its various modes of implementation. She is also studying the relation between corporate divestitures and other corporate development portfolio alternatives such as acquisitions and interorganizational relationships.

Denis Lacoste is Professor of Strategic Management at TBS Education. He has been a consultant and visiting professor at several universities in Europe, Latin America, and the United States. His research focuses on corporate strategies, international business, and service management. He has published numerous articles, books, and case studies on these topics.

Olimpia Meglio, PhD in Business Administration, is currently Associate Professor of Corporate Strategy at the University of Sannio. Her research interests revolve around corporate strategies, family business, and process research. Her works are regularly presented at international venues and published in leading academic journals such as the *Journal of Management Studies*, *Human Resource Management*, *Long Range Planning*, *Journal of Business Research*, and *R&D Management*.

Nicola Mirc is Professor of Strategic Management at TSM (Toulouse School of Management, University of Toulouse, CNRS, France). Nicola Mirc studies acquisitions, particularly the organizational challenges of synergy creation in innovative and knowledge-intensive sectors. She has published research in various international journals and book series on this topic.

Gonzalo Molina-Sieiro is an assistant professor of Strategy at Pontificia Universidad Católica de Chile. He received his PhD from Florida State University, and his research interests are international business strategy, including acquisitions. In particular, his research focuses on how contextual factors influence firm-level strategy.

Pankaj C. Patel is a professor of Management at Villanova University. His research interests are in entrepreneurship and innovation. He received his PhD from the University of Louisville.

Svante Schriber is a professor of Management at Stockholm Business School. He earned his PhD from the Stockholm School of Economics after a career as management consultant. His research covers strategic management, including how firms adjust to dynamic environment shifts using acquisitions and international business.

Elio Shijaku received his PhD from Autonomous University of Barcelona. He is currently Assistant Professor at University of Barcelona. His primary research interest is strategic alliances and performance feedback.

xii *About the contributors*

Satu Teerikangas is Professor of Management and Organization at University of Turku, Finland, and Honorary Professor at University College London. Her research centers on the management of acquisitions, including their cultural dynamics, as well as the change required toward securing ecologically sustainable futures. She is editor of the *Handbook of Mergers and Acquisitions* published by Oxford University Press.

Ainhoa Urtasun has a PhD in Economics from Universidad Carlos III de Madrid. She is an associate professor at Universidad Pública de Navarra. Data analysis is her main research interest.

Peter Zámborský is a senior lecturer in Management and International Business at the University of Auckland Business School in New Zealand. He earned his PhD from Brandeis University's International Business School, and his research focuses on foreign direct investment, foreign market entry modes, and global innovation strategy.

Nan Zhang has a PhD from University of Illinois at Urbana-Champaign, and she is Assistant Professor of Management in the College of Business Administration at California State University, Stanislaus. Her research interests encompass international business and strategic management while focusing on firm internationalization activities and strategic responses to policy and institutional factors.

Reflection on corporate restructuring research

David R. King

Introduction

Research on corporate restructuring began a century ago (Dewing, 1921), and research interest on related topics has risen with the pervasiveness of acquisitions, alliances, and divestment. Corporate restructuring is a complex event that spans different phases and impacts multiple different stakeholders. For acquisitions, processes associated with selection, completion, and integration are generally examined separately (Graebner, Heimeriks, Huy, & Vaara, 2017; King, Wang, Samimi, & Cortes, 2021; Welch, Pavićević, Keil, & Laamanen, 2020). Different disciplines have also focused on different theories and variables (Bauer & Matzler, 2014; King, Bauer, & Schriber, 2018). For example, a variable unique to management research is whether an acquirer and target operate in related industries (Wan, Hoskisson, Short, & Yiu, 2011). The combined result is research fragmentation that limits aggregating knowledge (King et al., 2021).

A less recognized concern is that research has largely focused on well-trodden paths where data are available and associated firm decisions are visible. For example, research has traditionally emphasized deal characteristics at acquisition completion and stock market announcement returns (Meglio & Risberg, 2010) that are imperfect predictors of long-term acquisition performance (Cording, Chrismann & Weigelt, 2010; King, Slotegraaf, & Kesner, 2008; Papadakis & Thanos, 2010). As a result, fundamental questions on acquisition activity and performance remain unexamined. The intent behind this book is to showcase promising areas of research that can advance our knowledge of corporate restructuring. The foundation is provided by acquisition research that is more common and where I have focused my research efforts.

Evolution of acquisition research

To better understand the status of where we are and where we can go, I summarize books, reviews, and meta-analysis associated with improving my understanding of acquisitions. While inherently incomplete, the identified

DOI: 10.4324/9781003188308-1

2 David R. King

Table I.1 Focus of research by acquisition phase

Selection	Completion	Integration
Welch, Pavićević, Keil & Laamanen (2020)	Datta, Pinches & Narayanan (1992); Sirower (1997); King, Dalton, Daily & Covin (2004); Homberg, Rost & Ostrloh (2009); Campbell, Sirmon & Schijven (2016); Hernandez & Menon (2019); Maas, Heugens & Reus (2019)	
	Ravenscraft & Scherer (1987); Stahl & Voigt (2008); Haleblian, Dever, McNamara, Carpenter & Davidson (2009); King, Wang, Samimi & Cortes (2021)	
	Hitt, Harrison & Ireland (2001); King, Bauer & Schriber (2018)	

studies present important milestones in developing my understanding of acquisitions. Even a limited review shows that research largely focuses on limited aspects of the acquisition process (see Table I.1). Specifically, the majority of research has focused on deal characteristics at acquisition completion with limited consideration of multiple phases of acquisitions, or relationships between acquisitions and other strategic activities by firms.

A book by Ravenscraft and Scherer (1987) provides a good summary of acquisition mechanics with descriptions of the difference between purchase and pooling of interests accounting.[1] Due to acquisitions increasing the assets of a company, they identify that return on assets (ROA) presents a negatively biased measure of acquisition performance. Despite this recognition, ROA continues to be frequently used in management research. They also describe the Federal Trade Commission (FTC) database that covered US manufacturing firms from 1974 to 1977 that was predominantly used in acquisition research published before 1990. Ravenscraft and Scherer (1987) also note that acquisitions and divestments are related with 40 percent of acquisitions later being divested. Still, research infrequently examines acquisitions and divestment together, and this is the focus of Chapter 3 by Kochura, Mirc, and Lacoste.

Haspeslagh and Jemison (1991) is a book based on eight case studies that examined how target firms are integrated into an acquirer that is associated with an increase in management research on acquisitions (Ferreira et al., 2014). The book develops a 2×2 matrix based on tension between strategic interdependence and need for autonomy to identify four approaches to acquisition integration: preservation, symbiosis, absorption, and holding. The authors also identify acquisitions as offering the

---

1 In 2001, the Financial Accounting Standards Board (FASB) restricted firms to using purchase accounting (Moehrle and Reynolds-Moehrle, 2001).

Reflection on corporate restructuring 3

opportunity for managers to renew an organization, as well as greater speed and control than internal development and alliances, respectively. While research examining the relationship acquisitions have with internal development and alliances is infrequent, it is the focus of Chapter 1 by Shijaku, King, and Urtasun.

The first meta-analysis aggregation acquisition research was performed by Datta, Pinches, and Narayanan (1992). The meta-analysis aggregated research results from 41 studies and the impact of regulatory changes, number of bidders, type of transaction (tender offer/merger), method of payment (cash/stock), and type of acquisition (conglomerate/non-conglomerate), a classification from the FTC database. Of studied variables, they find that stock payment has a negative and significant impact on acquirer firm wealth effects. Wealth effects involved stock market announcement returns aggregated from studies using event windows within a 21-day period (−10, +10).

A book by Mark Sirower (1997) developed the impact of the premium paid for a target firm that had not been widely considered in management research. He outlines how the premium paid is a major predictor in the performance of acquisitions with higher premiums associated with lower acquisition performance at acquisition announcement for multiple event windows.

Hitt, Harrison, and Ireland (2001) authored a book on acquisitions that identifies them as one of the most important corporate strategy tools. The book summarizes different aspects of acquisitions, including due diligence, financing, learning from acquisition experience, and cross-border acquisitions (CBA), to offer insights for how to create value from acquisitions. The book identifies the importance of complementary resources in acquisitions and an impact of acquisitions on firm innovation.

King, Dalton, Daily, and Covin (2004) provide a second meta-analysis of acquisition research that summarized results from 93 studies for stock market and accounting measures of performance. While they did not find research aggregated on four variables (conglomerate, relatedness, method of payment, acquisition experience) predicted acquisition performance, they found that acquisitions had a slightly negative impact on firm performance and that there was significant unexplained variance in acquisition performance.

Stahl and Voigt (2008) examine CBA, a specific subset of deals, in a meta-analysis summarizing the impact of cultural differences on acquisition performance. Based on 46 studies on the impact of cultural differences, the expectation that cultural distance represents an obstacle received inconclusive support for stock market and accounting measures of performance. This is also the first meta-analysis to summarize research on acquisition integration.

Haleblian, Dever, McNamara, Carpenter, and Davidson (2009) review acquisition research to identify research needs. They document a consistent research interest in acquisitions and highlight human aspects of

4 *David R. King*

acquisitions related to change and perceptions of fairness, as well as regulatory impacts to acquirer and target returns. Learning from acquisitions and the impact of resources are identified as promising areas of research.

Homberg, Rost, and Ostrloh (2009) perform a meta-analysis of acquisition research with a focus on different dimensions of relatedness (industry, technology, culture and size) using 67 studies. While general results support positive impacts of business and technology relatedness and negative effects of culture and size relatedness, their results highlight the importance of context for research variables and their impact on acquisition performance.

Campbell, Sirmon, and Schijven (2016) employ fuzzy logic to identify four configurations of "good" and "bad" acquisitions that may be obscured by regression analysis. Based on archival data (2,403 deals completed 1990 to 2004), good acquisitions are associated with geographic expansion and related diversification. Meanwhile, bad acquisitions involve merger or equals, efforts to turnaround unrelated businesses, or overextension with acquisitions that are highly leveraged or pay a high premium using stock.

Graebner et al. (2017) review research on acquisition integration and identify the importance of coordination (interdependence) and control (autonomy) identified by Haspeslagh and Jemison (1991) in making appropriate integration decisions. Associated integration decisions are important, as the process of integration is what enables reconfiguration of firm resources, structure, and routines that can create value from an acquisition. They also identify leadership traits as an important area of research, and that acquisition experience is a necessary, but insufficient condition for learning.

King et al. (2018) summarize acquisition research within the context of organizational change that considers content, context, process, and outcomes. Content considers how acquisitions relate to other corporate strategies and motives for using acquisitions. Context identifies the need to consider multiple stakeholders impacted by an acquisition. Acquiring firm shareholders are the primary stakeholder considered in acquisition research (Meglio & Risberg, 2010), but there is also a need to consider impacts to employees, suppliers, customers, and competitors. Not considering the influence of different stakeholders on acquisition performance likely introduces unexplained variance in many studies. While the book focuses on summarizing existing research, the process of change needs to consider interrelationships between earlier and later events during the acquisition process (Jemison & Sitkin, 1986). For outcomes, different measures of acquisition performance are reviewed with recognition that all performance variables have advantages and disadvantages, leading to the need for research to consider multiple measures of performance.

Hernandez and Menon (2018) take a novel perspective of acquisitions by considering network effects. From this viewpoint, acquisitions collapse nodes in alliance networks. Working from the insight that alliance network centrality has value, they develop how acquisitions can increase the prominence of an acquirer in an alliance network. Centrality can provide greater insight and access into network resources. Consideration of network effects begins to explain the effects of corporate strategy (e.g., acquisitions, alliances and divestment) on a firm's alliance network and help explain observed firm behavior.

Maas, Heugens, and Reus (2019) examine the impact of variance in country institutions on CBA performance using meta-analytic regression analysis to combine results from multiple single-country studies. Archival data were collected for 73 countries to consider the impact of country-level institutions on published research. They find that institutions that address principal-agent problems have unintentional consequences for firms. Specifically, legal protections that restrict manager discretion tend to decrease value generated from acquisitions.

Welch et al. (2020) perform a review of research considering the phase of acquisition selection (pre-deal) and the quality of acquisition decisions. They identify that focusing only on completed acquisitions can bias findings, as it may be more important to understand how firms can avoid 'bad' deals. They also identify the need to consider seller motivations, leadership traits, due diligence, and temporal effects in acquisitions.

King et al. (2021) aggregate research findings using meta-analysis on 19 variables from 220 studies across five measures of acquisition performance to identify significant effects for 16 variables. They find support for signaling theory (Cornell and Shapiro, 1987) with variables at acquisition announcement serving as significant predictors of acquisition performance with the most consistent result involving a negative impact of stock payment on several measures of acquisition performance. The latter result confirms a similar finding (Datta et al., 1992). This study is the first meta-analysis to summarize research findings for managerial assessment (survey) of performance, and results are largely consistent with accounting measures of acquisition performance.

Summary

While a strong foundation of acquisition research exists, there is limited overlap across studies, acquisition phases, or combined consideration of acquisitions with other corporate restructuring options. This book provides general topics for where research can expand to broaden our understanding and integrate different areas of research on corporate restructuring, while examining complexities associated with acquisitions. The three sections of the book are devoted to fundamental research questions: (1) How do acquisitions relate to other corporate strategy options; (2) what helps to predict acquisition performance; and (3) what are persistent acquisition research issues? While this introduction looks at where we have been, the rest of the book looks at where we are at, and the

6 David R. King

conclusion offers predictions of where corporate restructuring research is going. The next section begins by considering how acquisitions relate to other corporate restructuring options.

References

Bauer, F., & Matzler, K. (2014). Antecedents of M&A success: The role of strategic complementarity, cultural fit, and degree and speed of integration. *Strategic Management Journal, 35*(2), 269–291.

Campbell, J., Sirmon, D., & Schijven, M. (2016). Fuzzy logic and the market: A configurational approach to investor perceptions of acquisition announcements. *Academy of Management Journal, 59*(1), 163–187.

Cording, M., Christmann, P., & Weigelt, C. (2010). Measuring theoretically complex constructs: The case of acquisition performance. *Strategic Organization, 8*(1), 11–41.

Cornell, B., & Shapiro, A. (1987). Corporate stakeholders and corporate finance. *Financial Management, 16*(1), 5–14.

Datta, D., Pinches, G., & Narayanan, V. (1992) Factors influencing wealth creation from mergers and acquisitions: A meta-analysis. *Strategic Management Journal, 13*(1), 67–84.

Dewing, A. (1921). A statistical test of the success of consolidations. *Quarterly Journal of Economics, 36*(1), 84–101.

Ferreira, M., Santos, J., de Almeida, M., & Reis, N. (2014). Mergers and acquisitions research: A bibliometric study of top strategy and international business journals, 1980–2010. *Journal of Business Research, 67*(12), 2550–2558.

Graebner, M., Heimeriks, K., Huy, Q., & Vaara, E. (2017). The process of postmerger integration: A review and agenda for future research. *Academy of Management Annals, 11*(1), 1–32.

Haleblian, J., Devers, C., McNamara, G., Carpenter, M., & Davison, R. (2009). Taking stock of what we know about mergers and acquisitions: A review and research agenda. *Journal of Management, 35*(3), 469–502.

Haspeslagh, P. C., & Jemison, D. B. (1991). *Managing acquisitions: Creating value through corporate renewal* (Vol. 416). New York: Free Press.

Hernandez, E., & Menon, A. (2018). Acquisitions, node collapse, and network revolution. *Management Science, 64*(4), 1652–1671.

Hitt, M., Harrison, J., & Ireland, R. (2001). *Mergers & acquisitions: A guide to creating value for stakeholders*. Oxford: Oxford University Press.

Homberg, F., Rost, K. & Ostrloh, M. (2009). Do synergies exist in related acquisitions? A meta-analysis of acquisition studies. *Review of Management Science, 3*, 75–116.

Jemison, D., & Sitkin, S. (1986). Corporate acquisitions: A process perspective. *Academy of Management Review, 11*(1), 145–163.

King, D., Bauer, F., & Schriber, S. (2018). *Mergers & acquisitions: A research overview*. Oxford: Routledge.

King, D., Dalton, D., Daily, C., & Covin, J. (2004). Meta-analyses of post-acquisition performance: Indications of unidentified moderators. *Strategic Management Journal, 25*(2), 187–200.

King, D., Slotegraaf, R., & Kesner, I. (2008). Performance implications of firm resource interactions in the acquisition of R&D-intensive firms. *Organization Science*, *19*(2), 327–340.

King, D., Wang, G., Samimi, M., & Cortes, F. (2021). A meta-analytic integration of acquisition performance prediction. *Journal of Management Studies*, *58*(5), 1198–1236.

Maas, A., Heugens, P., & Reus, T. (2019). Viceroys or emperors? An institution-based perspective on merger and acquisition prevalence and shareholder value. *Journal of Management Studies*, *56*(1), 234–269.

Meglio, O., & Risberg, A. (2010). Mergers and acquisitions—Time for a methodological rejuvenation of the field? *Scandinavian Journal of Management*, *26*(1), 87–95.

Moehrle, S., & Reynolds-Moehrle, J. (2001). Say good-bye to pooling and goodwill amortization. *Journal of Accountancy*, *192*(3), 31–38.

Papadakis, V., & Thanos, I. (2010). Measuring the performance of acquisitions: An empirical investigation using multiple criteria. *British Journal of Management*, *21*(4), 859–873.

Ravenscraft, D., & Scherer, F. (1987) *Mergers, sell-offs, and economic efficiency*. Washington, DC: Brookings Institution.

Sirower, M. (1997). *The synergy trap: How companies lose the acquisition game*. New York: Simon and Schuster.

Stahl, G., & Voigt, A. (2008). Do cultural differences matter in mergers and acquisitions? A tentative model and examination. *Organization Science*, *19*(1), 160–176.

Wan, W., Hoskisson, R., Short, J., & Yiu, D. (2011). Resource-based theory and corporate diversification: Accomplishments and opportunities. *Journal of Management*, *37*(5), 1335–1368.

Welch, X., Pavićević, S., Keil, T., & Laamanen, T. (2020). The pre-deal phase of mergers and acquisitions: A review and research agenda. *Journal of Management*, *46*(6), 843–878.

Section I

How do acquisitions relate to other corporate strategy options?

David R. King

Many divestments are acquired (Laamanen, Brauer, & Junna, 2014; Weston, 1989) and a substantial percentage of acquisitions experience some form of divestment (Ravenscraft & Scherer, 1987; Weston, 1989), making the strategic options inexorably linked. However, divestment and acquisitions are rarely studied together. Divestment generally occurs during integration or the later stages of an acquisition. Meanwhile, target selection, the start of the acquisition process, is influenced by alliances (Porrini, 2004). Again, there is limited research with a combined focus on alliances and acquisitions (Shi, Sun, & Prescott, 2012). Further, international strategy and foreign market entry is often presented as a choice between cross-border acquisitions (CBA) and foreign direct investment (FDI), and what drives choices between these alternatives remains unclear (Tsang & Yamanoi, 2016). The problem of understanding corporate strategy from focusing only on the role acquisitions play is akin to only studying one side of a six-sided dice to describe the whole. The result is an incomplete picture of important relationships. This section raises awareness of this issue, and it also takes initial steps to address it by presenting research that compares acquisitions with alliances, divestment, and FDI.

In Chapter 1, Elio Shijaku, David King, and Ainhoa Urtasun examine how characteristics associated with transaction costs in the exchange of strategic resources with alliances contribute to acquisition activity. Increased awareness of different firm capabilities from a focal firm's portfolio of alliances can inform acquisition decisions, leading to observations that alliances often precede acquisitions. In examining internalization of prior alliances with an acquisition, they argue it is more likely when there are market failures associated with uncertainty and opportunism. Empirical analysis finds that more than one source of market failure is often needed before a firm completes an acquisition of an alliance partner.

DOI: 10.4324/9781003188308-2

10   *David R. King*

In a review of divestment research, Sina Amiri, David King, and Samuel DeMarie in Chapter 2 find (similar to the study of acquisitions) there is a need to integrate theoretical perspectives and look at divestment more holistically. For example, context associated with a firm's environment, ownership (e.g., family firm), or experience appears to be important antecedents to restructuring. Additionally, how investors react to divestment is influenced by whether divestments are made as part of a firm's larger acquisition strategy (Bingham, Heimeriks, Schijven, & Gates, 2015), suggesting the need to consider portfolio theory in acquisition research. Further, shared processes across acquisition and divestment activity may facilitate development of firm restructuring capabilities (Doan, Sahib, & van Witteloostuijn, 2018).

In Chapter 3, Oleksandra Kochura, Nicola Mirc, and Denis Lacoste provide a closer look at how strategy scholars approach and study divestitures and acquisitions, including the different ways they can be combined to restructure a firm's portfolio of businesses. By arguing that acquisitions and divestitures are sequential on their own, the authors demonstrate that in business configurations, any one of these can precede another. Through the consolidation of the temporal interrelationships between acquisition and divestiture, this chapter aims to advance our understanding of various possible corporate restructuring patterns.

In Chapter 4, Nan Zhang and Joseph Clougherty examine the relationship between CBA and greenfield investments (GI). The establishment-mode choice literature considers these to be substitutes for conducting business in a host nation. Recent scholarship, however, posits a more complex relationship where distinctness, partial substitution, and even complementarity might better characterize the relationship between investment modes. This lack of consensus is partly driven by the presence of empirical challenges and potential endogeneity. To surmount these challenges, the authors invoke an estimation approach based on cross-price elasticities. US merger-policy enforcement constitutes a "price" directly affecting CBA that only indirectly affects GI via a substitutive or complementary relationship. Employing firm-level data covering 1,763 firms situated in 58 industries from 2003 to 2017, their panel-data empirical testing indicates that merger-policy investigations deter cross-border horizontal acquisitions and attract greenfield investments. In other words, empirical results support GI substituting for CBA.

References

Bingham, C., Heimeriks, K., Schijven, M., & Gates, S. (2015). Concurrent learning: How firms develop multiple dynamic capabilities in parallel. *Strategic Management Journal*, 36(12), 1802–1825.

Doan, T.., Sahib, P., & van Witteloostuijn, A. (2018). Lessons from the flipside: How do acquirers learn from divestitures to complete acquisitions? *Long Range Planning*, 51(2), 252–266.

Laamanen, T., Brauer, M., & Junna, O. (2014). Performance of acquirers of divested assets: Evidence from the US software industry. *Strategic Management Journal*, 35(6), 914–925.

Porrini, P. (2004). Can a previous alliance between an acquirer and a target affect acquisition performance? *Journal of Management*, 30(4), 545–562.

Ravenscraft, D., & Scherer, F. (1987) *Mergers, sell-offs, and economic efficiency*. Brookings Institution: Washington, DC.

Shi, W., Sun, J., & Prescott, J. (2012). A temporal perspective of merger and acquisition and strategic alliance initiatives: Review and future direction. *Journal of Management*, 38(1), 164–209.

Tsang, E. & Yamanoi, J. (2016). International expansion through start-up or acquisition: A replication. *Strategic Management Journal*, 37(11), 2291–2306.

Weston, J. F. (1989). Divestitures: Mistakes or learning. *Journal of Applied Corporate Finance*, 2(2), 68–76.

1 Alliances as precursors to an acquisition

Elio Shijaku, David R. King, and Ainhoa Urtasun

Introduction

While research has established that alliances and acquisitions allow for the exchange of resources (Hess & Rothaermel, 2011; McCann, Reuer, & Lahiri, 2016; Van de Vrande, 2013), alliances and acquisitions are often treated separately in research (Achtenhagen, Brunninge, & Melin, 2017; Arora, Fosfuri, & Gambardella, 2001; Chen & Chen, 2003; Yang, Lin, & Peng, 2011). One explanation for this separation is that firms develop preferences for either alliances or acquisitions (Capron & Mitchell, 2010), but firm preferences can vary under different conditions (Hagedoorn & Duysters, 2002). We develop how characteristics associated with transaction costs in the exchange of strategic resources (Chi, 1994; Williamson, 1979) using alliances can contribute to acquisition activity.

Alliance research frequently applies transaction cost economics (TCE) (Panico, 2017; Reuer & Ariño, 2002), reflecting that alliances involve hazards that contribute to a failure rate over 50 percent (Dyer, Kale, & Singh, 2001; Saxton & Dollinger, 2004). While this may involve alliances helping to resolve uncertainty that they were created to address (Schilling, 2015), alliances often precede acquisitions (Porrini, 2004; Stahl et al., 2013). As a result, market failure likely contributes to firms making transactions under an alliance internal to a firm (Williamson, 1975). Still, alliances may not provide motivation to acquire an alliance partner, and simply increase awareness of a partner firm's capabilities (Yang et al., 2011). Increased awareness of different firm capabilities likely extends across a focal firm's portfolio of alliances, including indirect ties of an alliance network, and this can provide information for acquisition decisions (Wassmer, 2010; Yang et al., 2011). Still, the motives behind an alliance and their context likely influence a firm's acquisition propensity (Mellewigt, Thomas, Weller, & Zajac, 2017).

We develop and test how different types of alliance activity and contextual factors are associated with acquisition propensity. In demonstrating the applicability of TCE (Williamson, 1975) in predicting acquisition activity, we develop and demonstrate that uncertainty associated with exploration alliances is not sufficient in driving firms to internalize

DOI: 10.4324/9781003188308-3

transactions through an acquisition. However, after adding information on resource similarity and rivalry (Chen, 1996; Upson, Ketchen, Connelly, & Ranft, 2012), we demonstrate that the combination of uncertainty and opportunism (Williamson, 1975) can drive internalizing transactions through an acquisition. As a result, exploration alliances and uncertainty may represent a necessary, but insufficient element in predicting acquisition activity. The need to consider additional contextual factors in predicting acquisitions from exploration and exploitation alliances is consistent with existing research (Yang et al., 2011; Yu, Umashankar, & Rao, 2016), and it may begin to explain conflicting research findings on ambidexterity (Junni, Sarala, Taras, & Tarba, 2013).

Theory and hypotheses

TCE provides insight into when resource exchanges will be internalized within a firm (Williamson, 1975, 1979). In predicting acquisition activity, we distinguish between R&D and non-R&D alliances. March (1991) outlined two independent approaches to organizational learning involving either: (1) the exploration of new possibilities, or (2) the exploitation of old certainties. R&D alliances explore new resources, and other alliances more likely exploit existing resources (Rothaermel & Deeds, 2004). We anticipate that pursuing new resources with R&D alliances exhibits higher uncertainty and scarcity that corresponds to increased market failures that contribute to increased acquisition activity. This relates to concepts of bounded rationality and the reduction of uncertainty (Williamson, 1975). However, we anticipate context is also important (Ryu, McCann, & Reuer, 2018). Specifically, we anticipate that acquisition activity is more likely, when the resource profiles of competitors are more similar to an acquirer. A positive interaction of resource similarity on acquisition activity relates to concerns of opportunism and asset specificity (Williamson, 1975). As a result, firms are more likely to acquire needed resources to ensure access and also deny it to competitors. Anticipated relationships are displayed in Figure 1.1, and further developed in the following subsections.

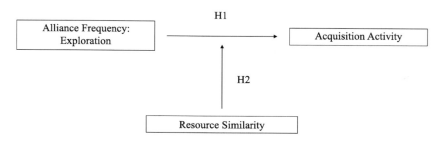

Figure 1.1 Precursors influencing acquisition activity.

Alliance frequency

Alliances are common and driven by strategic resource needs (Asgari, Singh, & Mitchell, 2017; Eisenhardt & Schoonhoven, 1996; Rothaermel & Deeds, 2004). For example, two common alliance motives involve exploring new resources or exploiting existing firm resources (Dittrich, Duysters, & de Man, 2007; Rothaermel & Deeds, 2004; Yang et al., 2011). Exploration and exploitation are not always equally important (Puranam, Powell, & Singh, 2006), and firms can provide alternating patterns for exploration and exploitation (Boumgarden, Nickerson, & Zenger, 2012; Jansen, Tempelaar, & van den Bosch, 2009). We maintain that firms are able to temporally manage the mix of R&D and non-R&D alliances over time, and that R&D alliances (exploration) are more likely to correspond to exploration and exhibit market failure.

Consistent with meeting different needs, alliances pursuing exploration or exploitation display differences. For example, exploration alliances tend to experience greater turnover in alliance partners and pursuit of partners with different technologies (Dittrich et al., 2007). In contrast, exploitation alliances place a greater emphasis on efficiency (Yang et al., 2011), and include measurable operational objectives that simplify monitoring (Koza & Lewin, 2000). Research suggests that acquisitions are more likely to follow exploration alliance activity (Yang et al., 2011). This likely reflects that acquisitions provide greater control over identified resource needs versus internal benefits from scale and scope efficiencies from alliances that exploit existing resources. As a result, when a firm has an increased frequency of R&D alliances, it is more likely engaging in exploration or a search for appropriate resources. Further, we anticipate that uncertainty reduction as part of this search is associated with acquisition activity (Williamson, 1975). Therefore, we propose:

> Hypothesis 1 (H1): Greater R&D alliance frequency, or an exploration focus is more likely to result in acquisition activity.

Resource similarity

An important contextual factor that positively influences acquisition propensity is resource similarity across competing firms. Chen (1996, p. 107) defines resource similarity as the extent competitors possess comparable strategic endowments in terms of both type and amount. The extent of resource similarity is important, as it relates to increase rivalry (Chen, 1996; Kilduff, Elfenbein, & Staw, 2010). A key principle of competitive rivalry involves acting before rival firms (Ferrier, 2001), and this applies to acquisitions. Acquisitions earlier in a wave tend to perform better from being able to pick better targets and paying lower premiums (Martynova & Renneboog, 2008). The use of an exploration alliance involves a search for information and firms with better information are able to

16   *Elio Shijaku et al.*

make acquisitions more quickly than rivals to access resources (Carow, Heron, & Saxton, 2004; Duysters, Lavie, Sabidussi, & Stettner, 2018; Haleblian, McNamara, Kolev, & Dykes, 2012). Further, acquisitions of similar resources are more common than acquisitions of complementary resources (Zaheer, Castañer, & Souder, 2013), and we anticipate this relates to concerns of opportunism and asset specificity (Williamson, 1975). Therefore, we propose:

> Hypothesis 2 (H2): Resource similarity of competitors with a firm increases the likelihood that R&D alliance frequency (exploration) results in acquisition activity.

Method

We apply purposive sampling to examine our hypotheses in the global pharmaceutical industry that displays needed alliance and acquisition activity. We restricted our sample to the top pharmaceutical firms by selecting those that, for 2002–2013, appeared at least once in the list of the top 50 firms that the Pharmaceutical Executive Magazine yearly published. Alliance and acquisition activity for the 68 identified firms was hand collected from the publicly available Pharma and Medtech Business Intelligence database. Our resulting sample includes 11,855 alliances and 1,724 acquisitions between 1 January 1991 and 31 December 2012 for 56 global, pharmaceutical firms. Financial and other information was collected from Compustat, Datastream, and firm annual reports. Overall, results are based on 657 firm-year observations.

Dependent variable

Our dependent variable reflects acquisition activity by firms in our sample. Acquisition activity is measured as a count of yearly acquisition announcements for each firm in our sample.

Independent variables

Exploration alliance frequency is measured as the ratio of new R&D alliances (count of R&D alliances/12) to new non-R&D alliances by a firm in a year with higher values indicating greater exploration alliance frequency.

Resource similarity is measured as the extent that competitors possess similar strategic resource endowments to a focal firm (Chen, 1996; Upson et al., 2012). Specifically, we created a matrix of the Euclidean distances between every pair of firms in our sample provided by the following equation:

$$D_{ab} = SQRT\left(F_a - F_b\right)^2 + \left(P_a - P_b\right)^2 + \left(T_a - T_b\right)^2 + \left(H_a - H_b\right)^2$$

where F_a or F_b are the standardized scores of the financial resources of firms a and b, P_a or P_b are the standardized scores of the physical resources of firms a and b,

T_a or T_b are the standardized scores of the technological resources of firms a and b,

H_a or H_b are the standardized scores of the human resources of firms a and b.

Finally, to obtain a firm-level measure of *resource similarity*, we averaged the Euclidean distance (D_{ab}) across the total sample of firms.

The financial dimension was captured using firms' debt-to-equity ratio (Greenley & Oktemgil, 1998), while the physical dimension was measured as investments in property, plant, and equipment (Upson et al., 2012). Meanwhile, the technological dimension was captured via the total number of yearly patents assigned to each firm (Bloom & Reenen, 2002), while the human resources dimension was measured using a ratio of firm sales to the number of employees (Morbey & Reithner, 1990).

Control variables

We also include several control variables anticipated to influence relationships among our variables or to display alternate interpretations. First, we control for the degree of market commonality, as it can provide an alternate explanation for acquisition activity under competitive dynamics (Chen, 1996). In measuring market commonality, we follow (Upson et al., 2012) and measure market commonality as the highest degree of presence that any competitor manifests in markets in which it overlaps with a focal firm. We calculated this variable by creating a matrix of market commonalities between every pair of firms in our sample using the following equation:

$$M_{ab} = \Sigma \left[\left(P_{ai}/P_a \right) \times \left(P_{bi}/P_i \right) \right]$$

where Pai = sales by firm a in product-market i,
Pa = total sales by firm a,
Pbi = sales by firm b in product-market i,
Pi = total sales of all firms in product-market i, and
i = all product-markets in which firms a and b compete.

To obtain a firm-level measure of market commonality, we averaged the market commonality measure across the total sample of firms. Second, we control for absorptive capacity by including a ratio of a firm's R&D expenditures to sales for each year. Third, we control for organizational

18   *Elio Shijaku et al.*

slack using a firm's current ratio (current assets/current liabilities) for each year. Fourth, firm size is included as a control using the log of total assets each year. Fifth, firm age is controlled for using a count variable for each year of our sample. Sixth, we control for equity alliances as a count for each firm and year, as equity alliances are an alternate governance mechanism to address alliance hazards (Asgari, Tandon, Singh, & Mitchell, 2018). Seventh, we control for a firm's alliance experience by calculating the number of alliances formed by a firm between year t-1 and year t-4, using a discount of 0.75. Eighth, we control for acquisition experience by calculating the number of acquisitions by a firm of alliance partners between year t-1 and year t-4 using a discount of 0.75. Ninth, we control for firm's patent ability using the yearly number of patents per firm.

Results

Table 1.1 reports descriptive statistics and pairwise correlations for our variables. Observed correlations align with expectations and are below levels that may raise concerns of multicollinearity (Gujarati, 2003). For example, alliance and acquisition experience display a significant, positive correlation ($r = 0.57$, $p < 0.001$). Additionally, consistent with their representing different constructs, market commonality and resource similarity are not significantly correlated ($r = -0.04$, $p > 0.10$). However, acquisition activity is significantly and negatively related to exploration alliance frequency ($r = -0.009$, $p < 0.001$).

Table 1.2 reports the results of our maximum likelihood estimation using generalized Poisson analysis performed in statsmodels with python (Cameron & Trivedi, 1998) with study variables added in a stepwise fashion. Model 1 reports the results for our control variables. Consistent with prior research (Villalonga & Mcgahan, 2005), prior acquisition experience is a significant predictor of acquisition activity ($\beta = 0.61$, $p = 0.000$). A firm with one additional prior acquisition will be 6.1 percent more likely to complete an acquisition. Additionally, firm size is a significant predictor of acquisition activity ($\beta = 0.52$, $p = 0.001$). However, acquisitions are less likely if firms are in common markets ($\beta = -0.17$, $p = 0.005$), and this could relate to antitrust review or firm growth relying on moving into new areas.

In model 2, variables with hypothesized effects are added. Hypothesis 1 expected increased acquisition activity from exploration (R&D) alliances and the opposite effect is found. The impact of exploration alliance frequency is significant and negative ($\beta = -0.22$, $p = 0.043$). For a one unit increase in exploration alliances, firms are 2.2 percent less likely to compete an acquisition. Meanwhile, a direct effect of resource similarity is not significant in prediction acquisition activity. In model 3, the interaction between exploration alliance and resource similarity is positive and significant ($\beta = 0.18$, $p = 0.021$). This supports Hypothesis 2, and it is consistent with TCE expectations that market failure is greater when

Table 1.1 Variable means, standard deviation, and correlations

	mean	std	1	2	3	4	5	6	7	8	9	10	11
1 Acquisitions	1.4	2.1											
2 Alliance experience	16.71	19.34	0.57***										
3 Acquisition experience	2.39	3.12	0.7***	0.68***									
4 Patent ability	14.03	24.45	0.1***	0.29***	0.16***								
5 Absorptive ability	0.26	0.78	−0.08***	−0.08***	−0.11***	−0.07**							
6 Current ratio	2.97	2.9	−0.16***	−0.24***	−0.21***	−0.19***	0.42***						
7 Firm size	8.65	1.75	0.27***	0.49***	0.35***	0.39***	−0.37***	−0.47***					
8 Firm age	76.16	56.32	0.05	0.13***	0.07**	0.08***	−0.2***	−0.24***	0.52***				
9 Market commonality	0.4	0.14	−0.06**	0.03	−0.04	0.02	0.07**	0.01	0	0			
10 Equity alliances	0.63	1.27	0.34***	0.61***	0.38***	0.07***	−0.01	−0.06**	0.17***	0.03	0.03		
11 Exploration alliance frequency	1.22	1.14	−0.09***	−0.12***	−0.09**	−0.06*	0	0.07*	−0.05	0.05	−0.04	−0.06*	
12 Resource similarity	2.95	0.67	−0.02	0.01	0.02	0.14***	0.06*	−0.08**	0.1***	0.02	−0.04	−0.03	−0.01

*** p < 0.001, ** p < 0.01, * p < 0.05.

Table 1.2 Results for predicting alliances and acquisitions

Variables	Model 1			Model 2			Model 3		
	dy/dx	Robust SE	p-value	dy/dx	Robust SE	p-value	dy/dx	Robust SE	p-value
Alliance experience	0.17	0.12	0.163	0.15	0.12	0.229	0.14	0.12	0.264
Acquisition experience	0.61	0.08	0.000	0.6	0.08	0.000	0.60	0.08	0.000
Patent ability	-0.13	0.07	0.071	-0.12	0.07	0.087	-0.12	0.07	0.084
Absorptive capacity	-0.13	0.17	0.469	-0.12	0.18	0.488	-0.11	0.17	0.506
Current ratio	-0.07	0.11	0.496	-0.07	0.11	0.533	-0.06	0.11	0.546
Firm size	0.52	0.15	0.001	0.53	0.15	0.000	0.54	0.15	0.000
Firm age	-0.15	0.09	0.078	-0.14	0.09	0.118	-0.13	0.09	0.144
Market commonality	-0.17	0.06	0.005	-0.18	0.06	0.004	-0.18	0.06	0.003
Equity alliances	0.09	0.06	0.181	0.09	0.06	0.155	0.09	0.06	0.145
H1: Exploration alliance frequency				-0.22	0.11	0.043	-0.28	0.1	0.005
Resource similarity				-0.06	0.08	0.475	-0.04	0.08	0.575
H2: Exploration alliance frequency × resource similarity							0.18	0.08	0.021
N	657			657			657		
Pseudo-R squared	0.130			0.132			0.135		
Likelihood-ratio (p-value)				6 (0.049)			6.20 (0.012)		

Note: Maximum likelihood estimation of generalized Poisson; average marginal effects as coefficients; standard errors are heteroskedastic and first-order autocorrelation robust; all models include year dummies (not shown in the table); likelihood ratios compare model 1 with model 2, and model 2 with model 3, respectively, showing that model 2 is significantly superior to model 1 and model 3 is significantly superior to model 2.

exploration alliances are in areas with similarity to competitor resources. The interaction was confirmed through a graph that shows exploration alliances are more likely to be acquired when they have resource similarity. However, exploration alliances alone are not sufficient condition for internalizing resources within a firm using an acquisition. Additionally, the highest acquisition likelihood is for exploitation alliances with low resource similarity.

Discussion

Alliances represent one means for balancing conflicting demands for exploration and exploitation (Lavie & Rosenkopf, 2006; Stadler, Rajwani, & Karaba, 2014). However, alliances involve risk and display high failure rates that include acquisition of alliance partners (Porrini, 2004). TCE (Williamson, 1975) offers a theoretical foundation for predicting when alliances will display market failures that contribute to acquisition activity. Our results suggest that alone exploration alliances and uncertainty are not sufficient in predicting acquisition activity, and the direct effect of exploration alliances actually reduces acquisition activity. This may relate to our data not providing insight into when uncertainty from exploration is resolved, or other unmeasured effects. For example, asymmetry in alliance partner goals for exploration and exploitation could increase alliance failure (Koza & Lewin, 2000). However, we confirm the importance of considering additional contextual factors in predicting acquisitions of exploration alliances (Yang et al., 2011). Additional implications for research and management are described next.

Research implications

We demonstrate that the applicability of TCE (Williamson, 1975) in predicting acquisition activity may benefit from adding information on resource similarity and rivalry (Chen, 1996). Our results suggest that individual elements of TCE (Williamson, 1975) by themselves may not be sufficient to drive acquisition activity. For example, we find that uncertainty associated with exploration alliances actually is significantly associated with lower acquisition activity, and that potential opportunism and asset specificity does not have a significant direct effect. However, in combination, exploration alliances and resource similarity are significant predictors of acquisition activity. Overall, we demonstrate the importance of contextual factors in understanding acquisition activity. Alliances and acquisitions are complex phenomena, and our understanding of associated decisions needs a theoretical basis that considers interactions and context (King, Dalton, Daily, & Covin, 2004; King, Wang, Samimi, & Cortes, 2021).

22 Elio Shijaku et al.

Managerial implications

We provide insight for managers considering alliances to better understand when governance mechanisms short of internalization through acquisition can be effective. For example, uncertainty or potential opportunism (by themselves) can likely be managed through contractual monitoring or equity investments. It is when contextual circumstances present multiple aspects of market failure that acquisition activity is more likely. As acquisitions require increased resource investment and absorb management attention (Cording, Christmann, & King, 2008), additional insights into circumstances associated with higher acquisition activity can be important.

Limitations and future research directions

We used a purposive sample of firms in the global pharmaceutical industry, and aspects of this industry may be unique. As a result, additional research is needed to validate whether our findings generalize to other industries. Our data also have limitations in determining whether the timing of uncertainty reduction from exploration alliances is important. If uncertainty persists over multiple years, then this begins to explain our finding that exploration alliances are associated with less acquisition activity. Further, we do not compare alliance partner motives in an alliance, and asymmetry in strategic goals for exploration and exploitation by alliance partners may increase failure (Koza & Lewin, 2000). Another limitation is that we look at a firm's overall alliance and acquisition activity in predicting acquisitions. In other words, we do not examine the acquisition of specific alliance partners. Existing research suggests that alliances with a specific firm can predict acquisition (Porrini, 2004), but this is not always the case (Yang et al., 2011). Our generalized examination of a firm use of alliances and acquisitions enables insight into the broader impact of alliances on acquisitions.

In closing, alliances and acquisitions are common organizational phenomena that are frequently considered separately despite recognition that they are related and both offer firms the means to access strategic resources. We develop and test that the combined elements of TCE (Williamson, 1975) can help to identify when alliances will contribute to acquisition activity. However, additional research is needed to understand how alliances and acquisitions are used together by firms.

References

Achtenhagen, L., Brunninge, O., & Melin, L. (2017). Patterns of dynamic growth in medium-sized companies: Beyond the dichotomy of organic versus acquired growth. *Long Range Planning, 50*(4), 457–471.

Arora, A., Fosfuri, A., & Gambardella, A. (2001). *Markets for technology: The economics of innovation and corporate strategy.* Boston, MA: MIT Press.

Asgari, N., Singh, K., & Mitchell, W. (2017). Alliance portfolio reconfiguration following a technological discontinuity. *Strategic Management Journal*, *38*(5), 1062–1081.

Asgari, N., Tandon, V., Singh, K., & Mitchell, W. (2018). Creating and taming discord: How firms manage embedded competition in alliance portfolios to limit alliance termination. *Strategic Management Journal*, *39*(12), 3273–3299.

Bloom, N., & Reenen, J. (2002). Patents, real options and firm performance. *Economic Journal*, *112*(478), C97–C116.

Boumgarden, P., Nickerson, J., & Zenger, T. (2012). Sailing into the wind: Exploring the relationships among ambidexterity, vacillation, and organizational performance. *Strategic Management Journal*, *33*(6), 587–610.

Cameron, A., & Trivedi, P. (1998). *Regression analysis of count data*. Cambridge: Cambridge University Press.

Capron, L., & Mitchell, W. (2010). Finding the right path. *Harvard Business Review*, *88*(7–8), 102–107.

Carow, K., Heron, R., & Saxton, T. (2004). Do early birds get the returns? An empirical investigation of early-mover advantages in acquisitions. *Strategic Management Journal*, *25*(6), 563–585.

Chen, H., & Chen, T.-J. (2003). Governance structures in strategic alliances: Transaction cost versus resource-based perspective. *Journal of World Business*, *38*(1), 1–14.

Chen, M.-J. (1996). Competitor analysis and interfirm rivalry: Toward a theoretical integration. *Academy of Management Review*, *21*(1), 100–134.

Chi, T. (1994). Trading in strategic resources: Necessary conditions, transaction cost problems, and choice of exchange structure. *Strategic Management Journal*, *15*(4), 271–290.

Cording, M., Christmann, P., & King, D. (2008). Reducing causal ambiguity in acquisition integration: Intermediate goals as mediators of integration decisions and acquisition performance. *Academy of Management Journal*, *51*(4), 744–767.

Dittrich, K., Duysters, G., & de Man, A.-P. (2007). Strategic repositioning by means of alliance networks: The case of IBM. *Research Policy*, *36*(10), 1496–1511.

Duysters, G., Lavie, D., Sabidussi, A., & Stettner, U. (2018). What drives exploration? Convergence and divergence of exploration tendencies among alliance partners and competitors. *Academy of Management Journal*, doi: 10.5465/amj.2017.1409.

Dyer, J., Kale, P., & Singh, H. (2001). How to make strategic alliances work. *MIT Sloan Management Review*, *42*(4), 37–43.

Eisenhardt, K, & Schoonhoven, C. (1996). Resource-based view of strategic alliance formation: Strategic and social effects in entrepreneurial firms. *Organization Science*, *7*(2), 136–150.

Ferrier, W. (2001). Navigating the competitive landscape: The drivers and consequences of competitive aggressiveness. *Academy of Management Journal*, *44*(4), 858–877.

Greenley, G., & Oktemgil, M. (1998). A comparison of slack resources in high and low performing British companies. *Journal of Management Studies*, *35*(3), 377–398.

Gujarati, D. (2003). *Basic econometrics*. New York: McGraw-Hill.

24 Elio Shijaku et al.

Hagedoorn, J., & Duysters, G. (2002). External sources of innovative capabilities: The preference for strategic alliances or mergers and acquisitions. *Journal of Management Studies*, 39(2), 167–188.

Haleblian, J., McNamara, G., Kolev, K., & Dykes, B. (2012). Exploring firm characteristics that differentiate leaders from followers in industry merger waves: A competitive dynamics perspective. *Strategic Management Journal*, 33(9), 1037–1052.

Hess, A., & Rothaermel, F. (2011). When are assets complementary? Star scientists, strategic alliances, and innovation in the pharmaceutical industry. *Strategic Management Journal*, 32(8), 895–909.

Jansen, J., Tempelaar, M., van den Bosch, F., & Volberda, H. (2009). Structural differentiation and ambidexterity: The mediating role of integration mechanisms. *Organization Science*, 20(4), 797–811.

Junni, P., Sarala, R., Taras, V., & Tarba, S.Y. 2013. Organizational ambidexterity and performance: A meta-analysis. *Academy of Management Perspectives*, 27(4), 299–312.

Kilduff, G., Elfenbein, H., & Staw, B. (2010). The psychology of rivalry: A relationally dependent analysis of competition. *Academy of Management Journal*, 53(5), 943–969.

King, D., Dalton, D., Daily, C., & Covin, J. (2004). Meta-analyses of post-acquisition performance: Indications of unidentified moderators. *Strategic Management Journal*, 25(2), 187–200.

King, D., Wang, G., Samimi, M., & Cortes, F. (2021). A meta-analytic integration of acquisition performance prediction, *Journal of Management Studies*, 58(5), 1198–1236.

Koza, M., & Lewin, A. (2000). Managing partnerships and strategic alliances: Raising the odds of success. *European Management Journal*, 18(2), 146–151.

Lavie, D., & Rosenkopf, L. 2006. Balancing exploration and exploitation in alliance formation. *Academy of Management Journal*, 49(4), 797–818.

Martynova, M., & Renneboog, L. (2008). A century of corporate takeovers: What have we learned and where do we stand, *Journal of Banking and Finance*, 32(10), 2148–2177.

March, J. (1991). Exploration and exploitation in organizational learning. *Organization Science*, 2(1), 71–87.

McCann, B., Reuer, J., & Lahiri, N. (2016). Agglomeration and the choice between acquisitions and alliances: An information economics perspective. *Strategic Management Journal*, 37(6), 1085–1106.

Mellewigt, T., Thomas, A., Weller, I., & Zajac, E. (2017). Alliance or acquisition? A mechanisms-based, policy-capturing analysis. *Strategic Management Journal*, 38(12), 2353–2369.

Morbey, G., & Reithner, R. (1990). How R&D affects sales growth, productivity and profitability. *Research-Technology Management*, 33(3), 11–14.

Panico, C. (2017). Strategic interaction in alliances. *Strategic Management Journal*, 38(8), 1646–1667.

Porrini, P. (2004). Can a previous alliance between an acquirer and a target affect acquisition performance? *Journal of Management*, 30(4), 545–562.

Puranam, P., Powell, B., & Singh, H. 2006. Due diligence failure as a signal detection problem. *Strategic Organization*, 4(4), 319–348.

Reuer, J., & Ariño, A. (2002). Contractual renegotiations in strategic alliances. *Journal of Management*, 28(1), 47–68.

Rothaermel, F., & Deeds, D. (2004). Exploration and exploitation alliances in biotechnology: A system of new product development. *Strategic Management Journal*, 25(3), 201–221.

Ryu, W., McCann, B., & Reuer, J. (2018). Geographic co-location of partners and rivals: Implications for the design of R&D alliances. *Academy of Management Journal*, 61(3), 945–965.

Saxton, T., & Dollinger, M. (2004). Target reputation and appropriability: Picking and deploying resources in acquisitions. *Journal of Management*, 30(1), 123–147.

Schilling, M. (2015). Technology shocks, technological collaboration, and innovation outcomes. *Organization Science*, 26(3), 668–686.

Stadler, C., Rajwani, T., & Karaba, F. (2014). Solutions to the exploration/exploitation dilemma: Networks as a new level of analysis. *International Journal of Management Reviews*, 16(2), 172–193.

Stahl, G., Angwin, D., Very, P., Gomes, E., Weber, Y., Tarba, S., Noorderhaven, N., Benyamini, H., Bouckenooghe, D., Chreim, S., Durand, M., Hassett, M., Kokk, G., Mendenhall, M., Mirc, N., Miska, C., Park, K., Reynolds, N., Rouzies, A., et al. (2013). Sociocultural integration in mergers and acquisitions: Unresolved paradoxes and directions for future research. *Thunderbird International Business Review*, 55(4), 333–356.

Upson, J., Ketchen, D., Connelly, B., & Ranft, A. (2012). Competitor analysis and foothold moves. *Academy of Management Journal*, 55(1), 93–110.

Van de Vrande, V. (2013). Balancing your technology-sourcing portfolio: How sourcing mode diversity enhances innovative performance. *Strategic Management Journal*, 34(5), 610–621.

Villalonga, B., & Mcgahan, A. (2005). The choice among acquisitions, alliances, and divestitures. *Strategic Management Journal*, 26(13), 1183–1208.

Wassmer, U. (2010). Alliance portfolios: A review and research agenda. *Journal of Management*, 36(1), 141–171.

Williamson, O. (1975). *Markets and hierarchies: Analysis and antitrust implications*. New York: Free Press.

Williamson, O. (1979). Transaction-cost economics: The governance of contractual relations. *Journal of Law and Economics*, 22(2), 233–261.

Yang, H., Lin, Z., & Peng, M. (2011). Behind acquisitions of alliance partners: Exploratory learning and network embeddedness. *Academy of Management Journal*, 54(5), 1069–1080.

Yu, Y., Umashankar, N., & Rao, V. (2016). Choosing the right target: Relative preferences for resource similarity and complementarity in acquisition choice. *Strategic Management Journal*, 37(8), 1808–1825.

Zaheer, A., Castañer, X., & Souder, D. (2013). Synergy sources, target autonomy, and integration in acquisitions. *Journal of Management*, 39(3), 604–632.

2 Review of divestment research[1]

Sina Amiri, David R. King, and Samuel M. DeMarie

Introduction

Divestiture involves removing firm assets or operations using sell-offs, spin-offs, equity carve-outs, or split-offs (Amiri, King & DeMarie, 2020), and they display important differences as spin-offs do not generate cash proceeds for a firm. Traditionally, divestitures have been viewed as the opposite of acquisitions, but contemporary research recognizes that divestiture represents a strategic alternative or complement to acquisitions for corporate restructuring (Brauer, 2006; Mulherin & Boone, 2000; Villalonga & McGahan, 2005). For example, research shows over one third of acquisitions are later divested (Ravenscraft & Scherer, 1987; Weston, 1989). However, there is less research on divestiture than on acquisitions (Brauer, 2006; Lee & Madhavan, 2010). Further, divestment research is fragmented across topics and disciplines with economics research viewing divestiture as means of overcoming diversification discount (Feldman & McGrath, 2016) and management research viewing divestiture as means of refocusing, correcting prior mistakes (Markides & Singh, 1997), innovating (Moschieri & Mair, 2011), or adapting to environmental changes (Berry, 2013; Funk & Luo, 2015).

The complexity of divestment activity is reflected in illustrative examples. In a well-known example, General Electric (GE) proactively planned series of divestitures, including even high performing units, during Jack Welch's tenure as Chief Executive Officer (CEO) (Dranikoff, Koller, & Schneider, 2002). This example highlights the role of a firm's leadership in corporate restructuring. Meanwhile, General Motors (GM) divested its loss-making European Opel/Vauxhall in 2017, after it retreated from an initial attempt in 2009 due to government intervention (McDermott & Luethge, 2013). This example suggests that divestment decisions are not entirely internal. The combined implications of less research attention, fragmentation of what research exists, and divestment reflecting complex circumstances reinforce the need to consolidate and integrate findings to inform future research.

---

1 This chapter was independently edited by Olimpia Meglio who coordinated blind reviews.

DOI: 10.4324/9781003188308-4

Review of divestment research 27

We review divestment research and to identify how they relate to acquisitions, we organize it around antecedents, process, and outcomes. Examination of antecedents, process, and outcomes (Dominguez, Galán-González, & Barroso, 2015; Pettigrew, Woodman, & Cameron, 2001) is common in acquisition research (Birkinshaw, Bresman, & Hakanson, 2000; Cording, Christmann, & King, 2008; Haspeslagh & Jemison, 1991). However, reviews of antecedents and processes in divestment research are largely missing. For example, Moschieri and Mair (2008) summarize research on divestment performance. While Brauer (2006) examines antecedents, process, and outcomes, this review is becoming dated and it overlooks significant research that followed its publication (Alaix, 2014; Kolev, 2016; Lee & Madhavan, 2010; Thywissen, 2015; Veld & Veld-Merkoulova, 2009). We present a cross-disciplinary review of empirical research on antecedents, processes, and outcomes of corporate divestiture that makes two primary contributions. First, we summarize theoretical arguments and constructs used in divestment research. This enables a comparison with acquisition research. Second, we clarify where divestment and acquisition research overlaps and where each area is distinct.

Method

To collect a sample of articles, we employed a computerized keyword search within major databases, including the ProQuest ABI/Inform Global and Web of Science, as well as of leading journals in accounting, finance, management, and marketing. We applied proven review techniques to limit our review to journal publications of empirical research identified from a keyword search (Haleblian, Devers, McNamara, Carpenter, & Davison, 2009; Podsakoff, Mackenzie, Bachrach, & Podsakoff, 2005). Our search of article titles and abstracts used: divest, divestment, divestiture, spin-off, sell-off, and corporate unbundling. Also, to make sure our sample was comprehensive in covering relevant works, we applied a manual backward ancestry approach combined with a forward-looking snowball approach by tracing the works which respectively were cited by and cited in major review papers (Brauer, 2006; Moschieri, & Mair, 2008) and foundational works (Lee & Madhavan, 2010; Weston, 1989) using Google Scholar. Next, we read identified papers and excluded those that were irrelevant to the context. Our final sample includes 112 articles.

Literature review

Our review covers divestiture antecedents, process, and outcomes. Research on each stage is summarized in Figure 2.1 and covered in more detail in the following sections.

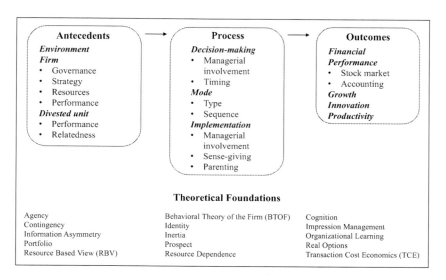

Figure 2.1 Overview of divestment research.

Antecedents

We categorize divestment antecedents into three groups: (1) environment, (2) firm, and (3) divested unit.

Environment. A firm's external general and industry environment influence its strategic decisions and actions (Porter, 1980), and research has considered both external and internal aspects of a firm's environment.

In the general environment, volatility in the general economy or exchange rates, and instability of governmental policy are associated with higher costs in managing a portfolio of businesses (Alexander, 1991) that can drive restructuring (Mitchell & Mulherin, 1996) through divestitures and acquisitions (Hoskisson & Hitt, 1994; Markides, 1995). Still, research offers conflicting expectations with positive (Hill & Hoskisson, 1987; Jones & Hill, 1988) and negative (Belderbos & Zou, 2009; O'Brien & Folta, 2009) effects of general environment uncertainty on corporate restructuring. However, Hamilton and Chow (1993) find general economy and industry growth as significant determinants that are negatively related to firms' decision to divest.

Still, research does support an impact of institutions and economic growth on corporate restructuring. Divestment is influenced by institutional (e.g., tax, international trades, ownership) stability (Henisz & Delios, 2004). Instability in macro level policies and regulations brings about uncertainty that managers of firms reduce through business exit and divestment (cf. Cyert & March, 1963). For example, research shows a higher chance of divestment in countries with more unstable legal and political systems (Berry, 2013; Hoskisson & Hitt, 1990). Meanwhile, globalization has increased standardization of institutions that lowers the inter-firm transaction costs (Farrell & Saloner, 1985; Porter, 2008). For example, transaction costs can drive firms to divest their vertically expanded operations over the value chain (Baldwin, 2008). Additionally, Funk and Luo (2015, p. 59) show that the emergence of industry standards resulted in vertical disintegration by firms to the extent that these "standard modules" increased the entrance of resource-constrained entrepreneurial firms and reduced the "transaction costs of having work done by multiple agents". Additionally, growth implies higher future market demand, gain, performance improvement, and less intense competition, influencing firms' level of diversification and scope of operations (Chang, 1996). Growing markets may cause managers to postpone or give up their divestment decision in those markets. Benito (1997) finds an inverse relation between economic growth and divestments among Norwegian firms, and Berry (2013) shows that higher country growth significantly decreases the divestiture of low performing international units by their US parent firms.

In studying the industry environment, firms in stigmatized industries respond to media attacks differently by evading media coverage, while a public response can incur reputational damage and hostile scrutiny (Durand & Vergne, 2015). Divestment of operations in a stigmatized industry is an effective strategy to fix a damaged firm's reputation (Love & Kraatz, 2009). Durand and Vergne (2015) show that media attacks on focal firms and their peers in stigmatized industries increase the likelihood of firms divesting their businesses.

Firm. Internal to a firm, governance is a significant determinant of corporate divestiture (Ahn & Walker, 2007; Kolev, 2016). For example, managerial incentives (e.g., bonuses and ownership stakes) can enhance managers' risk tolerance and encourage them to undertake value-generating strategies like divestitures (Denis, Denis, & Sarin, 1999). A recent stream of research extends agency theory to consider the impact of family firms (Feldman, Amit, & Villalonga, 2016; Praet, 2013). Family owners that strongly identify with the firm inherit the ownership and management over generations, leading to socioemotional wealth (Gómez-Mejía, Haynes, Núñez-Nickel, Jacobson, & Moyano-Fuentes, 2007; Zellweger & Dehlen, 2012). Therefore, Feldman and colleagues (2016) argue that the associated total costs of divestitures are higher for family firms than non-family firms, leading family firms to avoid divestments unless they generate higher value. Additionally, Feldman and colleagues (2016) posit that family CEOs are less likely to undertake divestiture, but when they do, their divestment is more likely to generate higher value than those run by non-family firms. Meanwhile, Praet (2013) finds an inverted U-shaped relationship between family ownership and divestment activities, arguing that an increase in family ownership (up to a point)

30 *Sina Amiri et al.*

attenuates the agency problem within a firm. However, as the share of family ownership becomes large, the risk of entrenchment and adoption of non-economic goals arises, decreasing the likelihood of divestment activities. Overall, family ownership may represent an important context that needs to be controlled for by researchers studying acquisitions or divestment. In considering manager characteristics, shorter CEO tenure drives corporate divestiture due to less inertia (Shimizu & Hitt, 2005) or an association with newer CEOs' higher responsiveness to shareholder pressure for enhancing performance (Feldman, 2014).

For firm strategy, Kolev (2016) finds a positive relationship between level of diversification and divestment. Over-diversification is source of inefficiency (Hoskisson & Turk, 1990), as it potentially drives complexities in resource allocation (Ravenscraft & Scherer, 1987), increased bureaucratic costs (Nayyar, 1992), and decreased information-processing capabilities (Berger & Ofek, 1995). Bergh and colleagues (2008) argue that managers employ different types of divestitures (e.g., sell- or spin-offs) to create value out of the "information asymmetry" derived from diversification. However, divestitures are not costless to firms, and divestitures may signal lack of efficiency (Dranikoff et al., 2002) or they can remove, valuable, shared resources (Semadeni & Cannella, 2011). Divestment also relates to a firm's internationalization strategy, as Berry (2010) finds positive impacts on divestiture for firms' global expansion. As firms' cross-border and domestic operations compete over limited resources, global firms tend to move operations to foreign countries where the cost of production is lower (Blonigen, 2001).

A parallel consideration of diversification is the level that different business units of a firm are related, and this influences divestment. In general, research shows that firms are less likely to divest related businesses (Brauer, 2006; Chang, 1996; Chang & Singh, 1999; Duhaime & Grant, 1984; Moschieri & Mair, 2008; Xia & Li, 2013; Zuckerman, 2000). However, it has different implications for different theories. On one hand, RDT views relatedness as a source of parent-unit interdependence negatively associated with the likelihood of unit divestiture. For example, excessive dependence on a given business unit may result in a power imbalance, increasing the risk of units' opportunistic behavior (Xia & Li, 2013). On the other hand, resource-based view (RBV) views related units as sources of tacit knowledge and competitive advantage, but unrelated businesses as revenue hedges (Bergh, Johnson, & Dewitt, 2008). Meanwhile, intra-firm redeployability of related resources may reduce economic sunk costs that facilitate divestment (Lieberman, Lee, & Folta, 2017).

A firm's internal resources also influence divestiture activity. For example, firms may spin-off a unit to place its resources under more efficient management (Rose & Ito, 2005), or to use cash proceeds from a sell-off to acquire or develop new resources (Borisova & Brown, 2013). Another resource is a firm's prior experience that develops knowledge and routines that can facilitate divestiture (Bergh & Lim, 2008; Humphery-Jenner, Powell, & Zhang, 2019) through improving subsequent restructuring decisions (Donaldson, 1990), reducing the process costs, and lessening the risk of competency traps (Bergh & Lim, 2008). Shimizu and Hitt (2005) argue that excess slack creates inertia in firms that limits major strategic change (i.e., divestiture) of poor performing units. However, resource scarcity tends to drive managers to take on more risk (Palmer & Wiseman, 1999; Shimizu, 2007; Teece, 1980).

Another consideration internal to a firm is its performance at the firm and unit level that represents the most commonly studied divestiture antecedents (Kolev, 2016). Behavioral theory contends that firms constantly compare their performance with aspiration levels, and that performance below aspiration triggers "problemistic" search (Greve, 2003). Divestitures can help to restore efficiency (Dranikoff et al., 2002), implying an inverse relation between firm performance and corporate divestiture (Ravenscraft & Scherer, 1987; Shimizu, 2007). Prospect theory (Kahneman & Tversky, 1979) refines the behavioral perspective by adding a "reference point" to decision-making. Higher firm performance enables managers overlook underperforming units based on overall firm favorable performance, implying a direct association between firm performance and the likelihood of divesting under-preforming units (Hayward & Shimizu, 2006).

Divested unit. Units within a firm also receive considerable attention as antecedents to divestiture comparable to firm and environment criteria (Moschieri & Mair, 2008). For example, poor unit performance is a major driver of corporate divestiture (Berry, 2013; Brauer, 2006; Duhaime & Grant, 1984; Hamilton & Chow, 1993; Kolev, 2016; Markides, 1992; Shimizu & Hitt, 2005; Ravenscraft & Scherer, 1987). Portfolio considerations suggest that managers evaluate businesses and drop underperforming units and retain those with satisfactory performance (Dranikoff et al., 2002; Hoskisson & Turk, 1990). Meanwhile, performance beyond aspiration levels creates inertia reducing divestiture (Greve, 2003). Using prospect theory, Shimizu (2007) argues that firms' divestiture behavior varies based on managers' risk preferences at different levels of unit performance. When unit performance is moderately low, managers show higher risk tolerance and less likely to divest underperforming units; however, when low performance passes the threat point, managers become more risk averse and more likely to divest. Wang and Jensen (2019) extend the field by viewing unit performance within a firm's identity to argue that low performing units are considered inconsistent with firm identity and more likely to be divested. Moreover, Xia, Jifeng, and Yijia (2019) argue that sub-units with peripheral operations are less powerful, and more likely to be divested. Still, Schlingemann, Stulz, and Walkling (2002) suggest that liquidity of a unit is the main determinant of divestment.

32 *Sina Amiri et al.*

Divestiture processes

Divestment is a complex strategic process (Brauer, Mammen, & Luger, 2017), requiring managerial decisions and implementation (Dean & Sharfman, 1996; Thywisson, 2015). Success or failure depends on how a divestment is structured and implemented (Bergh et al., 2008). Still, there is less research in this area, and we found only four empirical journal articles on divestiture processes. We found two empirical studies on divestment decision-making (Elfenbein & Knott, 2015; Elfenbein, Knott, & Croson, 2017) and two on implementation (Cheyre, Klepper, & Veloso, 2014; Gopinath & Becker, 2000). As a result, we also include qualitative studies (e.g., case studies), as inductive studies dominate the research on decision-making and implementation processes that we organize into three categories: decision-making, mode of divestiture, and implementation.

Decision-making. We recognize two subthemes on decision-making process of managerial involvement and timing.

First, managerial involvement provides authority behind a divestiture decision, and Ghertman (1988) suggests restructuring decisions follow a top-down pattern among multinational firms. However, Burgelman (1994, 1996) stresses that internal selection processes are dominated by mid-level managers. The contrasting perspectives may be resolved using a contingency perspective from Brauer (2009) who provides a typology of different types of divestitures based on corporate and unit manager involvement. For example, spin-offs are driven by external sources (shareholders) and represent high degree of both corporate and unit manager involvement, and entrepreneurial spinouts are internally driven divestments by unit managers with low corporate manager involvement.

With respect to the timing of divestiture decisions, Nees (1983) finds that a lengthy decision process deteriorates employee morale. Elfenbein and Knott (2015) outline that managerial biases underlie delays in making timely divestment decisions within US banking industry. Additionally, Elfenbein and colleagues (2017) find that managerial incentives (e.g., equity stakes) can delay divestment decisions by making managers overly optimistic.

Mode of divestiture. Following the decision to divest, managers choose a divestment mode (e.g., spin-off or sell-off). Duhaime and Schwenk (1985) argue that effective decision-making drives the right choice of divestiture mode and successful implementation. In our review, we categorize research by divestiture mode and sequential divestment.

In distinguishing between spin-off and sell-offs, Bergh and colleagues (2008) find that higher corporate degree of diversification and unit un-relatedness to firm core operations associate with more sell-offs, as managers try to turn information asymmetry into financial benefit. Bergh and Sharp (2015) find that large outside stockholder ownership and unit size are directly associated with greater use of spin-offs. Meanwhile, Bergh and Lim (2008) find that contemporaneous experience is associated with more spin-off decisions, while distant and accumulated repetitive experience leads to more of sell-offs. Still, Hildebrandt and colleagues (2018) develop a comprehensive fuzzy model implying that the success of divestitures is contingent on a set of internal and external factors.

Implementation. Research on divestiture implementation examines what follows a decision to divest, and we group research on implementation into managerial involvement, sense-giving, and parenting.

Managerial involvement focuses on how different organizational levels take part in divestment implementation. Nees (1981) finds that corporate managers need to involve unit managers in divestiture implementation process. When corporate managers make divestiture decisions without involving divisional managers, divisional managers are more likely to resist separation from the parent due to perceived ambiguity in the future of the unit. Similarly, Moschieri (2011) finds that sense of opportunity, created through unit's independence and managerial involvement, creates higher unit performance through enhancing unit managers' commitment, motivation, and identification. This is closely related to research finding a positive impact of sense-giving and communications on corporate restructuring (Balogun & Johnson, 2004).

For sense-giving during implementation, Gopinath and Becker (2000) find that communicating with unit managers and employees enhances their perceptions of procedural justice regarding the divestment decision and its consequent layoffs. Perception of procedural justice, in turn, raises trust and commitment, which are critical to divestiture success. Corley and Gioia (2004) argue for the necessity of managerial sense-giving actions through better communicating divestiture underlying logics, insights, and perspectives to alleviate the tensions arisen by change and identity ambiguities as part of divestiture implementation process.

Finally, parenting examines the relationship between divested unit and parent. Arguing that divestitures are recurrent and multifaceted programs that should not be studied in isolation, Moschieri and Mair (2012) find that retaining a relationship with the divested unit enables former parent firms to efficiently manage its portfolio of businesses, while providing a parent firm with an option to buy the divested unit back (Moschieri & Mair, 2011). Assessing and recruiting new employees is important in spin offs, as a divested unit cannot hire all employees required from the parent firm (Cheyre et al., 2014). Still, the process of divestment remains largely unexplored with available research often providing conflicting findings.

Outcomes

Financial performance (i.e., stock market and accounting) is the most common dependent variable, but we also summarize research on firm growth, innovation, and productivity.

34 *Sina Amiri et al.*

Financial performance. We organize our review around different theoretical expectations. From an agency perspective, divestitures will generally lead to positive financial performance (Berger & Ofek, 1995) by aligning the interests of managers and owners (Denning, 1988). Feng, Nandy, and Tian (2015) suggest that interest alignment effect of incentives in CEO compensations is more effective than strong governance or disciplining to keep firm performance high post-divestment. Still, Pathak, Hoskisson, and Johnson (2014) find that boards compensate CEOs for risk proportional to the size of refocusing divestiture programs. As a result, governance moderates the performance by diminishing the agency conflicts and spurring value creation. For example, Chesbrough (2003) and Semadeni and Cannella (2011) find that continued parent's ownership and board representation in the spun-off unit can begin to harm a unit's market performance. Chesbrough (2003) finds that parents' active presence in the spun-off unit management restrains units' search scope and creativity; however, the presence of venture capitalists in the board mitigates the negative effect of parent presence. Moreover, Feldman (2015) finds that spin-offs clarify operations and performance of the separated unit to better align the compensation of spun-off unit managers with the performance. Chen and Feldman (2018) also find evidence that external hedge fund investors can fulfill the role of strong external governance by inducing managers to make value creating divestment decisions. In general, large blockholders may address agency problems between managers and owners. However, unbalanced ownership can create a conflict of interest among shareholders (e.g., type 2 agency problem). For example, Peruffo and colleagues (2014) argue that the presence of family owners could exacerbate the negative effect of information asymmetry among investors by increasing the risk of family owners' opportunistic behavior against others.

Reducing information asymmetry between managers and investors (Sanders & Boivie, 2004) is also a consideration of institutional theory, and deal characteristics may signal whether a focal divestment is driven by managers' independent strategic intents or mimetic isomorphism. Brauer and Wiersema (2012) find a U-shaped relation between divestment timing over a wave and market response, arguing that divestments in the middle of a wave signal imitation. If managers divest units with performance below aspiration to signal brighter prospects, then investors react positively (Feldman, 2014; Markides, 1992; Zuckerman, 2000). However, Golder, Markovitch, and O'Brien (2018) find a negative moderating effect for pre-divestiture relative performance on market reaction to divestment. Still, this may be moderated by CEO background, as Huang (2014) finds that CEOs are less attached and more likely to divest units where they have less expertise. Meanwhile, Feldman (2014) argues that newer CEOs are more concerned with meeting the performance aspirations and they are also less attached to older businesses, making new CEOs more likely to make suboptimal divestment decisions.

Organizational learning theory implies that routines and knowledge developed from accumulated experience can improve the quality of corporate practices (Levitt & March, 1988), including decision-making practices (Berg & Lim, 2008; Brauer, Mammen, & Luger, 2017; Haleblian, Kim, & Rajagopalan, 2006). Hence, experience can enhance divestiture performance by boosting individual performance, as well as reducing process costs, risk of competency traps, and anxiety, over the stages of identification, transaction timing and negotiations, detachment, and reallocation of released resources (Bergh & Lim, 2008). Prior divestiture experience can help to improve strategic flexibility and restructuring learnings, enabling firms to acquire riskier targets and pay less premiums (Bertrand, Betschinger, & Petrina, 2014). In support of these expectations, Humphery-Jenner and colleagues (2019) find a positive link between divestment experience and market response. Doan and colleagues (2018) argue that there is spillover between acquisitions and divestitures, and that prior divestitures facilitate both experiential learning and vicarious learning over restructuring procedures applicable to future acquisition practices. Bingham and colleagues (2015) extend the positive effect of experience across restructuring activities, arguing that corporations can learn concurrently from their distinct restructuring practices. However, Bergh and colleagues (2008) argue that spin-offs' idiosyncratic and rare nature does not allow for learning through repetition and accumulation of explicit knowledge into routines applicable to the learning curve.

RBV anticipates that divestitures can improve performance by helping firms gain competitive advantage through improving the fitness and complementarity among remaining assets, as well as releasing resources to reinvest into corporations' future prosperity. As a result, firms can use existing resources and restructure resource combinations (Teece, Pisano, & Shuen, 1997) to gain competitive advantage. Additionally, Zschoche (2016) finds that favorable macro environment (e.g., labor costs) facilitate efficiency gains that enhance restructuring performance. Prior performance also acts as a moderator by signaling the incentives behind divestment, as well as corporations' capabilities to reinvest the released resources. For example, Vidal and Mitchell (2018) find that higher pre-divestment performance enables firms to reinvest divestment proceeds in assets and growth, but lower performance increases the risk of closure or takeover.

Transaction cost economics (TCE) examines parent-unit relationships following spin-off to explain the performance consequences. TCE assumes a positive market reaction as spin-offs believed to enhance performance through units' increased contract efficiency, new partners, and autonomy from parents' restraining bureaucracy (Makhija, 2004). Meanwhile, continued post spin-off parent-unit relations can reduce costs of their mutual transactions. Research finds parent control over the spun-off unit in forms of ownership stake and board representation as moderators of performance. Moderate level of parent ownership

36 *Sina Amiri et al.*

and board representative in the spun-off units positively influence both parties' stuck return; nonetheless, investors perceive parents' involvement beyond a certain level as too much that obstructs units progress, and separate identity (Semadeni & Cannella, 2011). Feldman (2016) finds that the presence of dual directors in the spun-off unit's board creates conflict of interest, leading to dual directors exercising their power to the benefit of parent firms.

Growth. Chesbrough (2003) argues that parents' ownership stakes or presence of dual directors in the board of technology spin-offs is counterproductive to unit growth, but the presence of venture capitalists (VCs) on the board mitigates agency issues. Meanwhile, Rose and Ito (2005) find that macro environment (i.e., national culture) and relatedness moderate the relation between divestment type and divested units' growth, making unrelated units less of a concern to parent firms. However, Sapienza, Parhankangas, and Autio (2004) find an inverted U-shaped relationship between unit relatedness and spun-off unit growth, arguing that moderate levels of knowledge similarity maximize learning capacity and growth. In studying the growth consequences of divestiture to the former parent, Vidal and Mitchell (2018) find that firm performance and financial well-being moderate divestment growth outcomes to provide high performance firms with better opportunities to reinvest the resources.

Innovation. Divestitures can improve innovativeness (Moschieri & Mair, 2008). For example, over-diversified firms can employ divestitures to restore their strategic control, which may be lost due to excessive corporate restructuring activities (Hitt, Hoskisson, Johnson, & Moesel, 1996). Moreover, the intangible nature and uncertainty of R&D projects cause information asymmetry, raising the cost of external financing for R&D projects to encourage managers to use proceeds from divestitures as a source of funding (Borisova & Brown, 2013). Alternatively, firms can form spin-offs as incubators of new projects to develop a new technology or enter a new market (Parhankangas & Arenius, 2003). However, Lindholm (1997) does not find any significant difference in terms of innovativeness and growth between spin-offs and other Swedish new technology start-ups, suggesting the potential for confounding influential factors on innovation outcomes. For instance, Chesbrough and Rosenbloom (2002) argue that business model mediates the effect of divestiture on innovation.

Productivity. Research also considers divestitures' performance outcomes to productivity outcomes in order to explain the underlying sources and mechanisms of value generation in divestments. Chemmanur and colleagues (2014) find that spin-offs are associated with enhanced productivity. Additionally, Engel and Procher (2013) find that the cost of protecting knowledge intensive properties makes foreign divestments and relocation of operations to major home sites increases productivity in high-technology industries. This contrasts with expectations that firms tend to divest and relocate their local operations abroad in pursuit of more favorable labor costs (Berry, 2010).

Discussion

Our review of research on divestiture antecedents, processes, and outcomes shows that research largely overlooks the divestiture process (Thywissen, 2015), as well as its links with antecedents and performance. While process research examines multiple topics, including divestiture decision-making and implementation, antecedents set the foundation for later outcomes for acquisitions and divestment (Jemison & Sitkin, 1986). Consistent with an emphasis on process and antecedents, restructuring programs are recognized to result in higher performance (Brauer & Schimmer, 2010; Barkema & Shijven, 2008). We also find overlap across acquisition and divestment research, including common shortcomings, as well as relevant differences.

First, acquisition and divestment research do overlap. For example, relatedness of business units is a focus of research in both divestment and acquisitions (Brauer, 2006; King, Meglio, Gomez-Mejia, Bauer, & De Massis, 2021) with firms less likely to divest related business units (Xia & Li, 2013). While the predominant focus is on acquisition and divestment outcomes associated with financial performance, there is need to consider the impact of acquisitions and divestment on firm survival (King, Bauer, & Schriber, 2018; Lee & Madhavan, 2010). Insights from research on acquisition and divestment processes also suggest a general tendency to anticipate better outcomes from acting quickly to implement divestment and acquisition decisions (Angwin, 2004; Nees, 1983).

Next, acquisition and divestment research also display common shortcomings. Acquisitions are heterogeneous (Bower, 2001) and so are divestitures, but this is not consistently reflected in research. For example, family firms tend to engage in fewer corporate restructuring (e.g., acquisitions and divestment) activities than other firms (Feldman et al., 2016; King et al., 2022). This may reflect family owners displaying opportunistic behavior toward other shareholders (Peruffo, Perri, & Oriani, 2014). However, there is limited research that controls for family ownership in research on acquisitions or divestitures (King et al., 2022; Meglio & King, 2019), so the implications of family firms are largely unknown.

Finally, divestments are also more than a mirror image of an acquisition, and this drives additional considerations for research. Observed differences in market reactions are not understood. For example, stock market reactions to divestment announcements are generally positive (Humphery-Jenner et al., 2019), while reactions to acquisitions are generally not positive (King, Dalton, Daily, & Covin, 2004, Amiri et al., 2020). Further, there is a problem of perspective and comparison. While divestments often involve an acquisition by another organization,

38 Sina Amiri et al.

business unit can also be spun-off into a separate organization. The latter drives an additional focus in divestment research on parenting effects that may lead a firm to re-acquire a divested unit (Moschieri & Mair, 2012). Another difference is that corporate portfolio considerations are more commonly considered in divestment research (Dranikoff et al., 2002), and this offers an opportunity for acquisition research. Our review offers additional implications for research and practice.

Research implications

For research, we summarize implications for theory, antecedents, outcomes, and moderators, as well as methodology.

Theory. There is a need for research on divestment to integrate multiple theoretical perspectives, as a variety of theories are applied in divestment research. This is more obvious from research on divestment outcomes and different theories being associated with different variables. Greater integration of theoretical perspectives and commonality of variables used in corporate restructuring research is needed (King et al., 2021). We find the most common theories in divestment research are agency, TCE, RBV, portfolio, BTOF, and organizational learning. Future research can expand theoretical boundaries by combining perspectives. For example, scholars can draw from psychological identity and managerial cognition theories to examine the impact of the interplay between managers' role and social identities and cognitive characteristics on divestiture decisions. This relates to our review identifying a lack of research on TMT and CEO psychological characteristics, such as managerial personality, narcissism, or hubris, in the context of divestiture.

Antecedents. Research needs to study environmental factors as antecedents to divestiture as only Hamilton and Chow (1993) consider both general and task environments. For example, the general economy influences acquisition and divestment decisions with divestments in contracting industries funding acquisitions made in growing industries (Borisova & Brown, 2013; Hamilton & Chow, 1993; Heeley, King, & Covin, 2006); however, positive outcomes may be limited to higher performing firms with better opportunities (Vidal & Mitchell, 2018). Foreign direct investment opportunities for both domestic firms and international firms in a certain market can also have implications for divestitures. Better opportunities abroad or attractiveness of the domestic market to foreign investors can impact divestitures.

Outcomes. Financial performance, captured through market and accounting returns, followed by innovation and growth are the most common outcomes considered by research on divestments. While research uses abnormal returns and returns on stocks as measures for long-term market returns, future studies can use changes in market value to measure long-term performance consequences of divestitures. Additionally, we recommend future studies to use Tobin's Q as a proxy for performance as it is a mix of market and accounting measures; however, its application is not common (Feldman et al., 2016). Management research can also make wider use of multiple measures, including the addition of quality of analyst coverage (Feldman, 2015) tied to divestment motives.

Moderator. Another opportunity for future research is to study the relationship between the former parent and divested units (e.g., parenting) for divested units established as a separate firm (i.e., spin-offs, MBOs) in order to study its impacts on both firms. Anticipated benefits may depend on the perspective of each party. For example, a divested unit can benefit from complementary resources provided by its former parents, while parent can gain access to the potential new technology developed inside the unit, as well as unit's network and market. Additionally, the impacts of parenting on each partner may not be symmetric or all positive. Overall, greater consideration of moderators can help develop expectations of contingent relationships in corporate restructuring (King et al., 2021).

Methodology. With respect to the methodology, research on the divestment process is outnumbered by studies on antecedent and outcomes. This is a striking shortcoming as research reportedly emphasizes the need for viewing divestitures as a holistic process. To gain a deeper and more precise understanding of divestiture decision, its mode, and its performance consequences, scholars need to step beyond econometric analysis of archival data to conduct qualitative research. This guarantees a better understanding of issues such as unit and firm managerial involvement, employees' perceptions of opportunity, responsibility, and motivation.

Process studies can also provide better insights over issues, like efficiency of decision-making, resource allocation, and asset redeployment, as addressed by research applying RBV perspective (Capron, Mitchell, & Swaminathan, 2001; Capron & Mitchell, 2010) in studying corporate divestitures. Also, process studies facilitate better measurement of latent variables in studying resources such as absorptive capacity in divestiture studies. Additionally, processes between divestment and acquisition decisions display commonalities that enable experiential learning (Bingham, Heimeriks, Schijven, & Gates, 2015; Doan, Sahib & van Witteloostuijn, 2018). However, learning may be restricted to sell-offs (Bergh & Lim, 2008).

Managerial implications

Our review suggests managers should be cautious in generalizing inferences from experience, and that they can generate value from matching the mode of divestiture with the organization's history of prior divestments. In other words, it is easier to apply lessons from prior sell-offs to another sell-off. Additionally, communication with employees and perceptions of justice are important in both acquisitions and divestment (Bansal & King, 2020; Gopinath & Becker, 2000), implying a role for managerial sensegiving during restructuring (Corley & Gioia, 2004).

40 Sina Amiri et al.

Limitations

Several limitations to our review are worth noting and provide opportunities for additional research. Our primary limitation is from categorization that decreased the level of detail provided, and our comments are on general findings and not all variables or theories applied. While we identify theories used in each of the reviewed studies in appendices, there remains an opportunity for more focused reviews that develop integrated variable relationships. Future research can also investigate corporate restructuring implications of divestments and acquisitions. In closing, we hope an increased awareness of divestment in corporate restructuring encourages more research.

References

Ahn, S., & Walker, M. (2007). Corporate governance and the spinoff decision. *Journal of Corporate Finance, 13*(1), 76–93.

Alaix, J. (2014). The CEO of Zoetis on how he prepared for the top job. *Harvard Business Review, 92*(6), 41–44.

Alexander, J. (1991). Adaptive change in corporate control practices. *Academy of Management Journal, 34*(1), 162–193.

Amiri, S., King, D., DeMarie, S. (2020). Divestiture of prior acquisitions: Competing explanations of performance. *Journal of Strategy and Management, 13*(1), 33–50.

Angwin, D. (2004). Speed in M&A integration: The first 100 days. *European Management Journal, 22*(4), 418–430.

Baldwin, C. (2008). Where do transactions come from? Modularity, transactions, and the boundaries of firms. *Industrial and Corporate Change, 17*(1), 155–195.

Balogun, J., & Johnson, G. (2004). Organizational restructuring and middle manager sensemaking. *Academy of Management Journal, 47*(4), 523–549.

Bansal, A., & King, D. (2020). Communicating change following an acquisition. *International Journal of Human Resource Management.* https://doi.org/10.1080/09585192.2020.1803947

Barkema, H., & Schijven, M. (2008). Toward unlocking the full potential of acquisitions: The role of organizational restructuring. *Academy of Management Journal, 51*(4), 696–722.

Belderbos, R., & Zou, J. (2009). Real options and foreign affiliate divestments: A portfolio perspective. *Journal of International Business Studies, 40*(4), 600–620.

Benito, G. (1997). Divestment of foreign production operations. *Applied Economics, 29*(10), 1365–1378.

Berger, P., & Ofek, E. (1995). Diversification's effect on firm value. *Journal of Financial Economics, 37*(1), 39–65.

Bergh, D., Johnson, R., & Dewitt, R. (2008). Restructuring through spin-off or sell-off: transforming information asymmetries into financial gain. *Strategic Management Journal, 29*(2), 133–148.

Bergh, D., & Lim, E. (2008). Learning how to restructure: Absorptive capacity and improvisational views of restructuring actions and performance. *Strategic Management Journal, 29*(6), 593–616.

Bergh, D., & Sharp, B. (2015). How far do owners reach into the divestiture process? Blockholders and the choice between spin-off and sell-off. *Journal of Management, 41*(4), 1155–1183.

Berry, H. (2010). Why do firms divest? *Organization Science, 21*(2), 380–396.

Berry, H. (2013). When do firms divest foreign operations? *Organization Science, 24*(1), 246–261.

Bertrand, O., Betschinger, M., & Petrina, Y. (2014). Organizational spillovers of divestiture activity to M&A decision-making. In *Advances in mergers and acquisitions* (pp. 65–83). Bingley: Emerald Group Publishing Limited.

Bingham, C., Heimeriks, K., Schijven, M., & Gates, S. (2015). Concurrent learning: How firms develop multiple dynamic capabilities in parallel. *Strategic Management Journal, 36*(12), 1802–1825.

Birkinshaw, J., Bresman, H., & Håkanson, L. (2000). Managing the post-acquisition integration process: How the human integration and task integration processes interact to foster value creation. *Journal of Management Studies, 37*(3), 395–425.

Blonigen, B. (2001). In search of substitution between foreign production and exports. *Journal of International Economics, 53*(1), 81–104.

Borisova, G., & Brown, J. (2013). R&D sensitivity to asset sale proceeds: New evidence on financing constraints and intangible investment. *Journal of Banking & Finance, 37*(1), 159–173.

Bower, J. (2001). Not all M&As are alike – and that matters. *Harvard Business Review, 79*(3), 92–101.

Brauer, M. (2006). What have we acquired and what should we acquire in divestiture research? A review and research agenda. *Journal of Management, 32*(6), 751–785.

Brauer, M. (2009). Corporate and divisional manager involvement in divestitures— A contingent analysis. *British Journal of Management, 20*(3), 341–362.

Brauer, M., Mammen, J., & Luger, J. (2017). Sell-offs and firm performance: A matter of experience? *Journal of Management, 43*(5), 1359–1387.

Brauer, M., & Schimmer, M. (2010). Performance effects of corporate divestiture programs. *Journal of Strategy and Management, 3*(2), 84–109.

Brauer, M., & Wiersema, M. (2012). Industry divestiture waves: How a firm's position influences investor returns. *Academy of Management Journal, 55*(6), 1472–1492.

Burgelman, R. (1994). Fading memories: A process theory of strategic business exit in dynamic environments. *Administrative Science Quarterly, 39*(1), 24–56.

Burgelman, R. (1996). A process model of strategic business exit: Implications for an evolutionary perspective on strategy. *Strategic Management Journal, 17*(S1), 193–214.

Capron, L., & Mitchell, W. (2010). Finding the right path. *Harvard Business Review, 88*(7), 102–107.

Capron, L., Mitchell, W., & Swaminathan, A. (2001). Asset divestiture following horizontal acquisitions: A dynamic view. *Strategic Management Journal, 22*(9), 817–844.

Chang, S. (1996). An evolutionary perspective on diversification and corporate restructuring: Entry, exit, and economic performance during 1981–89. *Strategic Management Journal, 17*(8), 587–611.

42 Sina Amiri et al.

Chang, S., & Singh, H. (1999). The impact of modes of entry and resource fit on modes of exit by multibusiness firms. *Strategic Management Journal*, 20(11), 1019–1035.

Chemmanur, T., Krishnan, K., & Nandy, D. (2014). The effects of corporate spin-offs on productivity. *Journal of Corporate Finance*, 27, 72–98.

Chen, S., & Feldman, E. (2018). Activist-impelled divestitures and shareholder value. *Strategic Management Journal*, 39(10), 2726–2744.

Chesbrough, H. (2003). The governance and performance of Xerox's technology spin-off companies. *Research Policy*, 32(3), 403–421.

Chesbrough, H., & Rosenbloom, R. (2002). The role of the business model in capturing value from innovation: Evidence from Xerox Corporation's technology spin-off companies. *Industrial and Corporate Change*, 11(3), 529–555.

Cheyre, C., Klepper, S., & Veloso, F. (2014). Spinoffs and the mobility of US merchant semiconductor inventors. *Management Science*, 61(3), 487–506.

Cording, M., Christmann, P., & King, D. (2008). Reducing causal ambiguity in acquisition integration: Intermediate goals as mediators ofintegration decisions and acquisition performance. *Academy of Management Journal*, 51(4), 744–767.

Corley, K., & Gioia, D. (2004). Identity ambiguity and change in the wake of a corporate spin-off. *Administrative Science Quarterly*, 49(2), 173–208.

Cyert, R., & March, J. (1963). *A behavioral theory of the firm* (Vol. 2). Englewood Cliffs, NJ.: Prentice Hall.

Dean, J., & Sharfman, M. (1996). Does decision process matter? A study of strategic decision-making effectiveness. *Academy of Management Journal*, 39(2), 368–392.

Denis, D., Denis, D., & Sarin, A. (1999). Agency theory and the influence of equity ownership structure on corporate diversification strategies. *Strategic Management Journal*, 20(11), 1071–1076.

Denning, K. (1988). Spin-offs and sales of assets: An examination of security returns and divestment motivations. *Accounting and Business Research*, 19(73), 32–42.

Doan, T., Sahib, P., & van Witteloostuijn, A. (2018). Lessons from the flipside: How do acquirers learn from divestitures to complete acquisitions? *Long Range Planning*, 51(2), 252–266.

Dominguez, M., Galán-González, J., & Barroso, C. (2015). Patterns of strategic change. *Journal of Organizational Change Management*, 28(3), 411–431.

Donaldson, G. (1990). Voluntary restructuring: The case of General Mills. *Journal of Financial Economics*, 27(1), 117–141.

Dranikoff, L., Koller, T., & Schneider, A. (2002). Divestiture: Strategy's missing link. *Harvard Business Review*, 80(5), 74–83, 133.

Duhaime, I., & Grant, J. (1984). Factors influencing divestment decision-making: Evidence from a field study. *Strategic Management Journal*, 5(4), 301–318.

Duhaime, I., & Schwenk, C. (1985). Conjectures on cognitive simplification in acquisition and divestment decision making. *Academy of Management Review*, 10(2), 287–295.

Durand, R., & Vergne, J. (2015). Asset divestment as a response to media attacks in stigmatized industries. *Strategic Management Journal*, 36(8), 1205–1223.

Elfenbein, D., & Knott, A. (2015). Time to exit: Rational, behavioral, and organizational delays. *Strategic Management Journal*, 36(7), 957–975.

Elfenbein, D., Knott, A., & Croson, R. (2017). Equity stakes and exit: An experimental approach to decomposing exit delay. *Strategic Management Journal*, 38(2), 278–299.

Engel, D., & Procher, V. (2013). Home firm performance after foreign investments and divestitures. *World Economy*, 36(12), 1478–1493.

Farrell, J., & Saloner, G. (1985). Standardization, compatibility, and innovation. *RAND Journal of Economics*, 16(1), 70–83.

Feldman, E. (2014). Legacy divestitures: Motives and implications. *Organization Science*, 25(3), 815–832.

Feldman, E. (2015). Managerial compensation and corporate spinoffs. *Strategic Management Journal*, 37(10), 2011–2030.

Feldman, E. (2016). Dual directors and the governance of corporate spinoffs. *Academy of Management Journal*, 59(5), 1754–1776.

Feldman, E., Amit, R., & Villalonga, B. (2016). Corporate divestitures and family control. *Strategic Management Journal*, 37(3), 429–446.

Feldman, E., & McGrath, P. (2016). Divestitures. *Journal of Organization Design*, 5(1), 1–16.

Feng, Y., Nandy, D., & Tian, Y. (2015). Executive compensation and the corporate spin-off decision. *Journal of Economics and Business*, 77, 94–117.

Funk, J., & Luo, J. (2015). Open standards, vertical disintegration and entrepreneurial opportunities: How vertically-specialized firms entered the US semiconductor industry. *Technovation*, 45, 52–62.

Ghertman, M. (1988). Foreign subsidiary and parents' roles during strategic investment and divestment decisions. *Journal of International Business Studies*, 19(1), 47–67.

Golder, P., Markovitch, D., & O'Brien, J. (2018). When do investors reward acquisitions and divestitures? The contrasting implications of normative and behavioral economic theories. *Managerial and Decision Economics*, 39(2), 226–239.

Gómez-Mejía, L., Haynes, K., Núñez-Nickel, M., Jacobson, K., & Moyano-Fuentes, J. (2007). Socioemotional wealth and business risks in family-controlled firms: Evidence from Spanish olive oil mills. *Administrative Science Quarterly*, 52(1), 106–137.

Gopinath, C., & Becker, T. (2000). Communication, procedural justice, and employee attitudes: Relationships under conditions of divestiture. *Journal of Management*, 26(1), 63–83.

Greve, H. (2003). A behavioral theory of R&D expenditures and innovations: Evidence from shipbuilding. *Academy of Management Journal*, 46(6), 685–702.

Haleblian, J., Devers, C., McNamara, G., Carpenter, M., & Davison, R. (2009). Taking stock of what we know about mergers and acquisitions: A review and research agenda. *Journal of Management*, 35(3), 469–502.

Haleblian, J., Kim, J., & Rajagopalan, N. (2006). The influence of acquisition experience and performance on acquisition behavior: Evidence from the US commercial banking industry. *Academy of Management Journal*, 49(2), 357–370.

Hamilton, R., & Chow, Y. (1993). Why managers divest—Evidence from New Zealand's largest companies. *Strategic Management Journal*, 14(6), 479–484.

44 *Sina Amiri et al.*

Haspeslagh, P., & Jemison, D. (1991). The challenge of renewal through acquisitions. *Planning Review, 19*(2), 27–30.

Hayward, M., & Shimizu, K. (2006). De-commitment to losing strategic action: Evidence from the divestiture of poorly performing acquisitions. *Strategic Management Journal, 27*(6), 541–557.

Heeley, M., King, D., & Covin, J. (2006). Effects of firm R&D investment and environment on acquisition likelihood. *Journal of Management Studies, 43*(7), 1513–1535.

Henisz, W., & Delios, A. (2004). Information or influence? The benefits of experience for managing political uncertainty. *Strategic Organization, 2*(4), 389–421.

Hildebrandt, P., Oehmichen, J., Pidun, U., & Wolff, M. (2018). Multiple recipes for success: A configurational examination of business portfolio restructurings. *European Management Journal, 36*(3), 381–391.

Hill, C., & Hoskisson, R. (1987). Strategy and structure in the multiproduct firm. *Academy of Management Review, 12*(2), 331–341.

Hitt, M., Hoskisson, R., Johnson, R., & Moesel, D. (1996). The market for corporate control and firm innovation. *Academy of Management Journal, 39*(5), 1084–1119.

Hoskisson, R., & Hitt, M. (1990). Antecedents and performance outcomes of diversification: A review and critique of theoretical perspectives. *Journal of Management, 16*(2), 461–509.

Hoskisson, R., & Hitt, M. (1994). *Downscoping: How to tame the diversified firm.* New York: Oxford University Press.

Hoskisson, R., & Turk, T. (1990). Corporate restructuring: Governance and control limits of the internal capital market. *Academy of Management Review, 15*(3), 459–477.

Huang, S. (2014). Managerial expertise, corporate decisions and firm value: Evidence from corporate refocusing. *Journal of Financial Intermediation, 23*(3), 348–375.

Humphery-Jenner, M., Powell, R., & Zhang, E. (2019). Practice makes progress: Evidence from divestitures. *Journal of Banking & Finance, 105*, 1–19.

Jemison, D., & Sitkin, S. (1986). Corporate acquisitions: A process perspective. *Academy of Management Review, 11*(1), 145–163.

Jones, G., & Hill, C. (1988). Transaction cost analysis of strategy-structure choice. *Strategic Management Journal, 9*(2), 159–172.

Kahneman, D., & Tversky, A. (1979). Prospect theory: An analysis of decision under risk. *Econometrica: Journal of the Econometric Society, 47*(2), 263–292.

King, D., Bauer, F., Schriber, S. (2018). *Mergers & acquisitions: A research overview.* Oxford: Routledge.

King D., Dalton D, Daily C., & Covin J. (2004). Meta-analyses of post-acquisition performance: Indications of unidentified moderators. *Strategic Management Journal, 25*(2), 187–200.

King, D., Meglio, O., Gomez-Mejia, L., Bauer, F., & De Massis, A. (2022). Family business restructuring: A review and research agenda. *Journal of Management Studies, 49*(1), 197–235. https://onlinelibrary.wiley.com/doi/pdf/10.1111/joms.12717

King, D., Wang, G., Samimi, M., & Cortes, F. (2021). A meta-analytic integration of acquisition performance prediction, *Journal of Management Studies, 58*(5), 1198–1236.

Kolev, K. (2016). To divest or not to divest: A meta-analysis of the antecedents of corporate divestitures. *British Journal of Management, 27*(1), 179–196.

Lee, D., & Madhavan, R. (2010). Divestiture and firm performance: A meta-analysis. *Journal of Management, 36*(6), 1345–1371.

Levitt, B., & March, J. (1988). Organizational learning. *Annual Review of Sociology,* 319–340.

Lieberman, M., Lee, G., & Folta, T. (2017). Entry, exit, and the potential for resource redeployment. *Strategic Management Journal, 38*(3), 526–544.

Lindholm, A. (1997). Growth and inventiveness in technology-based spin-off firms. *Research Policy, 26*(3), 331–344.

Love, E., & Kraatz, M. (2009). Character, conformity, or the bottom line? How and why downsizing affected corporate reputation. *Academy of Management Journal, 52*(2), 314–335.

Makhija, M. (2004). The value of restructuring in emerging economies: The case of the Czech Republic. *Strategic Management Journal, 25*(3), 243–267.

Markides, C. (1992). Consequences of corporate refocusing: Ex ante evidence. *Academy of Management Journal, 35*(2), 398–412.

Markides, C. (1995). Diversification, restructuring and economic performance. *Strategic Management Journal, 16*(2), 101–118.

Markides, C., & Singh, H. (1997). Corporate restructuring: A symptom of poor governance or a solution to past managerial mistakes? *European Management Journal, 15*(3), 213–219.

McDermott, M., & Luethge, D. (2013). Anatomy of a reversed foreign divestment decision: General Motors and its European subsidiary, Opel. *GSTF Business Review, 3*(1), 147.

Meglio, O. and King, D. (2019). Family businesses: Building a merger and acquisition research agenda. In Cooper, C. L. and Finkelstein, S. (Eds.), *Advances in mergers and acquisitions.* Bingley: Emerald Publishing Limited, Vol. 18, pp. 83–98.

Mitchell, M., & Mulherin, J. (1996). The impact of industry shocks on takeover and restructuring activity. *Journal of Financial Economics, 41*(2), 193–229.

Moschieri, C. (2011). The implementation and structuring of divestitures: The unit's perspective. *Strategic Management Journal, 32*(4), 368–401.

Moschieri, C., & Mair, J. (2008). Research on corporate divestitures: A synthesis. *Journal of Management & Organization, 14*(4), 399–422.

Moschieri, C., & Mair, J. (2011). Adapting for innovation: Including divestitures in the debate. *Long Range Planning, 44*(1), 4–25.

Moschieri, C., & Mair, J. (2012). Managing divestitures through time—Expanding current knowledge. *Academy of Management Perspectives, 26*(4), 35–50.

Mulherin, J., & Boone, A. (2000). Comparing acquisitions and divestitures. *Journal of Corporate Finance, 6*(2), 117–139.

Nayyar, P. (1992). On the measurement of corporate diversification strategy: Evidence from large US service firms. *Strategic Management Journal, 13*(3), 219–235.

Nees, D. (1981). Increase your divestment effectiveness. *Strategic Management Journal, 2*(2), 119–130.

Nees, D. (1983). Simulation: A complementary method for research on strategic decision-making processes. *Strategic Management Journal, 4*(2), 175–185.

O'Brien, J., & Folta, T. (2009). Sunk costs, uncertainty and market exit: A real options perspective. *Industrial and Corporate Change, 18*(5), 807–833.

Palmer, T., & Wiseman, R. (1999). Decoupling risk taking from income stream uncertainty: A holistic model of risk. *Strategic Management Journal, 20*(11), 1037–1062.

Parhankangas, A., & Arenius, P. (2003). From a corporate venture to an independent company: A base for a taxonomy for corporate spin-off firms. *Research Policy, 32*(3), 463–481.

Pathak, S., Hoskisson, R., & Johnson, R. (2014). Settling up in CEO compensation: The impact of divestiture intensity and contextual factors in refocusing firms. *Strategic Management Journal, 35*(8), 1124–1143.

Peruffo, E., Perri, A., & Oriani, R. (2014). Information asymmetries, family ownership and divestiture financial performance: Evidence from Western European countries. *Corporate Ownership & Control, 11*(4), 43–57.

Pettigrew, A., Woodman, R., & Cameron, K. (2001). Studying organizational change and development: Challenges for future research. *Academy of Management Journal, 44*(4), 697–713.

Podsakoff, P., Mackenzie, S., Bachrach, D., & Podsakoff, N. (2005). The influence of management journals in the 1980s and 1990s. *Strategic Management Journal, 26*(5), 473–488.

Porter, M. (1980). *Competitive strategy: Techniques for analyzing competitors and industries.* New York: Free Press.

Porter, M. (2008). The five competitive forces that shape strategy. *Harvard Business Review, 86*(1), 2–17.

Praet, A. (2013). Family firms and the divestment decision: An agency perspective. *Journal of Family Business Strategy, 4*(1), 34–41.

Ravenscraft, D., & Scherer, F. (1987). Life after takeover. *Journal of Industrial Economics, 36*(2), 147–156.

Rose, E., & Ito, K. (2005). Widening the family circle: Spin-offs in the Japanese service sector. *Long Range Planning, 38*(1), 9–26.

Sanders, W., & Boivie, S. (2004). Sorting things out: Valuation of new firms in uncertain markets. *Strategic Management Journal, 25*(2), 167–186.

Sapienza, H., Parhankangas, A., & Autio, E. (2004). Knowledge relatedness and post-spin-off growth. *Journal of Business Venturing, 19*(6), 809–829.

Schlingemann, F., Stulz, R., & Walkling, R. (2002). Divestitures and the liquidity of the market for corporate assets. *Journal of Financial Economics, 64*(1), 117–144.

Semadeni, M., & Cannella, A. (2011). Examining the performance effects of post spin-off links to parent firms: Should the apron strings be cut? *Strategic Management Journal, 32*(10), 1083–1098.

Shimizu, K. (2007). Prospect theory, behavioral theory, and the threat-rigidity thesis: Combinative effects on organizational decisions to divest formerly acquired units. *Academy of Management Journal, 50*(6), 1495–1514.

Shimizu, K., & Hitt, M. (2005). What constrains or facilitates divestitures of formerly acquired firms? The effects of organizational inertia. *Journal of Management, 31*(1), 50–72.

Teece, D. (1980). Economies of scope and the scope of the enterprise. *Journal of Economic Behavior & Organization, 1*(3), 223–247.

Teece, D., Pisano, G., & Shuen, A. (1997). Dynamic capabilities and strategic management. *Strategic Management Journal, 18*(7), 509–533.

Thywissen, C. (2015). Divestiture decisions: Conceptualization through a strategic decision-making lens. *Management Review Quarterly, 65*(2), 69–112.

Veld, C., & Veld-Merkoulova, Y. (2009). Value creation through spin-offs: A review of the empirical evidence. *International Journal of Management Reviews, 11*(4), 407–420.

Vidal, E., & Mitchell, W. (2018). Virtuous or vicious cycles? The role of divestitures as a complementary Penrose effect within resource-based theory. *Strategic Management Journal, 39*(1), 131–154.

Villalonga, B., & McGahan, A. (2005). The choice among acquisitions, alliances, and divestitures. *Strategic Management Journal, 26*(13), 1183–1208.

Wang, P., & Jensen, M. (2019). A bridge too far: Divestiture as a strategic reaction to status inconsistency. *Management Science, 65*(2), 859–878.

Weston, J. (1989). Divestitures: Mistakes or learning. *Journal of Applied Corporate Finance, 2*(2), 68–76.

Xia, J., Jifeng, Y., & Yijia, L. (2019). Periphery, overlap, and subunit exit in multiunit firms: A subunit power perspective. *Journal of Management, 45*(3), 881–908.

Xia, J., & Li, S. (2013). The divestiture of acquired subunits: A resource dependence approach. *Strategic Management Journal, 34*(2), 131–148.

Zellweger, T., & Dehlen, T. (2012). Value is in the eye of the owner: Affect infusion and socioemotional wealth among family firm owners. *Family Business Review, 25*(3), 280–297.

Zschoche, M. (2016). Performance effects of divesting foreign production affiliates: A network perspective. *Long Range Planning, 49*(2), 196–206.

Zuckerman, E. (2000). Focusing the corporate product: Securities analysts and de-diversification. *Administrative Science Quarterly, 45*(3), 591–619.

3 What follows what?

Sequences and combinations of acquisitions and divestitures

Oleksandra Kochura, Nicola Mirc, and Denis Lacoste

Introduction

Acquisitions and divestitures both act as "vehicles" of corporate restructuring that mark a change in the firm's internal configuration of businesses (Bowman & Singh, 1993; Brauer, 2006) and a shift in a firm's boundaries and scope (Chang, 1996). Firm management constantly administers to a corporate development portfolio by sequencing, combining, and choosing between acquisitions and divestitures to reset the firm's boundaries. As acquisitions and divestitures are modes that help firms pursue different strategies, such as refocusing, diversification, or repositioning, both modes can contribute to strategy realization. For instance, both restructuring actions can be part of a defensive mechanism to correct past decisions (Hopkins, 1991), to react to environmental shocks (Mulherin & Boone, 2000), or as a mechanism to adjust corporate scope in reaction to technological innovation produced within the firm or by rival firms (Kaul, 2012). Even though acquisitions are resource-consuming investments and divestitures free resources to narrow a firm's focus (Kuusela, Keil, & Maula, 2017), both aim to improve a firm's competitive position. Firms attempt to use a fundamental rationale when engaging in divestiture or acquisition— value and competitive advantage creation (Brauer, 2006; Feldman & McGrath, 2016; Haleblian, Devers, McNamara, Carpenter, & Davison, 2009; Moschieri & Mair, 2008). Firms often focus on their core activities and strive to align their products within the industry (Ito, 1995), while supporting synergy creation (Hoskisson, Johnson, & Moesel, 1994), by divesting peripheral businesses (Brauer, 2006; Chen & Guo, 2005; Haynes, Thompson, & Wright, 2003) or acquiring complementary assets (Bauer & Matzler, 2014; King, Dalton, Daily, & Covin, 2004; King, Wang, Samimi, & Cortes, 2021). Thus, both divestitures and acquisitions help firms strengthen their market position in terms of sales growth in the post-acquisition (Vidal & Mitchell, 2018) and address the gap between their aspired and actual performance (Kuusela et al., 2017).

DOI: 10.4324/9781003188308-5

Acquisitions and divestitures 49

Despite their shared importance in achieving firm goals and forming part of the corporate restructuring process (Bowman & Singh, 1993; Weston, 1989), divestitures and acquisitions are often studied separately. However, their sequential and simultaneous character has been acknowledged in academic research (Johnson, 1996), indicating that imprecise judgments have been made about their individual effects on firm performance (Schönhaar, Nippa, & Pidun, 2014). Recent research has illustrated that divestitures and acquisitions are "causes and consequences of each other" (Ma & Wang, 2018), which has resulted in a continuous shift toward considering divestitures and acquisitions as sequential strategic transactions rather than the static view of strategy moves (Bennett & Feldman, 2017; Karim & Mitchell, 2000; Schilke & Jiang, 2019; Vidal & Mitchell, 2018). Acknowledging that acquisitions and divestitures can occur in the same period (e.g., when down-scoping firms simultaneously pursue acquisitions in addition to commonly accepted divestitures) means that these processes cannot be studied separately (Hoskisson et al., 1994). Consequently, each of these corporate restructuring actions contributes to only part of the intended strategic change (Keum, 2020). Put differently, the role of acquisition and divestiture sequence cannot be neglected.

Possible relationships between acquisitions and divestitures by firms can be complex. For example, acquisitions can be conducted with the anticipation of some divestiture action as part of a long-term strategy (Ma & Wang, 2018). Divestiture could also be a sign of acquisition failure (Bergh, 1997), or offer a way for confronting rival firms (Haleblian et al., 2009). In scholarly publications, a common proxy for acquisition failure is divestiture (Barkema & Schijven, 2008; Montgomery & Wilson, 1986; Porter, 1976; Ravenscraft & Scherer, 1987; Schoenberg, 2006), but this does not provide a comprehensive list of the reasons for acquiring firms to divest previous acquisitions. In fact, acquisition success or failure may also depend on the firm's prior divestiture activity. For example, divestiture preceding an acquisition enables firms to release managerial and financial resources for future expansion strategies (Arcot, Gantchev, & Sevilir, 2020; Bennett & Feldman, 2017). Additionally, managers may test divestiture options before taking possible reacquisition actions (Gleason, Madura, & Pennathur, 2006; Moschieri & Mair, 2012) to help unlock the full value of an acquisition (Amiri, King, & DeMarie, 2020). Further, firms often have to make divestitures before acquisitions or complete acquisitions before divestitures due to regulatory and antitrust requirements. Overall, divestitures and acquisitions are clearly interlinked.

By stating that corporate strategy mechanisms are not exclusive and can therefore create more value when combined (Feldman, 2020; Johnson, 1996), we assume that the classification system provided in this chapter advances our understanding of every conceivable acquisition and divestiture pattern. Taking stock of various transaction programs, we assert that there is a need to stress on causal and temporal interrelationships in

50 *Oleksandra Kochura et al.*

firms' acquisitions and divestitures, as the two actions can occur through a series of sequences and combinations in the course of adjusting a firm's business portfolio.

The remainder of this chapter is structured as follows. After a short account of the research that addresses the staged nature of acquisitions and divestitures as individual transactions or a series of transaction programs, we identify two types of acquisition and divestiture sequences. The first category concerns acquisitions that precede divestitures. Option 1 includes cases where previously acquired assets are fully divested. Option 2 includes acquisitions that occur before divestitures and do not necessarily involve the same target but are interlinked to some extent. The second category covers divestitures that precede acquisitions. Option 3 includes divestitures that occur before reacquisitions of the same target in both transactions. Option 4 includes divestitures that occur before acquisitions and have different targets, yet these transactions are causes or consequences of each other.

Acquisition and divestiture combinations

Both acquisitions and divestitures are corporate restructuring tools that help firms manage their corporate development portfolios and set boundaries. The role of sequences in corporate restructuring actions to develop a new portfolio configuration, such as acquisitions and divestitures, was first acknowledged by Bowman and Singh (1993). Since then, however, restructuring sequences have been largely studied independently of one another.

Another challenge is that when the sequence of restructuring activities is considered, different theoretical lenses are used (see Table 3.1). The role of sequences was previously explained by evolutionary models of firms continuously searching for and selecting product-market configurations (Chang, 1996) and transaction cost arguments when a business portfolio is constructed considering the trade-off between costs and benefits (Bergh & Lawless, 1998). From a resource reconfiguration perspective (Teece, Pisano, & Shuen, 1997), the sequence of acquisitions and divestitures is studied based on how firms add, redeploy, and recombine resources via internal development, alliances, acquisitions, and divestitures (Achtenhagen, Brunninge, & Melin, 2017; Karim, 2006; Karim & Capron, 2016).

From an organizational learning standpoint, the experience accumulation through corporate activities can spill into other corporate activities (Zollo & Reuer, 2010). Both divestitures and acquisitions enable firms to enhance their strategic flexibility and the learning effects from their past restructuring decisions (Bertrand, Betschinger, & Petrina, 2014; Shimizu & Hitt, 2005). Hence, transaction capabilities can be transferred from one restructuring alternative to another. For example, experience with divestitures can produce knowledge that is beneficial for completion of

Table 3.1 Different potential perspectives to study corporate restructuring sequences

Perspective	Unit of analysis	Examples of articles	Seminal research	Relevance for studying acquisition and divestiture sequences
Evolutionary theory	Routines	Chang, 1996; Miller & Yang, 2016; Karim & Mitchell, 2000.	Nelson & Winter, 1982; Hannan & Freeman, 1989; Feldman & Pentland, 2003	Firms are composed of routines, which are a source of organizational stability and change. Firms are operating in the context of corporate evolution leading to a continuous and gradual search, selection and modification of their activities through corporate restructuring sequences.
Resource reconfiguration	Resources	Kaul, 2012; Karim, 2006; Karim & Mitchell 2004; Capron et al., 2001	Teece et al., 1997; Karim & Capron, 2016	Firms proactively and deliberately match capabilities and markets in a dynamic context by adding, redeploying, recombining or divesting components.
Embeddedness	Relations, network ties, structural position	Schilke & Jiang, 2019; Karim, 2012	Granovetter, 1985; Uzzi, 1996; Gulati, 1998	Embeddedness within a firm's activities, firm's embeddedness within its environment and embeddedness across governance modes imply a series of governance and resource allocation decisions. Various facets of embeddedness allow a better understanding of the temporal nature of organizational boundary decisions.
Organizational learning	Experiences	Kolev, 2016; Bingham, Heimeriks, Schijven, & Gates, 2015; Bertrand et al., 2014; Zollo & Reuer, 2010; Kalnins, Swaminathan, & Mitchell, 2006	Levitt & March, 1988	Corporate restructuring sequences are triggered, facilitated or impeded by the focal firm's direct experience with corporate restructuring, spillovers from distinct corporate development initiatives or learning from the experience of others. Moreover, learning from past strategic actions can sustain subsequent strategic initiatives.

(continued)

Table 3.1 Cont.

Perspective	Unit of analysis	Examples of articles	Seminal research	Relevance for studying acquisition and divestiture sequences
Transaction cost theory	Transactions, contracts	Villalonga & McGahan 2005, Bergh & Lawless, 1998	Williamson, 1999; Langlois, 1992	Even though the transaction cost theory is static, some dynamic developments manifest: not only ex-ante but also ex-post conditions for a specific governance choice are necessary. In the same vein, governance modes are adapted over time. These considerations imply intertemporal application of transaction cost reasoning in sequences of corporate restructuring actions.
Real option	Investments, disinvestments	Moschieri & Mair, 2017; Damaraju, Barney, & Makhija, 2015; Chi, 2000	Dixit & Pindyck, 1994; Bowman & Hurry, 1993; Kogut & Kulatilaka, 2001	The real options perspective suggests that under conditions of uncertainty firms make a compromise between commitment and flexibility by sequenced, staged and reversible investments and disinvestments. Firms relying on a diverse set of alternatives by choosing some options simultaneously. This perspective may help particularly to explain corporate restructuring sequences, like reacquisitions, series of staged acquisitions and staged divestitures.

| Resource dependence theory | Dependencies | Xia & Li, 2013 | Pfeffer & Salancik, 1978 | Resource dependence theory regards firm interactions with environmental constraints and contingencies to access resources for survival. The power-dependence relations within a focal firm and outside the firm imply organizational actions and change. These relations are dynamic, and their change might trigger various sequential corporate restructuring actions. Notably, subsequent increase or decrease of the dependence relation and level of autonomy between the focal firm and acquired entities and/or divested entities result in subsequent divestitures and/or acquisitions. |

54 *Oleksandra Kochura et al.*

acquisitions (Doan, Rao Sahib, & van Witteloostuijn, 2018), and this leads to a greater ability to make divestiture decisions and master the selling procedure (Moliterno & Wiersema, 2007). The learning effect is enhanced when a prior sell-off increases the likelihood of acquisition completion in the future. As a sell-off implies the disposal of the divesting parent firm's assets through sale to another company, transaction similarities become more salient. Factors such as overlapping duties and similarities in the preparation process for potential deals for both divestors and acquirers and experience with market evaluation and timelines can help future acquirers better gauge the needs and expectations of the divesting party (Doan et al., 2018).

The potential perspectives to study corporate restructuring sequences also include embeddedness, real option, and resource dependence theories. A combination of different theoretical angles to handle these dynamic processes should result in a production of novel contributions to theory and practice. But again, despite various examples of possible trade-offs and complementarity between acquisitions and divestitures, these processes have been examined rather independently from one another.

Acquisition and divestiture programs

The relationship between acquisition and divestiture is apparent in cases where firms are pursuing large acquisition or divestiture programs simultaneously with a change in their strategy. For example, in 2014, Siemens launched its Vision 2020 strategy program focused on gaining new market shares in the industrial digitalization, the Internet of Things, and electric mobility fields. In line with its formulated strategy, Siemens proceeded with a series of acquisitions and divestitures to reorganize the firm into three separately operating entities. The series of sell-offs, spin-offs, and acquisitions were intended to create more entrepreneurial freedom for the separate companies produced. The active management of a firm's corporate portfolio through a balance of divestitures and acquisitions delivers substantially more shareholder value than if firms avoid any form of corporate restructuring or rely exclusively on acquisitions or divestitures (Dranikoff, Koller, & Schneider, 2002).

Thus, in practice, acquisitions and divestitures are often not mutually exclusive activities but rather elements of an acquisition and divestiture restructuring program aimed at changing a firm's corporate strategy and business portfolio. It has been recognized not only that firms can pursue acquisition programs and engage in single deals (Laamanen & Keil, 2008) but also that acquisition sequencing and timing are important elements in such activity (Chatterjee, 2009). Divestitures are sequential rather than "stand-alone" transactions (Brauer & Schimmer, 2010), and a series of divestitures can help a firm implement its corporate strategy as well as adapt its governance structure and leadership (Dranikoff et al.,

Acquisitions and divestitures 55

2002). Further, firms regularly engage in acquisitions and divestitures in the same year or during the same period. For instance, firms pursue acquisitions along with divestitures during down-scoping processes. Vidal (2021) illustrated that it is common for pharmaceutical firms to concurrently implement acquisitions and divestitures.

Typologies of sequential divestiture and acquisition

We can classify acquisition and divestiture sequences into two main groups: acquisitions that precede divestitures, henceforth referred to as "acquisition before divestiture", and divestitures that precede acquisitions, henceforth referred to as "divestiture before acquisition". Transactions in either group can concern the same target or only part of the same target or even not involve the target at all in future transactions. Therefore, we also distinguish between sequences that involve the same or different targets, as the explanatory factors differ between sequences with these varying targets. This multiplicity stems from the complexity of acquisitions and divestitures and the fact that they can be staged or progressive. This issue is important for understanding that firms may not acquire or divest other entities completely, or transactions may be partial. A firm might divest partially, allowing later reacquisition, or may acquire partially and, after reconfiguring its internal resources, divest only a part of a newly formed entity. However, as the focus of this chapter is on suggesting different combinations and sequences of acquisitions and divestitures, we walk through four possible scenarios. The four likely sequences are simplified here, functioning like poles on a continuum that contains much more nuance (see Table 3.2).

Acquisition before divestiture involving the same target (Option 1)

As noted above, divestiture can be a consequence of a prior acquisition. In this section, we illustrate the conditions where the strategic intent of

Table 3.2 Four scenarios of acquisition and divestiture sequence

	Sequences		
		Acquisition before divestiture	Divestiture before acquisition
Overlap	Involves the same target	Firm A acquires X and later divests X	Firm A divests X and later reacquires X
		Option 1	*Option 3*
	Does not necessarily involve the same target	Firm A acquires X and later divests Y	Firm A divests X and later acquires Y
		Option 2	*Option 4*

acquisition leads to a reversal of the previous decision and thus to the divestiture of the acquired target. In these circumstances, firms are not fully redeploying and integrating the acquired business, thus leading to the complete divestiture of the acquired entity. However, acquisitions can also be staged, leading to the partial divestiture of previously acquired assets. For example, at the end of 2020, pharmaceutical firm Merck & Co divested its stake in vaccine-maker Moderna, which it had previously acquired in 2015; similarly, Etihad divested its 20 percent stake in Air Seychelles in 2021 that it had previously acquired in 2012. The first divestiture is an example of Merck & Co seizing an opportunity due to growth in the stock price of Moderna; the second one is the result of the failed strategy of investing in other airlines.

In any divestiture of previously acquired assets, it can be asked whether the action is a reversal of a previous decision after acknowledging having made a mistake or just the result of a change in the firm's strategy. Since Weston's (1989) work, there have generally been two dominant opinions on the matter: an acquisition-turned-divestiture may be the result of a failed acquisition or simply a reflection of a change in corporate strategy (Weston, 1989). In the latter condition, for example, a refocusing or reorientation implies that the firm is divesting noncore operations to grow through more core- or new core-related acquisitions. For instance, the legacy business of Electrolux, a multinational home appliance manufacturer, from the beginning was vacuum cleaner manufacturing. However, in 2016, the company shifted its focus to strong small appliance categories and divested the previously acquired Eureka company. Following this divestiture, Electrolux engaged in a series of acquisitions focusing on innovative solutions in the home appliance market, such as the acquisition of Anova, a smart kitchen appliance company. Generally, the most common rationale for the divestiture of previously acquired assets is a misalignment between the parent firm and the acquired business. This misalignment can take the form of acquisition failure due to failed integration, the form of a strategic change originated within or outside the focal firm, or an apparent misfit between an acquired target and an acquirer. We discuss these hereinafter by supplementing with the performance implications for acquisitions-turned-divestitures.

Misalignment owing to acquisition failure. Divestiture is a possible outcome of both related and unrelated acquisition activities (Montgomery & Wilson, 1986) and is a frequent phenomenon (Bergh, 1997; Wang & Larimo, 2020). The ongoing debate on acquisition performance and acquisition survival illustrates that divestiture commonly serves as a proxy for these concepts (Meschi & Métais, 2015; Nadolska & Barkema, 2007; Wang & Larimo, 2020). The decision to divest a previously acquired target is a matter of misalignment between the expected and actual outcomes of such an acquisition. This kind of reverse action is often attributed to acquisition failure (Bergh, 1997; Ravenscraft & Scherer, 1987). From an acquisition outcomes perspective, scholars associate divestiture with the inability of an acquisition to achieve the expected performance-related outcomes, thus leading to accounting losses (Kaplan & Weisbach, 1992), and the inability of the acquired business to contribute to the acquirer's cash flow and acquirer's financial synergies (Bergh, 1997).

Based on a sample of divested and retained unrelated acquisitions, Bergh (1997) illustrated that the initial acquisition motives, such as financial synergies, market power, and economies of scale and scope, impact future divestiture decisions. When the conditions and motives of an acquisition are satisfied, firms tend to keep previously acquired unrelated businesses; when these fail to meet expectations, firms divest (Bergh, 1997). One example of an acquisition that did not achieve the intended result is Adidas's acquisition of Reebok in 2006, which was undertaken to increase Adidas's competitiveness with its rival, Nike. In 2020, Adidas announced its intention to divest Reebok, as it had succeeded in limiting its competitive gap with Nike. Despite the parent firm's statements regarding the successful outcome of acquisition, independent analysts suggested that the objectives formulated for the 2006 acquisition were not achieved and that sales for Reebok had recently dropped significantly.

Acquisition failure can originate from the decision-making or integration phases. Some acquisition "mistakes" already occur during the decision-making phase. Acquiring firms can overestimate the benefits of acquiring the given business (Roll, 1986), which can also result in high-price acquisition (Hitt et al., 2012) and lead to future divestiture options for the business. Similar financial arguments are that acquisitions-turned-divestitures are a correction of previous strategic mistakes that are valued with the positive reaction to the divestiture announcement (Weston, 1989) and that the acquired business can improve the acquiring firm's performance at the time of the transaction.

Divestiture can originate from a previous acquisition following the inability of the acquirer to successfully integrate the target. Schilke and Jiang (2019) show that alliances before acquisitions help limit the probability of later divestitures. They explain that embeddedness between allies can help provide precise information about compatibility between the parties and generate an important level of trust, which can then lead to smooth integration if acquisition is pursued (Schilke & Jiang, 2019) as well as maximize the ability of the acquirer to secure synergistic benefits (Lumineau & Mulotte, 2019). On the one hand, if the integration process fails, the acquired target can later be divested (Meschi & Métais, 2015). But on the other hand, the massive managerial focus on integration of acquired businesses might lead to inability to learn from the process leading to subsequent divestiture (Hayward, 2002).

Misalignment owing to strategic change. Another reason for the divestiture of previously acquired businesses include a change in the firm's strategy. Firms can not only unintentionally acquire redundant activities that need to be carved out at a later point in time (Brauer,

58   *Oleksandra Kochura et al.*

2006) but also intentionally acquire some activities where a divestiture option has already been considered at the time of acquisition. The intention of a firm to acquire with the intention to divest later is explained by the investment purpose argument and the option of seizing an opportunity today with a plan to let it go later (Weston, 1989). Firms pursuing an acquisition before a divestiture may do so while searching for new opportunities (Dranikoff et al., 2002) or due to a change in their business environment or governance (Johnson, 1996). Thus, these findings refute the view that considers divestiture only the result of a failure and supports the notion that divestiture is a dynamic process occurring in response to changes in market dependencies (Jun, Yu, & Lin, 2019) expressed through changes in the strategic importance of the market for a firm in terms of the revenues that the specific market can bring (Gimeno, 1999).

Misalignment owing to acquired targets' characteristics. Statistically, previously acquired businesses are more often divested than those developed through greenfield investments (Benito, 1997) or other internal development options (Karim, 2006). First, it is easier to pursue divestiture for previously acquired businesses (Colombo & Rabbiosi, 2014). Second, academic studies illustrate that R&D operations are more often affected by divestiture decisions for businesses that were previously acquired than for those owned initially by the acquiring firm (Capron, 1999). However, not all previously acquired businesses are later divested, and sometimes the misalignment between the target and acquirer after acquisition can result in the subsequent divestiture of the former.

Previously acquired targets that are candidates for divestiture are more often involved in activities that are unrelated to the acquirer's core operations (Bergh, 1997) and those that are poorly performing (Shimizu & Hitt, 2005). For a more extensive review of corporate divestiture antecedents, please refer to Chapter 2 of this book. However, even loss-inducing acquired targets can be protected from divestiture decisions. Delay in the decision to divest underperforming previously acquired targets is explained by particular managerial attention to the integration process, managerial attachment to the acquired businesses, and organizational inertia (Shimizu & Hitt, 2005; Xia & Li, 2013).

The divestiture of previously acquired businesses is facilitated within firms with strong governance mechanisms. Long-tenured CEOs may postpone divestiture decisions, leading to harmful risk-seeking behavior (Shimizu & Hitt, 2005) and the ineffectiveness of the divestiture decisions that are made (Thywissen, Pidun, & zu Knyphausen-Aufseß, 2018). However, CEOs who manage the firm with increasingly strong performance are more likely to reverse past strategic actions and divest previously acquired units (Hayward & Shimizu, 2006). Nevertheless, the appointment of new outside CEOs and new outside directors produces a more effective reexamination of prior management teams' mistakes, prompts changes in the dominant logic to highlight opportunities that

Acquisitions and divestitures 59

divestiture can bring for poorly performing acquired units (Shimizu & Hitt, 2005).

As mentioned previously, divestitures are more likely to happen when previously acquired assets do not benefit from a pre-acquisition alliance. In terms of a firm's network embeddedness, premerger alliances reduce the plausibility of subsequent divestitures, including the impact of prior alliance governance choice (Schilke & Jiang, 2019) and the availability of information about acquirer–target fit (Lumineau & Mulotte, 2019) on the likelihood of an acquisition turning into a divestiture. From the resource dependence theory lens, the divestiture of previously acquired subunits is a matter of the low mutual dependence between divested and retained businesses and increasing subunit power through consequent acquisitions and alliances completed by the subunit (Xia & Li, 2013).

Performance implication of divestitures of previously acquired businesses. Acquisitions leading to subsequent divestiture can positively impact firms' market value. This mechanism is more salient when the original acquisition was aimed at increasing synergetic value, but with time, this synergy weakened or disappeared (Benito, 1997). The possible losses from divestitures of previously acquired businesses vary from financial (depletion of financial resources), organizational (departure of managers), or reputational (damage of institutional identity) (Bergh, 1997). Nevertheless, the performance implications for acquisition-turned-divestiture activities are better for acquirers that have received a better market reaction to acquisition events (Amiri et al., 2020). To mitigate the negative effect of acquisition-turned-divestiture, in the frame of unbundling, acquiring firms sometimes partially divest previously acquired assets. This happens when the acquirer retains valuable resources from the target and divests unnecessary ones (Capron, Mitchell, & Swaminathan, 2001), and this sequence is developed next.

Acquisition before divestiture, not necessarily involving the same target (Option 2)

A divestiture might encompass part of a previously acquired target or even some assets that have been internally recombined and reconfigured with internally developed businesses following the acquisition. The divestitures, in this case, include those assets that are unnecessary or redundant, cannot be redeployed in acquiring firms, or simply were unintentionally acquired as a part of the acquired target. For example, FedEx's acquisition of TNT was followed by a series of organizational restructurings to avoid duplicate job positions.

In addition, firms may acquire specific assets but divest some of their activities that were not necessarily acquired in a previous acquisition. For example, in 2020, Worldline, a French payment and transactional services company acquired Ingenico Group, a company operating in the payment terminals market. Having barely completed its acquisition

60 *Oleksandra Kochura et al.*

of Ingenico, Worldline began selling its payment terminal activities, refocusing on electronic payments. In such circumstances, the activities that are divested are not necessarily those that were previously acquired; acquisition can be a trigger for future divestiture options.

In the same vein, divestitures following acquisitions can defend interests in a hostile situation and be a way to mitigate antitrust problems. For example, Veolia's 2021 hostile takeover of Suez, two competing environmental services companies, was successful, as Suez accepted the acquisition only when a spin-off alternative for some of its assets was agreed upon. Another example of the role of regulatory requirements is the obligation imposed by the US Justice Department for Novelis to divest a portion of the acquired company Aleris as a condition of is acquisition activity.

Divestitures following acquisitions can also be a way to create new growth opportunities. This sequence applies more often to the spin-off or split-up of a firm. For example, in 2021, Dell announced a spin-off of its 81 percent equity VMware, a cloud computing company. In 2015, multinational computer technology company Dell acquired VMware as a part of its acquisition of EMC Corp. The announced spin-off was meant to enable additional growth opportunities by maintaining strong collaboration between the two now independent firms. Another example of the emergent divestiture of the previously acquired business is the spin-off of DirecTV by AT&T. In 2015, the world's largest telecommunication company acquired DirecTV, a company operating in the satellite television industry. Six years later, AT&T announced that it was preparing to spin off DirecTV, U-Verse, and AT&T TV, which would operate as standalone firms. This demonstrates that the acquirer's reconfiguration efforts can also be aimed at preparing the part of the target to operate as a standalone company. At the same time, these examples illustrate how firms are constantly adapting their corporate development portfolios by acquiring and divesting in search of the optimal configuration. Below we separately develop three reasons firms may make divestitures that do not necessarily involve the same target.

Resource reconfiguration after acquisition. Acquisition-turned-divestiture activity that does not necessarily imply the acquired business was largely viewed through a resource reconfiguration lens. Reconfiguration and renewal are strategic perspectives for studying the post-acquisition integration process and examining how resources, competencies, and knowledge are aligned between acquired and acquiring firms (Graebner, Heimeriks, Huy, & Vaara, 2017). The reconfiguration of acquirers and acquired targets occurs by redeploying, adding, or divesting resources, product lines, or entire businesses (Bodner & Capron, 2018; Karim, 2006; Karim & Capron, 2016). Following an acquisition, the major activities of integration involve resource reconfiguration through the alteration of the firm's resource and competence asset structure to continuously adapt to a rapidly changing environment (Teece et al., 1997) or the change and recombination of the resources of the acquiring firm and the acquired business (Capron, Dussauge, & Mitchell, 1998; Karim & Mitchell, 2000).

Acquiring firms spend exert effort to integrate acquired targets (Hambrick & Cannella, 1993), and a divestiture during this time can serve as a mechanism for reducing the inefficiency, bureaucracy, and complexity deriving from numerous acquisition and increased diversification activities (Kolev, 2016). Barkema and Schijven (2008) illustrated that the recombination of subunits, as a form of organizational restructuring following an acquisition, can reduce existing organizational inefficiencies and provide long-term benefits for an acquiring firm. Although these authors distinguish between divestiture and organizational restructuring, prior studies have illustrated that divestiture activity tends to be intense during organizational restructuring periods (Bowman & Singh, 1993). Organizational restructuring following an acquisition can be a matter of high information asymmetries at the time of acquisition and the bounded rationality associated with the organizational complexity that additional acquisitions can bring. Therefore, firms tend to implement organizational restructuring that can unlock their full synergistic potential and act as an important step in the post-acquisition integration process (Barkema & Schijven, 2008).

Misalignment following reconfiguration. Divestitures are an integral part of the post-acquisition integration process (Barkema & Schijven, 2008). From a resource reconfiguration standpoint, acquisitions are tools for accessing and obtaining resources and capabilities that enable value creation, while divestitures are a means to remove less valuable resources and change a firm's portfolio of businesses to be more effective (Feldman, 2020). Acquisitions that generate economies of scope can require divestitures to cut the cost of the targets' redundant resources (Helfat & Eisenhardt, 2004). Divestiture, as an important element of reconfiguration (Berry, 2010), enables firms to secure the most added value by recombining resources and to increase strategic flexibility (Karim, 2006). Acquired units are recombined and divested faster than internally developed units (Karim, 2006), and R&D assets are more likely to be divested from acquired firms than from acquiring firms (Capron, 1999).

Due to the different routines, procedures, and information flow of acquired units and internally developed units, acquiring firms reconfigure the former and weed out resources that are not needed (Karim, 2006). An example of this sequence is Hachette, a French publishing company that acquired the company Perseus and then divested some of the latter's client services businesses that it did not need to Ingram, a US book distribution company. As part of the initial negotiations, Hachette planned to fully acquire the business and then divest unnecessary activities that were not intended to be integrated and would hence be relatively easy to separate. However, the deal was called off in 2014 because of concerns over

62 *Oleksandra Kochura et al.*

the complexity of such actions, and Hachette finally acquired Perseus's publishing assets and imprints and Ingram acquired its distribution assets two years later. Therefore, even firms considering certain sequences of acquisition followed by divestiture may find that in practice, these plans are not always easily implemented.

Misalignment due to the incapacity to reconfigure. Acquisitions can be followed by partial divestitures where only a portion of previously acquired assets is divested (Colombo & Rabbiosi, 2014). In an acquisition, firms can also acquire resources that they do not need and then divest those resources. Divestiture candidates are resources that were not redeployed or were not intended for redeployment in the acquiring firm during post-acquisition integration. The resources that are divested are those that do not provide any synergistic gains (Lumineau & Mulotte, 2019), but they do not necessarily involve previously acquired targets. Sometimes the impact of divesting even partially previously acquired assets damages long-term acquisition performance. For instance, the divestiture of resources from previously acquired targets may not help develop revenue-enhancing capabilities, such as market coverage and innovation, and may even damage these capabilities. Less commonly, the divestiture of an acquirer's assets following acquisition has a positive impact on cost savings (Capron, 1999).

Divestiture before acquisition involving the same target (Option 3)

Prior evidence implies that between 19 and 50 percent of divestitures are reacquired by their former parent firms, thus equating to three out of ten divested units (Klein, Rosenfeld, & Beranek, 1991; Ma & Wang, 2018; Moschieri & Mair, 2012; Schipper & Smith, 1986). These reacquired assets and businesses were divested previously through equity carve-outs, spin-offs, or sell-offs. Reacquisition decisions are analyzed during the divestiture decision-making stage (Moschieri & Mair, 2012), emerge from changes in the divestor's strategy or the external environment (Dietz & Zu Knyphausen-Aufseß, 2017), or arise in response to negative market reactions to announcements that signal that the divestiture was a mistake (Gleason et al., 2006). In addition, reacquisition can take place in the framework of regulatory requirements. The Japanese Nidec Corporation, a company operating in the variable-speed compressor market, was forced to divest its manufacturing line according to an agreement with the European Commission regarding its acquisition of Embraco. However, following divestiture, the increasing risk of closing the manufacturing line prompted the former parent firm to request the reacquisition of the previously divested activity. This reflects different reasons for reacquiring a prior divestiture related to either reassessment or adaptation.

Partial divestiture, flexibility and reassessment of the previous decision. Finance scholars have provided evidence that subsidiary listings can lead to reacquisition by parent firms. Equity carve-outs, a type of divestiture

Acquisitions and divestitures 63

alternative, generally involve two stages in which the firm initially carves out some shares and either completely divests the remaining interest or reacquires publicly traded shares (Klein et al., 1991). The second stage can then be realized by third-party acquisition (sell-off), spin-off, or reacquisition by the parent firm (Vijh, 2002). An example of reacquisition following equity carve-out is the case of Telefonica and Terra, companies operating in the telecommunication industry. Telefonica reacquired Terra in 2004 after the former's successful initial public offering (IPO) of the latter in 1999. However, the great valuation of Terra at the time of the IPO was ultimately unstable and declined, prompting the former parent reacquire the subsidiary for a lower price.

In such cases, the firm's decision to fully divest through the temporary alternative of asset restructuring can be explained either as an initially planned two-staged divestiture process or as the parent firm seeking to disclose more information about the subsidiary that would result in a broader market for acquisition and potential buyers for the business. The decision to reacquire the subsidiary thus signifies that the firm has failed to receive satisfactory offers from the market for acquisition (Klein et al., 1991) or that after the first divestiture event, the subsidiary is undervalued (Otsubo, 2009). In Klein et al.'s (1991) data sample, reacquisition decisions occurred, on average, 5 years after the first equity carve-out and while parent firms still retained a large percentage of their subsidiary shares (Klein et al., 1991). The reacquisition of a previously listed subsidiary is more likely when a strong business relationship with the parent firm is maintained, and the presence of board interlocks and low dividend policies in a listed subsidiary can produce conflicts of interest (Otsubo & Miyoshi, 2009).

Adaptability to new contingencies. Reacquisitions are means for a divestor to adapt to evolving industry business models, to ensure the continuity of its operations, or to diminish the threat of a third party, such as a competitor, taking over the business (Moschieri & Mair, 2012). Through a qualitative study, Dietz and Zu Knyphausen-Aufseß (2017) showed that 13 out 14 studied reacquisition cases were not planned at the time of divestiture, and only one divestiture was implemented with reacquisition planned in the future. In this single case, the divestiture occurred because of regulatory requirements. When firm management is confident that reacquisition is likely, they make various interorganizational arrangements. After acquisition, the acquiring firm obtains control over the targets. At the same time, divesting firms can maintain relationships with former targets in the post-divestiture period by outsourcing contracts, commercial agreements, board member interlocks (Moschieri & Mair, 2012), and dual directors (Feldman, 2016).

Possible reasons for unplanned reacquisitions are heterogenous and involve changes in the parent firm's strategy or external environment, partnership failure, and pressure from initial investors. In the case of dis-synergies appearing within the parent firm following the acquisition

64   *Oleksandra Kochura et al.*

or of potential new synergies arising from reacquisition due to market and technology changes, firms may reconsider the decision to acquire the business back. Some previously divested businesses become more attractive by providing new business opportunities, or they threaten to become a rival of the parent firm, making past divestiture a poor business decision. Additional causes of the reacquisition of previously partially divested activities include the failure of the partnership due to conflicts of interests, culture clashes, and failed projects leading to deficient synergies (Dietz & Zu Knyphausen-Aufseß, 2017).

Performance implications of reacquisitions. The market may react positively to reacquisition announcements for both parent firms and subsidiaries (Gleason et al., 2006). In such cases, the reacquisition is efficient (Aron, 1991) and can be value-adding even if it comes at a premium (Moschieri & Mair, 2012). However, contradictory findings suggest that the divesting firm's excess returns from the announcement of the reacquisition of carved-out and sold-off units are insignificant (Klein et al., 1991). Still, before reacquisition, the market capitalization of subsidiaries may be lower than the activities that were divested (Thompson, 2013).

Reacquisition as a response to the undervaluation of a target can be motivated by the need to improve the divestor's performance. In such cases, the market also reacts positively to reacquisitions and is more favorable to the full reacquisition and reintegration of a previously divested business (Gleason et al., 2006). For example, Withings, a French consumer electronics company, following its initial acquisition and further integration by Nokia Health, was reacquired by a co-founder two years later. Following its reacquisition, Withings showed an improved innovation capacity by introducing innovative new products. However, even though the former owner of Withings, entrepreneur Eric Carreel, justified this reacquisition by citing the strong attachment to the company, the sequence of the divestiture before the reacquisition resulted in a significant loss of talent.

Divestiture before acquisition, not necessarily involving the same target (Option 4)

Divestitures that precede acquisitions, but do not necessarily involve the same businesses, can be used to obtain greater flexibility for future expansion objectives and greater adaptability to changing market conditions, as well as to respond to regulatory obligations. Frequently, firms are forced to divest because there is a risk that their future acquisitions will need to be abandoned because of pressure from regulators. In anticipation of such obstructions, firms might choose to divest ex ante to avoid legal and regulatory difficulties (Hite & Owers, 1983). For example, in 2021, EssilorLuxottica, a manufacturer and distributor of ophthalmic lenses, frames, and sunglasses, was required to divest more than 300 shops in

Italy, the Netherlands, and Belgium to obtain European Union antitrust approval for the acquisition of GrandVision.

Organizational restructuring can also facilitate acquisition. For example, the resource planning software company SAP announced the spin-off of Qualtrics to "make smaller 'tuck-in' acquisitions" in 2021. Additionally, Alitalia, an Italian national airline carrier, started significant employee downsizing in preparation for a merger with AirFrance-KLM in 2003. Despite often being triggered by regulatory requirements, divestitures that occur before acquisitions and involve different targets can likewise be part of a deliberate strategic decision. Specifically, divestiture can unlock resources.

Resource-freeing in anticipation of acquisition. Acquisitions require substantial managerial involvement and financial resources. Divestitures can form part of a future expansion strategy, as they release the necessary resources to finance acquisitions or raise funds (Lang, Poulsen, & Stulz, 1995) and facilitate managerial attention within an organization (Bennett & Feldman, 2017). In this vein, divestiture before acquisition is a means for freeing financial resources and refocusing managerial attention on future corporate portfolio development (Kaul, 2012; Vidal & Mitchell, 2015, 2018) and in anticipation of subsequent acquisitions.

Divestiture can also serve as a tool for the separation of activities that no longer fit within the firm, thus freeing resources for additional growth opportunities (Kaul, 2012). Divesting firms subsequently become more focused and invest more than diversified firms (Nanda & Narayanan, 1999). Divestiture helps generate cash, which can be used for further investments. This can be important as cash payment for acquisition payments generate better acquisition performance than stock-financed payments (King et al., 2021). Thus, organizational growth and transformation can be attained through divestiture, as such activity helps a firm reorient or reshape itself and can support subsequent acquisitions (Brauer, 2006; Dranikoff et al., 2002).

Performance implications of divestitures before acquisitions. A divestiture before an acquisition has a different impact on parent firms. Despite being driven by the desire to increase managerial attention and seize new market opportunities through subsequent acquisitions, divestiture may also increase the risk of the divesting firm being acquired itself. Whether a divesting firm acquires other entities or is acquired itself remains largely dependent on the firm's financial performance prior to divestiture. Divestiture helps low-performing firms increase their profits, but it might increase the risk of being acquired. When high-performing firms use such actions as an opportunity for growth, investment in current acquisitions can significantly diminish the risk of being acquired (Vidal & Mitchell, 2018).

The "divest to acquire" motive may be a solution to a misinterpreted view of acquisitions driven by managerial agency costs and empire-building purposes. Arcot et al. (2020) demonstrated that firms use divestitures as an ex ante proactive strategy to secure greater gains from future acquisitions. For example, divestiture can declutter a firm before acquisition enabling the more efficient integration of newly acquired assets. The sequence of divestiture before acquisition results in greater value creation for the acquiring firm shareholders, especially when large divestitures are followed by large acquisitions. However, large acquisitions have greater risk of destroying value, suggesting that a divestiture undertaken one to three years before a large acquisition can mitigate a negative performance effect (Arcot et al., 2020). Perhaps this effect is related to experience, as firms can learn from divestitures from the target's perspective to inform future acquisitions (Doan et al., 2018). In such cases, acquisitions followed by divestitures provide additional familiarity along with organizational learning about how to complete acquisition deal-making and integration processes.

Conclusion

We outline examples of various sequences and configurations of acquisitions and divestitures. We illustrated that divestitures and acquisitions are both types of corporate restructuring aimed at reshaping a firm's scope and portfolio of businesses. Both types can be combined in different acquisition and divestiture sequences and programs, and both can be progressive or partial. In the context of market uncertainty, firms may seek to retain the option to undo a transaction decision or proceed with complete resource-consuming and resource-freeing investments. The typologies presented highlight evidence that firms are constantly adapting their corporate portfolios in search of optimum asset allocation. Both divestitures and acquisitions help firms achieve these portfolio efficiency objectives. We demonstrated that there are two types of sequences: (1) acquisitions preceding divestitures, and (2) divestitures preceding acquisitions. In addition, these two sequences can involve the partial or full target, or not involve that target at all. We found that the "acquisitions preceding divestitures" configuration has been acknowledged in the literature following Weston's (1989) work, but the "divestitures preceding acquisitions" configuration remains counterintuitive to most researchers. This drives several implications for research.

First, acquisitions before divestitures may involve the same target in two transactions. In this configuration, firms mostly acquire targets with a specific rationale that is not subsequently fulfilled. In such conditions, firms use reversal action and divest previously acquired assets. This sequence of events is not necessarily related to acquisition failure, as has been proposed in existing research. Rather, it may be the outcome of a misalignment between the businesses the company operates in and the added value of acquired businesses to the firm's strategic objectives.

Second, acquisitions before divestitures may involve different targets in two transactions that are nevertheless linked. In such cases, acquiring

Acquisitions and divestitures   67

firms aim to implement reconfiguration efforts and commonly integrate the acquired businesses. Resources that cannot be recombined or that remain unnecessary are further divested. In contrast, the firm may divest resources that were not necessarily acquired but no longer fit within the desired business portfolio. In such circumstances, following an acquisition, a firm can continue refocusing or reorientation efforts by making a divestiture. This sequence is pursued to source for new resources, competencies, and knowledge through such acquisition. Subsequent divestiture is then a result of a misalignment between what the firm aspired to achieve and what it actually achieved.

Third, divestitures that occur before acquisitions may involve the same target in two transactions. In such cases, a firm executes a full or partial divestiture but later reacquires the same business that it previously divested. This emergent action of reversal can be interpreted as an example of sharp alteration and adaptability to changing market conditions and new growth opportunities. In some cases, reacquisition is planned from the beginning as a part of a deliberate strategy to test the ability of the divested business to operate separately from the parent firm. Nevertheless, reacquisition is ensured through diverse forms of relationship maintenance between parent firms and divested targets.

Fourth, divestitures before acquisitions may not involve the same target in two transactions. These divestitures are rather deliberate actions aimed at focusing managerial and financial resources to support upcoming acquisitions. Adjusting a business portfolio through divestiture before acquisition may occur because firms seek to secure subsequent acquisitions but must consider regulatory difficulties and antitrust laws.

This classification of the interrelations between acquisitions and divestitures has various business applications. For managers, it suggests that acquisitions may be complemented by divestitures and vice versa. The list of different corporate portfolio management choices may allow firms to pursue several options at the time or use divestitures and acquisitions in different time frames to facilitate the benefits of each option. We also outline when different choices may be advantageous to firms.

Future research agenda

As acquisitions and divestitures are traditionally studied independently, their interrelated character has not been sufficiently examined. By merging two streams of literature, we illustrate that firms engage in both acquisition and divestiture to implement an intended strategy. If we assume that divestitures and acquisitions are unrelated, we may misunderstand the motivations behind these decisions. For example, if we consider a firm's market expansion as an acquisition rationale, but the firm also divests some operations within the same market, the rationale for such actions is faulty. Additionally, if firms are deliberately acquiring with the intent to divest, they will probably avoid integration, implying consequences for

68 *Oleksandra Kochura et al.*

post-acquisition performance. Further, it can lead to misunderstanding why firms might acquire in order to divest, or divest in order to acquire or reacquire.

A closer look at divestitures and acquisitions with the order in which they occur suggests that it is perhaps not possible to understand the motives and performance implications of these transactions without considering their sequence. Both acquisitions and divestitures are important elements of portfolio management and should not be studied in isolation. In general, a deliberate acquisition decision with the intent to divest or deliberate divestiture with the intent to acquire is not well understood. The same holds true for the sequences of acquisition and divestiture, and their impact on performance remains unexamined (for an exception, see Amiri et al., 2020). However, in practice, firms combine acquisitions and divestitures to reshape their strategy (Dranikoff et al., 2002); thus, the use of one tool (i.e., acquisition or divestiture) in managing a firm's corporate portfolio can precede the use of the other.

In considering limitations, we acknowledge that we cover only two-step sequences of acquisition and divestiture, and many more steps are possible, as practical evidence reveals. For example, firm A can acquire X and then divest X to finance acquisition Y. This is the case for one "divestiture before acquisition" example given for the 2021 spin-off of Qualtrics by SAP (Option 4). However, 20 months before SAP acquired Qualtrics, the acquisition was criticized by investors because of the overestimation of the target and the high payment of $8 billion in an all-cash deal. Consequently, this might be a sign of misalignment owing to acquisition failure (Option 1). If SAP appropriated any resources, competencies, and knowledge from the target before the spin-off or reconfigured its asset base with those of the acquired target, then the spun-off Qualtrics was no longer the one that was acquired (Option 2). We can suppose that SAP might consider reacquiring part or all of Qualtrics, leading to a reverse of a strategic action (Option 3). There is also the question of other corporate portfolio options, such as sequences of equity and nonequity alliances (Shi and Prescott, 2011), and the role they play in sequences of corporate restructuring.

Another major puzzle in such classification lies in the fact that divestitures and acquisitions sometimes involve a triad of participants: a divesting firm, a divested entity, and an acquiring firm. In such cases, the divestiture of one firm can become the acquisition of another. For example, let us consider the case of Cisco and Permira. In 2012, Cisco acquired NDS, a videoscape business owned by the private equity company Permira. After six years under the umbrella of Cisco, NDS was reacquired by its former owner, Permira (Option 3). However, by 2018, Cisco had recombined the video technology provider business with its internal legacy operations. Consequently, the divestiture by Cisco included not only previously acquired NDS assets but also video security services, software, and cloud solutions that were a part of Cisco

(Option 2). Associated complexity surrounding corporate restructuring decisions is common.

In closing, a "sequence view" of acquisitions and divestitures can be extended in future research. It is important to understand how firms achieve optimal business portfolio configurations. The best way to elaborate on the sequences discussed here is to track a firm's acquisitions and divestitures by using longitudinal case studies or collecting panel or historical data. These methods are useful for revealing the interplay of a specific strategy and the way in which acquisitions and divestitures support the strategy implementation. We suggest that others continue examining what we know about acquisition and divestiture sequences and further research the rationales pushing firms to combine these two corporate restructuring mechanisms. For example, the sequences of these activities reveal that under certain conditions, acquisitions and divestitures may be motivated by their anteceding counterparts. When considering these sequences, we have to explore the temporality of these actions to determine the best time to divest after acquisition and to reacquire after divestiture. Overall, our understanding of the possible interrelations between acquisitions and divestitures suggests that their value-enhancing mechanisms require considering sequential relationships.

References

Achtenhagen, L., Brunninge, O., & Melin, L. (2017). Patterns of dynamic growth in medium-sized companies: Beyond the dichotomy of organic versus acquired growth. *Long Range Planning, 50*(4), 457–471.

Amiri, S., King, D., & DeMarie, S. (2020). Divestiture of prior acquisitions: Competing explanations of performance. *Journal of Strategy and Management, 13*(1), 33–55.

Arcot, S., Gantchev, N., & Sevilir, M. (2020). Divest to acquire. *SSRN Electronic Journal*: http://dx.doi.org/10.2139/ssrn.3554632

Aron, D. (1991). Using the capital market as a monitor: Corporate spinoffs in an agency framework. *RAND Journal of Economics, 22*(4), 505–518.

Barkema, H. & Schijven, M. (2008). Toward unlocking the full potential of acquisitions: The role of organizational restructuring. *Academy of Management Journal, 1*(4), 696–722.

Bauer, F., & Matzler, K. (2014). Antecedents of M&A success: The role of strategic complementarity, cultural fit, and degree and speed of integration. *Strategic Management Journal, 35*(2), 269–291.

Benito, G. (1997). Divestment of foreign production operations. *Applied Economics, 29*(10), 1365–1378.

Bennett, V., & Feldman, E. (2017). Make room! Make room! A note on sequential spinoffs and acquisitions. *Strategy Science, 2*(2), 100–110.

Bergh, D. (1997). Predicting divestiture of unrelated acquisitions: An integrative model of Ex Ante conditions. *Strategic Management Journal, 18*(9), 715–731.

Bergh, D., & Lawless, M. (1998). Portfolio restructuring and limits to hierarchical governance: The effects of environmental uncertainty and diversification strategy. *Organization Science, 9*(1), 87–102.

70   *Oleksandra Kochura et al.*

Berry, H. (2010). Why Do Firms Divest? *Organization Science, 21*(2), 380–396.

Bertrand, O., Betschinger, M., & Petrina, Y. (2014). Organizational spillovers of divestiture activity to M&A decision-making. In *Advances in mergers and acquisitions*. Bingley: Emerald Publishing, pp. 65–83.

Bingham, C. B., Heimeriks, K. H., Schijven, M., & Gates, S. (2015). Concurrent learning: How firms develop multiple dynamic capabilities in parallel. *Strategic Management Journal, 36*(12), 1802–1825.

Bodner, J., & Capron, L. (2018). Post-merger integration. *Journal of Organization Design, 7*(1), 1–20.

Bowman, E., & Singh, H. (1993). Corporate restructuring: Reconfiguring the firm. *Strategic Management Journal, 14*(S1), 5–14.

Brauer, M. (2006). What have we acquired and what should we acquire in divestiture research? A review and research agenda. *Journal of Management, 32*(6), 751–785.

Brauer, M., & Schimmer, M. (2010). Performance effects of corporate divestiture programs. *Journal of Strategy and Management, 3*(2), 84–109.

Capron, L. (1999). The long-term performance of horizontal acquisitions. *Strategic Management Journal, 20*(11), 987–1018.

Capron, L., Dussauge, P., & Mitchell, W. (1998). Resource redeployment following horizontal acquisitions in Europe and North America, 1988–1992. *Strategic Management Journal, 19*(7), 631–661.

Capron, L., & Mitchell, W. (2012). *Build, borrow or buy: Solving the growth dilemma*. Boston, MA: Harvard Business Review Press.

Capron, L., Mitchell, W., & Swaminathan, A. (2001). Asset divestiture following horizontal acquisitions: A dynamic view. *Strategic Management Journal, 22*(9), 817–844.

Chang, S. (1996). An evolutionary perspective on diversification and corporate restructuring: Entry, exit and economic performance during 1981–89. *Strategic Management Journal, 17*(8), 587–611.

Chatterjee, S. (2009). The keys to successful acquisition programmes. *Long Range Planning, 42*(2), 137–163.

Chen, H., & Guo, R. (2005). On corporate divestiture. *Review of Quantitative Finance and Accounting, 24*(4), 399–421.

Chi, T. (2000). Option to acquire or divest a joint venture. *Strategic Management Journal, 21*(6), 665–687.

Colombo, M., & Rabbiosi, L. (2014). Technological similarity, post-acquisition R&D reorganization, and innovation performance in horizontal acquisitions. *Research Policy, 3*(6), 1039–1054.

Damaraju, N., Barney, J., & Makhija, A. (2015). Real options in divestment alternatives. *Strategic Management Journal, 36*(5), 728–744.

Dietz, B., & zu Knyphausen-Aufseß, D. (2017). Beyond a one-size-fits-all explanation for reacquisitions—A cluster-based analysis of reacquisition motives and their influence on the involved firms. *Schmalenbach Business Review, 18*(1), 1–28.

Dixit, A., & Pindyck, R. (1994). *Investment under Uncertainty*. Princeton, NJ: Princeton University Press.

Doan, T., Rao Sahib, P., & van Witteloostuijn, A. (2018). Lessons from the flipside: How do acquirers learn from divestitures to complete acquisitions? *Long Range Planning, 51*(2), 252–266.

Dranikoff, L., Koller, T., & Schneider, A. (2002). Divestiture: Strategy's missing link. *Harvard Business Review, 80*(5), 74–83, 133.

Feldman, E. (2016). Dual Directors and the Governance of Corporate Spinoffs. *Academy of Management Journal, 59*(5), 1754–1776.

Feldman, E. (2020). Corporate strategy: Past, present and future. *Strategic Management Review, 1*(1), 179–206.

Feldman, E., & McGrath, P. (2016). Divestitures. *Journal of Organization Design, 5*(1), 1–16.

Feldman, M., & Pentland, B. (2003). Reconceptualizing organizational routines as a source of flexibility and change. *Administrative Science Quarterly, 48*(1), 94–118.

Gimeno, J. (1999). Reciprocal threats in multimarket rivalry: Staking out 'spheres of influence' in the U.S. airline industry. *Strategic Management Journal, 20*(2), 101–128.

Gleason, K., Madura, J., & Pennathur, A. K. (2006). Valuation and performance of reacquisitions following equity carve-outs. *Financial Review, 41*(2), 229–246.

Graebner, M., Heimeriks, K., Huy, Q., & Vaara, E. (2017). The process of postmerger integration: A review and agenda for future research. *Academy of Management Annals, 11*(1), 1–32.

Granovetter, M. (1985). Economic action and social structure: The problem of embeddedness. *American journal of sociology, 91*(3), 481–510.

Gulati, R. (1998). Alliances and networks. *Strategic Management Journal, 19*(4), 293–317.

Haleblian, J., Devers, C., McNamara, G., Carpenter, M., & Davison, R. (2009). Taking stock of what we know about mergers and acquisitions: A review and research agenda. *Journal of Management, 35*(3), 469–502.

Hambrick, D., & Cannella, A. (1993). Relative standing: A Framework for understanding departures of acquired executives. *Academy of Management Journal, 36*(4), 733–762.

Hannan, M., & Freeman, J. (1989). *Organizational ecology*. Cambridge, MA: Harvard University Press.

Haynes, M., Thompson, S., & Wright, M. (2003). The impact of divestment on firm performance: Empirical evidence from a panel of UK companies. *Journal of Industrial Economics, 50*(2), 173–196.

Hayward, M. (2002). When do firms learn from their acquisition experience? Evidence from 1990 to 1995. *Strategic Management Journal, 23*(1), 21–39.

Hayward, M., & Shimizu, K. (2006). De-commitment to losing strategic action: Evidence from the divestiture of poorly performing acquisitions. *Strategic Management Journal, 27*(6), 541–557.

Helfat, C., & Eisenhardt, K. (2004). Inter-temporal economies of scope, organizational modularity, and the dynamics of diversification. *Strategic Management Journal, 25*(13), 1217–1232.

Hite, G., & Owers, J. (1983). Security price reactions around corporate spin-off announcements. *Journal of Financial Economics, 12*(4), 409–436.

Hitt, M., King, D., Krishnan, H., Makri, M., Schijven, M., Shimizu, K., & Zhu, H. (2012). Creating value through mergers and acquisitions: challenges and opportunities. In D. Faulkner, S. Teerikangas & R. Joseph (Eds.) *The handbook of mergers and acquisitions*. Oxford: Oxford University Press, pp. 71–113.

72 Oleksandra Kochura et al.

Hopkins, H. (1991). Acquisition and divestiture as a response to competititve position and market structure. *Journal of Management Studies, 28*(6), 665–677.

Hoskisson, R., Johnson, R., & Moesel, D. (1994). Corporate divestiture intensity in restructuring firms: Effects of governance, strategy, and performance. *Academy of Management Journal, 37*(5), 1207–1251.

Ito, K. (1995). Japanese spinoffs: Unexplored survival strategies. *Strategic Management Journal, 16*(6), 431–446.

Johnson, R. (1996). Antecedents and outcomes of corporate refocusing. *Journal of Management, 22*(3), 439–483.

Jun, X., Yu, J., & Lin, Y. (2019). Periphery, Overlap, and Subunit Exit in Multiunit Firms: A Subunit Power Perspective. *Journal of Management, 45*(3), 881–908.

Kalnins, A., Swaminathan, A., & Mitchell, W. (2006). Turnover events, vicarious information, and the reduced likelihood of outlet-level exit among small multiunit organizations. *Organization Science, 17*(1), 118–131.

Kaplan, S., & Weisbach, M. (1992). The Success of Acquisitions: Evidence from Divestitures. *Journal of Finance, 47*(1), 107–138.

Karim, S. (2006). Modularity in organizational structure: The reconfiguration of internally developed and acquired business units. *Strategic Management Journal, 27*(9), 799–823.

Karim, S. (2012). Exploring structural embeddedness of product market activities and resources within business units. *Strategic Organization, 10*(4), 333–365.

Karim, S., & Capron, L. (2016). Reconfiguration: Adding, redeploying, recombining and divesting resources and business units. *Strategic Management Journal, 37*(13), E54–E62.

Karim, S., & Mitchell, W. (2000). Path-dependent and path-breaking change: Reconfiguring business resources following acquisitions in the U.S. medical sector, 1978–1995. *Strategic Management Journal, 21*(10–11), 1061–1081.

Karim, S., & Mitchell, W. (2004). Innovating through acquisition and internal development: A quarter-century of boundary evolution at Johnson & Johnson. *Long Range Planning, 37*(6), 525–547.

Kaul, A. (2012). Technology and corporate scope: Firm and rival innovation as antecedents of corporate transactions. *Strategic Management Journal, 33*(4), 347–367.

Keum, D. (2020). Cog in the wheel: Resource release and the scope of interdependencies in corporate adjustment activities. *Strategic Management Journal, 41*(2), 175–197.

King, D., Dalton, D., Daily, C., & Covin, J. (2004). Meta-analyses of post-acquisition performance: Indications of unidentified moderators. *Strategic Management Journal, 25*(2), 187–200.

King, D., Wang, G., Samimi, M., & Cortes, A. F. (2021). A meta-analytic integration of acquisition performance prediction. *Journal of Management Studies, 58*(5), 1198–1236.

Klein, A., Rosenfeld, J., & Beranek, W. (1991). The two stages of an equity carve-out and the price response of parent and subsidiary stock. *Managerial and Decision Economics, 2*(6), 449–460.

Kogut, B., & Kulatilaka, N. (2001). Capabilities as real options. *Organization Science, 12*(6), 744–758.

Kolev, K. (2016). To divest or not to divest: A meta-analysis of the antecedents of corporate divestitures. *British Journal of Management, 27*(1), 179–196.

Acquisitions and divestitures 73

Kuusela, P., Keil, T., & Maula, M. (2017). Driven by aspirations, but in what direction? Performance shortfalls, slack resources, and resource-consuming vs. Resource-freeing organizational change. *Strategic Management Journal,* 38(5), 1101–1120.

Laamanen, T., & Keil, T. (2008). Performance of serial acquirers: Toward an acquisition program perspective. *Strategic Management Journal,* 29(6), 663–672.

Lang, L., Poulsen, A., & Stulz, R. (1995). Asset sales, firm performance, and the agency costs of managerial discretion. *Journal of Financial Economics,* 37(1), 3–37.

Langlois, R. (1992). Transaction-cost economics in real time. *Industrial and Corporate Change,* 1(1), 99–127.

Levitt, B., & March, J. (1988). Organizational learning. *Annual Review of Sociology,* 14(1), 319–338.

Lumineau, F., & Mulotte, L. (2019). How governance modes intertwine over time: Beyond an embeddedness-based approach to post-acquisition divestitures. *Academy of Management Discoveries,* 5(2), 201–204.

Ma, Q., & Wang, S. (2018). A unified theory of forward- and backward-looking M&As and divestitures. *European Financial Management,* 24(3), 418–450.

Meschi, P., & Métais, E. (2015). Too big to learn: The effects of major acquisition failures on subsequent acquisition divestment: Too big to learn. *British Journal of Management,* 26(3), 408–423.

Miller, D., & Yang, H. (2016). The dynamics of diversification: Market entry and exit by public and private firms. *Strategic Management Journal,* 37(11), 2323–2345.

Moliterno, T., & Wiersema, M. (2007). Firm performance, rent appropriation, and the strategic resource divestment capability. *Strategic Management Journal,* 28(11), 1065–1087.

Montgomery, C., & Wilson, V. (1986). Research note and communication mergers that last: A predictable pattern? *Strategic Management Journal,* 7(1), 91–96.

Moschieri, C., & Mair, J. (2008). Research on corporate divestures: A synthesis. *Journal of Management and Organization,* 14(4), 399–422.

Moschieri, C., & Mair, J. (2012). Managing divestitures through time-expanding current knowledge. *Academy of Management Perspectives,* 26(4), 35–50.

Moschieri, C., & Mair, J. (2017). Corporate entrepreneurship: Partial divestitures as a real option. *European Management Review,* 14(1), 67–82.

Mulherin, J., & Boone, A. (2000). Comparing acquisitions and divestitures. *Journal of Corporate Finance,* 6(2), 117–139.

Nadolska, A., & Barkema, H. (2007). Learning to internationalise: The pace and success of foreign acquisitions. *Journal of International Business Studies,* 38(7), 1170–1186.

Nanda, V., & Narayanan, M. (1999). Disentangling value: Financing needs, firm scope, and divestitures. *Journal of Financial Intermediation,* 8(3), 174–204.

Nelson, R., & Winter, S. (1982). *An Evolutionary Theory of Economic Change.* Cambridge, MA: Belknap Press of Harvard University Press.

Otsubo, M. (2009). Gains from equity carve-outs and subsequent events. *Journal of Business Research,* 62(11), 1207–1213.

Otsubo, M., & Miyoshi, Y. (2009). Empirical study on subsidiary reacquisition among Japanese companies. *Japanese Economy,* 36(4), 31–60.

74 *Oleksandra Kochura et al.*

Pfeffer, J., & Salancik, G. (1978). *The External Control of Organizations: A Resource Dependence Perspective.* New York: Harper & Row.

Porter, M. (1976). Please note location of nearest exit. *California Management Review, 19*(2), 21–33.

Ravenscraft, D., & Scherer, F. (1987). Life after takeover. *Journal of Industrial Economics, 36*(2), 147–156.

Roll, R. (1986). The hubris hypothesis of corporate takeovers. *Journal of Business, 59*(2), 197–216.

Schilke, O., & Jiang, H. (2019). Embeddedness across governance modes: Is there a link between premerger alliances and divestitures? *Academy of Management Discoveries, 5*(2), 137–151.

Schipper, K., & Smith, A. (1986). A comparison of equity carve-outs and seasoned equity offerings. Share price effects and corporate restructuring. *Journal of Financial Economics, 15*(1–2), 153–186.

Schoenberg, R. (2006). Measuring the performance of corporate acquisitions: An empirical comparison of alternative metrics. *British Journal of Management, 17*(4), 361–370.

Schönhaar, S., Nippa, M., & Pidun, U. (2014). From patchwork to theory development: Mapping and advancing research about business portfolio restructuring. *Management Review Quarterly, 64*(3), 157–200.

Shi, W., & Prescott, J. (2011). Sequence patterns of firms' acquisition and alliance behaviour and their performance implications. *Journal of Management Studies, 48*(5), 1044–1070.

Shimizu, K., & Hitt, M. (2005). What constrains or facilitates divestitures of formerly acquired firms? The effects of organizational inertia. *Journal of Management, 31*(1), 50–72.

Teece, D., Pisano, G., & Shuen, A. (1997). Dynamic capabilities and strategic management. *Strategic Management Journal, 18*(7), 509–533.

Teerikangas, S., & Thanos, I. (2018). Looking into the 'black box'—unlocking the effect of integration on acquisition performance. *European Management Journal, 36*(3), 366–380.

Thompson, T. (2013). An examination of the long-term performance of reacquired carve-outs. *Managerial Finance, 39*(6), 569–583.

Thywissen, C., Pidun, U., & zu Knyphausen-Aufseß, D. (2018). Process matters— The relevance of the decision making process for divestiture outcomes. *Long Range Planning, 51*(2), 267–284.

Uzzi, B. (1996). The sources and consequences of embeddedness for the economic performance of organizations: The network effect. *American Sociological Review, 61*: 674–698.

Vidal, E. (2021). Divestitures, value creation, and corporate scope. *Strategic Management Review, 2*(2), 413–435.

Vidal, E., & Mitchell, W. (2015). Adding by subtracting: The relationship between performance feedback and resource reconfiguration through divestitures. *Organization Science, 26*(4), 1101–1118.

Vidal, E., & Mitchell, W. (2018). Virtuous or vicious cycles? The role of divestitures as a complementary Penrose effect within resource-based theory. *Strategic Management Journal, 39*(1), 131–154.

Vijh, A. M. (2002). The positive announcement-period returns of equity carveouts: Asymmetric information or divestiture gains? *Journal of Business, 75*(1), 153–190.

Villalonga, B., & McGahan, A. (2005). The choice among acquisitions, alliances, and divestitures. *Strategic Management Journal*, 26(13), 1183–1208.

Wang, Y., & Larimo, J. (2020). Survival of full versus partial acquisitions: The moderating role of firm's internationalization experience, cultural distance, and host country context characteristics. *International Business Review*, 29(1), 101605.

Weston, J. (1989). Divestitures: Mistakes or learning. *Journal of Applied Corporate Finance*, 2(2), 68–76.

Williamson, O. (1999). Strategy research: governance and competence perspectives. *Strategic Management Journal*, 20(12), 1087–1108.

Xia, J., & Li, S. (2013). The divestiture of acquired subunits: A resource dependence approach: Subunit Divestiture and Resource Dependence. *Strategic Management Journal*, 34(2), 131–148.

Zollo, M., & Reuer, J. (2010). Experience spillovers across corporate development activities. *Organization Science*, 21(6), 1195–1212.

4 Cross-border acquisition and greenfield investment
Substitutes or complements?[1]

Nan Zhang and Joseph A. Clougherty

Introduction

Firms can invest abroad via portfolio investments, licenses, contracts, franchising, outsourcing, sub-contracting, and other means (Hennart, 1989; Odebunwi, 2017). Yet foreign direct investment (FDI) typically occurs through two dominant establishment modes: cross-border acquisitions (CBA) and greenfield investments (GI). CBA involves purchasing businesses that have already been operating in a host nation; thus this mode entails acquiring existing firms and corporate assets. GI involves foreign firms establishing operations from the ground up to engage in host-nation business activities; thus this mode entails the creation of new establishments, plants, facilities, and human capital via direct investment. From a capital and ownership perspective, CBA represent a transfer in the ownership of pre-existing assets, while GI represent a net addition to the host-nation's capital stock.

A sizable literature considers the factors driving the choice between the two establishment modes. While Slangen and Hennart (2007) review the management literature tackling this topic, a fair amount of recent economic scholarship (Davies, Desbordes, & Ray, 2018; Moghadam, Mazlan, Chin, & Ibrahim, 2019; Nguyen, Luu, & Do, 2021; Nocke & Yeaple, 2007, 2008) has considered the choice between CBA and GI. This focus on establishment-mode choice as a concept of interest is reflected by the literature's prevailing operationalization of the dependent variable: a dummy construct that usually flips to one for a GI and zero for a CBA (Barkema & Vermeulen, 1998; Brouthers & Brouthers, 2000; Drogendijk & Slangen, 2006; Harzing, 2002). Despite this focus on the choice between establishment modes, a consistent lament from both management and economics scholars (e.g., Brouthers & Brouthers, 2000; Slangen & Hennart, 2007; Nocke & Yeaple, 2007, 2008; Odebunmi, 2017) over the last two decades has been the lack of consistent empirical findings.

---

1 This chapter was blind reviewed.

DOI: 10.4324/9781003188308-6

Cross-border acquisition and greenfield investment 77

To begin unraveling the inconsistencies in the establishment-mode choice literature, we first echo the observation by Davies et al. (2018) that this literature considers the number of foreign investments to be set and given. Indeed, the dichotomous dependent construct that is most-frequently employed in the literature assumes that a foreign investment will be undertaken and that the foreign firm simply chooses between the appropriate mode—CBA versus GI—under prevailing circumstances. In essence, employing such a dichotomous dependent construct involves a forced counter-factual, as every realized GI could have been a CBA, and every realized CBA could have been a GI. Accordingly, the prevailing relationship between CBA and GI has been assumed to be substitutive in nature.

Bertrand, Hakkala, and Norbäck (2007) observe that there has been growing evidence that CBA and GI are not perfect substitutes due to the presence of systematic differences in the modes. For instance, Davies et al. (2018) highlight how the literature finds CBA to be affected by geographic and cultural barriers, exchange-rate fluctuations, and host-nation institutions, while GI is affected by home-nation competitive advantages and host-nation taxes. Further, the vast majority of CBAs take place in developed nations, while the majority of GIs take place in emerging nations (Calderón, Loayza, & Servén, 2004; Davies et al., 2018; UNCTAD, 2014). This conceptual distinction between the two modes has been recognized by a number of scholars (Blonigen, 1997; Moghadam et al., 2019; Nocke & Yeaple, 2007, 2008; Odebunwi, 2017). The upshot of these considerations is that the investment modes might not often substitute in practice. Instead of representing an actual choice made by foreign firms investing in host markets, CBA would be appropriate in certain contexts while GI would be appropriate in other contexts. As Moghadam et al. (2019, p. 750) succinctly surmise, these two investment modes might "not completely substitute for each other".

In addition to CBA and GI potentially being imperfect substitutes (i.e., not strongly related), some empirical work supports the existence of a complementary relationship between CBA and GI. For instance, Calderón et al. (2004) find increases in CBA activities lead to subsequent increases in GI in samples of industrial, emerging, and Latin American nations. Further, Nguyen et al. (2020) find evidence that CBAs generate future GIs in the Vietnamese context. Moreover, if CBA and GI are driven by fundamentally different strategic motives and represent distinct choices undertaken by internationalizing firms, then the prevailing practice in the empirical literature to force a choice between the establishment modes via a dichotomous dependent construct may reside behind the inconsistent empirical findings.

It stands to reason then that the relationship between CBA and GI must be established. The establishment-mode choice literature assumes a substitutive relationship; however, there exist indications that this relationship is either faintly substitutive or complementary. Despite the

78 *Nan Zhang and Joseph A. Clougherty*

importance of setting this relationship, we could only identify two studies (Calderón et al., 2004; Nguyen et al., 2021) that openly attempt to establish the CBA-GI relationship. This omission in the literature is all the more striking once one recognizes the substantial amount of literature attempting to define the relationship between trade and FDI (Belderbos & Sleuwaegen, 1998; Blonigen, 2001; Clausing, 2000; Forte & Silva, 2017; Grubert & Mutti, 1991; Head & Ries, 2001; Hejazi & Safarian, 2001). Since a degree of uncertainty exists with respect to whether multinationals actually substitute GI for CBA, the principal aim of this chapter is to establish the true CBA-GI relationship.

Estimating a relationship between CBA and GI has been partially hindered by the potential for endogeneity bias (also see Chapter 9). While simultaneity and measurement error constitute two of the three sources of endogeneity bias, the omitted-variable concern (a third source of endogeneity bias) has received the greatest amount of scholarly attention (Bascle, 2008; Wooldridge, 2013). Indeed, the omitted-variable concern represents the most-salient endogeneity threat to the methodological approach employed in the narrow literature factoring the CBA-GI relationship (Calderón et al., 2004; Nguyen et al., 2021). That approach involves a measure of GI activities being regressed upon a measure of CBA activities: where a positive (negative) coefficient estimate for CBA indicates a complementary (substitutive) relationship. Yet this estimation approach is particularly vulnerable to endogeneity bias and the detection of a complementary relationship, as omitted constructs are likely to positively co-vary with both CBA and GI activities.

Our methodological approach attempts to surmount these issues in following Clausing (2000) and Grubert and Mutti (1991) by addressing the endogeneity issue via a cross-price elasticity approach. Specifically, if CBA and GI are complements, then as the price of engaging in CBAs increases, both CBA and GI activities will decrease. Accordingly, factors which increase the cost of engaging in CBA will not only reduce CBA activities, but they also decrease GI activities via that complementary relationship. However, if CBA and GI are substitutes, then as the price of engaging in CBAs increases, CBA activities will decrease but GI activities will increase. Accordingly, factors which increase the cost of engaging in CBA will reduce CBA activities, but increase GI activities via that substitutive relationship. This methodological approach relies on the idea that a change in the exogenous price of CBA directly affects the level of CBA activity but does not directly affect the level of GI activity. Greenfield activity is instead only indirectly affected by changes in the price of engaging in CBA—an indirect relationship that will either be substitutive (i.e., leading to decreased greenfield activity) or complementary (i.e., leading to increased greenfield activity).

To capture a "price" paid by foreign firms that directly affects the costs of engaging in CBAs without directly affecting the costs for GI, we consider the existence of merger policy. Namely, US antitrust authorities—i.e., the

US Federal Trade Commission (FTC) and the US Department of Justice (DOJ)—are charged with undertaking reviews where they screen, remedy, and prohibit deals that lead to a significant lessening of competition (Clougherty, 2005). The logical implication of the presence of merger policy is that increased scrutiny by antitrust authorities generates deterrence effects as firms curtail their acquisition activities due to stepped-up enforcement of merger policy. While Clougherty and Seldeslachts (2013) establish the presence of deterrence effects for both domestic and foreign firms in the US merger-policy context, Clougherty and Zhang (2021) take the next step by focusing on foreign firms. Specifically, they find that US merger enforcement in a sector yields substantial deterrence effects with respect to foreign investors, as greater levels of investigative scrutiny generate substantially reduced levels of foreign investor's—as compared to domestic investor's—acquisitions of US targets.

While the presence of merger policy represents a cost to foreign firms interested in operating in a host-nation market via CBA, the presence of US merger policy does not directly affect the costs involved with engaging in GI. Foreign firms initially entering a host market via GI actually increase market competition, as such investments increase the number of market competitors and will generally be welcomed by antitrust authorities mandated with protecting consumer welfare (Clougherty, 2001; Neven & Röller, 2005; Scherer, 1996). Further, if the foreign firm already had a presence in the local market via trade, then GI does not change the number of competitors in the host-nation market and again does not necessarily negatively affect domestic consumer welfare. Accordingly, GI is generally pro-competitive with respect to the competition taking place in a host-nation market, and, as such, GI is infrequently the target of antitrust authorities (Johnson & Li, 2018; Kovacic, 2003; Kwoka & White, 2008). Indeed, antitrust agencies are authorized to regulate deals to preserve effective competition in a national market, but GI is generally exempt from such merger reviews.

While the above testifies to the lack of a direct relationship between the application of merger policy and GI activities, an indirect relationship may present. Specifically, GI may be substituted for CBA by foreign firms in the presence of enhanced merger policy. Thus, greater levels of merger-policy enforcement increase the costs of engaging in CBA, and as a result, foreign firms will move toward the GI option. In line then with a substitutive CBA-GI relationship, the enforcement of merger policy may lead to increased levels of GI.

Our study accordingly considers the impact of US merger-policy enforcement on foreign firm investments in the US market via these two different establishment modes. Employing data on the CBAs and GIs undertaken by foreign firms in the US, we consider whether US merger-policy investigations at the industry level affect the mix of these firm-investment activities. Our firm-level data cover 1,763 firms situated in 58 different industries over the 2003–2017 period. The panel-data empirical

80   Nan Zhang and Joseph A. Clougherty

testing indicates that merger-policy investigations deter cross-border horizontal acquisitions and attract GI. These results support the prior that foreign firms substitute GI for CBA, and that a complementary relationship does not exist.

Hypothesis development

The presence of merger policy can negatively impact foreign firms by slowing down the onset of foreign investments, by leading to restrictions on investments that curtail profitability, and by even resulting in the outright prohibition of foreign investment (Clougherty, 2005). Accordingly, Oliveira, Hochstetler, and Kalil (2001) note that many observers advise countries to not emphasize such a policy as it could deter inward investment via the creation of additional regulatory barriers and risks for foreign firms. Yet to comprehensively understand how merger-policy enforcement influences foreign investment activities, it is necessary to distinguish between CBA and GI activities and consider the effects on these investment modes individually. We accordingly turn to a more-detailed discussion of whether and how merger-policy enforcement affects these two foreign-investment modes.

Cross-border horizontal acquisitions

Horizontal acquisitions are characterized by the acquirer and target having operated in overlapping industries in the pre-transaction period. Importantly, cross-border investments tend to be more horizontal and related in nature as compared to domestic investments (Makaew, 2012). US antitrust authorities have also long considered horizontal transactions as potentially anti-competitive, whereas non-horizontal (unrelated or vertical) transactions are more rarely considered to involve anti-competitive effects (Clougherty & Seldeslachts, 2013; Viscusi, Vernon, & Harrington, 1995). It is then horizontal CBAs which face scrutiny from US antitrust authorities. Accordingly, vigorous enforcement of merger policy will substantially impair inward-horizontal CBA activities, as the CBA of US firms with horizontal overlap are of principal concern for antitrust authorities.

A number of scholars in international business (Dunning & Pitelis, 2008; Forsgren, 2013; Hymer, 1970, 1976) have highlighted that market-power incentives represent an important driver of cross-border investment activity. Yet as Hymer (1970, 1979) long ago observed, the presence of merger policy represents a direct institutional counter to a multinational's ability to earn supra-normal profits by stifling local competition and harming consumer welfare when engaging in FDI activities. Accordingly, the presence of vigorous merger policy in a host nation attenuates market power as a motive behind foreign investment and therefore deters foreign firms from engaging in horizontal CBA (Brewer, 1993; Clougherty & Zhang, 2021).

Cross-border acquisition and greenfield investment 81

We should also note that the presence of host-nation merger policy involves additional transaction costs that foreign firms must factor when deciding upon whether—and to what extent—to invest in a particular nation. For instance, navigating the host nation's merger review process involves several direct costs to clear the transaction, such as fees for filing, and the obtaining of advisory and legal counsel (Hemphill, 2010). Further, the presence of host-nation merger policy exerts internal costs for foreign firms engaging in CBA as navigating the merger-review process requires a substantial amount of managerial time and commitment (Clougherty & Zhang, 2021). In addition to these costs, the merger review process can negatively impact foreign firms by slowing down the onset of foreign investment (Clougherty, 2005). The varied costs involved with the presence of host-nation merger policy ultimately deter the willingness of foreign firms to engage in cross-border horizontal acquisitions.

Summarizing the above, the enhanced enforcement of merger policy in a nation will negatively influence CBAs of local targets by foreign firms via three pertinent mechanisms. First, horizontal-CBA activities are of particular interest to both foreign firms and antitrust authorities; thus the presence of substantial conflict between foreign firms and local antitrust authorities generates robust deterrence effects. Second, the enforcement of host-nation merger policy attenuates the market-power rationales residing behind foreign-firm interest in CBA activities, thereby reducing the incentive for foreign firms to undertake CBA. Third, the enforcement of host-nation merger policy involves additional direct and indirect costs for foreign firms when attempting to navigate the merger-review process, which, in turn, generates additional deterrence effects for foreign firms. Based then on these three mechanisms, our first theoretical prior can be formulated as follows:

> Hypothesis 1 (H1): Increases in host-nation merger-policy enforcement deter foreign firms from engaging in future cross-border acquisitions of host-nation targets.

Greenfield investment

When commencing or enhancing foreign business operations, firms can choose between a GI or the acquisition of an existing business in the host-nation market. GI offers greater control over local operations but requires a substantial contribution of know-how and a long amount of time to fully establish (Chang & Rosenzweig, 2001). CBAs, on the other hand, may involve reduced uncertainties, increased efficiency, and capitalizing on target-firm resources. The upsides involved with CBA have generally led to their being the most popular form of FDI in recent years (Moghadam et al., 2019; UNCTAD, 2016).

Yet when horizontal CBAs are deterred by enhanced merger-policy enforcement, foreign investment behavior will necessarily adjust.

82 Nan Zhang and Joseph A. Clougherty

Most obviously, foreign firms may curtail their acquisition behavior in markets experiencing greater merger-review scrutiny and instead search for alternative host-nation markets with laxer merger enforcement. However, foreign firms may also seek to counter host-nation impediments by identifying substitutive investments that are less subject to merger-review concern. GI are where a foreign firm creates a subsidiary and builds a host-nation business operation from the ground up— represent an obvious alternative to CBA investments for firms seeking to serve customers in a particular host nation. Moreover, GI is not directly subject to merger-policy review, as only acquiring firms are required to report agreed-upon investments to antitrust officials for approval prior to transaction consummation (Johnson & Li, 2018; Kovacic, 2003; Kwoka & White, 2008).

Accordingly, foreign firms facing substantial policy risks as to whether and when a CBA can be legally achieved via successful navigation of the merger-review process in a host nation might seek to substitute GI for CBA in such a context. GI may then not be directly affected by the conduct of host-nation merger policy; however, greenfield can be indirectly positively affected via a substitutive relationship with CBA. Thus, as the merger-policy costs involved with conducting horizontal CBAs become higher in a particular market, foreign firms shift to GI as an alternative operation mode. In sum, when horizontal CBAs are deterred by the conduct of merger policy, GI represents a viable alternative. Based then on the above reasoning, our second theoretical prior can be formulated as follows:

> Hypothesis 2 (H2): Increases in host-nation merger-policy enforcement spur foreign firms to engage in future greenfield investments in the host nation.

Data and methodology

Data coverage

We build a dataset for empirical testing based upon annual firm-level observations over the 2003 through 2017 period. Specifically, the annual proclivities of foreign firms to engage in GI and CBA targeted at the US market form the basis of our empirical analysis. To build this dataset, we compiled and matched observations from five separate data sources: (1) the 'SDC Platinum' dataset from Thomson; (2) the 'fDi Markets' dataset from the *Financial Times*; (3) the 'Annual Reports to Congress on HSR Antitrust Enforcement' from the FTC and DOJ; (4) the 'Gross Domestic Product (GDP) by Industry' dataset from the US Bureau of Economic Analysis (BEA); and (5) the 'Compustat' database from Wharton Research Data Services (WRDS).

Cross-border acquisition and greenfield investment 83

These data sources are combined to create measures of CBA activities, GI activities, merger-policy investigations, and an extensive list of controls. Importantly, CBA and GI activities both allow for a firm-year level of analysis: where we have observations on 1,763 foreign (non-US) firms over the 2003–2017 period. The merger-policy-investigations variable and the control constructs are all at the industry-year level, as our sampled firms hail from 58 different three-digit level industries that conform to the North American Industry Classification System (NAICS) standard. These industry-level measures are matched up with the firm-level measures via the main industry of the foreign firm. The compilation and matching of the different variables from different data sources yield an unbalanced panel-data estimation sample consisting of 23,092 foreign-firm observations. Due to the employment of lagged structures in the regression estimations, this estimation sample reduces to 19,733 foreign-firm observations for empirical testing.

Dependent variables

We first require a measure of CBA activity to serve as the dependent variable of interest for testing our first theoretical prior. Thomson's SDC Platinum database provides transaction-level data that allow identifying foreign acquisitions of US-based targets where the foreign acquiring firm can gain full, majority, or minority control. The SDC data also allow differentiating between horizontal and non-horizontal acquisitions of US-based targets. We specifically define horizontal transactions as those involving four-digit overlap in the product space of the acquiring and target firms; thus, we employ a relatively narrow definition of a horizontal acquisition. Based on this criterion, we compiled the SDC transaction-level data into an annual measure of the number of horizontal acquisitions of US targets undertaken by a specific foreign firm (hereafter referred to as *Cross-Border-Acquisitions*). This measure of foreign-firm acquisition activities in the US market captures the degree to which specific foreign firms invest in the US via horizontal acquisitions.

We also require a measure of GI activity to serve as the dependent variable of interest for testing our second theoretical prior. The 'fDi Markets' database is one of the most comprehensive sources of greenfield-investment data, as it involves extensive coverage of greenfield projects from around the world. While this database has generally not been used in the establishment-mode choice literature, recent scholarship employs this data (Davies et al., 2018; Moghadam et al., 2019). Importantly, the 'fDi Markets' database provides transaction-level data on GI projects that allow building a firm-based measure of the count of GIs in the US market. Accordingly, we compiled this transaction-level data into an annual measure of the number of GIs undertaken by a specific foreign firm in the US market (hereafter referred to as *Greenfield Investments*). This

84 Nan Zhang and Joseph A. Clougherty

measure of foreign-firm greenfield activities in the US market captures the degree to which specific foreign firms invest in the US via GI. This variable operationalization for firm-level GI substantially improves upon the norm in the economics literature (Calderón et al., 2004; Moghadam et al., 2019; Nguyen et al., 2021) to empirically capture industry- or country-level GI activities by subtracting CBA activities from total FDI activities.

Explanatory variables

Both of our theoretical priors require a measure of US merger-policy enforcement for empirical testing, as increases in merger-policy enforcement are conjectured to deter foreign firms from CBAs but encourage foreign firms to make GI. Fortunately, the 'Annual Reports to Congress on HSR Antitrust Enforcement' provide detailed data on the number of annual investigations undertaken by the DOJ and the FTC in a specific three-digit sector. As observed by Motta (2004), the US Hart-Scott-Rodino (HSR) merger-review process requires reporting transactions to US antitrust authorities for approval. The large majority of transaction notifications are cleared within a month; however, a number of transactions receive what is referred to as a 'second-request investigation' (Shapiro, 2010). Second-request investigations require additional information and documentation from the merging parties, and usually imply that the transaction will remain in the review process for an additional period of time. We should also note that investigations represent a necessary procedural step prior to the application of more serious merger-policy measures such as structural remedies and prohibitions (Kovacic, 2003). It is no surprise then that Clougherty (2005) regards second-request investigations as a source of substantial holdup for managers attempting to engage in acquisition activities. Accordingly, we use the DOJ and FTC data on the number of annual second-request investigations in a three-digit industrial sector as our principal explanatory variable for empirical testing (hereafter referred to as *Merger-Policy-Investigations*). This time-varying measure of the investigative activity taking place in a sector proxies for the level of merger-policy enforcement—or merger scrutiny—in a particular industry.

To generate stronger causal inferences, we compile a series of industry-level controls. We first created a set of controls that reflect the industry-level investment waves that might, respectively, affect foreign firm proclivities to engage in CBA and GI. Indeed, a substantial amount of finance literature (Andrade & Stafford, 2004; Harford, 2005) suggests that firm-level investment activities must be factored within the wave-like context in which they manifest. Further, Blonigen (1997) finds domestic-acquisition activities to be correlated with foreign-acquisition activities in the US context. Thus, to help better specify a CBA equation, we create industry-level count measures of inward CBA, domestic acquisitions, and

Cross-border acquisition and greenfield investment 85

outward CBA. These industry-level controls were created by compiling the transaction-level data from Thomson's SDC Platinum database. Thus, the annual number of foreign-firm horizontal acquisitions of US targets in a particular sector (hereafter referred to as *Industry-Inward-CBA*), the annual number of US-firm horizontal acquisitions of US targets in a particular sector (hereafter referred to as *Industry-Domestic-M&A*), and the annual number of US-firm horizontal acquisitions of foreign targets in a particular sector (hereafter referred to as *Industry-Outward-CBA*) were all added as controls to capture the respective acquisition waves influencing foreign-firm proclivities to engage in CBAs of US targets. To help better specify a GI equation, we create an industry-level count measure of the GI undertaken by foreign firms in a particular US industry by compiling the project-level data from 'fDi Markets'. Accordingly, the annual number of foreign-firm GI projects in a particular sector (hereafter referred to as *Industry-Greenfield*) was added as a control to capture the investment wave influencing foreign-firm proclivities to employ greenfields when investing in the US.

While the industry controls noted above are specific to the respective CBA and GI equations, we also introduce a series of ten additional industry-level controls that are common to both equations. Following Clougherty and Seldeslachts (2013), we construct annual measures of sales growth in an industry (hereafter referred to as *Industry-Growth*). Following Harford (2005), we construct annual measures of the cash present in an industry (hereafter referred to as *Industry-Cash*). Following Andrade and Stafford (2004), we employ the Compustat data to calculate annual Herfindahl-Hirschman-Index (HHI) measures for each industry (hereafter referred to as *Industry-HHI*). Following Clougherty and Zhang's (2021) identification of domestic experience as an important factor, we construct an annual measure capturing the percentage of domestic acquirers in a sector with US acquisition experiences in the preceding five years (hereafter referred to as *Industry-Domestic-Experience*). Following Grosse and Trevino's (2005) highlighting market size as salient, we construct an annual measure of the value-added in a sector (hereafter referred to as *Industry-Value-Added*).

In addition to the first five industry-level controls outlined above, Hitt, Li, and Xu (2016) observe that foreign firms are often interested in US sectors endowed with learning opportunities, i.e., industries with college-trained employees and high levels of R&D. Accordingly, we construct an annual measure of wage expenditures on college-trained employees in an industry (hereafter referred to as *Industry-Skilled-Labor*) to control for the degree to which a sector intensively uses skilled labor. Further, we construct an annual measure of R&D expenditures with respect to the gross output in an industry (hereafter referred to as *Industry-R&D*) to control for a sector's R&D intensity. Beyond these controls relating to learning opportunities, we construct three additional industry-level control constructs for comprehensiveness. First, we construct an annual

86 Nan Zhang and Joseph A. Clougherty

measure of an industry's expenditures on materials with respect to gross output (hereafter referred to as *Industry-Materials*), as the presence of intermediate material inputs may attract foreign investment. Second, we construct an annual measure of an industry's profitability by taking the gross operating surplus with respect to the value-added in the sector (hereafter referred to as *Industry-Profit-Rate*), as industry profit opportunities may attract foreign investment. Third, we construct an annual measure of an industry's tax burden by taking the taxes on production and imports—less subsidies—with respect to the value-added in the sector (hereafter referred to as *Industry-Tax-Rate*).

For all of the variable constructs, detailed descriptions and data sources are provided in Appendix 4.1, and Table 4.1 reports descriptive statistics (means and standard deviations) and pairwise-correlation coefficients.

Estimation strategy

Following through on our theoretical priors, we aim to empirically test whether merger-policy investigations deter horizontal CBAs and, in turn, attract GI as a substitutive option for foreign investment. Taking advantage of the data's panel structure, we estimate two equations to test our theoretical priors: where regression equation 1 tests hypothesis 1; and regression equation 2 tests hypothesis 2. Those two regression equations can be represented as follows:

$$
\begin{aligned}
\textit{Cross-Border-Acquisitions}_{it} &= \beta_0 + \beta_1 \\
\textit{Merger-Policy-Investigations}_{j, \sum_{k=1}^{3} t-k} &\\
+ \sum_{k=1}^{3} \beta_{k+1} \; & \textit{Cross-Border-Acquisitions}_{i,t-k} \\
+ \sum_{k=0}^{3} \beta_{k+5} \; & \textit{Industry-Inward-CBA}_{j,t-k} \\
+ \sum_{k=0}^{3} \beta_{k+9} \; & \textit{Industry-Domestic-M\&A}_{j,t-k} \\
+ \sum_{k=0}^{3} \beta_{k+13} \; & \textit{Industry-Outward-CBA}_{j,t-k} \\
+ \; \delta \, X_{jt} + \alpha_i + \mathrm{w}_t + \varepsilon_{it} & \qquad\qquad (1)
\end{aligned}
$$

$$
\begin{aligned}
\textit{Greenfield-Investments} &= \beta_0 + \beta_1 \\
\textit{Merger-Policy-Investigations}_{j, \sum_{k=1}^{3} t-k} &\\
+ \sum_{k=1}^{3} \beta_{k+1} \; & \textit{Greenfield-Investments}_{i,t-k} \\
+ \sum_{k=0}^{3} \beta_{k+5} \; & \textit{Industry-Greenfield}_{j,t-k} \\
+ \; \delta \, X_{jt} + \alpha_i + \mathrm{w}_t + \varepsilon_{it} & \qquad\qquad (2)
\end{aligned}
$$

Table 4.1 Descriptive statistics and pairwise correlations

	Mean	S.D.	1	2	3	4	5	6	7	8	9	10	11	12	13	14	15	16	17
1 Cross-Border-Acquisitions	0.06	0.31	1.00																
2 Greenfield-Investments	0.28	0.87	0.05	1.00															
3 Merger-Policy-Investigations	1.77	2.06	0.02	−0.001	1.00														
4 Industry-Inward-CBA	4.28	9.44	0.06	−0.03	0.16	1.00													
5 Industry-Domestic-M&A	13.46	35.32	0.03	−0.01	0.06	0.26	1.00												
6 Industry-Outward-CBA	4.06	10.68	0.03	−0.03	0.13	0.49	0.14	1.00											
7 Industry-Greenfield	25.62	20.51	0.02	0.11	0.38	−0.06	−0.07	−0.08	1.00										
8 Industry-Growth	0.04	0.08	0.01	−0.03	−0.05	−0.03	−0.01	−0.02	−0.16	1.00									
9 Industry-Cash	0.002	0.01	0.001	0.002	−0.03	0.02	−0.02	−0.01	0.02	0.003	1.00								
10 Industry-HHI	0.05	0.05	0.01	−0.04	−0.28	0.17	0.13	0.11	−0.41	0.07	0.09	1.00							
11 Industry-Domestic-Experience	0.44	0.08	0.01	−0.02	0.10	0.13	0.13	0.13	−0.12	0.05	0.14	−0.04	1.00						
12 Industry-Value-Added	0.26	0.21	0.04	0.08	0.14	−0.05	−0.01	−0.05	0.12	0.03	−0.10	−0.31	0.04	1.00					

(*continued*)

Table 4.1 Cont.

		Mean	S.D.	1	2	3	4	5	6	7	8	9	10	11	12	13	14	15	16	17
13	Industry-Skilled-Labor	76.67	88.97	0.02	−0.02	−0.07	-0.03	0.03	−0.02	0.16	0.08	−0.12	−0.07	−0.14	0.48	1.00				
14	Industry-R&D	0.02	0.07	−0.0003	−0.01	0.02	0.03	−0.01	0.02	−0.05	−0.01	−0.01	0.08	−0.05	−0.11	−0.06	1.00			
15	Industry-Materials	0.24	0.22	−0.03	0.05	0.18	−0.14	−0.20	−0.14	0.12	−0.01	0.06	−0.13	−0.12	−0.31	−0.63	0.14	1.00		
16	Industry-Profit-Rate	0.20	0.12	0.03	0.03	0.21	0.30	0.26	0.19	−0.11	−0.003	0.004	−0.02	0.29	0.31	−0.19	−0.01	−0.12	1.00	
17	Industry-Tax-Rate	0.03	0.03	0.01	0.004	0.03	−0.02	0.10	−0.05	−0.24	0.03	−0.02	−0.05	0.12	0.47	0.16	−0.09	−0.31	0.35	1.00

The above are based on the estimation sample of 23,092 observation.

Cross-border acquisition and greenfield investment   89

where the subscripts i, j, and t, respectively, stand for firm, industry, and year; and where k allows for convenient expression. Vector X refers to the series of ten contemporaneous industry-level control constructs, and δ refers to the respective coefficient estimates for these ten controls. The term (w_t) reflects the employment of time-specific fixed effects, while the term (α_i) reflects the employment of firm-specific fixed effects. Our employing firm-level fixed effects compares favorably to the norms in the establishment-mode choice literature where cross-sectional analysis represents the common approach—Barkema and Vermeulen (1998) represent a noteworthy exception to this observation. Lastly, ε_{it} refers to an idiosyncratic error term.

The first point to notice in the above regression equations is that the merger-policy investigations construct involves taking the thrice-lagged sum of second-request investigations. This practice follows the pre-existing merger-policy deterrence literature where it is commonly understood that the actions undertaken by antitrust authorities involve deterrence in subsequent years, or the impact of merger policy on firm-investment behavior is not contemporaneous and persists for a few years (Clougherty, Duso, Lee, & Seldeslachts, 2016; Clougherty & Seldeslachts, 2013; Clougherty & Zhang, 2021; Seldeslachts, Clougherty & Barros, 2009). Indeed, Davies and Majumdar (2002) observe that the FTC considers its enforcement efforts to involve a two-year window in terms of deterrence benefits. While the pre-existing deterrence literature tends to consider industry-level effects due to changes in merger-policy enforcement, our firm-level context indicates the appropriateness of a three-year window for deterrence.

In light of our lacking data with respect to appropriate firm-level control constructs, both regression equations include lagged-dependent variables to achieve better model specification. Including lagged-dependent variables is certainly appropriate when the dependent variable is not created anew each period (Finkel, 1995). The proclivity of foreign firms to engage in CBAs and GIs when operating in the US might also reflect such dependencies over time. Moreover, Wooldridge (2002) observes that a dynamic panel-data approach is often intended to simply control for the presence of omitted variables. The inclusion of lagged-dependent variables in our context is very much driven by the lack of firm-level controls, but also by the presence of autoregressive dynamics. Accordingly, both regression equations involve three lags of the dependent construct and thereby indicate that a foreign firm's previous investment levels are held constant, which generates coefficient estimates for the principal variable of interest—merger-policy-investigations—that should be interpreted as measuring short-term, not long-term, effects on the relevant dependent variable.

In addition to including lagged-dependent variables in both regression equations, we also control for sets of industry-level controls to generate stronger causal inferences. Unique to equation 1 (the CBA equation) is

90 *Nan Zhang and Joseph A. Clougherty*

that we control for the contemporaneous and thrice lagged measures of Industry-Inward-CBA, Industry-Domestic-M&A, and Industry-Outward-CBA. Unique to equation 2 (the GI equation) is that we control for the contemporaneous and the thrice lagged measures of Industry-Greenfield. Accounting for the lagged structures in these four industry-control variables in this manner (where the t, t–1, t–2, and t–3 measures are nested) follows precedent (Bertrand et al., 2007; Calderón et al., 2004; Nguyen et al., 2021) and represents a comprehensive approach that is agnostic as to the appropriate causal lags. Finally, the series of ten contemporaneous industry-level control constructs represented by vector X are common to both regression equations.

An additional econometric issue of importance is that the dependent variables in both regression equations exhibit a substantial degree of left censoring, i.e., where the dependent construct manifests a clustering of zeros on the left-hand side of the distribution. This left-censoring indicates the appropriateness of a left-sided Tobit estimation (Tobin, 1958). We, therefore, undertake left-sided Tobit estimations to correct for the substantial left censoring in both regression estimations. Finally, our regression estimations follow standard practice with panel-data estimations by employing robust standard errors clustered on the foreign firm.

Empirical results

Table 4.2 reports the empirical results for our estimations of regression equations 1 and 2, i.e., the respective CBA and GI equations. The pseudo R-squared for the two Tobit estimations (0.259 and 0.194, respectively) indicate that both models are reasonably well specified. Importantly, McFadden (1979) highlights how pseudo R-squared is systematically lower than the values of a standard R-squared. In addition to the goodness-of-fit statistics, the control variables also generally conform to expectations—which also indicates well-specified regression models. Before considering the results for the principal explanatory variable—merger-policy-investigations—in both Tobit estimations, we discuss the results for the control variables.

We first focus on the controls in the Tobit estimation of equation 1 where the level of CBA by foreign firms represents the dependent variable of interest. Evident from that estimation is that the lagged-dependent constructs substantially affect a foreign firm's proclivity to engage in CBAs of US targets. Specifically, the three lagged-dependent variables all yield negative and statistically significant (at the one-percent level) coefficient estimates. These results are in line with the idea that CBAs involve a substantial commitment of time and resources on the part of an acquirer; thus, foreign firms are not, on average, serial acquirers of US firms on a year-to-year basis. Indeed, these are encompassing events; hence, higher levels of CBA in one period partly preclude firms from engaging in near-future CBAs.

Cross-border acquisition and greenfield investment 91

Table 4.2 Tobit estimation results for two regression equations

	Eq. 1: Cross-Border-Acquisitions	Eq. 2: Greenfield-Investments
Merger-Policy-Investigation $\sum_{k=1}^{3}$ t-k	−0.022*** (0.0003)	0.018* (0.0115)
Cross-Border-Acquisitions $_{t-1}$	−0.110*** (0.0040)	
Cross-Border-Acquisitions $_{t-2}$	−0.093*** (0.0049)	
Cross-Border-Acquisitions $_{t-3}$	−0.164*** (0.0044)	
Industry-Inward-CBA $_t$	0.002*** (0.0004)	
Industry-Inward-CBA $_{t-1}$	0.0001 (0.0004)	
Industry-Inward-CBA $_{t-2}$	−0.009*** (0.0004)	
Industry-Inward-CBA $_{t-3}$	−0.001 (0.0006)	
Industry-Domestic-M&A $_t$	0.001*** (0.0001)	
Industry-Domestic-M&A $_{t-1}$	0.001*** (0.0001)	
Industry-Domestic-M&A $_{t-2}$	−0.001*** (0.0001)	
Industry-Domestic-M&A $_{t-3}$	−0.003*** (0.0001)	
Industry-Outward-CBA $_t$	−0.005*** (0.0004)	
Industry-Outward-CBA $_{t-1}$	−0.004*** (0.0006)	
Industry-Outward-CBA $_{t-2}$	−0.008*** (0.0006)	
Industry-Outward-CBA $_{t-3}$	−0.001 (0.0005)	
Greenfield-Investments $_{t-1}$		0.039 (0.0360)
Greenfield-Investments $_{t-2}$		−0.061 (0.0426)
Greenfield-Investments $_{t-3}$		−0.120*** (0.0319)
Industry-Greenfield $_t$		0.041*** (0.0040)
Industry-Greenfield $_{t-1}$		−0.007** (0.0034)
Industry-Greenfield $_{t-2}$		−0.002 (0.0035)
Industry-Greenfield $_{t-3}$		−0.007* (0.0036)
Industry-Growth $_t$	0.451*** (0.0628)	1.232** (0.4839)

(*continued*)

92 *Nan Zhang and Joseph A. Clougherty*

Table 4.2 Cont.

	Eq. 1: Cross-Border-Acquisitions	Eq. 2: Greenfield-Investments
Industry-Cash $_t$	3.070***	−0.953
	(0.1585)	(3.3618)
Industry-HHI $_t$	1.271***	0.755
	(0.0344)	(1.7447)
Industry-Domestic-Experience $_t$	−0.247***	−0.502
	(0.0067)	(0.4387)
Industry-Value-Added $_t$	1.216***	2.064*
	(0.0072)	(1.1019)
Industry-Skilled-Labor $_t$	0.001***	−0.002
	(0.0002)	(0.0022)
Industry-R&D $_t$	−0.182***	0.153
	(0.0058)	(1.7192)
Industry-Materials $_t$	2.313***	1.370
	(0.0066)	(1.1349)
Industry-Profit-Rate $_t$	0.669***	−0.929
	(0.0108)	(0.8192)
Industry-Tax-Rate $_t$	13.103***	11.436*
	(0.0437)	(6.2017)
Constant	−13.372***	−4.387***
	(0.0028)	(0.7597)
Number of observations	19,773	19,773
Pseudo R-squared	0.259	0.194

Robust standard errors clustered at the firm level in parentheses.

Significance at the one-percent, five-percent, and ten-percent levels is represented by ***, **, and *, respectively.

All estimations involve left-sided Tobit censoring, as well as firm-specific and year-specific fixed effects.

Turning to the industry-level controls of industry-inward-CBA and industry-domestic-M&A, the results for these two variables conform to our priors regarding investment waves—or more specifically, merger waves. Indeed, both variables manifest positive coefficient estimates for the contemporaneous and once-lagged measures (t and t–1); yet both variables also manifest negative coefficient estimates for their twice-lagged and thrice-lagged measures (t–2 and t–3). These results for the lagged constructs are in line with the approach and findings in the economics literature concerning the modeling of merger waves (Gugler, Mueller & Weichselbaumer, 2012; Seldeslachts, Clougherty & Barros, 2009). We should note that the industry-domestic-M&A construct manifests greater significance as compared to the industry-inward-CBA construct; thus, domestic activities appear to principally define the merger wave. The industry-level control of industry-outward-CBA, however, manifests a different pattern as the coefficient estimates are negative throughout

Cross-border acquisition and greenfield investment   93

and statistically significant at the one-percent level for the t, t–1, and t–2 measures. These results suggest that sectors with high levels of outward CBA activities are sectors where US firms have a competitive advantage; moreover, this competitive advantage for US firms appears to reduce the ability of foreign firms to acquire US targets. Finally, the ten contemporaneous industry-level controls all manifest statistical significance at the one-percent level in the CBA equation. These ten controls indicate that industries characterized by high growth, more cash, larger HHI, low domestic acquisition experience, greater value-added, more skilled labor, less R&D, increased materials, higher profitability, and steeper taxes incur higher levels of CBAs by foreign firms.

We now consider the controls in the Tobit estimation of equation 2 where the level of GI by foreign firms represents the dependent variable of interest. Interestingly, the first two lags of the dependent construct do not manifest statistical significance, though the third lag of the dependent construct manifests a negative and significant coefficient estimate at the one-percent level. These results appear to indicate that previous GI projects in the US by foreign firms do not substantially preclude firms from engaging in future greenfield projects. While this finding contrasts with the preclusion effect characteristic of CBA activities, it does stand to reason in that greenfield projects are generally much smaller investments as compared to CBAs. The smaller nature of greenfield projects means that these investments are not so encompassing, thus allowing for recurring GI.

Turning to the industry-level control of industry-greenfield, the results for this construct conform to our priors regarding the presence of investment waves. Akin to the pattern of coefficient estimates supporting the relevance of merger waves, the coefficient estimates for industry-GI initially exhibit a positive sign though additional lags exhibit negative coefficient estimates. Specifically, industry-greenfield manifests a positive coefficient estimate for the contemporaneous measure (t), but manifests negative coefficient estimates for the once-lagged, twice-lagged, and thrice-lagged measures (t–1, t–2, and t–3). Further, all of these coefficient estimates are statistically significant with the exception of the twice-lagged construct. Finally, the contemporaneous industry-level controls do not manifest the robust statistical significance across all the controls in the GI equation that was present in the CBA equation. Nevertheless, the empirical results for these contemporaneous industry-level controls indicate that industries characterized by high growth, greater value-added, and larger taxes incur higher levels of GI by foreign firms.

We can now turn to discussing the empirical results for the explanatory variable of principal interest, merger-policy-investigations, in both regression equations. In support of H1, the coefficient estimate for merger-policy-investigations is negative and significant at the one-percent level in the Tobit estimation of equation 1. Accordingly, increases in second-request investigations at the sectoral level by US antitrust authorities lead to decreased horizontal CBAs of US targets by foreign firms in subsequent years. This finding is consistent with the merger-policy deterrence literature by suggesting that the enforcement of US merger policy negatively affects foreign-investor acquisition activities. In terms of the economic significance of this coefficient estimate, a one-standard-deviation increase in merger-policy investigations leads, on average, to 0.0451 fewer horizontal CBAs for each foreign firm.

In support of H2, the coefficient estimate for merger-policy investigations is positive and significant at the ten-percent level in the Tobit estimation of equation 2. Accordingly, increases in second-request investigations at the sectoral level by US antitrust authorities lead to increased GI by foreign firms in subsequent years. Moreover, this finding—in conjunction with the results from equation 1—is consistent with the prior that GI activities substitute for CBA activities. Foreign firms appear to decrease CBAs but increase their GI in the US in the face of stricter merger-policy enforcement. In terms of the economic significance of this coefficient estimate, a one-standard-deviation increase in merger-policy investigations leads, on average, to 0.0379 more GIs for each foreign firm.

Discussion

The establishment-mode choice literature holds that CBA and GI represent viable alternatives to set up an organizational presence in a host-nation. As such, a substitutive relationship between CBA and GI activities is generally assumed within the establishment-mode choice literature. Yet the potential exists for a complementary—or even a partially substitutive—relationship between CBAs and GIs, and to date the nature of this relationship has not been definitively established. We explore the relationship between CBA and GI activities by employing a cross-price elasticities estimation approach. Specifically, we use merger-policy enforcement as a 'price' that directly impacts CBA but only indirectly impacts GI. Moreover, that indirect relationship between merger-policy enforcement and GI reflects whether the prevailing relationship between CBAs and GIs is either substitutive or complementary. Panel-data estimation techniques applied to data covering 1,763 foreign firms investing in the US over the 2003–2017 period support the presence of a substitutive relationship. While our empirics yield clear implications with respect to the CBA-GI relationship, the results also provide salient research implications for the greater literature on CBAs and establishment-mode choice.

Research implications

Hennart and Park (1993) first discerned a lack of empirical work considering the factors determining whether firms enter a foreign nation

Cross-border acquisition and greenfield investment   95

via CBA or GI. The subsequent three decades have borne witness to a substantial increase in empirical—as well as theoretical—scholarship in both management and economics addressing this important question. Despite this progress, Demirbag, Tatoglu, and Glasiter (2008) observe that the literature considering the choice between CBA and GI pales in comparison to the literature considering the parallel choice between wholly- and jointly-owned foreign subsidiaries. The difficulties involved with empirically capturing GI may partly explain this relative neglect. This study—employing detailed data on GI projects by foreign firms investing in the US—represents an important empirical contribution that attempts to rebalance the empirical literature.

Our analysis also involves some distinction as it bridges the management and economics literature on establishment-mode choice. While Slangen and Hennart (2007) review the extensive literature in management where the establishment-mode question was first posed, Nocke and Yeaple (2007) recognize a growing literature within economics on the factors determining the choice between CBAs and GIs. Yet outside a few notable exceptions (Bertrand et al., 2007; Davies et al., 2018), the vast majority of this literature remains mono-disciplinary in that the works fail to recognize the progress made in the other discipline. In our analysis, the recent literature in economics helped illuminate that substitution between CBA and GI activities was a taken for granted assumption in the management literature; further, the cross-price elasticities approach from economics (Clausing, 2000; Grubert & Mutti, 1991) was instrumental in helping establish that the relationship between CBA and GI is in fact largely substitutive in nature.

The most important implication of our research involves finding evidence in support of a substitutive CBA-GI relationship. As already noted, Slangen and Hennart (2007), Odebunmi (2017), and others recognize the inconsistent empirical results in the establishment-mode choice literature. Brouthers and Brouthers (2000) express similar concerns when noting the lack of a coherent conceptual framework in this literature. If CBA and GI were best characterized as complements—or, at best, partial subsitutes—then the conceptual and empirical inconsistences in the literature might be based on a false-dichotomous choice between the two investment modes. The fact that our evidence indicates a substitutive relationship is reassurring for the establishment-mode choice literature. For example, it allows re-focusing research efforts in line with prescriptions of Slangen and Hennart (2007) and Nocke and Yeaple (2007, 2008) to move the research agenda on CBA and GI forward.

Managerial implications

Our empirical results clearly indicate that firms deterred from engaging in horizontal CBA activities, due to increased merger-policy enforcement in a host nation, will substitute GI for CBA. GI certainly involves the greatest

96 Nan Zhang and Joseph A. Clougherty

contribution of technology and know-how, requires a longer period to establish, and offers substantial control over local operations (Chang & Rosenzweig, 2001). Yet, GI also allows foreign firms to bypass national conduct of merger control. Indeed, GI does not require vetting by antitrust authorities; thus there is no mandatory reporting of these transactions for merger review. Accordingly, GI represents a viable substitute for CBA activities, when merger-policy enforcement in the host market is particularly stringent. For example, GI represents a superior establishment mode for investments in the US and EU, as these jurisdictions have relatively strong merger policies. Moreover, the proliferation of merger policy to over 90 nations in the last few decades (Dikova, Sahib & Witteloostuijn, 2010) and the stepped-up enforcement of merger policy in developed and emerging nations yield clear managerial implications. Specifically, it behooves firms interested in broadly internationalizing to increasingly employ GI as a means to circumvent the continued establishment and strengthening of merger policies in the cross-national context for global business.

Limitations and future research

Our analysis does involve some limitations that call for future research. First, our empirical analysis lacks the appropriate firm-level controls that the pre-existing literature considers relevant to determining the choice between CBA and GI activities. Accordingly, future empirical analysis should compile a full set of firm-level controls akin to those assembled by Drogendijk and Slangen (2006) and complete a similar analysis to ours to establish the nature of the CBA-GI relationship. That said, we should reiterate the point that our empirical analysis invokes the appropriate firm-level fixed effects (which yields estimators based on within-firm variation) that most establishment-mode choice studies neglect. Second, our cross-price elasticities approach to detecting the CBA-GI relationship is certainly a sound method that avoids the endogeneity bias that plagues the pre-existing approaches (Calderón et al., 2004; Nguyen et al., 2021). Nevertheless, we would strongly encourage alternative approaches to studying CBA-GI relationships. For instance, Blonigen (2001) established substitution between trade and FDI by employing data with exacting detail, while Belderbos and Sleuwaegen (1998) established substitution by factoring substantial exogenous shocks. Third, our study necessarily considers the relationship between different forms (CBA and GI) of horizontal cross-border investments. However, future research should consider the relationship between vertical cross-border investments. It is an open question as to the degree to which firms substitute between CBA and GI when engaging in vertical foreign investments. Fourth, and most obviously, we would strongly support conducting similar analyses outside of the US host-nation context to enhance the generalizability of findings. Yet, the fact that the US has generally been considered a paragon of exemplary antitrust and a nation where inward FDI is welcomed suggests that our findings would be echoed in the cross-national context for antitrust.

In closing, our empirical analysis provides clear implications with respect to how CBA activities relate to internal development activities via GI. These two investment modes do indeed represent alternative (substitutive) choices made by firms seeking to expand in foreign markets. Recent scholarship has expressed the concern that CBA and GI involve a complementary, or a partially substitutive, relationship. A complementary relationship would be troubling for the establishment-mode choice literature, as the fundamental premise behind this literature is that these two modes can be employed interchangeably for foreign-investment purposes. In line with the establishment-mode choice literature, our empirical evidence indicates that CBA and GI are not fully distinct investment modes and are instead employed as substitutes. Accordingly, the main implication of this study is simple, but important: CBA and GI are indeed characterized by a substitutive relationship.

References

Andrade, G., & Stafford, E. (2004). Investigating the economic role of mergers. *Journal of Corporate Finance*, 10(1), 1–36.

Barkema, H., & Vermeulen, F. (1998). International expansion through start-up or acquisition: A learning perspective. *Academy of Management Journal*, 41(1), 7–26.

Bascle, G. (2008). Controlling for endogeneity with instrumental variables in strategic management research. *Strategic Organization*, 6(3), 285–327.

Belderbos, R., & Sleuwaegen, L. (1998). Tariff jumping DFI and export substitution: Japanese electronics firms in Europe. *International Journal of Industrial Organization*, 16(5), 601–638.

Bertrand, O., Hakkala, K., & Norbäck, P.-J. (2007). Cross-border acquisition or greenfield entry: Does it matter for affiliate R&D?. IFN Working Paper No. 693, Research Institute of Industrial Economics (IFN), Stockholm.

Blonigen, B. (1997). Firm-specific assets and the link between exchange rates and foreign direct investment. *American Economic Review*, 87(3), 447–465.

Blonigen, B. (2001). In search of substitution between foreign production and exports. *Journal of International Economics*, 53(1), 81–104.

Brewer, T. (1993). Governments, policies, market imperfections, and foreign direct investment. *Journal of International Business Studies*, 24(1), 101–120.

Brouthers, K., & Brouthers, L. (2000), Acquisition or greenfield start-up? Institutional, cultural and transaction cost influences. *Strategic Management Journal*, 21(1), 89–97.

Calderón, C., Loayza, N., & Servén, L. (2004). Greenfield foreign direct investment and mergers and acquisitions: Feedback and macroeconomic effects. World Bank Policy Research Paper No. 3192, Washington, DC.

98 *Nan Zhang and Joseph A. Clougherty*

Chang, S., & Rosenzweig, P. (2001). The choice of entry mode in sequential foreign direct investment. *Strategic Management Journal*, 22(8), 747–776.

Clausing, K. (2000). Does multinational activity displace trade? *Economic Inquiry*, 38(2), 190–205.

Clougherty, J. (2001). Globalization and the autonomy of domestic competition policy: An empirical test on the world airline industry. *Journal of International Business Studies*, 32(3), 459–478.

Clougherty, J. (2005). Antitrust holdup source, cross-national institutional variation, and corporate political strategy implications for domestic mergers in a global context. *Strategic Management Journal*, 26(8), 769–790.

Clougherty, J., Duso, T., Lee, M., & Seldeslachts, J. (2016). Effective European antitrust: Does EC merger policy generate deterrence. *Economic Inquiry*, 54(4), 1884–1903.

Clougherty, J., & Seldeslachts, J. (2013). The deterrence effects of US merger policy instruments. *Journal of Law, Economics, and Organization*, 29(5), 1114–1144.

Clougherty, J., & Zhang, N. (2021). Foreign investor reactions to risk and uncertainty in antitrust: U.S. merger policy investigations and the deterrence of foreign acquirer presence. *Journal of International Business Studies*, 52(3), 454–478.

Davies, R., Desbordes, R., & Ray, A. (2018). Greenfield versus merger and acquisition FDI: Same wine, different bottles? *Canadian Journal of Economics*, 51(4), 1151–1190.

Davies, S., & Majumdar, A. (2002). *The development of targets for consumer savings arising from competition policy.* London, U.K.: Office of Fair Trading.

Demirbag, M., Tatoglu, E., & Glaister, K. (2008). Factors affecting perceptions of the choice between acquisition and greenfield entry: The case of western FDI in an emerging market. *Management International Review*, 48(1), 1–34.

Dikova, D., Sahib, P., & Witteloostuijn, A. (2010). Cross-border acquisition abandonment and completion: The effect of institutional differences and organizational learning in the international business service industry. *Journal of International Business Studies*, 41(2), 223–245.

Drogendijk, R., & Slangen, A. (2006). Hofstede, Schwartz, or managerial perceptions? The effects of different cultural distance measures on establishment mode choices by multinational enterprises. *International Business Review*, 15(4), 361–380.

Dunning, J., & Pitelis, C. (2008). Stephen Hymer's contribution to international business scholarship: An assessment and extension. *Journal of International Business Studies*, 39(1), 167–176.

Finkel, S. (1995). *Causal analysis with panel data.* Thousand Oaks, CA: Sage.

Forsgren, M. (2013). *Theories of the multinational firm.* Northampton, MA: Edward Elgar.

Forte, R., & Silva, V. (2017). Outward FDI and home country exports: Theoretical approaches and empirical evidence. *The International Trade Journal*, 31(3), 245–271.

Grosse, R., & Trevino, L. (2005). New institutional economics and FDI location in Central and Eastern Europe. *Management International Review*, 45(2), 123–145.

Cross-border acquisition and greenfield investment   99

Grubert, H., & Mutti, J. (1991). Taxes, tariffs and transfer pricing in multinational corporate decision making. *Review of Economics and Statistics*, 73(2), 285–293.

Gugler, K., Mueller, D., & Weichselbaumer, M. (2012). The determinants of merger waves: An international perspective. *International Journal of Industrial Organization*, 30(1), 1–15.

Harford, J. (2005). What drives merger waves? *Journal of Financial Economics*, 77(3), 529–560.

Harzing, A. (2002). Acquisitions versus greenfield investments: International strategy and management of entry modes. *Strategic Management Journal*, 23(3), 211–227.

Head, K., & Ries, J. (2001). Overseas investment and firm exports. *Review of International Economics*, 9(1), 108–122.

Hejazi, W., & Safarian, A. (2001). The complementarity between US foreign direct investment stock and trade. *Atlantic Economic Journal*, 29(4), 420–437.

Hemphill, T. (2010). The 'new protectionism': Industrial policy barriers to cross-border mergers and acquisitions. *Competition & Change*, 14(2), 124–148.

Hennart, J. (1989). Can the "new forms of investment" substitute for the "old forms?" A transaction costs perspective. *Journal of International Business Studies*, 20(2), 211–234.

Hennart, J., & Park, Y. (1993). Greenfield vs. acquisition: The strategy of Japanese investors in the United States. *Management Science*, 39(9), 1054–1070.

Hitt, M., Li, D., & Xu, K. (2016). International Strategy: From local to global and beyond. *Journal of World Business*, 51(1), 58–73.

Hymer, S. (1970). The efficiency (contradictions) of multinational corporations. *American Economic Review*, 60(2), 441–448.

Hymer, S. (1976). *The international operations of national firms: A study of direct foreign investment*. Cambridge, MA: MIT Press.

Hymer, S. (1979). The multinational corporation and the law of uneven development. In R. Cohen, N. Felton, M. Nkosi, & J. van Liere (Eds.), *The multinational corporation: A radical approach* (pp. 54–74). Cambridge: Cambridge University Press.

Johnson, A., & Li, Q. (2018). Regime type and FDI: A transaction cost economics approach to the debate. *Oxford Research Encyclopedia of Politics*. Retrieved 22 Dec. 2021, from https://oxfordre.com/politics/view/10.1093/acrefore/9780190228637.001.0001/acrefore-9780190228637-e-578

Kovacic, E. (2003). The modern evolution of U.S. competition policy enforcement norms. *Antitrust Law Journal*, 71(2), 377–478.

Kwoka, J., & White, L. (2008). *The antitrust revolution: Economics, competition, and policy*. Oxford: Oxford University Press.

Makaew, T. (2012). Waves of international mergers and acquisitions. Mimeo, University of South Carolina. https://papers.ssrn.com/sol3/papers.cfm?abstract_id=1786989

McFadden, D. (1979). Quantitative methods for analysing travel behaviour of individuals: Some recent developments. In D. Hensher & P. Stopher (Eds.), *Behavioural travel modelling* (pp. 279–318). London: Croom Helm.

Moghadam, A., Mazlan, N., Chin, L., & Ibrahim, S. (2019). Mergers and acquisitions and greenfield foreign direct investment in selected ASEAN countries. *Journal of Economic Integration*, 34(4), 746–765.

Motta, M. (2004). *Competition policy: Theory and practice*. Cambridge: Cambridge University Press.

Neven, D., & Röller, L. (2005). Consumer surplus vs. welfare standard in a political economy model of merger control. *International Journal of Industrial Organization, 23*(9–10), 829–848.

Nguyen, H., Luu, H., & Do, N. (2021). The dynamic relationship between greenfield investments, cross-border M&As, domestic investment and economic growth in Vietnam. *Economic Change and Restructuring, 54*(4), 1065–1089. https://doi.org/10.1007/s10644-020-09292-7

Nocke, V., & Yeaple, S. (2007). Cross-border mergers and acquisitions vs. greenfield foreign direct investment: The role of firm heterogeneity. *Journal of International Economics, 72*(2), 336–365.

Nocke, V., & Yeaple, S. (2008). An assignment theory of foreign direct investment. *Review of Economic Studies, 75*(2), 529–557.

Odebunmi, I. (2017). Model uncertainty in foreign direct investment: Greenfield versus mergers and acquisitions. Thesis, University of Calgary. https://prism.ucalgary.ca/bitstream/handle/11023/3774/ucalgary_2017_odebunmi_iyanuoluwa.pdf?sequence=1

Oliveira, G., Hochstetler, R., & Kalil, C. (2001). Competition policy and foreign direct investment: Possible relationships and aspects from the recent Brazilian experience. *Transnational Corporations, 10*(1), 69–87.

Scherer, F. (1996). International trade and competition policy. Discussion Paper No. 96–18, Zew Industrial Economics and International Management Series, Mannheim Germany.

Seldeslachts, J., Clougherty, J., & Barros, P. (2009). Settle for now but block for tomorrow: The deterrence effects of merger policy tools. *Journal of Law & Economics, 52*(3), 607–634.

Shapiro, C. (2010). The 2010 horizontal merger guidelines: From hedgehog to fox in forty years. *Antitrust Law Journal, 77*, 701–759.

Slangen, A., & Hennart, J. (2007). Greenfield or acquisition entry: A review of the empirical foreign establishment mode literature. *Journal of International Management, 13*(4), 403–429.

Tobin, J. (1958). Estimation of relationships for limited dependent variables. *Econometrica, 26*(1), 24–36.

UNCTAD. (2014). *World investment report: Investing in the SDGs: An action plan*. New York, NY.

UNCTAD. (2016). *World investment report: Investor nationality: Policy challenges*. New York, NY.

Viscusi, W., Vernon, J., & Harrington, J. (1995). *Economics of regulation and antitrust*. Cambridge, MA: The MIT Press.

Wooldridge, J. (2002). *Econometric analysis of cross section and panel data*. Cambridge, MA: MIT Press.

Wooldridge, J. (2013). *Introductory econometrics: A modern approach*. Mason, OH: Thomson South-Western.

Appendix 4.1 Variable descriptions by data source

Variable	Description
Source: Thomson SDC Platinum	
Cross-Border-Acquisitions	Annual number of cross-border horizontal acquisitions of US targets by foreign firm i.
Industry-Inward-CBA	Annual number of foreign-acquirer horizontal acquisitions of US targets in industry j.
Industry-Domestic-M&A	Annual number of domestic-acquirer horizontal acquisitions of US targets in industry j.
Industry-Outward-CBA	Annual number of US-acquirer horizontal acquisitions of foreign targets in industry j.
Industry-Growth	Average net sales growth over the past year—$((Sales_{j,t-1})/ Sales_{j,t-1}))$—in industry j.
Industry-Cash	Average earnings before interest and taxes (EBIT) over gross output in industry j.
Industry-Domestic-Experience	Percentage of domestic acquirers in industry j with a US acquisition experience in the preceding five years.
Source: fDi Markets	
Greenfield-Investments	Annual number of greenfield-investment projects in the US by foreign firm i.
Industry-Greenfield	Annual number of foreign greenfield investment projects in the US for industry j.
Source: Annual Reports to Congress on Hart-Scott-Rodino Antitrust Enforcement	
Merger-Policy-Investigations	Three-year sum of FTC and DOJ second-request investigations in industry j.
Source: GDP by Industry dataset from US BEA.	
Industry-Value-Added	Gross output less intermediate inputs ($tril.) in industry j.
Industry-Skilled-Labor	College worker's compensation ($bil) in industry j.
Industry-R&D	R&D capital contribution as a percent of gross output in industry j.
Industry-Materials	Materials' contribution as a percent of gross output in industry j.
Industry-Profit-Rate	Gross operating surplus as a percent of gross output in industry j.
Industry-Tax-Rate	Net tax on production & imports as percent of gross output in industry j.
Source: Compustat Database from WRDS.	
Industry-HHI	Herfindahl-Hirschman-Index calculation based on the largest four firms in industry j.

Section II

What helps to predict acquisition performance?

David R. King

Firm performance is the primary dependent variable in management research (Hoskisson, Wan, Yiu, & Hitt, 1999; Richard, Devinney, Yip, & Johnson, 2009), but a variety of measures exist and they all have advantages and disadvantages (see Table II.1). Further, performance is a multidimensional construct and individual measures have a limited ability to provide multidimensional insights (Richard et al., 2009). A potential exception is innovation performance for firms in high-technology industries where multiple measures provide similar results (Hagedoorn & Cloodt, 2003). For acquisition research, different measures of performance often provide conflicting results, making selection of the performance measure an important part of research design (Cording, Christmann, & Weigelt, 2010; King, Wang, Samimi, & Cortes, 2021; Papadakis & Thanos, 2010; Schoenberg, 2006; Zollo & Meier, 2008).

The complexity of acquisitions suggests a need to increase the use of managerial surveys designed to evaluate anticipated relationships (Junni, Sarala, Taras, & Tarba, 2013) in combination with other measures of performance to enable triangulation and comparison of findings (King et al., 2021; Richard et al., 2009). For example, managerial surveys can be used to measure whether acquisition goals were achieved, and this may provide an intermediate step needed to improve firm performance from an acquisition (Cording, Chrismann, & King, 2008). This also suggests that research needs to consider measures that better reflect the motives behind an acquisition, as well as the context where they occur. The chapters in this section begin to address these concerns.

In Chapter 5, Svante Schriber develops the argument that dynamic capabilities can be central to improving our understanding of acquisition processes and performance. The chapter integrates dynamic capabilities with a process view of acquisitions that have largely developed in parallel to develop a theoretical framework based on acquisition characteristics. The framework highlights how key acquisition choices affect the conditions for dynamic capabilities, or the ability of managers to sense external change, monitor and reallocate firm capabilities and

DOI: 10.4324/9781003188308-7

104   David R. King

Table II.1 Measures of acquisition performance

	Advantages	*Disadvantages*
Accounting	• Considers performance following an acquisition • Facilitates comparison of firms • Repeatable measure	• Limited to public firms • Historical focus • Difficulty comparing across industries and nations • Managers can influence • Does not consider risk • Confounding events
Innovation	• Different measures provide similar results in high-technology industries • Patent measures are also available for private firms	• Difficulty comparing across industries • Not all innovations are patented • Not all firms report R&D
Managerial survey	• Facilitates measuring multiple dimensions of performance • Enables study of private firms • Can evaluate acquisition goals	• Concerns about bias (recall, etc.)
Stock (short)	• Assumption of market efficiency normally holds • Facilitates comparison of firms • Repeatable measure	• Limited to public firms • Better predictor than measure of performance • Information asymmetry between managers and investors
Stock (long)	• Considers performance following an acquisition • Repeatable measure	• Limited to public firms • Potential for confounding events • Difficult to compare across nations
Tobin's Q	• Hybrid of stock and accounting measures that considers multiple dimensions of performance • Repeatable measure	• Limited to public firms • Accounting component based on historical versus replacement costs

resources to adjust to a firm's changing environmental conditions. The chapter uses the context of acquisitions to outline how dynamic capabilities develop and impact firm competitiveness, and it offers testable propositions. Managerial advice is provided.

Pankaj Patel and David King, in Chapter 6, examine acquirers that seek to improve the operations of target firms. Specifically, firms with lower pollution rates can generate value by transferring green capabilities to polluting targets through the market for corporate control. Importantly, empirical analysis finds that green capabilities (a firm's efficiency in converting environmental-related inputs into environmental performance) help decrease a target firm's pollution and improve overall financial performance after an acquisition, and this is enhanced for chemically related targets.

In Chapter 7, Camilla Jensen, Peter Zámborský, and David King aggregate research on cross-border acquisition (CBA) performance to identify impacts of cultural distance, and home and host country effects. Using predictive modeling that uses a nonlinear classification with machine learning to identify patterns, they find research that supports an overall positive impact of cultural distance on CBA performance. However, host and home country effects, and the home country setting of acquirers may be as important or more important than host country and cultural distance. Nonlinear predictive modeling of CBA performance reveals relationships that have not explicitly been explored previously, and it questions the usefulness of cultural distance in CBA performance research in comparison to considering country effects.

References

Cording, M., Christmann, P., & King, D. (2008). Reducing causal ambiguity in acquisition integration: Intermediate goals as mediators of integration decisions and acquisition performance. *Academy of Management Journal*, *51*(4), 744–767.

Cording, M., Christmann, P., & Weigelt, C. (2010). Measuring theoretically complex constructs: The case of acquisition performance. *Strategic Organization*, *8*(1), 11–41.

Junni, P., Sarala, R., Taras, V., & Tarba, S. (2013). Organizational ambidexterity and performance: A meta-analysis. *Academy of Management Perspectives*, *27*(4), 299–312.

Hagedoorn, J., & Cloodt, M. (2003). Measuring innovative performance: Is there an advantage in using multiple indicators? *Research Policy*, *32*(8), 1365–1379.

Hoskisson, R., Wan, W., Yiu, D., & Hitt, M. (1999). Theory and research in strategic management: Swings of a pendulum. *Journal of Management*, *25*(3), 417–456.

King, D., Bauer, F., Schriber, S. (2018). *Mergers & acquisitions: A research overview*. Oxford: Routledge.

King, D., Wang, G., Samimi, M., & Cortes, A. (2021). A meta-analytic integration of acquisition performance prediction. *Journal of Management Studies*, *58*(5), 1198–1236.

Papadakis, V., & Thanos, I. (2010). Measuring the performance of acquisitions: An empirical investigation using multiple criteria. *British Journal of Management*, *21*(4), 859–873.

Richard, P., Devinney, T., Yip, G., & Johnson, G. (2009). Measuring organizational performance: Towards methodological best practice. *Journal of Management*, *35*(3), 718–804.

Schoenberg, R. (2006). Measuring the performance of corporate acquisitions: An empirical comparison of alternative metrics. *British Journal of Management*, *17*(4), 361–370.

Zollo, M., & Meier, D. (2008). What is M&A performance? *Academy of Management Perspectives*, *22*(3), 55–77.

5 Merging dynamic capabilities and acquisition process research

Toward an integrative theoretical framework[1]

Svante Schriber

Introduction

Research increasingly highlights the relation between corporate acquisitions and dynamism in the competitive landscape, and repeating acquisitions especially constitutes an important option for adjusting to environmental change. Acquisitions can provide access to new markets, customers, logistics networks, patents, knowledge, and many other valuable resources (King, Slotegraaf, & Kesner, 2008; Lee & Lieberman, 2010). Alongside longstanding insights that internal dynamism from cultural tensions pose challenges to acquisitions (Stahl & Voigt, 2008; Teerikangas & Very, 2006; Zaheer, Castañer, & Souder, 2013) research increasingly acknowledges that acquiring firms may continuously and over time need to handle dynamism in their competitive environment (Junni, Sarala, Tarba, & Weber, 2015; Schriber, King, & Bauer, 2018).

Alongside but largely isolated from acquisition research, dynamic capabilities research has grown into one of the most influential strategic management research streams. This approach aims to explain why certain firms survive or even thrive in circumstances that change unpredictably and dramatically (Helfat & Peteraf, 2009; Teece, Pisano, & Shuen, 1997; Teece, 2007). Specifically, dynamic capabilities research highlights how firms become aware of and adjust firm resources through skill-based, repeated, organizational processes (Danneels, 2011; Eisenhardt & Martin, 2000). This framework has been applied in various strategic circumstances, and it has had a profound impact on both conceptual (Barreto, 2010) and empirical strategic management research (Drnevich & Kriauciunas, 2011; Schilke, 2014).

Against this background, the lack of integration between these two research streams is both surprising and problematic. Although sometimes combined, acquisition and dynamic capabilities research have been applied in parallel rather than been integrated (Junni et al., 2015; Meyer-Doyle, Lee, & Helfat, 2019) with application largely limited to

---

1 This chapter was blind reviewed.

DOI: 10.4324/9781003188308-8

the integration phase (Heimeriks, Schijven, & Gates, 2012). Dynamic capabilities provide a structured theoretical approach to address why certain acquiring firms adjust more effectively to dynamism than others. Specifically, it can illuminate how key acquisition choices help to shape the conditions for the organizational processes that constitute dynamic capabilities. In turn, this responds to calls for more research into why acquisitions fall short of intended goals (King, Dalton, Daily, & Covin, 2004; King, Wang, Samimi, & Cortes, 2021), and it is highly relevant as acquisitions typically occur in dynamic environments (Haleblian, McNamara, Kolev, & Dykes, 2012; McNamara, Haleblian, Kolev, & Dykes, 2008).

This chapter aims to systematically integrate dynamic capabilities and acquisition research. It emphasizes firms conducting repeated acquisitions and builds on process research (Jemison & Sitkin, 1986), a broad and largely empirically driven stream that identifies that several key managerial choices during the acquisition process affect conditions for dynamic capabilities. Dynamic capabilities, in turn, are regarded as organizational processes whose efficiency is contingent on their organizational context (Winter, 2003). This conceptual integration results in testable propositions regarding how key managerial choices during acquisition processes shape conditions for dynamic capabilities, and thereby a firm's ability to adjust to environmental dynamism. This chapter therefore makes several contributions to theory. First, it integrates dynamic capabilities and acquisition process research in the form of a theoretical framework. Second, it extends acquisition research by theorizing how acquisitions perform in dynamic environments. Lastly, it contributes to dynamic capabilities by concretizing the sources of such capabilities in acquisitions.

Acquisitions as embedded processes

Acquisitions are generally considered as processes, or events playing out in time, where previous events contribute to shaping the conditions of subsequent events and acquisition outcomes. In their seminal paper, Jemison and Sitkin (1986) outlined that acquisition processes involve a variety of managerial challenges, developed further in research. Since then, research has identified that several challenges inside or between involved firms can prevent acquisitions from reaching their aims. For instance, the combination of firms may not provide sufficiently beneficial overlap of technology (Pehrsson, 2006) or markets (Homburg & Bucerius, 2006), cultures and identities (Stahl & Voigt, 2008). Further, managers facing bounded rationality (Cyert & March, 1963) struggle to handle these conditions during the typically complex integration (Steigenberger, 2017).

More recently, the interdependence between acquisitions and their competitive context has been recognized (Rouzies, Colman, & Angwin, 2019; Schriber, 2016), as rival firms may attempt to hinder the acquisition

Dynamic capabilities and acquisition processes 109

reaching its aims (Bauer, King, Schriber, & Kruckhauser, 2021b; Keil, Laamanen, & McGrath, 2013; Schriber, King, & Bauer, 2021). As an example, acquisitions may cause customers to seek new suppliers (Öberg, 2014). The interdependence with the surrounding environment means similar integration efforts can have different outcomes depending on institutional conditions (Bauer, Schriber, Degischer, & King, 2018). Despite the recognition that acquisition processes evolve in a continuous interaction with a dynamic external environment, little systemic integration has taken place between acquisition research and theories focusing on firm adaptation to dynamism.

Dynamic capabilities research

The concept of dynamic capabilities has been proposed to explain a firm's strategic ability to handle external change, or how it is able to survive or even thrive under various levels of environmental dynamism (Teece et al., 1997). In stable, gradually or predictably changing environments, firms can compete successfully based on resources that are essentially unchanged; however, associated sources of competitive advantage can erode quickly when environments shift, giving dynamic capabilities a special role in explaining how firms are able to adapt to dynamic environments (Helfat et al., 2007).

The commonly accepted starting point of dynamic capabilities research is evolutionary economics, and the concept of routines. Organizational achievements can fruitfully be understood as resulting from pre-defined, collective, skill-based routines. Such routines are combined into organizational behavior (Nelson & Winter, 1982) that together with resources of various sorts allow firms to form more complex organizational capabilities, conceptualized hierarchically. Zero-level or basic organizational capabilities allow firms to perform basic processes such as producing goods and services at a certain level of efficiency. First-level, operational capabilities operate on and allow refining, but are unable to fundamentally alter, zero-level capabilities. Second-order, higher-order, or dynamic capabilities are required to change the direction of lower-order capabilities to adjust to environmental dynamism. Accordingly, dynamic capabilities are higher-ordered routines that induce change onto a firm's lower-order capabilities and resources, and the existence and proficiency of such higher-order routines ultimately explain why certain firms can adjust to sudden dynamism better than others (Schriber & Löwstedt, 2015; Winter, 2003).

More recent research on dynamic capabilities has relaxed the emphasis on strict routines. Eisenhardt and Martin (2000) suggest that capabilities can rather be considered robust processes, much like best practices, that are steadily enacted by social actors. As such, they constantly develop as a result of changing conditions, frictions, learning, and forgetting (Schriber & Löwstedt, 2020). This highlights multiple organization variables

110   *Svante Schriber*

matter for how dynamic capabilities evolve and operate. Consequently, explanations of dynamic capabilities must consider their organizational conditions, in turn, shaped, for instance, by managerial choices.

Specifically, dynamic capabilities operate through three underpinning processes. First, a firm needs to recognize, or sense, change in the external environment, to assess what changes are necessary (Teece et al., 1997). Second, it needs to evaluate, or monitor, the current state of available resources and how it matches the external requirements (Danneels, 2011). Third, a firm needs to re-allocate, or orchestrate, its capabilities and resources to fit the new situation (Sirmon, Hitt, Ireland, & Gilbert, 2011). Considering how these processes are shaped by managerial choices thereby offers a theoretically founded way of illuminating the conditions for dynamic capabilities.

Dynamic capabilities appear useful in addressing the question of how choices in the acquisition process affect the ability of firms to adjust to environmental dynamism. As can be expected from a broad and growing stream, this research encompasses slightly different foci and definitions (Barreto, 2010; Giudici & Reinmoeller, 2012); however, it is arguably more coherent compared to related concepts such as organizational flexibility (Brozovic, 2018). Moreover, it may add more theoretical rigor to acquisition research that is largely phenomenon-driven.

The usefulness is visible also in clear overlaps between acquisitions and dynamic capabilities. Acquisitions and dynamic capabilities center on a firm's ability to adjust to competitive pressures by orchestrating its capabilities or resources such as adding, combining, recombining, and dispensing with resources and capabilities controlled by a focal firm (Danneels, 2011; Ranft & Lord, 2002). Both acquisitions and resource orchestration constitute processes, where interaction effects, delays, intervals, and pace matter (Haspeslagh & Jemison, 1991; Schriber & Löwstedt, 2018). Lastly, the view of dynamic capabilities as knowledge-based and evolving processes (Schriber & Löwstedt, 2020) echoes organizational learning having important role in acquisitions and acquisition processes (Zollo & Singh, 2004). Taken together, an integration between acquisition process and dynamic capabilities research appears to offer potential for cross-fertilization.

An integrative framework for dynamic capabilities in acquisition processes

Acquisitions in competitive markets are inherently intertwined with and depend on relations with their environment (Rouzies et al., 2019). This exposes them to positive and negative changes in the environment (Junni et al., 2015). While some changes are predictable, others, including competitive retaliation that are deliberately prepared in secrecy, are difficult or even impossible to foresee. Combined, this suggests acquisitions are likely exposed to external dynamism, lending

Dynamic capabilities and acquisition processes 111

weight to dynamic capabilities for explaining how well the involved firms are able to adapt. The organizational conditions for these capabilities vary, and central acquisition choices during the acquisition process shape these conditions.

Dynamic capabilities are understood here to support firm adjustment to environment dynamism through the three analytically distinct underpinning processes of sensing, monitoring, and re-allocating. Illuminating how key choices in the acquisition process affect these processes offers a concrete path to understand the conditions for dynamic capabilities, and, in turn, how an acquisition is able to adjust to and perform in less than stable environments. A theoretical framework connecting dynamic capabilities and acquisition processes is outlined in Figure 5.1.

The key argument of this chapter is shown in Figure 5.1. The acquisition process spans three broad and not always clearly distinguishable phases: before, during, and after. Each phase includes key managerial choices identified in acquisition research, phrased as propositions positively impacting the conditions for dynamic capabilities. In turn, dynamic capabilities are proposed to positively impact the ability of acquisitions to adjust to unpredicted dynamic environments. Overall and in accordance with the dynamic capabilities approach underlying this framework, this is assumed to have a positive effect on acquisition performance in less stable competitive environments.

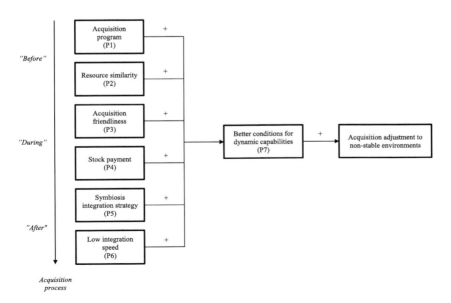

Figure 5.1 Framework combining acquisition process and dynamic capabilities influence on firm adaptation.

112   Svante Schriber

The figure does not aspire to completeness, and additional choices in acquisition processes can be added once receiving more research attention. Moreover, choices can vary with regard to the degree of consciousness where certain decisions may be highly deliberate and articulated, others made without much consideration or for reasons of convenience or habit. Lastly, in line with the dynamic capabilities view, the argument is limited to such environmental dynamism that is unpredicted by key decision-makers in the firm, and at a level that can influence firm performance.

Acquisition programs

Research increasingly recognizes that many firms pursue more than one acquisition. However, when firms acquire repeatedly, the degree of deliberation can differ. While this may simply be a number of opportunistic deals (Bauer, Friesl, & Dao, 2021a), research recognizes that certain acquirers pursue a deliberate idea or plan for future acquisitions, or an acquisition program (Laamanen & Keil, 2008). An acquisition program here means "a group of acquisitions driven by a core business logic, often with significant interdependencies" (Chatterjee, 2009, p. 138). Dynamic capabilities evolve gradually, and they are more likely to develop with deliberate, coherent acquisition programs.

Acquisition research has produced a vast amount of research on the effects of acquisition experience (Barkema & Schijven, 2008a; Schriber & Degischer, 2020). Research has found a positive correlation between the number of prior deals and subsequent acquisition performance (Bruton, Oviatt, & White, 1994), but also that firms can misapply (Ellis, Reus, Lamont, & Ranft, 2011) or overestimate their competence (Zollo, 2009), leading to negative effects. A key insight is that acquisition skills do not develop automatically, but instead require deliberate efforts such as creating checklists and formalized decision processes (Zollo & Singh, 2004). Moreover, acquirers pursuing an acquisition program are more likely to invest in a specific organizational department or unit responsible for acquisitions. This can involve identifying potential targets, scrutinize how they fit an acquirer's strategic needs, as well as conduct valuation, negotiations, and other tasks (Trichterborn, zu Knyphausen-Aufsess, & Schweizer, 2016). Acquisition programs also have better chances to develop routines for the evaluation process (Angwin, Paroutis, & Connell, 2015) or increase the chance of detecting key assets in a target. In short, dynamic capabilities are most likely to apply to acquisitions when they develop in and are applied in a series of acquisitions.

Sensing external dynamism likely benefits from an intended acquisition program. First, it may lead to the adoption of a specialized acquisition team (Trichterborn et al., 2016) with experience from prior deals. Moreover, the investment in developing necessary adjustment skills (Heimeriks et al., 2012) becomes easier to motivate if future acquisitions

Dynamic capabilities and acquisition processes 113

are planned. Such skills can improve the ability to recognize whether competitors will respond to an acquisition (Bauer et al., 2021b; Keil et al., 2013; Schriber et al., 2021). Thus, acquisition programs likely improve the conditions for dynamism sensing compared to firms repeatedly pursuing acquisitions but without a plan to do so.

Compared to opportunistic acquirers, acquirers pursuing an acquisition program are more likely to invest in the skills to assess targets. For instance, an acquisition program makes investing in an organizational department specifically responsible for acquisitions easier, something that has been found to benefit acquisition performance (Trichterborn et al., 2016). They also have better chances to develop routines for the evaluation process (Angwin et al., 2015), all likely to increase the chance of detecting key assets in the target.

An acquisition program also likely furthers resource reallocation during integration. Firms deliberately trying to benefit from prior experience are more successful at integrating (Zollo & Singh, 2004). In particular, experienced acquirers are able to not only execute prior routinized capabilities, but dynamic capabilities allow adjusting and tailor such routines to specific targets, thereby increasing the likelihood of integration success (Heimeriks et al., 2012). This suggests that adapting experience from past unique events also could benefit adjusting to external events. Therefore, the following is proposed:

> Proposition 1: Acquisitions within an acquisition program create better conditions for dynamic capabilities in acquisitions, than opportunistic acquisitions.

Resource similarity

Acquisitions are not homogenous. One fundamental difference is the degree that acquirers seek targets that are similar or different from themselves. There is an abundance of frameworks categorizing acquisition types such as the Federal Trade Commission (FTC) framework (Lubatkin, Srinivasan, & Merchant, 1997). Additionally, Shelton (1988) proposes four acquisition types depending on the degree of product and market similarity of the involved firms. The underpinning thought is that the gains that can be achieved in acquisitions correlate with the degree of resource similarity between the involved firms. Resources broadly denote what a firm needs to compete, including fixed assets, skills, capabilities, and knowledge (Barney, 1991). While research mainly has found a mixed connection between resource similarity and acquisition performance (King et al., 2004) and the terms have been criticized for not sufficiently clarifying the value resulting from resource complementarity (Zaheer et al., 2013), the present focus is on resource similarities and the effects on the conditions for dynamic capabilities.

114 *Svante Schriber*

The degree of resource similarity between the involved firms can influence the sensing of external dynamism in acquisitions. With dissimilar resources between acquirer and target, the amount of new information increases, further straining often already overwhelmed integration managers (Lamont, King, Maslach, Schwerdtfeger, & Tienari, 2019) and their limited cognitive capacity (Cyert & March, 1963). The combined implication is reduced attention to sensing external events (Cording, Christmann, & King, 2008).

For similar reasons, integration is more challenging when resources are unfamiliar to an acquirer compared to when they are familiar. In general, most acquisitions share a certain lack of information about the target (Coff, 1999); however, this is likely more problematic when resources differ and when the acquirer cannot draw on familiarity from working with similar resources. The same unfamiliarity relates also to resource monitoring, meaning it likely suffers more when resources differ, compared to when they are similar.

Lastly, resource reconfiguring is also likely easier in acquisitions with similar resources. The new capability connections in unrelated acquisitions can be thought of as valuable options that the acquirer can choose to execute (Smit & Moraitis, 2010) to handle new, unexpected events in the environment. However, a lack of knowledge about the target resources means integration managers are at a disadvantage, making it likely such potentials remain untapped. Therefore, it is proposed that:

> Proposition 2: Acquisitions between firms with similar resources create better conditions for dynamic capabilities than acquisitions with different resources.

Acquisition friendliness

Whether or not a deal is hostile likely affects the conditions for dynamic capabilities. In friendly acquisitions, a potential buyer approaches a target firm's managers to discuss a potential deal. This offers an opportunity to probe a target's appetite for the takeover, as well as draw on insights about how a joint firm could develop. In contrast, during hostile acquisitions, a target firm's board and managers are by-passed to purchase shares from target firm shareholders directly through a tender offer (Muehlfeld, Sahib, & van Witteloostuijn, 2007). Further, discord from hostile bids is higher as they are often publicly fought in media with the bidder attacking the incumbent target managers, and the latter attempting to defend themselves. Fights also include adopting "poison pills" that make acquisitions unpalatable or more arduous (Mallette & Fowler, 1992). Although the terms friendly and hostile mark ends of a spectrum and acquisitions in practice are of a matter of degrees, these terms are useful for predicting impact on the conditions for dynamic capabilities.

Dynamic capabilities and acquisition processes   115

A first impact relates to an acquirer's ability to sense external dynamism. Hostile takeovers involve less information sharing, thus hampering insights into the target (Harding & Rouse, 2007). They also are associated with heightened levels of stress and a sense of resentment in the target (Schneider & Dunbar, 1992). Even if takeovers in general can come with a sense of loss or failure, these feelings are accentuated in hostile takeovers. Marks, Mirvis, and Brajkovich (2001, p. 87) state that "[i]n a hostile deal or one imposed by the board, there is from the start a sense of violation: Executives we have interviewed have likened it to a rape and described their buyer as an attacker or barbarian." In hostile deals, such sentiments are less likely to create willingness to pass on crucial information relevant to sudden market change.

For similar reasons, hostility also impairs the ability to monitor vital capabilities and resources inside the target. Hostile takeovers are typically associated with higher employee turnover, as target firm top managers are almost always replaced in hostile deals (Walsh, 1988). Stress and sense of bereavement is also associated with employee turnover (Napier, 1989) and withdrawal (Tian et al., 2021). This leads to loss in knowledge assets and capability in the target, and likely significantly reduces employees' willingness to monitor vital resources or pass on such information, compared to in friendly acquisitions.

Similar mechanisms also likely hamper the ability of hostile acquisitions to reallocate resources in response to environmental dynamism. While some have argued that hostile takeovers fulfill a disciplinary function by replacing underperforming managers of the target (Jensen & Ruback, 1983), hostile takeovers amplify subsequent resistance to resource reallocation during integration (Franks & Mayer, 1996). Such resistance hinders integration (Larsson & Finkelstein, 1999), and it can also impede reallocation of capabilities and resources. Overall, this leads to the following proposed relationship:

> Proposition 3: Friendly acquisitions create better conditions for dynamic capabilities than hostile acquisitions.

Form of payment

A central choice in acquisitions has to do with the form of payment, or whether a firm is paid for in stock or in cash (Rappaport & Sirower, 1999). Paying in stock means an acquirer trades its own shares for ownership in the target, while paying in cash implies buyers giving sellers cash to give up ownership of the target. While acquisitions paid in cash tend to outperform those paid in shares (King et al., 2021; Linn & Schweitzer, 2001), the form of payment likely has consequences for the conditions for dynamic capabilities. Specifically, the underpinning argument here is that the limited cash funds facing many firms hamper the conditions for dynamic capabilities. Payment also can be mixed, and the following

116 *Svante Schriber*

arguments apply proportionally to how payment forms are mixed. However, for the sake of simplicity, only pure stock or cash options are discussed here.

Cash deals are often partly financed with debt (Hitt, Harrison, & Ireland, 2001), suggesting financial funds can be in short supply. Overpayment in cash deals does not only imply a value transfer in terms of buyers' stock to sellers, and it typically requires workforce reductions (Krishnan, Hitt, & Park, 2006; Siegel & Simons, 2010). Associated employee stress, anxiety, and feelings of loss among remaining employees (Seo & Hill, 2005) can lead to open resistance (Larsson & Finkelstein, 1999). This, in turn, leads to employee withdrawal and unwillingness to share information (Tian et al., 2021). Further, loss of target firm managers can reduce the ability to understand target firm resources to enable valuable resource combinations (Graebner, 2004). In sum, cash payment may associate with conditions with less slack that reduce the willingness for cooperation and communication necessary to adapt to environmental dynamism and monitoring of resources.

Similarly, a reduction in available cash and subsequent reductions can hamper resource reallocation in response to environmental dynamism. Arguably, cash is the most fungible asset and cash acquisitions leave fewer fungible assets to meet unexpected events. For instance, product development, marketing, or other costly efforts may be needed to adjust to rapidly changing environments (Steenkamp, Hanssens, Dekimpe, & Marnik, 2005). Cash is also often needed to add resources (e.g., patents or new staff), and for reallocation costs (Schriber & Löwstedt, 2018). In short, a reduction in cash threatens the reallocation of resources that is necessary for dynamic capabilities, more than acquisitions paid in stock. Put differently:

> Proposition 4: Acquisitions paid with stock create better conditions for dynamic capabilities compared to acquisitions paid in cash.

Integration strategy

Reaching acquisition aims typically requires a sufficient level of coordination between combining firms' marketing (Homburg & Bucerius, 2006), operations (Larsson & Finkelstein, 1999), and research and development activities (King et al., 2008). At the same time, integration typically creates employee tensions between cultures and identities of the involved organizations (Stahl & Voigt, 2008). As a complex process, integration spans a variety of managerial choices, often summarized in the form of types sharing similarities across key dimensions (Marks & Mirvis, 1998; Napier, 1989; Pablo, 1994).

Typically, these typologies take their starting point in the challenge of balancing the opposing needs both for integration and autonomy. Arguably the most commonly referenced framework by Haspeslagh and

Dynamic capabilities and acquisition processes 117

Jemison (1991) proposes three forms of integration (i.e., preservation, absorption, or symbiosis), excluding holding acquisitions that largely do not integrate a target. *Preservation* involves very limited integration of the target. *Absorption* represents a full and forceful consolidation of the target into the acquirer. Lastly, *symbiosis* involves handling the need for target autonomy while integrating requiring delicate balance. Although this framework has been criticized for instance for not sufficiently distinguishing associated complexity (Zaheer et al., 2013), the Haspeslagh and Jemison (1991) framework still largely captures an essential acquisition choice between autonomy or integration. As a result, integration conducted as these types can be anticipated to influence the conditions for dynamic capabilities.

Integration is a task typically added to the daily running of the firm, and research has identified managerial attention as a limiting factor (Cording et al., 2008; Lamont et al., 2019; Larsson & Finkelstein, 1999). In consequence, the ability to perceive relevant information about conditions in the environment likely is reduced proportionally to the degree of integration. Hence, the rapid and close integration between firms typical to absorption acquisitions reduces managers' ability to scan the environment (for competitive retaliation; King & Schriber, 2016). In contrast, the lack of integration of reporting and communication (Shrivastava, 1986) in preservation acquisitions means the communication channels necessary for passing on news of environment dynamism may not be developed. Meanwhile, the relatively limited strain on integration management and the level of integration achieved in symbiosis acquisitions likely enhances detecting and addressing environmental dynamism

Also, the rapid and forceful integration in absorption acquisitions likely reduces ability to monitor resources, as does the low integration in preservation deals. Full integration is associated with increasing employee stress (Ranft & Lord, 2002), as well as unwanted or unexpected management and employee turnover (Napier, 1989; Walsh, 1988). In turn, absorption acquisitions likely hamper the ability to monitor where in the involved organizations valuable resources and capabilities reside. Simultaneously, the less acquiring managers engage with the target, the more likely it is that such capabilities remain unknown (Graebner, 2004). Thus, if the firms are not to be integrated, such as in preservation acquisitions, the ability to monitor resources is reduced.

Both the turbulence and lack of integration in absorption and preservation acquisitions, respectively, can hamper the ability to fruitfully reconfigure resources in response to environmental dynamism, for different reasons. Absorption acquisitions often create organizational fatigue that can create an unwillingness to engage in further change (Napier, 1989). Separately, a target that has not been integrated may react strongly to later efforts to reconfigure resources. Not having been integrated, a preservation acquisition may (rightly) be perceived by employees as performing

118　*Svante Schriber*

sufficiently. Thereby, an acquirer, may miss a "window of opportunity" immediately following an acquisition (Ranft & Lord, 2002) before integration becomes more difficult (Angwin, 2004). Altogether, a symbiosis integration appears most conducive to dynamic capabilities, compared to absorption and preservation acquisitions. Therefore, the following is proposed:

> Proposition 5: Acquisitions following a symbiosis integration strategy create better conditions for dynamic capabilities than acquisitions integrated as preservation or absorption.

Integration speed

A key choice in acquisitions is the pace that an acquirer attempts to complete planned integration. This emphasis on speed is exemplified in the importance attributed to "the first 100 days" (Angwin, 2004; Ashkenas, DeMonaco, & Francis, 1998). Homburg and Bucerius (2006) found that speed is beneficial under low external relatedness and high internal relatedness, but it has negative performance implications under opposite conditions. In contrast, Bauer and Matzler (2014) found no clear connection between speed and performance, and more recent findings suggest speed has varied effects on integration depending on the institutional context (Bauer et al., 2018). Still, there are reasons to assume that integration speed can impact the conditions for dynamic capabilities.

All things equal, attempting to achieve the same number of tasks in a shorter time equals more work per period, straining limited managerial integration capacity (Lamont et al., 2019). Research shows that more internal turbulence has been associated with employee turnover (Walsh, 1988) and reduced contact with or even loss of customers (Öberg, 2014). Both circumstances contribute to reduced information about market change and responses to it (Liao, Chang, Wu, & Katrichis, 2011). To integration managers already pressed for time with internal matters (Cording et al., 2008), a high integration pace therefore likely further reduces their ability to scan and sense external environment changes. Further, the less time available for conducting integration, the lower likelihood that managers can detect and monitor relevant capabilities and resources. Getting familiarized with a new organization requires time, especially detecting sensitive processes and skills underpinning organizational capabilities (Coff, 1999). This is even more relevant to capabilities depending on tacit knowledge (Ranft & Lord, 2002).

In summary, a higher pace of integration leaves less time to detect, map, and monitor valuable resources. Higher integration speed likely reduces the ability to efficiently reallocate resources and capabilities. Rapid integration also increases the risk of turmoil and fatigue among employees (Napier, 1989), reducing appetite for further change. Further, even in cases where available integration routines exist, successful

Dynamic capabilities and acquisition processes 119

implementation requires adaptation to the relevant situation (Heimeriks et al., 2012), and time pressure may impede adaptation and result in suboptimal resource allocation. Therefore, it is proposed that:

> Proposition 6: Low integration speed creates better conditions for dynamic capabilities than high integration speed.

Dynamic capabilities and adjusting to dynamic environments

The basic tenet of dynamic capabilities theory is that firms in possession of these capabilities can survive or even thrive under dynamic conditions (Teece et al., 1997). Although lower-order, ordinary capabilities can make important contributions to such change (Schriber & Löwstedt, 2020), it is dynamic capabilities that explain firm ability to adjust to hard-to-predict environmental change (Drnevich & Kriauciunas, 2011; Helfat et al., 2007). Specifically, research demonstrates that dynamic capabilities can assist in sensing, monitoring, and reallocating resources to ensure environmental fitness (Teece et al., 1997; Teece, 2007). In line with fundamental dynamic capabilities research, the following is proposed:

> Proposition 7: The better the conditions for dynamic capabilities in acquisitions, the higher the ability of acquisitions to adjust to dynamic environments.

Discussion

Acquisitions are an important means for how firms adjust to change in their competitive environment, and dynamic capabilities has proven useful for explaining how firms survive or even thrive in dynamic environments. Despite the potential for cross-fertilization, a systematic integration between these two research streams has been missing. A dynamic capabilities approach can illuminate how acquisitions can handle dynamic environments, especially in the context of repeated acquisitions. Specifically, acquisition processes occur within an external context whose dynamism can affect the acquisition process. Sources of dynamism range from involuntary customers loss (Öberg, 2014) to active competitive responses (King & Schriber, 2016; Schriber et al., 2021). As capabilities develop in use and over time, combining dynamic capabilities and acquisition process research is even more relevant when an acquirer pursues several acquisitions.

Integrating these research streams emphasizes the interconnectedness between acquisitions and their environment and has implications for theory on integration management. Specifically, if environments change, initial synergy potentials may also change. Integration efforts that are poorly adapted can then create costs and coordination where no potential exists. Simultaneously, new potential synergies created from changes

120 Svante Schriber

in the new competitive environment risk remaining unrecognized and unrealized (Schriber, 2016). Dynamic capabilities offer structure for analyzing the ability of acquiring firms to adjust to such environmental dynamism throughout the acquisition process. The framework developed in this chapter highlights how key acquisition choices affect the conditions for dynamic capabilities. Specifically, the ability to sense external change, monitor firm capabilities and resources, and reallocate resources to new environmental conditions is developed into testable propositions. This provides a systematic integration between the dynamic capabilities and acquisition research streams, and it makes multiple contributions to research.

Research implications

While initial connections have been made (Heimeriks et al., 2012), dynamic capabilities theory is sparsely used in acquisition research, and this chapter takes an important step in integrating them. Acquisition process research outlines how key managerial choices affect acquisition outcomes. The dynamic capabilities stream constitutes a coherent, theoretically founded and empirically tested framework for explaining firm performance in dynamic environments. Thus, the integrative framework developed here helps explicate a context where dynamic capabilities likely matter for firm competitiveness. Beyond the ability to adjust to dynamism (Drnevich & Kriauciunas, 2011; Schilke, 2014) the impact of dynamic capabilities has been shown for innovation (Berghman et al., 2013), alliances (Li, Eden, Hitt, & Ireland, 2008), and product innovation (Marsh & Stock, 2003). While research has established acquisitions as a means to access valuable capabilities (King et al., 2008; Puranam, Singh, & Chaudhuri, 2009), the present framework integrates dynamic capabilities and acquisition process research streams, and it confirms and extends the role of capabilities inside acquisitions (Heimeriks et al., 2012; Lamont et al., 2019).

The importance of dynamic capabilities in the context of acquisitions likely is higher than reflected in associated research. A fundamental challenge to acquirers is that acquisitions are paid for upfront. In comparison, costs are shared and can be adjusted incrementally for joint ventures and alliances. Still, acquisitions typically take very long time to execute, especially when they rely on organizational conditions (Haspeslagh & Jemison, 1991). Research shows that acquisitions can take up to five or seven years before potential gains are fully realized (Birkinshaw, Bresman, & Håkanson, 2000), or even 12 years (Barkema & Schijven, 2008b) or longer (Lu, 2014; Risberg, 1999). The consequence is a risk that the conditions motivating the initial payment change, making it impossible to extract intended values. While research points out the benefits of adjusting integration (Junni et al., 2015; Schriber et al., 2018), the current framework extends beyond integration to span the *entire* acquisition process. As a result, this chapter contributes to acquisition research, as it highlights dynamic capabilities as a key capability for acquisition success.

Specifically, the developed framework outlines why some acquisitions are better able to adjust to external dynamism than others. Establishing how key choices shape the conditions for the processes underpinning dynamic capabilities advances understanding of how acquisitions can adjust to, and ultimately perform in dynamic environments. This connects to research on retaliation against acquisitions (Bauer et al., 2021b) and the demands this raises on acquisition management (King & Schriber, 2016). Importantly, this also provides further theoretical underpinning to acquisition research that is largely phenomenon driven, and answers to calls for better explanations regarding acquisition outcomes (King et al., 2004).

These ideas also have consequences for dynamic capabilities research. By clarifying key choices during acquisition processes and their impact on the conditions for dynamic capabilities, the suggested framework helps concretizing the development of such capabilities. An area of criticism is that dynamic capabilities are vague and abstract (Danneels, 2011; Zahra, Sapienza, & Davidsson, 2006). A connection to acquisitions helps adding concrete understanding of when dynamic capabilities can be of value to firms. This contributes to existing research on the sources and development of dynamic capabilities (Zahra et al., 2006; Zollo & Winter, 2002), or their underpinning micro-foundations (Morris & Snell, 2014). Further, since acquisitions typically take place in dynamic environments, they can contribute to additional industry dynamism. Against this background, dynamic capabilities are singularly well-suited to improve our understanding for how acquisitions relate to adjusting to dynamism in the competitive environment.

Managerial implications

A managerial implication of the ideas developed show dynamic capabilities can help firms adjust to competitive dynamism using acquisitions, but developing such capabilities takes time. That is, very similar to any form of insurance, acquirers aspiring to such capabilities need to start nurturing relevant underpinning processes early on and persist in efforts to develop and refine them. Simply, dynamic capabilities are not for free. Direct costs may include the development and maintaining of collective skills to avoid capabilities becoming 'rusty' (Winter, 2003). Developing and using dynamics capabilities also may cause indirect costs, for instance, the cost of inhouse teams to manage the deal flow, select and evaluate candidates, and execute acquisitions (Trichterborn et al., 2016). Moreover, somewhat ironically, the very processes underpinning dynamic capabilities are under threat from internal organizational changes following acquisitions. These processes are typically skill-based, social, tacit, and take time to

122 Svante Schriber

develop. As managers in acquisitions are often pressed to produce tangible results, managers need to balance "quick wins", such as cut-backs, against the risk of harming dynamic capabilities. Overall, the benefits of dynamic capabilities in acquisitions must be weighed against the costs and care needed to develop and maintain them.

Limitations and future research

This chapter is a first attempt to systematically integrate the dynamic capabilities and acquisition research streams in a conceptual framework with testable propositions. However, it remains to be empirically tested. Additionally, being the first of its kind, the associated complexity makes the framework incomplete, or research is needed to develop relationships further. There are ample opportunities to refine the suggested framework and produce even more precise propositions from integrating dynamic capabilities and acquisition research.

References

Angwin, D. (2004). Speed in M&A integration: The first 100 days. *European Management Journal, 22*(4), 418–430.

Angwin, D., Paroutis, S., & Connell, R. (2015). Why good things don't happen: The micro-foundations of routines in the M&A process. *Journal of Business Research, 68*(6), 1367–1381.

Ashkenas, R., DeMonaco, L., & Francis, S. (1998). Making the deal real: How GE Capital integrates acquisitions. *Harvard Business Review, 76*(1), 165–178.

Barkema, H., & Schijven, M. (2008a). How do firms learn to make acquisitions? A review of past research and an agenda for the future. *Journal of Management, 34*(3), 594–634.

Barkema, H., & Schijven, M. (2008b). Toward unlocking the full potential of acquisitions: The role of organisational restructuring. *Academy of Management Journal, 51*(4), 696–722.

Barney, J. (1991). Firm resources and sustained competitive advantage. *Journal of Management, 17*(1), 99–120.

Barreto, I. (2010). Dynamic capabilities: A review of past research and an agenda for the future. *Journal of Management, 36*(1), 256–280.

Bauer, F., & Matzler, K. (2014). Antecedents of M&A success: The role of strategic complementarity, cultural fit, and degree and speed of integration. *Strategic Management Journal, 35*, 269–291.

Bauer, F., Friesl, M., & Dao, M.A. (2021a). Run or hide: Changes in acquisition behaviour during the COVID-19 pandemic. *Journal of Strategy and Management.* https://doi.org/10.1108/JSMA-02-2021-0046

Bauer, F., King, D., Schriber, S., & Kruckhauser, C. (2021b). Navigating challenging contexts: Costs and benefits of codified acquisition experience. Long Range Planning, *54*(6). https://doi.org/10.1016/j.lrp.2021.102088.

Bauer, F., Schriber, S., Degischer, D., & King, D. (2018). Contextualizing speed and cross-border acquisition performance: Labor market flexibility and efficiency effects. *Journal of World Business, 53*(1), 290–301.

Dynamic capabilities and acquisition processes 123

Berghman, L., Matthyssens, P., Streukens, S., & Vandenbempt, K. (2013). Deliberate learning mechanisms for stimulating strategic innovation capacity. *Long Range Planning*, 46(1–2), 39–71.

Birkinshaw, J., Bresman, H., & Håkanson, L. (2000). Managing the post-acquisition integration process: How the human integration and task integration processes interact to foster value creation. *Journal of Management Studies*, 37(3), 395–425.

Brozovic, D. (2018). Strategic flexibility: A review of the literature. *International Journal of Management Reviews*, 20(1), 3–31.

Bruton, G., Oviatt, B., & White, M. (1994). Performance of acquisitions of distressed firms. *Academy of Management Journal*, 37(4), 972–989.

Chatterjee, S. (2009). The keys to successful acquisition programmes. *Long Range Planning*, 42(2), 137–163.

Coff, R. (1999). How buyers cope with uncertainty when acquiring firms in knowledge-intensive industries: Caveat emptor. *Organization Science*, 10(2), 144–161.

Cording, M., Christmann, P., & King, D. (2008). Reducing causal ambiguity in acquisition integration: Intermediate goals as mediators of integration decisions and acquisition performance. *Academy of Management Journal*, 51(4), 744–767.

Cyert, R., & March, J. (1963). *A behavioral theory of the firm*. Upper Saddle River, NJ: Prentice Hall.

Danneels, E. (2011). Trying to become a different type of company: Dynamic capability at Smith Corona. *Strategic Management Journal*, 32(1), 1–31.

Drnevich, P., & Kriauciunas, A. (2011). Clarifying the conditions and limits of the contributions of ordinary and dynamic capabilities to relative firm performance. *Strategic Management Journal*, 32(3), 254–279.

Eisenhardt, K., & Martin, J. (2000). Dynamic capabilities: What are they? *Strategic Management Journal*, 21(10/11), 1105–1121.

Ellis, K., Reus, T., Lamont, B., & Ranft, A. (2011). Transfer effects in large acquisitions: How size-specific experience matters. *Academy of Management Journal*, 54(6), 1261–1276.

Franks, J., & Mayer, C. (1996). Hostile takeovers and the correction of managerial failure. *Journal of Financial Economics*, 40, 163–181.

Giudici, A., & Reinmoeller, P. (2012). Dynamic capabilities in the dock: A case of reification? *Strategic Organization*, 10(4), 436–449.

Graebner, M. (2004). Momentum and serendipity: How acquired leaders create value in the integration of technology firms. *Strategic Management Journal*, 25(8–9), 751–777.

Haleblian, J., McNamara, G., Kolev, K., & Dykes, B. (2012). Exploring firm characteristics that differentiate leaders from followers in industry merger waves: A competitive dynamics perspective. *Strategic Management Journal*, 33(9), 1037–1052.

Haspeslagh, P., & Jemison, D. (1991). *Managing acquisitions: Creating value through corporate renewal*. New York: Free Press.

Heimeriks, K., Schijven, M., & Gates, S. (2012). Manifestations of higher-order routines: The underlying mechanisms of deliberate learning in the context of postacquisition integration. *Academy of Management Journal*, 55(3), 703–726.

Helfat, C., & Peteraf, M. (2009). Understanding dynamic capabilities: Progress along a developmental path. *Strategic Organization*, 7(1), 91–102.

124 *Svante Schriber*

Helfat, C., Finkelstein, S., Mitchell, W., Peteraf, M., Singh, H., Teece, D., & Winter, S. (2007). *Dynamic capabilities: Understanding strategic change in organizations.* Malden, MA: Blackwell Publishing.

Hitt, M., Harrison, J., & Ireland, R. (2001). *Mergers and acquisitions: A guide to creating value for stakeholders.* Oxford: Oxford University Press.

Homburg, C., & Bucerius, M. (2006). Is speed of integration really a success factor of mergers and acquisitions? An analysis of the role of internal and external relatedness. *Strategic Management Journal, 27*(4), 347–367.

Jemison, D., & Sitkin, S. (1986). Corporate acquisitions: A process perspective. *Academy of Management Review, 11*(1), 145–163.

Jensen, M., & Ruback, R. (1983). The market for corporate control: The scientific evidence. *Journal of Financial Economics, 11*, 5–50.

Junni, P., Sarala, R., Tarba, S., & Weber, Y. (2015). The role of strategic agility in acquisitions. *British Journal of Management, 26*(4), 596–616.

Keil, T., Laamanen, T., & McGrath, R. (2013). Is a counterattack the best defense? Competitive dynamics through acquisitions. *Long Range Planning, 46*(3), 195–215.

King, D., Dalton, D., Daily, C., & Covin, J. (2004). Meta-analyses of post-acquisition performance: Indications of unidentified moderators. *Strategic Management Journal, 25*(2), 187–200.

King, D., & Schriber, S. (2016). Addressing competitive responses to acquisitions. *California Management Review, 58*(3), 109–124.

King, D., Slotegraaf, R., & Kesner, I. (2008). Performance implications of firm resource interactions in the acquisition of R&D intensive firms. *Organization Science, 19*(2), 327–340.

King, D., Wang, G., Samimi, M., & Cortes, A. (2021). A meta-analytic integration of acquisition performance prediction. *Journal of Management Studies, 58*(5), 1198–1236.

Krishnan, H., Hitt, M., & Park, D. (2006). Acquisition premiums, subsequent workforce reductions and post-acquisition performance. *Journal of Management Studies, 44*(4), 709–732.

Laamanen, T., & Keil, T. (2008). Performance of serial acquirers: Toward an acquisition program perspective. *Strategic Management Journal, 29*(6), 663–672.

Lamont, B., King, D., Maslach, D., Schwerdtfeger, M., & Tienari, J. (2019). Integration capacity and knowledge-based acquisition performance. *R&D Management, 49*(1), 103–114.

Liao, S., Chang, W., Wu, C., & Katrichis, J. (2011). A survey of market orientation research (1995–2008). *Industrial Marketing Management, 40*(2), 301–310.

Larsson, R., & Finkelstein, S. (1999). Integrating resource strategic, organizational, and perspectives on mergers acquisitions: A case survey of synergy realization. *Organization Science, 10*(1), 1–26.

Lee, G., & Lieberman, M. (2010). Acquisition vs. internal development as modes of market entry. *Strategic Management Journal, 31*(2), 140–158.

Li, D., Eden, L., Hitt, M., & Ireland, R. (2008). Friends, acquaintances, or strangers? Partner selection in R&D alliances. *Academy of Management Journal, 51*(2), 315–334.

Linn, S., & Switzer, J. (2001). Are cash acquisitions associated with better postcombination operating performance than stock acquisitions? *Journal of Banking & Finance, 25*(6), 1113–1138.

Dynamic capabilities and acquisition processes 125

Lu, Q. (2014). Is speed of post-acquisition integration manageable? Case study: Post-acquisition integration of HSBC with the Mercantile Bank, 1959–84. *Business History*, 56, 1262–1280.

Lubatkin, M., Srinivasan, N., & Merchant, H. (1997). Merger strategies and shareholder value during times of relaxed antitrust enforcement: The case of large mergers during the 1980s. *Journal of Management*, 23(1), 59–81.

Mallette, P., & Fowler, K. (1992) Effects of board composition and stock ownership on the adoption of poison pills. *Academy of Management Journal*, 35, 1010–1035.

Harding, D., & Rouse, T. (2007). Human due diligence. *Harvard Business Review*, 85(4), 124–131.

Marks, M., & Mirvis, P. (1998). *Joining forces. Making one plus one equal three in mergers, acquisitions, and alliances.* San Francisco, CA: Jossey-Bass Publishers.

Marks, M., Mirvis, P., & Brajkovich, L. (2001). Making mergers and acquisitions work: Strategic and psychological preparation. *Academy of Management Executive*, 15(2), 80–92.

Marsh, S., & Stock, G. (2003). Building dynamic capabilities in new product development through intertemporal integration. *Journal of Product Innovation Management*, 20(815), 136–148.

McNamara, G., Haleblian, J., & Dykes, B. (2008). The performance implications of participating in an acquisition wave. *Academy of Management Journal*, 51(1), 113–130.

Meyer-Doyle, P., Lee, S., & Helfat, C. (2019). Disentangling the microfoundations of acquisition behavior and performance. *Strategic Management Journal*, 40(11), 1733–1756.

Morris, S., Hammond, R., & Snell, S. (2014). A microfoundations approach to transnational capabilities: The role of knowledge search in an ever-changing world. *Journal of International Business Studies*, 45(4), 405–427.

Muehlfeld, K., Sahib, P., & van Witteloostuijn, A. (2007). Completion or abandonment of mergers and acquisitions: Evidence from the newspaper industry, 1981–2000. *Journal of Media Economics*, 20(2), 107–137.

Napier, N. (1989). Mergers and acquisitions, human resources issues and outcomes: A review and suggested typology. *Journal of Management Studies*, 23(3), 271–289.

Nelson, R., & Winter, S. (1982). *An evolutionary theory of economic change.* Cambridge, MA: Harvard University Press.

Öberg, C. (2014). Customer relationship challenges following international acquisitions. *International Marketing Review*, 31(3), 259–282.

Pablo, A. (1994). Determinants of acquisition integration level: A decision-making perspective. *Academy of Management Journal*, 37(4), 803–836.

Pehrsson, A. (2006). Business relatedness and performance: A study of managerial perceptions. *Strategic Management Journal*, 27(3), 265–282.

Puranam, P., Singh, H., & Chaudhuri, S. (2009). Integrating acquired capabilities: When structural integration is (un)necessary. Organization *Science*, 20(2), 313–328.

Ranft, A., & Lord, M. (2002). Acquiring new technologies and capabilities: A grounded model of acquisition implementation. *Organization Science*, 13(4), 420–441.

Rappaport, A., & Sirower, M. (1999). Stock or cash? *Harvard Business Review*, *77*(6), 147–147.

Risberg, A. (1999). *Ambiguities thereafter. An interpretive approach to acquisitions*. Lund, Sweden: Lund University Press.

Rouzies, A., Colman, H., & Angwin, D. (2019). Recasting the dynamics of post-acquisition integration: An embeddedness perspective. *Long Range Planning*, *52*(2), 271–282.

Schilke, O. (2014). Second-order dynamic capabilities: How do they matter? *Academy of Management Perspectives*, *28*(4), 368–380.

Schneider, S.C., & Dunbar, R. (1992). A psychoanalytic reading of hostile takeover events. *Academy of Management Review*, *17*, 337–567.

Schriber, S. (2016). Toward a competitive dynamics perspective on value potential in M&A. In A. Risberg, O. Meglio, & D. King (Eds.), *Companion to mergers and acquisitions* (pp. 324–336). Oxford: Routledge.

Schriber, S., & Degischer, D. (2020). Disentangling acquisition experience: A multilevel analysis and future research agenda. *Scandinavian Journal of Management*, *36*(2), 101097.

Schriber, S., & Löwstedt, J. (2015). Tangible resources and the development of organizational capabilities. *Scandinavian Journal of Management*, *31*(1), 54–68.

Schriber, S., & Löwstedt, J. (2018). Managing asset orchestration: A processual approach to adapting to dynamic environments. *Journal of Business Research*, *90*, 307–317.

Schriber, S., & Löwstedt, J. (2020). Reconsidering ordinary and dynamic capabilities in strategic change. *European Management Journal*, *38*(3), 377–387.

Schriber, S., King, D., & Bauer, F. (2018). Acquisition integration flexibility: Toward a conceptual framework. *Journal of Strategy and Management*, *11*(4), 434–448.

Schriber, S., King, D., & Bauer, F. (2021). Retaliation effectiveness and acquisition performance: The influence of managerial decisions and industry context. *British Journal of Management*. https://doi.org/10.1111/1467-8551.12480

Shelton, L. (1988). Strategic business fits and corporate acquisition: Empirical evidence. *Strategic Management Journal*, *9*(3), 279–287.

Shrivastava, P. (1986). Postmerger integration. *Journal of Business Strategy*, *17*(1), 65–76.

Siegel, D., & Simons, K. (2010). Assessing the effects of mergers and acquisitions on firm performance, plant productivity, and workers: New evidence from matched employer-employee data. *Strategic Management Journal*, *31*(8), 903–916.

Sirmon, D., Hitt, M., Ireland, R., & Gilbert, B. (2011). Resource orchestration to create competitive advantage: Breadth, depth, and life cycle effects. *Journal of Management*, *37*(5), 1390–1412.

Smit, H., & Moraitis, T. (2010). Serial acquisition options. *Long Range Planning*, *43*(1), 85–103.

Stahl, G., & Voigt, A. (2008). Do cultural differences matter in mergers and acquisitions? A tentative model and examination. *Organization Science*, *19*(1), 160–176.

Steenkamp, J.-B., Hanssens, D., Dekimpe, M., & Marnik, D. (2005). Competitive reactions promotion to advertising and attacks. *Marketing Science*, *24*(1), 35–54.

Steigenberger, N. (2017). The challenge of integration: A review of the M&A integration literature. *International Journal of Management Reviews*, *19*(4), 408–431.

Teece, D. (2007). Explicating dynamic capabilities: The nature and micro-foundations of (sustainable) enterprise performance. *Strategic Management Journal*, *28*, 1319–1350.

Teece, D., Pisano, G., & Shuen, A. (1997). Dynamic capabilities and strategic management. *Strategic Management Journal*, *18*, 509–533.

Teerikangas, S., & Very, P. (2006). The culture-performance relationship in M&A: From yes/no to how. *British Journal of Management*, *17*(S1), 31–48.

Tian, A., Ahammad, M., Tarba, S., Pereira, V., Arslan, A., & Khan, Z. (2021). Investigating employee and organizational performance in a cross-border acquisition—A case of withdrawal behavior. *Human Resource Management*, *60*(5), 1–17.

Trichterborn, A., zu Knyphausen-Aufsess, D., & Schweizer, L. (2016). How to improve acquisition performance: The role of a dedicated M&A function, M&A learning process, and M&A capability. *Strategic Management Journal*, *37*, 763–773.

Walsh, J. (1988). Top management turnover following mergers and acquisitions. *Strategic Management Journal*, *9*(2), 173–183.

Winter, S. (2003). Understanding dynamic capabilities. *Strategic Management Journal*, *24*(10), 991–995.

Zaheer, A., Castañer, X., & Souder, D. (2013). Synergy sources, target autonomy, and integration in acquisitions. *Journal of Management*, *39*(3), 604–632.

Zahra, S., Sapienza, H., & Davidsson, P. (2006). Entrepreneurship and dynamic capabilities: A review, model and research agenda. *Journal of Management Studies*, *43*, 917–955.

Zollo, M. (2009). Superstitious learning with rare strategic decisions: Theory and evidence from corporate acquisitions. *Organization Science*, *20*(5), 894–908.

Zollo, M., & Singh, H. (2004). Deliberate learning in corporate acquisition: Post-acquisition strategies and integration capabilities in U.S. bank mergers. *Strategic Management Journal*, *25*(13), 1233–1256.

Zollo, M., & Winter, S.G. (2002). Deliberate learning and the evolution of dynamic capabilities. *Organization Science*, *13*, 339–351.

6 Capability transfer
Improved performance from acquiring polluting targets

Pankaj C. Patel and David R. King

Introduction

While research finds some evidence that it "pays to be green" (Russo & Fouts, 1997, p. 534), a link between environmental management capabilities and firm performance remains inconclusive (Christmann, 2000). Still, external pressure can drive firms to evaluate their environmental strategy. Firms lacking a focus on environmental sustainability face lower legitimacy as they deviate from institutionalized norms of acceptable behavior (Diestre & Rajagopalan, 2011). Stakeholder pressure can influence choices for the sustainability of a firm's operations (Kassinis & Vafeas, 2002) and societal and regulatory pressure requires polluting firms to review their environmental initiatives (Barnett & Hoffman, 2008). Although this creates costs of non-compliance, green capabilities may also create unique economic opportunities for firms. Green capabilities refer to relative efficiency in converting inputs related to environmental initiatives (e.g., green patents) into improved performance (e.g. lower pollution).

Despite its increasing relevance, research on the impact of environmental management on competitive advantage remains an emerging area (Berchicci & King, 2007; Berchicci, Dowell, & King, 2012; Hofer, Cantor, & Dai, 2012). Generally, research has focused on the effects of environmental management capabilities on firm performance and there is less research on how acquirers can transfer green capabilities in acquisitions (Berchicci et al., 2012; Diestre & Rajagopalan, 2011). Acquirers with green capabilities may improve the environmental and economic performance of a polluting target by implementing a turnaround strategy using the market for corporate control (Berchicci et al., 2012; Brouthers, von Hastenburg, & van den Ven, 1998; Capron & Mitchell, 1998; Rhodes-Kropf & Robinson, 2008). Resources, such as green capabilities, are valuable and they can be transferred to a target firm to improve acquisition performance (Ahuja & Katila, 2001; Capron & Hulland, 1999; Capron & Mitchell, 1998; Christmann, 2000; Hart & Dowell, 2011; King, Slotegraaf, & Kesner, 2008). With the possible exception of Ahuja and Katila (2001) who examine a link between innovative input and output, acquisition research on capability transfer

DOI: 10.4324/9781003188308-9

Capability transfer in acquisitions 129

largely examines fit leading to increased synergies and improved financial performance. We more closely link capabilities transfer by tying an acquirer's green capabilities to lower pollution in a target firm's facilities after an acquisition. Specifically, we examine change in pollution from target firm facilities in the post-acquisition period to assess possible transfer of green capabilities. Overall, we extend existing research by examining how firms with green capabilities generate value by transferring them to polluting targets.

We build on resource-based theory (RBT) to extend research in environmental management and acquisitions by focusing on operational efficiency (conversion of environmental inputs to improved environmental outputs) explanations for improved performance (Hart, 1995; Lockett & Thompson, 2001; Peteraf & Barney, 2003). Our measure of green capabilities meets needs for empirical research for environmental management to link "green" resources to environmental performance (Christmann, 2000; Hart, 1995; Silverman, 1999). Also, the link between environmental sustainability and resources from technology development is often overlooked (Hart, 1997), and our measure of green capabilities considers both innovative inputs and related environmental outputs. Additionally, we meet recognized needs to consider moderators of the relationship between environmental management and firm performance (Berchicci & King, 2007; Christmann, 2000) and moderated relationships in acquisition performance (King, Dalton, Daily, & Covin, 2004). For example, we outline how green capabilities positively moderate acquirer and target fit (chemical relatedness) by matching relevant capabilities in an appropriate context to improve the efficiency of operations.

Our contributions involve both a replication and extension of prior research. Consistent with classical guidance that research use alternate methods, we reinforce and extend research on transfer of environmental capabilities through constructive replication and triangulation (Jick, 1979). We incorporate two studies that examine environmental capabilities and acquisitions. The first by Diestre and Rajagopalan (2011) examines the role of chemical relatedness and industry sanctions on firm diversification decisions. The second by Berchicci et al. (2012) examines the role of environmental capabilities and physical distance on acquisition likelihood. Both studies examine the impact of environmental capabilities on diversification, but each stops short of considering performance implications. We include the major constructs of both studies (e.g., chemical relatedness and physical distance) and confirm their role in acquisition decisions. In our extension, we identify an environmental motive for acquisitions that may represent an important subgroup of acquisition activity (Diestre & Rajagopalan, 2011), and we outline how capability transfer can improve operational performance of a target firm and an acquirer's financial performance. This theoretical contribution suggests improved acquisition performance results from efficiency gains.

Background and hypotheses

Higher environmental performance is an increasingly important source of competitive advantage and higher pollution is an indicator of operational inefficiency (Buysse & Verbeke, 2003; Christmann, 2000; Porter & van der Linde, 1995) that leads to lower firm asset values and performance (Diestre & Rajagopalan, 2011; King & Lenox, 2002; Mackey, Mackey, & Barney, 2007). For example, firms reporting toxic chemical use had significantly negative stock reactions with average loss of $4.1 million (Hamilton, 1995). The negative stock reaction from unfavorable environmental performance likely coincides with increased institutional pressures on firms in the same industry (Barnett & Hoffman, 2008; Barnett & King, 2008). For example, Dow Chemical helped to create a trade association for improving perceptions of the chemical industry (Barnett & Hoffman, 2008). Resulting external pressure from stakeholders may contribute to firms with green capabilities to attempt turnaround strategies with polluting firms.

Therefore, we suggest that firms could use green capabilities to improve environmental performance of polluting targets to realize improved financial performance. McWilliams, Van Fleet, and Cory (2002) find evidence of a defensive strategy where firms increase rival firm operating costs through heightened regulatory pressure. However, an offensive strategy in the market for corporate control could leverage green capabilities by acquiring polluting targets. Targets with higher levels of pollution are likely attractive to acquirers with higher green capabilities as they represent a relevant use for an acquirer's capabilities. Compared to acquirers with weaker green capabilities, acquirers with stronger green capabilities may realize greater financial benefits from acquiring polluting targets (Buysse & Verbeke, 2003; King & Lenox, 2002; Starik & Marcus, 2000). This is consistent with RBT explanations of competitive advantage based on differences in efficiency in converting inputs into performance (Penrose, 1959; Peteraf & Barney, 2003).

Acquisitions offer one way to transfer capabilities to targets where they can be productively applied (Capron & Hulland, 1999; Capron & Mitchell, 1998; King et al., 2008). By one estimate, half of acquisition research examines resource transfer or reconfiguration (Ranft, Butler, & Sexton, 2011), and transferring capabilities to target firms is fundamental to realizing higher acquisition performance (King et al., 2008; Uhlenbruck, Hitt, & Semadeni, 2006). Firms with green capabilities have the opportunity to increase efficiency from higher utilization of capabilities and improving target firm operations to achieve increased performance (Diestre & Rajagopalan, 2011). For example, Srinivasan and Mishra (2007) conclude that acquisitions raise the level of efficiency in less efficient targets. However, the effectiveness of capability transfer is likely contextual. We develop logic for the interaction of chemical relatedness

Capability transfer in acquisitions 131

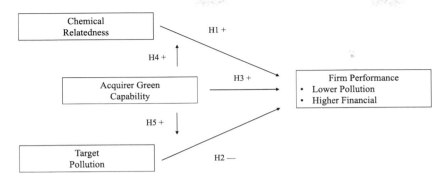

Figure 6.1 Conceptual framework on influence of green capabilities.

and target pollution with green capabilities. In the following sections, we outline the relationships in our conceptual model (see Figure 6.1).

Chemical relatedness

Relatedness involves opportunities unique to the combination of a given acquirer and target that create value (Bruton, Oviatt, & White, 1994; Finkelstein & Haleblian, 2002; Rhodes-Kropf & Robinson, 2008). Inconsistent empirical findings on the effect of relatedness on acquisition performance (Hitt et al., 2009; King et al., 2004) may result from problems with measuring relatedness at the industry level (Martin & Sayrak, 2003; Miller, 2006). The challenge of studying relatedness can be compared to how the skills and experience of a US soccer player may make them a good kicker in US football; however, the skills and experience of other US football players, such as lineman, can make them poor kickers even though they are in the same 'industry'.

Acquisition decisions within and across industries are not random (Montgomery & Hariharan, 1991), and similarities in firm operations that provide the foundation for the anticipated positive relationship between relatedness and acquisition performance. For example, the use of similar chemicals creates similar demands for management and work processes (Vaccaro, Jansen, Van de Bosch & Volberda, 2012). Chemical relatedness has been shown to influence diversification decisions (Diestre & Rajagopalan, 2011), and the next logical step is that firms chose chemically related targets because they enable increased performance through increased operational synergies and capability transfer. A positive impact can result from acquirers reducing pollution of familiar chemicals by improving process efficiency (Christmann, 2000; King & Lenox, 2002; Klassen & Whyback, 1999; Nameroff, Garant, & Albert, 2004; Sharma & Vredenburg, 1998). Context influences the development of intellectual capital (Kang & Snell, 2009) and the use of similar chemicals will

132   *Pankaj C. Patel and David R. King*

increase the application of knowledge and commonality of structures for its application. The preceding suggests lower pollution and improved financial performance following the acquisition of a chemically related target; therefore, we propose the following:

> Hypothesis 1 (H1): Acquisition of a chemically related target is associated with:
>
> *a)* Lower pollution in target firm facilities following the acquisition, and
> *b)* Higher financial performance in a combined firm.

Target firm pollution

Acquirers may be motivated to turnaround firms with less efficient environmental performance. However, integrating a target firm's less efficient operations likely has negative direct effects on environmental and financial performance. The relationship between hazardous chemical use and negative stock market reactions is cumulative (Hamilton, 1995), and the acquisition of a polluting target leads to higher toxic emissions in a combined firm. High joint emissions after an acquisition could make the combined firm more 'visible' to regulators and lower legitimacy among product market and institutional stakeholders. Additionally, the acquisition of an inefficient target may compound integration risks (Hitt et al., 2009). For example, targets with higher pollution levels may use different manufacturing processes from acquirers with proprietary acquirer processes. In the case of target firms with higher pollution, an acquirer also increases legal liabilities from hazardous chemicals (Barney, Edwards, & Ringleb, 1992). This means that beyond direct costs from higher toxic emissions an acquirer also accepts uncertainty in regulatory pressure, integration risks, and legal outcomes.

The challenge of incurring direct and indirect compliance costs and integration difficulties result in lower performance from acquiring polluting firms. Direct costs relate to additional compliance costs and retooling and recombination costs of integrating target firm pollution. Indirect costs stem from reduced legitimacy, regulatory compliance, and potential reputational impacts. For example, acquiring polluting firms may lower perceptions that an acquirer is green by stakeholders that result in a lower overall firm value (Zuckerman, 2004). As a result of increased costs and lower reputational advantages, the acquisition of environmentally inefficient or polluting firms is likely to result in higher emissions and lower financial performance. Therefore, we propose the following:

Capability transfer in acquisitions 133

Hypothesis 2 (H2): Acquiring a polluting target firm with lower environmental efficiency is associated with:

a) Higher pollution in target firm facilities following the acquisition, and
b) Lower financial performance in the combined firm.

Acquirer green capabilities

Firms with green capabilities likely represent an important subgroup of acquirers that have assets that can be productively leveraged in polluting targets to create value. Again, green capabilities relate to the ability of acquiring firms to convert inputs related to environmental initiatives (e.g., R&D intensity and green patents) into outputs (e.g., lower pollution levels) more efficiently than competitors. This means that more efficient acquirers have the opportunity to increase target efficiency by transferring green capabilities.

Green capabilities offer an advantage in resource transfer. First, green capabilities typically include codified knowledge embedded in tasks, tools, and processes that should be easier to transfer (e.g., patents, or environmentally friendly operational processes). Additionally, acquirers are better at redeploying their own resources to targets than assimilating target firm resources (Capron, 1999); therefore, acquirers with green capabilities can transfer their green capabilities to reduce target firm pollution. Second, applying and recombining acquirer green capabilities with a target firm's resources generates additional knowledge recombination to enhance performance (Montgomery & Hariharan, 1991). As an acquirer recombines green capabilities with a target firm's resource base, additional applications of green capabilities can emerge and offer an additional source of synergy as capabilities are stretched to new contexts and applications. Third, research suggests green capabilities indemnify firms from pollution events so they experience smaller losses (Flammer, 2013). In summary, the application of green capabilities should lower pollution in target firm facilities and offer improved financial performance and enhance an acquirer's green capabilities. Therefore, we predict the following:

Hypothesis 3 (H3): The level of an acquirer's green capabilities before an acquisition is positively associated with:

a) Lower pollution in target firm facilities following the acquisition, and
b) Higher financial performance of the combined firm.

134 *Pankaj C. Patel and David R. King*

Moderated relationships

Berchicci and King (2007, p. 525) suggest that the link between green capabilities and performance is likely contingent. An improved match between capabilities and opportunities likely provides increased efficiency gains. Specifically, we examine how an acquirer's green capabilities may modify the direct effect of chemical relatedness and target pollution on performance.

Acquirer green capabilities and chemical relatedness. Transfer of capabilities among chemically related firms is likely facilitated by a target and acquirer sharing common cognitive mindsets (Finkelstein & Haleblian, 2002), and process technologies (Puranam, Singh, & Zollo, 2006). Due to cognitive limitations, managers require "activity segmentation," and manage "expectational ambiguity" as they integrate resources (Birkinshaw, Bresman, & Håkanson, 2000, p. 398) and chemical relatedness increases context specificity of resources in a combined firm. Target firms with high chemical relatedness are likely to better assimilate knowledge from the acquirer due to shared cognitive, strategic, and technological bases that facilitate realignment and recontextualization of acquirer resources (Cassiman & Veugelers, 2006). Increased chemical relatedness involves greater strategic and operational fit that enables novel knowledge combinations between target firm resources and acquirer's green capabilities.

The likelihood of capability transfer is higher when acquiring and target firms display similarity (Finkelstein & Haleblian, 2002). Firms with green capabilities likely have unique and difficult to imitate resources that can be productively applied to targets in chemically related industries. From a pollution perspective, an acquirer with demonstrated capabilities to lower toxic emissions will have increased relevance, especially, when both the target and acquirer use chemically related processes. Put another way, green capabilities in chemically related industries likely provide a better fit that enables reducing emissions in target firm operations. From a synergy perspective, green capabilities likely have increased recombination potential when an acquirer has experience in a chemically related area. Therefore, we predict the following:

> Hypothesis 4 (H4): Firms with green capabilities that acquire targets with high chemical relatedness exhibit better performance. In other words, acquirer green capabilities moderate the relationship of chemically related targets on performance, such that:
>
> *a)* The interaction of green capabilities and chemical relatedness results in lower pollution in target firm facilities following the acquisition, and
>
> *b)* The interaction of green capabilities and chemical relatedness results in higher financial performance of the combined firm.

Acquirer green capabilities and target firm pollution. Transferring green capabilities to enhance performance requires both task and human integration (Birkinshaw et al., 2000). In considering target firm operations, the greatest benefit likely involves applying a firm's green capabilities to targets with higher levels of pollution. An acquirer's green capabilities can likely provide faster reductions to the direct environmental cost of target operations. Beyond the clear need for improving the efficiency of operations, higher levels of pollution may also facilitate resource transfer.

To the extent clear differences in environmental management are apparent, clear status differences can align employee expectations for needed resource transfer. For example, acquisitions involving distressed firms should perform better as a target displays the need for intervention (Bruton et al., 1994). Further, it is possible the higher status of green acquirers may transfer to target firm operations or provide reputational benefits by extending an acquirer's green image (Podolny, 1993). Operationally, green capabilities of an acquirer may facilitate employee acceptance and integration of needed improvements. When it comes to reputation, green capabilities broaden a target firm's product portfolio by including greener products, enhance organization image, and lower financing costs (Ghoul, Guedhami, Kwok, & Mishra, 2011). This suggests green capabilities can also reduce the indirect costs of acquiring polluting targets. Taken together acquirers with green capabilities likely have a higher potential for performance improvements. Therefore, we predict the following:

> Hypothesis 5 (H5): Firms with green capabilities that acquire polluting targets exhibit better performance. In other words, acquirer green capabilities moderate the relationship of polluting targets on performance, such that:

> *a)* The interaction of green capabilities and target pollution results in lower pollution in target firm facilities following the acquisition, and
> *b)* The interaction of green capabilities and target pollution results in higher financial performance of the combined firm.

Methods

To identify a sample of targets and acquirers with observable financial and environmental performance, we followed several steps. We start by identifying acquisitions of US public firms using Thomson's Securities Data Corporation (SDC) Platinum database between the years 1993 and 2005. This timeframe was chosen to minimize the effect of the 2008 recession on post-acquisition performance. Based on CUSIP number (COMPUSTAT identifier) and SIC and address match, we included an acquisition if: (a) it results in majority ownership; (b) the acquisitions value is more than USD 10 million but less than USD 500 million; (c) the

136 Pankaj C. Patel and David R. King

target is not financially distressed or its average stock price 21 days before acquisition should be greater than $3; (d) both target and acquirer are listed in EPA's toxic release inventory (TRI) database; (e) at least five years of financial information are available for both target and acquirer prior to the announcement date; and (f) at least three years of financial information are available for the acquirer after the acquisition. This resulted in an initial sample of 236 acquiring firms and 877 targets.

To match acquisitions with pollution information, we used Environmental Protection Agency (EPA) data that includes manufacturing plants using more than 10,000 pounds of 347 chemical compounds listed by the EPA and that have more than ten employees. The data provided on toxic release have been widely used in several studies (Barnett & King, 2008; Hamilton, 1995; King & Lenox, 2000, 2002). The TRI database provides toxic release information at the facility level and provides parent name (TRI database field id: parent) and the Dun and Bradstreet number (DUNS) for each parent (TRI database field id: pduns). For the acquirer, we identify facility level toxic releases using acquirer's DUNS in the pre- and post-acquisition periods. We identify target facilities' toxic releases prior to acquisition using target's DUNS, and, for the post acquisition toxic release, we identify toxic releases from a target's facilities listed under acquirer's DUNS in the post-acquisition phase by identifying geographic addresses of target's facilities before acquisition listed in TRI database. Although facilities of the target are listed under DUNS of the acquirer, the physical addresses of the target's facilities remain the same and enabling tracking acquired facilities to assess post-acquisition change in pollution performance. To link parent information from TRI to COMPUSTAT, we use DUNS-CUSIP concordance table in D&B Million Dollar Directory.

Next, we identified green patents held by acquiring and target firms. We matched the 207 acquiring firms and 738 target firms in the NBER-COMPUSTAT patent database to identify green patents.[1] We triangulated the identification of green patents using two approaches. First, we used an iterative search process using definitions and keywords described by Anastas and Warner (1998) and Anastas and Kirchhoff (2002), areas of green chemistry in OECD Sustainable Chemistry initiative (Tundo et al., 2000), and EPA's Green Chemistry program. While the search did not directly use names of chemical compounds, it captured concepts such as "use of alternative feedstocks, solvent-free processes, use of innocuous reagents, natural processes, use of alternative solvents, design of safer chemicals, development of alternative reaction conditions, and minimal energy consumption" (Nameroff et al., 2004: 962).[2] Using this first approach we identified 9,246 patents. Second, we applied the 2006 OECD Compendium on Patent Statistics methodology that identifies patents

---

1 Source: https://sites.google.com/site/patentdataproject/.
2 A full version of patent search filter is available at www.chemistry.org/green chemistryinstitute.

Capability transfer in acquisitions 137

based on environmental fields using a combination of IPC patent classes and keywords (see Appendix 6.2 for the list of keywords and patent classes used to identify patents). This approach focuses on end of pipe technologies that are easily identifiable and represent core technologies in limiting emissions. Using the OECD approach, we identified 10,017 patents. We combined the two methods for a final list of 9,424 green patents, where acquiring firms represented 6,519 green patents and target firms included 2,905 green patents.[3] Our final sample includes 207 acquiring firms with 738 targets acquired between 1993 and 2005 (1,674 firm-years).

Dependent variables

Five-year post-acquisition TRI change of target's facilities. To measure pollution performance, we collected data on the TRI change in emissions for five years after an acquisition for each target facility. We track a target firm's facilities in the post-acquisition phase using exact name and address matching in TRI database (TRI database field ids: address, city, county, state, spc [state postal code], zip, p_lat (latitude), p_long (longitude)). Next, based on guidelines developed by King and Lenox (2000), we measure toxicity adjusted emission levels in pounds for five calendar years after announcement year for all facilities acquired with a target.

Changes in emission levels of facilities in the post-acquisition phase could be driven by systematic changes such as increased capacity usage that could increase emission levels, or decreased capacity usage that could lower overall emissions and therefore an increase or decrease in toxic releases may not be directly driven by acquirer's green capabilities. Acquirers may also close facilities in the post-acquisition period and thereby lower overall emissions by the target's facilities. Further, industry level changes could also lower emission levels. Finally, year specific effects based on EPA administrative mandates could also lower emission levels. Therefore, changes in emission levels in the post-acquisition period by target firm's facilities could be divided into expected and unexpected components. Changes driven by green capabilities most likely relate to unexpected component of changes in emission levels.

We use autoregressive specification with one-year lag (AR(1)) to identify expected and unexpected changes in facilities' emission levels:

$$Toxicity - adjusted\,emissions_t = \beta_0 + \beta_1 Toxicity - \\ adjusted\,emissions_{t-1} + \beta_2 Number\,of\,Facilities\,closed_{t-1} \\ + \beta_{3i} \sum_{i=0}^{N} w_i \times median\,industry\,Toxicity - adjusted\,emissions_{t-1} \\ + \beta_4 \sum_{j=2}^{5} Year_j + \varepsilon_t$$

---

3 To minimize researcher bias, we only coded patents identified in both approaches.

Where *Toxicity – adjusted emissions$_t$* are the total toxicity adjusted emissions for all facilities of the target in year t (where $t = 1$ *to* 5 years) in the post-acquisition phase, that is predicted by *Toxicity – adjusted emissions$_{t-1}$* in the previous year, and changes in emission levels if one or more facilities were closed at $t - 1$. We code a facility as closed if a facility is not listed in TRI database for two consecutive years. Next, median emissions from facilities in each four digit SIC code (i) are weighted by relative emission of a target facility among all SIC codes where a target operated. For example, if a target has three facilities in SIC codes 2812, 2812, 2842 and the relative emission weights (w_i) are 0.3, 0.5, 0.2, respectively, then the total emission weight for SIC 2812 is 0.8, and for SIC 2842 it is 0.2. Next, median emission level in two unique SIC codes (N) at $t-1$ is identified and weighted by w_i to predict *Toxicity – adjusted emissions$_t$*. Industry pollution levels are compiled from TRI database. Using year of acquisition as the reference year, we control for year dummies (*Year$_j$*). The standardized residual from the regression (ε_t) is used as a proxy for unexpected change in five-year emission levels of a target firm's facilities. The measure is analogous to the measure of unsystematic return, firm returns after controlling for all firm- and industry-level systematic effects.

Financial performance. Cording and colleagues (2010) and King and colleagues (2021) called for short- and long-term measures of acquisition outcomes and we have incorporated both. For example, short-term measures represent an indication of 'potential' returns from an acquisition and long-term returns represent the success in unlocking that potential (Stahl & Voigt, 2008). Our specific performance measures are described in Appendix 6.1 and relate to: (1) three-day cumulative abnormal return (CAR) [-1,1]); (2) three-year average Return on Sales (ROS); (3) a 36-month buy and hold return (BHAR). Stock price information is compiled from Center for Research on Security Prices (CRSP).

Independent variables

Chemical relatedness. Our measure of chemical relatedness is an extension of the measure proposed by Diestre and Rajagolapan (2011). Specifically, we account for toxicity weights and multiple industry segments. From COMPUSTAT, we identified top three industry segments and calculated three-year average sales in each industry segment prior to announcement, and calculated percentage sales in each industry segment for both a target and acquirer. Next, we identified the distribution of 347 regulated chemicals across each four-digit SIC code industries of the target and acquirer. The emissions are further weighted by toxicity levels.

We created a 347 × 3 matrix for each acquirer and target. The rows consist of 347 regulated chemicals and columns consist of sales percentage weighted emissions in each industry segment. The similarity in

Capability transfer in acquisitions   139

industry segment weighted emission levels between the two matrices is the measure of chemical relatedness. If the emissions across the chemical classes are similar, then two industries have higher chemical relatedness.

$$
\begin{bmatrix}
w_{c^1} s_1 c_i^1 & w_{c^1} s_2 c_i^1 & w_{c^1} s_3 c_i^1 \\
w_{c^2} s_1 c_i^2 & w_{c^2} s_2 c_i^2 & w_{c^2} s_3 c_i^2 \\
& \cdot & \\
& \cdot & \\
& \cdot & \\
w_{c^{347}} s_1 c_i^{347} & w_{c^{347}} s_2 c_i^{347} & w_{c^{347}} s_3 c_i^{347}
\end{bmatrix}
$$

Where, $(w_{c^1} \dots w_{c^{347}})$ is the toxicity weight for 347 chemicals, (s_1, s_2, s_3) is the percentage of sales in top three industry segment a target or an acquirer operates in, and $(c_i^1 \dots c_i^{347})$ are the emission levels in industry i. Next, we created a one dimensional matrix for target and acquirer with industry-segment and toxicity weighted emissions for 347 chemicals.

Chemical relatedness between acquirer and target firms is represented as

$$
C_{acquirer,target,t} = \frac{C_{acquirer,t} C_{target,t'}}{\sqrt{(C_{acquirer,t} C_{acquirer,t'})(C_{target,t} C_{target,t'})}}
$$

The values range from 1, indicating high similarity, to 0, or no similarity.

Acquirer green capabilities and target pollution. Green capabilities relate to a firm's increased relative efficiency in converting environmental-related inputs to improve environmental performance. Acquirer green capabilities are related to efficiency in converting inputs to improving environmental performance, whereas target pollution is the inefficiency in converting inputs to improving environmental performance. We draw on earlier work by Dutta and others (1999, 2005), and Li, Shang, and Slaughter (2010), to measure capabilities as higher productivity for given inputs and associated outputs in comparison to a firm's industry. We defined industry competitors as all firms in the year of acquisition announcement in the same 4-digit SIC code, and used the stochastic frontier approach to assess relative input-output conversion capabilities among industry partners (Kumbhakar & Lovell, 2000; Li et al., 2010).

We used three inputs: (1) mean firm asset adjusted R&D intensity in the past five years; (2) mean firm asset adjusted capital expenditures in the past five years; and (3) total green patents filed in the past five years. For each firm listed in a four-digit SIC code, we identify patent portfolios based on NBER COMPUSTAT concordance table. Next, to

140 Pankaj C. Patel and David R. King

identify green patents for each firm in the industry we again triangulated using the approach proposed by Nameroff and others (2004) and key words and patent classes listed in OECD Compendium on Statistics (2006).

For output measures, we use five-year mean of seven environmental performance indicators prior to acquisition. The first indicator is the average sales- and toxicity-weighted emission levels in pounds over five calendar years prior to acquisition announcement. Second, based on EPA's *Docket database*, we count the number of cases or administrative actions filed against the target by the Justice Department (on behalf of EPA) for violating environmental law since 1988 (or, later, if a firm was established after 1988). Third, based on EPA's *Accidental Release Information Program* (ARIP), we count the chemical accidents per year between 1988 and 1995 (or, later, if a firm was established after 1988). Fourth, we estimate cancer- and non-cancer weighted TRI levels using *Tool for the Reduction and Assessment of Chemical Impacts* (TRACI) developed by the US EPA (Bare, 2002; Toffel & Marshall, 2004). Finally, to assess environmental management practices, we use data from TRI database's *Waste Quantity Reports* on three additional performance dimensions: (1) the fraction of toxic chemicals not recycled; (2) the fraction of toxic chemicals not combusted for energy recovery; and (3) the fraction of toxics not otherwise treated. We reverse code these three indicators to maintain parallel construction of the items.

As increasing pollution output indicates lower environmental performance, the 'efficiency' values estimated from the translog function indicate worse environmental performance, where firms with lower conversion 'efficiency' have higher environmental pollution for given level of inputs. The measure of target pollution is the conversion 'efficiency' derived from translog function. Higher values (range 0 to 1) indicate worse environmental performance, or higher target pollution and lower efficiency. Conversely, firms producing lower emissions for a given level of input have more green capabilities relative to their industry counterparts, or, for per unit of inputs, such firms have lower emission levels. Therefore, green capability is measured by subtracting the conversion 'efficiency' from 1. A firm with a conversion 'efficiency' of 1 has the highest level of emissions for a given level of inputs, subtracting conversion 'efficiency' from 1 reveals how far an acquirer is away from the emission frontier. This means higher values (range 0 to 1) indicate higher green capabilities and lower emissions.

Controls

Hitt and colleagues (2009) called for acquisition research to include common research variables to limit model misspecification; therefore, we applied multiple controls listed in Table 6.1.

Capability transfer in acquisitions   141

Analysis

Acquirers may share variance from completing multiple acquisitions, so we used the Breusch-Pagan test and the null hypothesis that residuals are homoscedastic and it was rejected (test statistic 25.617, p = 0.000). Therefore, we used GMM with Newey-West estimators to control for heteroscedasticity and shared variance.

Results

Variable mean, standard deviation, and zero-order correlations are available from the authors upon request. Still, we comment on several variables. The mean value of acquisition premium is 23.16 percent and it is lower than recent historical averages that range between 40 and 50 percent (Laamanen, 2007), suggesting that green firms have higher negotiating power. The mean value of chemical relatedness is 0.254, suggesting a low overlap in acquirer and target chemical use on average. Separately, a test of the means suggests that target pollution and acquirer green capabilities are significantly different ($p < 0.0001$; $t = 4.011$). While the mean values for the financial performance measures are all positive, zero is included within 1 standard deviation, or a result consistent with existing research (King et al., 2004). The financial performance measures are significantly ($p < 0.01$) correlated with target knowledge stock and this is consistent with bilateral transfer of resources in an acquisition. The five-year change in target facility emissions is positive on average, but this measure has greater variance than the financial measures and zero is within one standard deviation.

Table 6.2 reports the results of our analysis including beta coefficients and standard errors, and we comment on a few significant control variables. First, target knowledge stock is significant ($p < 0.05$ for all measures) across all the models and they relate to improved financial performance and lower toxic emissions. Again, this is consistent with a bilateral transfer of resources in an acquisition. Second, acquisition premium has a negative impact on financial performance ($p < 0.05$) and is associated with increased pollution in target facilities ($p < 0.05$). Third, market relatedness, or targets and acquirers in closer 4-digit SIC codes experience significantly improved financial performance (at least, $p < 0.05$ for all measures). Fourth, higher chemical dispersion reduces emissions ($p < 0.001$), suggesting the more chemicals used the greater the opportunity for reduced emissions. The highest VIF value is 5.68, or well below the recommended cut-off (O'Brien, 2007). Additionally, our models achieve R-squared values that explain approximately 40 percent of the variance, or a large improvement over research that on average explains 10 percent of acquisition performance variance (Sirower, 1997, p. 158).

The direct effects of hypothesized relationships are supported. Hypothesis 1 proposed that acquiring a chemically related target results

142 Pankaj C. Patel and David R. King

Table 6.1 Control variables

Variable	Measure/Source	Justification
Post-acquisition Acquirer Green Capabilities	Same calculation as our measure of acquirer green capabilities prior to an acquisition	Performance is measured after an acquisition and changes in performance could relate to changes in green capabilities
Acquirer knowledge stock	Total number of patents approved ten years prior the acquisition event (or, less than ten years if the firm us younger than ten years) from NBER's COMPUSTAT-patent concordance portfolio	Value may be created from transfer of knowledge other than an acquirer's green patents
Target knowledge stock	Same as above	Value may be created by recombining a target's knowledge
Acquirer prior alliances	The number of acquirer's alliances five years prior to acquisition event from SDC Platinum database	Alliances could impact legitimacy and/or knowledge transfer experience
Acquirer and target prior acquisitions	Count of the number of acquisitions in the past five years from SDC Platinum database	High tempo of acquisitions may interfere with capability transfer
Geographic distance	Linear distance based on longitude and latitude of the capital cities of the acquirer and the target	Proximity can impact diversification decisions (Berchicci et al., 2012)
Deal attitude	Categorical measure of whether an acquisition was hostile (1) or friendly (0)	Hostile acquisitions are likely less open to capability transfer
Acquisition premium	Percentage difference between final purchase price of the target firm and the trading price of the target firm stock 21 days before announcement	Acquisition premiums are generally considered to negatively impact performance
Market relatedness	Ratio of number of common three-digit technology codes assigned to acquirer and target firms to total number of technology codes between target and acquirer from SDC Platinum	Alternate explanation of value creation
Mean chemical dispersion	Blau's heterogeneity index between target and acquirer using the chemical products in target and acquirer portfolios	Mean level of dispersion helps control for possible recombination challenges resulting from greater diversity of emissions

Capability transfer in acquisitions   143

Table 6.1 Cont.

Variable	Measure/Source	Justification
Acquirer debt-to-equity	one calendar year before announcement from Compustat	Firm debt load may impact available slack
Ratio of acquirer' industry-adjusted ROA and target' industry-adjusted ROA	one calendar year before announcement from Compustat	Firm performance may be historically dependent
Ratio of acquirer to target size	Natural log of acquirer's and target's assets one calendar year before announcement from Compustat	Larger targets lower the impact of environmental management initiatives (Hofer et al., 2012)
Acquirer and Target regulatory sanctions	Total environmental fines in both target and acquiring firm's industries by four-digit SIC code adjusted by industry size by dividing natural log average fines in past three years by natural log of firms in an industry (Diestre and Rajagopalan, 2011)	Greater fines at the industry level indicate increased inability among industry participants in meeting environmental standards
Misspecification controls	Direct, squared and interaction effects of direct and square terms of target and acquirer industry regulatory sanctions	Diestre and Rajagopalan (2011) find that industry regulatory sanctions has an invertedU shaped relationship with acquisition likelihood and the relationship is stronger under increasing chemical relatedness

in lower toxic emissions from a target firm's facilities in the post-acquisition phase (H1a: $\beta = -0.202$, $p < 0.01$) and increases financial performance of the overall firm (H1b: 3-day CAR: $\beta = 0.079$, $p < 0.05$; 3-year average ROS: $\beta = 0.066$, $p < 0.05$; 36-month BHAR: $\beta = 0.157$, $p < 0.05$). Hypothesis 2 proposed that acquiring less efficient targets with more pollution leads to lower financial performance of the overall firm (H2b: 3-day CAR: $\beta = -0.126$, $p < 0.05$; 3-year average ROS: $\beta = -0.087$, $p < 0.05$; 36-month BHAR: $\beta = -0.074$, $p < 0.05$), and it coincides with higher toxic emissions from a target's facilities in the post-acquisition phase (H2a: $\beta = 0.089$, $p < 0.05$). This suggests that (on average) target inefficiency is persistent.

Hypothesis 3, acquirer green capabilities lower toxic emissions from a target firm's facilities in the post-acquisition phase (H3a: $\beta = -0.155$, $p < 0.01$), is strongly related to financial performance (3-day CAR: $\beta = 0.095$, $p < 0.05$; 3-year average ROA: $\beta = 0.127$, $p < 0.05$; 36-month BHAR:

Table 6.2 Results of analysis

		Five-year TRI change of target's facilities	3-day CAR ——— [-1,1]	3-year average ROS	36 month BHAR
Intercept		0.346***	0.013**	0.066***	0.062 ***
		−0.083	−0.005	−0.017	−0.019
Direct Effects (t)					
Chemical Relatedness	[H1]	−0.202**	0.079*	0.066*	0.157*
		−0.077	−0.036	−0.031	−0.061
Target Pollution	[H2]	0.089*	−0.126*	−0.087*	−0.074*
		−0.04	−0.058	−0.04	−0.031
Acquirer Green Capabilities	[H3]	−0.155**	0.095*	0.127*	0.153**
		−0.052	−0.037	−0.06	−0.056
Moderation Effects (t)					
Chemical relatedness × Green Capabilities	[H4]	−0.072*	0.065*	0.043*	0.102*
		−0.033	−0.03	−0.019	−0.085
Target Pollution × Green Capabilities	[H5]	−0.146**	0.086*	0.042*	0.113*
		−0.053	−0.041	−0.019	−0.045
Controls (t)Controls (t)Controls (t)					
Post–acquisition Acquirer green capabilities		−0.232**	−0.019	0.064*	0.088*
		−0.076	−0.033	−0.029	−0.039
Acquirer Knowledge Stock		−0.133*	0.015	0.009	0.019
		−0.061	−0.027	−0.012	−0.021
Target Knowledge Stock		−0.132*	0.067*	0.123*	0.077*
		−0.059	−0.033	−0.052	−0.031
Acquirer prior alliances		0.035	0.016	0.019	0.023
		−0.049	−0.017	−0.018	−0.012

Acquirer prior acquisitions	0.019	0.029	0.013	0.026
	−0.022	−0.018	−0.019	−0.019
Target prior acquisitions	0.017	0.032	0.041	0.022
	−0.071	−0.037	−0.054	−0.036
Geographic Distance	0.157*	0.018	0.015	0.02
	−0.072	−0.024	−0.013	−0.023
Deal Attitude	0.003	0.004	0.003	0.009
	−0.006	−0.005	−0.017	−0.008
Acquisition Premium	0.095*	−0.098*	−0.159**	−0.083*
	−0.04	−0.041	−0.062	−0.037
Market relatedness	−0.032	0.067	0.109*	0.088*
	−0.076	−0.032	−0.055	−0.04
Mean Chemical Dispersion	−0.341***	0.025	0.037	0.031
	−0.072	−0.016	−0.029	−0.018
Debt to Equity	−0.030*	−0.014	0.007	−0.013
	−0.014	−0.029	−0.015	−0.017
Ratio of acquirer to target industry– adjusted ROA	0.013	0.105*	0.046	0.076*
	−0.015	−0.052	−0.037	−0.03
Ratio of acquirer to target size	0.039	0.037	0.113*	0.029*
	−0.035	−0.039	−0.05	−0.013
Target Industry regulatory sanctions	0.032	−0.064	−0.028	−0.049
	−0.036	−0.069	−0.029	−0.036
Acquirer Industry regulatory sanctions	0.049	−0.029	−0.076*	−0.014
	−0.043	−0.041	−0.033	−0.019
Misspecification Controls				
Target Industry regulatory sanctions – square	0.016	0.042	0.009	0.012
	−0.022	-0.029	−0.016	−0.007

(continued)

Table 6.2 Cont.

	Five-year TRI change of target's facilities	3-day CAR ——— [-1,1]	3-year average ROS	36 month BHAR
Acquirer Industry regulatory sanctions – square	0.042 −0.027	0.029 -0.038	0.014 −0.02	0.049 −0.062
Target Industry regulatory sanctions – square × Chemical relatedness	0.028 −0.029	0.042 -0.027	0.042 −0.037	0.033 −0.036
Acquirer Industry regulatory sanctions – square × Chemical relatedness	0.022 −0.019	0.037 -0.066	0.036 −0.049	0.033 −0.047
Industry Dummies	Yes	Yes	Yes	Yes
Adjusted-R2	0.432	0.398	0.479	0.468
F-stat	78.544	82.654	104.556	128.674

$\beta = 0.153$, $p < 0.01$). Further, inconsistent with the findings of Diestre and Rajagopalan (2011) our misspecification controls with squared variable terms are not significant, or do not support an inverted-U shaped relationship for industry regulatory sanctions alone or under increasing chemical relatedness.

Moderated hypotheses involving acquirer green capabilities are examined by multiplying related variables together. Hypothesis 4a, mitigating effects of the negative relationship between chemical relatedness and pollution from a target firm's facilities in the post-acquisition phase ($\beta = -0.072$, $p < 0.05$), is supported. Both low and high levels of green capabilities lower changes in TRI pollution for target facilities for high chemical relatedness. Hypothesis 4b, a reinforcing effect of green capabilities on the positive relationship between chemical relatedness and performance, is supported for our financial measures (3-day CAR: $\beta = 0.065$, $p < 0.05$; 3-year average ROS: $\beta = 0.043$, $p < 0.05$; 36-month BHAR: $\beta = 0.102$, $p < 0.05$). The moderation effects of high levels of green capabilities on financial performance measures are significant, but there is less impact at low levels of green capabilities. Hypothesis 5a is supported with the interaction of green capabilities and target pollution resulting in lower emissions from a target firm's facilities in the post-acquisition phase ($\beta = -0.146$, $p < 0.01$). The change in target TRI emissions is higher for acquirers of polluting targets that have low green capabilities. Hypothesis 5b, a mitigating effect of green capabilities on the negative relationship between target pollution and financial performance, is supported for our financial measures (3-day CAR: $\beta = 0.086$, $p < 0.05$; 3-year average ROS: $\beta = 0.042$, $p < 0.05$; 36-month BHAR: $\beta = 0.113$, $p < 0.05$). High levels of green capabilities with increasing target pollution do not lead to an increase in financial performance, but lower levels of green capabilities result in lower financial performance for high target pollution.

Discussion

Our study makes important contributions to multiple streams of research. Consistent with efficiency explanations of performance, we find that acquiring firms can realize higher environmental and financial performance by leveraging green capabilities in polluting targets. Consistent with resource-based theory, we find that acquirers with higher green capabilities are able to transfer that capability to polluting firms to lower pollution in a target firm's facilities. Additionally, higher green capabilities mitigate the negative relationship of acquiring targets with higher pollution. Further, we find that the positive relationship between acquiring a chemically related target and performance is enhanced by an acquirer's green capabilities. Our research also has implications for management research and practice.

148 *Pankaj C. Patel and David R. King*

Research implications

Our results have several implications for acquisition research. First, we concur with the need to examine multiple measures of performance. While there is reason to expect that different performance measures may relate to different constructs that can help identify theoretical boundaries (Cording, Christmann & Weigelt, 2010), our results are consistent across different pollution and financial measures. For example, consistency in the performance measures suggests that financial performance may provide an indicator of environmental performance. Further, consistency of our short-term and long-term measures of performance suggests that expectations for improved performance at acquisition announcement are largely realized in long-term performance measures. We also demonstrate significant results that confirm long-held expectations that related acquisitions can lead to higher performance, and this outcome may relate to improved measures of relatedness based on chemical use that is specific to our context. Further, the impact of chemical relatedness is enhanced for an acquirer with more efficient green capabilities (conversion of inputs into related outputs) that likely results from applying capabilities in a relevant context (Cassiman & Veuglers, 2006).

With respect to environmental research, we demonstrate that firms with green capabilities can realize improved financial and pollution performance by acquiring polluting targets. Specifically, our results confirm that financial performance in acquisitions is related to efficiency in the form of pollution reduction (King & Lenox, 2002). To the extent that this holds, there is even a greater need to consider financial implications of green capabilities. This contributes to environmental research by showing that one way that it "pays to be green" is for firms to transfer green capabilities to polluting firms and improve their efficiency. This makes a contribution as increasing the acceptance of environmental management requires showing how environmental concerns impact shareholder value (Garrod & Chadwick, 1996).

Finally, our research has implications for resource-based theory. Our results support the conclusion that capabilities can be successfully transferred between an acquirer and target firm. The implication is that differences in firm efficiency (Leibenstein, 1966) extend to green capabilities and that related differences have performance implications. Additionally, our focus on efficiency suggests that resources are necessary, but insufficient for creating value. Rather, we find creating value depends on the efficiency of how resources are created and applied. Further, acquisitions appear to provide a viable option to efficiently apply resources by transferring them to new uses. In the case of green capabilities, it appears that increased resource combinations with a target firm bolster the underlying capability. The implication is that there are likely bilateral benefits of resource transfer that augment resource recombination.

Management implications

There are also implications for managers in that environmental capabilities appear to play a role in acquisition dynamics. First, our results show that firms display a capacity for self-regulation (Berchicci & King, 2007). Specifically, we show that polluting firms largely lacking environmental capabilities risk disciplinary acquisitions. This can provide an additional incentive for environmental management as acquisitions of polluting firms will likely experience management turnover (Krug & Shill, 2008). This is a byproduct of firms with developed green capabilities being able to successfully transfer and apply them to polluting firms. Beyond the potential for lower turnover, another selfish reason managers should pay more attention to environmental strategy is that shareholders appear to reward good environmental performance with higher CEO pay (Berrone & Gomez-Mejia, 2009). These reasons for paying heed to environmental management reinforce research that suggests managers need to adopt sustainability mindsets (Pagell & Gobeli, 2009).

Our results also suggest that differences in capabilities make environmental strategy firm-specific. In other words, value creation from acquiring polluting firms likely varies for different bidders. Capron and Pistre (2002) suggest liabilities from a target will be reflected in the price paid or will not influence acquisition performance. However, we find acquisition premium negatively impacts financial performance, or the premium paid limits value creation (Sirower, 1997). Higher premiums may drive financial controls that limit operational improvements. Therefore, while acquiring a polluting firm can lead to competitive advantage, following that strategy requires sustained investment by management to develop and maintain green capabilities (Buysse & Verbeke, 2003).

Limitations and research opportunities

While research recognizes a link between environmental management and stakeholders, we do not examine stakeholder relationships or strategies such as pushing for stronger regulation (Hart, 1995; Sharma & Vrendenburg, 1998). For example, Reinhardt (1999) reported that California refiners used regulations to create a local advantage, and examining political behavior of green firms represents a continued opportunity for additional research (Russo & Fouts, 1997). Further, firms may pursue multiple ways of profiting from environmental sustainability (Starik & Rands, 1995) and we only examine acquiring polluting firms. Additional research is needed to identify other circumstances where "being green" offers performance advantages or additional moderating effects. While our research sample goes beyond chemical firms to include manufacturing firms, it remains US based and examining

150 Pankaj C. Patel and David R. King

relationships in an international setting is needed. Further, while we discuss resource transfer and see evidence of it improving target facility efficiency through lowering toxic emissions, we do not examine the method of how the resources are transferred or its direction. We can only conclude that resource transfer between and acquirer and target is bilateral (Capron & Mitchell, 1998), and confirming resource transfer and direction is an opportunity for additional research. For example, green patents are largely codified and may be easier to transfer than tacit knowledge that may require greater care. Exploring contextual impacts of resource transfer also represents an opportunity for future research. In closing, we extend research by identifying unique advantages available to acquirers with green capabilities, and we find direct and indirect effects of green capabilities on improving pollution and financial performance from acquiring polluting targets.

References

Ahuja, G., & Katila, R. (2001). Technological acquisitions and the innovation performance of acquiring firm: A longitudinal study. *Strategic Management Journal*, 22(3), 197–220.

Anastas, T., & Kirchhoff, M. (2002). Origins, current status, and future challenges of green chemistry. *Accounts of Chemical Research*, 35(9), 686–694.

Anastas, P., & Warner, J. (1998). *Green chemistry theory and practice*. New York: Oxford University Press.

Bare, J. (2002). Traci--the tool for the reduction and assessment of chemical and other environmental impacts. *Journal of Industrial Ecology*, 6(3–4), 49–78.

Barney, J. B., Edwards, F. L., & Ringleb, A. H. (1992). Organizational responses to legal liability: Employee exposure to hazardous materials, vertical integration, and small firm production. *Academy of Management Journal*, 35(2), 328–349.

Barnett, M., & Hoffman, A. (2008). Beyond corporate reputation: Managing reputational interdependence. *Corporate Reputation Review*, 11(1), 1–9.

Barnett, M., & King, A. (2008). Good fences make good neighbors: A longitudinal analysis of an industry self-regulatory institution. *Academy of Management Journal*, 51(6), 1150–1170.

Berchicci, L., & King, A. (2007). Postcards from the edge: A review of the business and environment literature. *Academy of Management Annals*, 1(1), 513–547.

Berchicci, L., Dowell, G., & King, A. (2012). Environmental capabilities and corporate strategy: Exploring acquisitions among US manufacturing firms. *Strategic Management Journal*, 33(9), 1053–1071.

Berrone, P., & Gomez-Mejia, L. (2009). Environmental performance and executive compensation: An integrated agency-institutional perspective. *Academy of Management Journal*, 52(1), 103–126.

Birkinshaw, J., Bresman, H., & Håkanson, L. (2000). Managing the post-acquisition integration process: How the human integration and task integration processes interact to foster value creation. *Journal of Management Studies*, 37(3), 395–425.

Capability transfer in acquisitions 151

Brouthers, K., von Hastenburg, P., & van den Ven, J. (1998). If most mergers fail why are they so popular? *Long Range Planning, 31*(3), 347–353.

Bruton, G., Oviatt, B., & White, M. (1994). Performance of acquisitions of distressed firms. *Academy of Management Journal, 37*(4), 972–989.

Buysse, K., & Verbeke, A. (2003). Proactive environmental strategies: A stakeholder management perspective. *Strategic Management Journal, 24*(5), 453–470.

Capron, L. (1999). The long-term performance of horizontal acquisitions. *Strategic Management Journal, 20*(11), 987–1018.

Capron, L., & Hulland, J. (1999). Redeployment of brands, sales forces, and general marketing management expertise following horizontal acquisitions: A resource-based view. *Journal of Marketing, 63*(2), 41–54.

Capron, L., & Mitchell, W. (1998). Bilateral resource redeployment and capabilities improvement following horizontal acquisitions. *Industrial and Corporate Change, 7*(3), 453–484.

Capron, L., & Pistre, N. (2002). When do acquirers earn abnormal returns?. *Strategic Management Journal, 23*(9), 781–794.

Cassiman, B., & Veugelers, R. (2006). In search of complementarity in innovation strategy: Internal R&D and external knowledge acquisition. *Management Science, 52*(1), 68–82.

Christmann, P. (2000). Effects of "best practices" of environmental management on cost advantage: The role of complementary assets. *Academy of Management Journal, 43*(4), 663–680.

Cording, M., Christmann, P., & Weigelt, C. (2010). Measuring theoretically complex constructs: The case of acquisition performance'. *Strategic Organization, 8*(1), 11–41.

Diestre, L., & Rajagopalan, N. (2011). An environmental perspective on diversification: The effects of chemical relatedness and regulatory sanctions. *Academy of Management Journal, 54*(1), 97–115.

Dutta, S., Narasimhan, O., & Rajiv, S. (1999). Success in high-technology markets: Is marketing capability critical? *Marketing Science, 18*(4), 547–568.

Dutta, S., Narasimhan, O., & Rajiv, S. (2005). Conceptualizing and measuring capabilities: Methodology and empirical application. *Strategic Management Journal, 26*(3), 277–285.

Finkelstein, S., & Haleblian, J. (2002). Understanding acquisition performance: The role of transfer effects. *Organization Science, 13*(1), 36–47.

Flammer, C. (2013). Corporate social responsibility and shareholder reaction: The environmental awareness of investors. *Academy of Management Journal, 56*(3), 758–781.

Garrod, B., & Chadwick, P. (1996). Environmental management and business strategy: Towards a new strategic paradigm. *Futures, 28*(1), 37–50.

Ghoul, S., Guedhami, O., Kwok, C., & Mishra, D. (2011). Does corporate social responsibility affect the cost of capital? *Journal of Banking & Finance, 35*(9), 2388–2406.

Hamilton, J. (1995). Pollution as news: Media and stock market reactions to the toxics release inventory data. *Journal of Environmental Economics and Management, 28*(1), 98–113.

Hart, S. (1995). A natural-resource-based view of the firm. *Academy of Management Review, 20*(4), 986–1014.

152   *Pankaj C. Patel and David R. King*

Hart, S. (1997). Beyond greening: Strategies for a sustainable world. *Harvard Business Review, 75*(1), 66–76.

Hart, S., & Dowell, G. (2011). Invited editorial: A natural-resource-based view of the firm. *Journal of Management, 37*(5), 1464–1479.

Hitt, M., King, D., Krishnan, H., Makri, M., Schijven, M., Shimizu, K., & Zhu, H. (2009). Mergers and acquisitions: Overcoming pitfalls, building synergy and creating value. *Business Horizons, 52*(6), 523–529.

Hofer, C., Cantor, D., & Dai, J. (2012). The competitive determinants of a firm's environment management activities: Evidence from US manufacturing industries. *Journal of Operations Management, 30*(1–2), 69–84.

Jick, T. (1979). Mixing qualitative and quantitative methods: Triangulation in action. *Administrative Science Quarterly, 24*(4), 602–611.

Kang, S., & Snell, S. (2009). Intellectual capital architectures and ambidextrous learning: A framework for human resource management. *Journal of Management Studies, 46*(1), 65–92.

Kassinis, G., & Vafeas, N. (2002). Corporate boards and outside stakeholders as determinants of environmental litigation. *Strategic Management Journal, 23*(5), 399–415.

King, A., & Lenox, M. (2000). Industry self-regulation without sanctions: The chemical industry's responsible care program. *Academy of Management Journal, 43*(4), 698–716.

King A., & Lenox, M. (2002). Exploring the locus of profitable pollution reduction. *Management Science, 48*(2), 289–299.

King, D., Dalton, D., Daily, C., & Covin, J. (2004). Meta-analyses of post-acquisition performance: Indications of unidentified moderators. *Strategic Management Journal, 25*(2), 187–200.

King, D., Slotegraaf, R., & Kesner, I. (2008). Performance implications of firm resource interactions in the acquisition of R&D-intensive firms. *Organization Science, 19*(2), 327–340.

King, D., Wang, G., Samimi, M., & Cortes, F. (2021). A meta-analytic integration of acquisition performance prediction. *Journal of Management Studies, 58*(5), 1198–1236.

Klassen, R., & Whyback, D. (1999). The impact of environmental technologies on manufacturing performance. *Academy of Management Journal, 42*(6), 599–615.

Krug, J., & Shill, W. (2008). The big exit: Executive churn in the wake of M&As. *Journal of Business Strategy, 29*(4), 15–21.

Kumbhakar, S., & Lovell, C. (2000). *Stochastic frontier analysis*. Cambridge, UK: Cambridge University Press.

Laamanen, T. (2007). On the role of acquisition premium in acquisition research. *Strategic Management Journal, 28*(13), 1359–1369.

Leibenstein, H. (1966). Allocative efficiency vs. X-efficiency. *American Economic Review, 56*(3), 392–415.

Li, S., Shang, J., & Slaughter, S. (2010). Why do software firms fail? Capabilities, competitive actions, and firm survival in the software industry from 1995 to 2007. *Information Systems Research, 21*(3), 631–654.

Lockett, A., & Thompson, S. (2001). The resource-based view and economics. *Journal of Management, 27*(6), 723–754.

Mackey, A., Mackey, T., & Barney, J. (2007). Corporate social responsibility and firm performance: Investor preferences and corporate strategies. *Academy of Management Review, 32*(3), 817–835.

Martin, J., & Sayrak, A. (2003). Corporate diversification and shareholder value: A survey of recent literature. *Journal of Corporate Finance, 9*(1), 37–57.

McWilliams, A., Van Fleet, D., & Cory, K. (2002). Raising rivals' costs through political strategy: An extension of resource-based theory. *Journal of Management Studies, 39*(5), 707–724.

Miller, D. (2006). Technological diversity, related diversification, and firm performance. *Strategic Management Journal, 27*(7), 601–619.

Montgomery, C., & Hariharan, S. (1991). Diversified expansion by large established firms. *Journal of Economic Behavior and Organizations, 15*(1), 71–89.

Nameroff, T., Garant, R., & Albert, M. (2004). Adoption of green chemistry: An analysis based on US patents. *Research Policy, 33*(6–7), 969–974.

O'Brien, R. (2007). A caution regarding rules of thumb for variance inflation factors. *Quality & Quantity, 41*(5), 673–690.

Pagell, M., & Gobeli, D. (2009). How plant managers' experiences and attitudes toward sustainability relate to operational performance. *Production and Operations Management, 18*(3), 278–299.

Penrose, E. (1959). *The theory of the growth of the firm.* New York: John Wiley.

Peteraf, M., & Barney, J. (2003). Unraveling the resource-based tangle. *Managerial and Decision Economics, 24*(4), 309–323.

Podolny, J. (1993). A status-based model of market competition. *American Journal of Sociology, 98*(4), 829–872.

Porter, M., & van der Linde, C. (1995). Green and competitive. *Harvard Business Review, 73*(5), 120–134.

Puranam, P., Singh, H., & Zollo, M. (2006). Organizing for innovation: Managing the coordination-autonomy dilemma in technology acquisitions. *Academy of Management Journal, 49*(2), 263–280.

Ranft, A., Butler, F., & Sexton, J. (2011). A review of research progress in understanding the acquisition integration process: Building directions for future research. In Kellermanns, F., & Mazzola, P (Eds.), *Handbook of strategy research* (pp. 412–431). North Hampton, MA: Edward Elgar Publishing.

Reinhardt, F. (1999). Market failure and the environmental policies of firms. *Journal of Industrial Ecology, 3*(1), 9–134.

Rhodes-Kropf, M., & Robinson, D. (2008). The market for mergers and the boundaries of the firm. *Journal of Finance, 63*(3), 1169–1211.

Russo, M., & Fouts, P. (1997). A resource-based perspective on corporate environmental performance and profitability. *Academy of Management Journal, 40*(3), 534–559.

Sharma, S., & Vredenburg, H. (1998). Proactive corporate environmental strategy and the development of competitively valuable organizational capabilities. *Strategic Management Journal, 19*(8), 729–753.

Silverman, B. (1999). Technological resources and the direction of corporate diversification: Toward an integration of the resource-based view and transaction cost economics. *Management Science, 45*(8), 1109–1124.

Sirower, M. (1997). *The synergy trap: How companies lose the acquisition game.* New York: Free Press.

Srinivasan, R., & Mishra, B. (2007). Why do firms merge/acquire: An analysis of strategic intent in recent M&A activity among Indian firms. *IIMB Management Review, 19*, 388–402.

154 Pankaj C. Patel and David R. King

Stahl, G. K., & Voigt, A. (2008). Do cultural differences matter in mergers and acquisitions? A tentative model and examination. *Organization science*, 19(1), 160–176.

Starik, M., & Marcus, A. (2000). Introduction to the special research forum on the management of organizations in the natural environment: A field emerging from multiple paths, with many challenges ahead. *Academy of Management Journal*, 43(4), 539–546.

Starik, M., & Rands, G. (1995). Weaving an integrated web: Multilevel and multisystem perspectives of ecologically sustainable organizations. *Academy of Management Review*, 20(4), 908–935.

Toffel, M., & Marshall, J. (2004). Improving environmental performance assessment: A comparative analysis of weighting methods used to evaluate chemical release inventories. *Journal of Industrial Ecology*, 8(1–2), 143–172.

Tundo, P., Anastas, P., Black, D., Breen, J., Collins, T., Memoli, S., Miyamoto, J., Polyakoff, M., & Tumas, W. (2000). Synthetic pathways and processes in green chemistry. Introductory overview. *Pure and Applied Chemistry*, 72(7), 1207–1230.

Uhlenbruck, K., Hitt, M., & Semadeni, M. (2006). Market value effects of acquisitions involving internet firms: A resource-based analysis. *Strategic Management Journal*, 27(10), 899–913.

Vaccaro, I., Jansen, J., Van de Bosch, F., & Volberda, H. (2012). Management innovation and leadership: The moderating role of organizational size. *Journal of Management Studies*, 49(1), 28–51.

Zuckerman, E. (2004). Structural incoherence and stock market activity. *American Sociological Review*, 69(3), 405–432.

Appendix 6.1 Performance measures

Three-day CAR: Based on mainstream finance and economics literature, we use a standard event study methodology to measure cumulative abnormal return. Acquirer's predicted stock return is based on estimated daily returns from trading day t = −170 to ending day t = −21. Abnormal return is specified as:

$$r_t = \alpha + \beta rm_t + \varepsilon_t$$

where r_t is daily return on day t, and rm_t is the daily return for value-weighted Russell 3000, α is the intercept and β is firm-related risk parameter and ε_t is independent and identically distributed. As our data consist of a broad spectrum of publicly traded firms, we use Russell 3000 firms that is a comprehensive benchmark index that includes S&P 1500 firms. Using α and β we predict daily return, R_t on day t, or the day of the announcement, and subtract predicted return R_t from actual return r_t. The cumulative abnormal return is the sum of abnormal returns over the one-day window $(t-1)$ and two-day $(t+1)$, or $[-1, 1]$.

Return on Sales (ROS): We use three-year mean of return on sales for the 12-quarters following the acquisition announcement.

Buy and Hold Abnormal Return (BHAR): We calculate 36-month period BHAR using equation below:

$$BHAR_{iT} = \prod_{t=1}^{T}(1 + AR_{it}) - 1$$

Appendix 6.2 Compendium of patent statistics, OECD, 2006

The patent search strategy for environmental technology is built on a combination of IPC codes and search strings. It is divided into six major sub-areas, essentially end-of-pipe technologies, which partly also reflect integrated environmental technologies. For instance, improved engines with reduced energy consumption and reduced emissions of harmful chemicals are considered as integrated technologies. However, specific environmental characteristics are often not directly visible in patent applications.

- Waste disposal: A62D3 + {"exhaust", "effluent", "flue", "combustion", "waste"} & {"gas", "gases", "smoke", "air"}; [C02F,B01D53/(34,36)]; [B09B,B23G]; G21F9
- Recycling: {"waste", "refuse", "rubbish", "trash", "garbage", "scrap"} +[B03B7,B23D25/14,C10G1/10]; [A23J1/16,A23K1/(06,08,10),B02C18/(40,44),B02C19/14,B03B9/(04,06),B05B1/28,B05B15/04,B24B55/12,B27B33/20,B29B17,B30B9/32,B65D(65/46,81/36),B65H73,C04B7/(24,26,28),C04B11/26,C04B18,C05F(5/,7/,9/),C08J(11/,17/),C10L5/(46,48),C10G(19/08,17/10,21/28,25/12),C10M175,C11B13,C11D19,C12F3/(04,08),C12P7/08,(C12S3NOTC12S3/2*),C14C3/32,C22B(7/,19/28,19/30,25/06),C23F1/46,C23G1/36,C25F7/02,C25D21/(16,18,2*),D01C5,D01G11,D01F13,D06L1/10,D06B9/6,D21B1/08,D21B1/(10,32),D21C5/02,D21H(17/01,11/14),B65D90/(24,28,30),B67D5/378,C08L89/(04,06),F17D5/(04,06),G03C11/24
- Air cleaning technologies: [B03C3,A62D3,B01D(45,46,47,49,50,51,53)] + {"flue", "effluent", "exhaust", "combustion", "waste} & {"gas", "gases", "smoke", "air"}; [B01D53/(34,36),B24B55/(06,08,10)B28B17/04,B28D7/02,B25D17/(14,16,18),B65G69/18,C09K3/22,C10L10/02,D01H11,C21B7/22,C21C5/(38/40),E21F5,F01N3/(08,1*,2*,3*),F02M27/02,F23B5,F23C9/06,F27B1/18,F01N9]
- Water cleaning technologies: [B63B(29/16,35/32),B63J4,C09K3/32,C02F(1/,3/,7/,9/,11/),(E02B15 NOT E02B15/02),E03B3

156 *Pankaj C. Patel and David R. King*

- Noise protection: [B25D17/(11,12),E01F8,E03D9/14,(E04B1/8*
  NOT
  E04B1/80),E04B1/90,E04F15/20,E06B5/20,F01N(1/,7/02,7/
  04),F01B31/16,F02B77/13,F02C7/45,F02M35
  /(12,14),F42D5/055,G10K11/16,F16L55/
  033]&{"sound","noise"};[B60R13/08,B64F1/26,E01B19,E01C1,
  F02K1/(34,44),F42D5/05,F01p11/12,F02C7/(04,24),   F02K1/
  46,F16K47/02,F16L55/02] & {"absorb*",
  "reduc*", "abate*", "barrier", "prevent*", "deaden*", "dampen*,
  "anti"}; {"sound", "noise"} &{"absorb*", "reduc*", "abate*",
  "barrier", "prevent*", "deaden*", "dampen*, "anti"}; {"silencer"}
  NOTF01N; {"sound", "noise"} & {"absorb*", "reduc*", "abate*",
  "barrier", "prevent*", "deaden*","dampen*, "anti"} NOT[F41,G0
  1,H01,H02,H03,H04,H05]
- Environmental monitoring: G01N; {"toxi*","pollu*","contamin*"
  ,"monitor*"} &
  {"waters","water","air","airs","atmos*","soil","soils"};{"waters"
  ,"water","air","airs","atmos*","soil","soi
  ls"}&{"effluent","flue","exhaust","waste"};{"environment*"}&{"
  waters","water","air","airs","atmos*","
  soil","soils"};{"waters","water","air","airs","atmos*","soil","so
  ils"} & {"analys*","measure*"};(G01H
  NOT G01H1) & {"Noise"}; [G01N33/(18,24)];[G01T(1,7)] NOT
  [G01T1/(29,3*,40)]

For further details
International Patent Classification, 7th edition, 2000:
www.wipo.int/classifications/fulltext/new_ipc/index.htm;
Reformed IPC, 8th edition, 2006: www.wipo.int/classifications/ipc/ipc8.

7 Cross-border acquisition performance insights from predictive modeling

Camilla Jensen, Peter Zámborský, and David R. King

Introduction

Anyone traveling to another country has experienced the advantages and disadvantages of cultural distance, and associated complexity extends to CBA (Reus & Lamont, 2009). Acquisitions are an important strategic option for multinational firms (Aybar & Ficici, 2009; Cheng & Yang, 2017; Huang, Zhu, & Brass, 2017), and a growing body of research examines the impact of cultural distance on CBA performance. However, meta-analyses find inconclusive (Rottig, 2017; Stahl & Voigt, 2008) or negative impacts of cultural distance (Beugelsdijk, Kostova, Kunst, Spadafora, & van Essen, 2018), leaving what influences CBA performance unresolved. This may reflect that meta-analysis examining individual variable relationships (DV-IV) may represent too simplistic a view that provides evidence of moderating effects without testing them (Bergh et al., 2016; Lipsey & Wilson, 2001). Additionally, meta-analysis structural equation modeling depends on research reporting correlation matrixes for common measures in sufficient quantity (Jak, 2015; King, Wang, Samimi, & Cortes, 2021).

Cultural distance and CBA performance also represent umbrella constructs, or latent variables with multiple indicators (Beugelsdijk et al., 2018; Cording, Christmann, & Weigelt, 2010; Suddaby, 2010), resulting in fragmentation that restricts the application of meta-analytic structural equation modeling (Bergh et al., 2016). Meanwhile, predictive modeling can use small samples to identify the relative importance of variables and bridge content and statistical analysis (Shaikhina et al., 2019). Predictive modeling applies machine learning to find patterns in a dataset using a nonlinear set of binary decision rules (Breiman, Friedman, Stone, & Olshen, 1984). We apply predictive modeling as a relatively new option for aggregating research (Putka, Beatty, & Reeder, 2018; Tonidandel, King, & Cortina, 2018).

Our application of predictive modeling offers multiple contributions by aggregating research on CBA performance. By including reported effect sizes for cultural distance on CBA performance, we find an overall

DOI: 10.4324/9781003188308-10

158 *Camilla Jensen et al.*

positive effect of greater cultural distance on CBA performance. This is consistent with the benefits of CBA between culturally distant nations outweighing their costs (Vaara, Sarala, Stahl, & Björkman, 2012). Still, while confirming that cultural distance is important, including host and home country information provides further insight (Bauer, Schriber, Degischer, & King, 2018; He & Zhang, 2018; Marano, Arregle, Hitt, Spadafora, & van Essen, 2016), as competing explanatory variables of the effects of cultural distance on CBA performance exist (Kogut & Singh, 1988; Morosini, Shane, & Singh, 1998). Further, our prediction models suggest that home country effects of acquirers are potentially more important than those from a host country or cultural distance (He & Zhang, 2018; Marano et al., 2016; Zhu, Ma, Sauerwald, & Peng, 2019). Finally, our results suggest that CBA research methodological choices (e.g., sampling and controls) influence research results.

Theoretical background

There is an expectation that the benefits of cultural distance balance the costs, or firms would not continue to engage in CBA in culturally distant countries, but the study of variables that influence CBA performance has proliferated with limited theory building (Shimizu, Hitt, Vaidyanath, & Pisano, 2004). Still, scholars have examined the effects of cultural distance on CBA performance using multiple theories, such as organizational learning theory (Dikova & Sahib, 2013), resource-based view (Patel & King, 2016), transaction cost economics (Reuer, 2001), institutional theory (Bauer et al., 2018; Du & Boateng, 2015), and corporate governance (Chan & Emanuel, 2011). To a less extent, other perspectives, such as cultural friction (Popli, Akbar, Kumar, & Gaur, 2016; Schriber, King, & Bauer, 2018; Stahl & Voigt, 2008) and absorptive capacity (Park & Ghauri, 2011), have also been applied. Appendix 7.1 provides an overview of theories used in 59 studies on CBA performance and distance in our sample. The implication is that research on CBA performance reflects "theoretical endogeneity", or different perspectives fail to account for variables important to other frameworks (Busenbark, Krause, Boivie, & Graffin, 2016, p. 236).

By aggregating results, our review offers to identify important variables that can further theoretical development. For example, with the rise of acquisitions in and out of emerging markets, institutional theory is increasingly relevant in explaining CBA performance (Cho & Ahn, 2017). Additionally, it is important to distinguish between effects of home and host country's informal (cultural distance) and formal institutions and their interrelationships (Holmes, Miller, Hitt, & Salmador, 2013). However, there is limited research applying both cultural distance and formal institutions in studying CBA performance (Du & Boateng, 2015). In our sample, only 14 studies included host country effects, and only seven included home country effects with the effects of cultural distance in their analysis of CBA performance, (see Appendix 7.2). Still, it is important to distinguish between informal (cultural) and formal institutional distance (Gubbi, Aulakh, Ray, Sarkar, & Chittoor, 2010). For example, emerging markets have dynamic institutional settings (e.g., regulatory and legal environment) that differ from OECD countries (Verbeke, 2019).

Selection of research methods may also explain inconsistent research findings, as treating country differences as symmetric may contribute to inconsistency in research findings. For example, Nicholson and Salaber (2013) find that Indian (but not Chinese) acquirers are more likely to benefit from deals with less culturally distant countries as Indian bidders face relatively lower cultural disadvantages from its colonial heritage and widespread use of English. Additionally, Anglo-Saxon countries may have an inherent advantage for acquisitions from legal traditions, greater use of acquisitions, or advantages of English commonly being used as the language of business (Rao-Nicholson & Salaber, 2013; von Eije & Wiegerinck, 2010). Still, Rottig (2017) suggests that multinational firms are more successful when acquiring targets located in culturally distant emerging markets than in culturally distant developed markets. Meanwhile, research largely assumes that different forms of "distance" between two countries are the same, or it does not matter whether a firm in a country pair is an acquirer or a target (Weber, Tarba, & Reichel, 2009).

Method

We conducted an extensive search to identify relevant research published between 2000 and 2017. First, we used Google Scholar to search the keywords: 'cross-border acquisition performance' and 'performance' (all) with 'acquisition M&A merger' (one of) to identify articles. Second, we used a descendent search of the seminal articles by Stahl and Voigt (2008) and Kogut and Singh (1988). These two steps identified over 10,000 articles; however, most articles were either not empirical or they did not include the necessary statistical constructs for our analysis. Reviewing papers to identify needed information resulted in an initial sample of 81 articles, and information was coded from these papers. Following recommendations at least 20 percent of the coded papers were cross-checked amongst the author team (Gaur & Kumar, 2018). A final sample of coded papers consisted of 59 studies that include a quantifiable measure of CBA performance and at least one of the following explanatory factors of acquirer performance: acquisition experience, relatedness and/or cultural, administrative, geographic, and/or economic distance. The sample of events studied is 39,683 acquisitions, but individual studies likely use overlapping samples.

Study variables

Heterogeneity in measurement of constructs exists for our primary variables of interest. Summarized research used a variety of constructs to

160 Camilla Jensen et al.

measure CBA performance and for the Cultural Distance (CD) construct two samples (33 articles/33 observations, and 46 articles/93 observations) derived from the full sample of 59 coded articles. To avoid bias, we adopt the particular CBA performance and cultural distance constructs used in each study as control variables when building our prediction models.

Analysis

There are multiple approaches to aggregating research (Feld & Heckemeyer, 2011). We gathered data for the Z-score of Y (sample 1 with 33 studies and observations) and both T-stat (sample 2 with 46 studies and 93 observations) (see Table 7.1). This enabled a comparison of a traditional linear Z-score approach and T-stat approach using predictive modeling, as standardization methods used in the Z-score approach can result in errors (Cummings, 2011). Predictive algorithms complement traditional methods of synthesizing research, because predictive algorithms allow for a wider use of classification models such as decision trees (Tonidandel et al., 2018). While decision tree models

Table 7.1 Constructs underlying study variables

	Sample 1	Sample 2
	33 articles/33 obs.	*46 articles/93 obs.*
Performance variables		
Cumulative abnormal return (CAR)	8	40
Manager's self-assessment (survey)	4	3
Tobin's Q	3	5
BHAR (Jensen's Alpha)	2	9
Innovativeness (patents)	2	2
ROA	1	4
Other	13	28
Total	33	93
Cultural distance (CD) variables		
Globe	15	19
Kogut & Singh	10	11
Hofstede	3	39
World Value Survey	2	5
Linguistic distance	2	5
Shared cultural characteristics	1	10
Country of origin	–	3
Acculturation index	–	1
Total	33	93

Note: Sample 1 includes all studies that included pairs of observations on the Z-score and a CD construct but without repeating any single paper in the sample (e.g. without replacement), sample 2 includes all studies with paring acquisitions with a CD construct, but with replacement. Replacement in sample 1 would involve repetition of the same dependent variable in the sample, whereas this is not the case in sample 2 because every pair of observations creates a unique dependent variable (i.e. T-stat).

Cross-border acquisition performance insights 161

Table 7.2 Transforming the effect size (T-stat for cultural distance) into a categorical variable

Group	Sign of T-stat	Significance of T-stat	Frequency in our Sample 2
1 – NI	Negative	Insignificant	16
2 – NS	Negative	Significant	21
3 – PI	Positive	Insignificant	31
4 – PS	Positive	Significant	25

Note: PS stands for positive and significant, PI for positive and insignificant, NI for negative and insignificant, and NS for negative and significant. The cutting point for the T-stat being significant is set at +/–1.5 which has a p-value of 0.1 for all samples and 0.05 for most samples.

are computationally complex, interpretation is possible with a limited number of variables (James, Witten, Hastie, & Tibshirani, 2013; Liaw & Wiener, 2002; Viechtbauer, 2010).

Using a T-stat-based measure with decision tree prediction required converting the continuous variable of the T-stat into a categorical variable for several reasons. First, converting our continuous T-stat measure into a categorical variable avoided the problem of outliers to improve modeling validity and decision tree classification. Second, the T-stat measure has the advantage of having the same sign as the original beta. Finally, whether the T-stat is significant or not is another yardstick that can categorize results, and we place each study into the four groups (see Table 7.2). More studies reported a positive effect size (59 percent), but roughly half (47 of the 93 T-stats) of the sampled effect sizes are insignificant.

Results

Sample 1: Z-scores as dependent variable in linear prediction model

We report results for sample 1 using Z-scores in Table 7.3. Model 1 includes controls for the type of data used in each study (i.e., archival or survey), and the measurement of constructs. In selecting additional control factors, we are constrained by the small number of observations (33) available. Model 2 adds information about the host and home countries involved for each research study with country of origin (home country) as our main variable of interest. Acquirers from specific home countries may be more or less likely to be successful at integrating a target for reasons other than cultural distance. In Model 3, we re-estimated the model without the CD construct.

In Model 1, CD has a lower importance score and an average negative impact on CBA performance. Additionally, it was not significant when testing different partitions for the training and testing datasets (not shown). In Model 1, the results suggest that the use of survey or archival data was the most predictive factor of the results in the underlying

162 Camilla Jensen et al.

Table 7.3 Linear prediction modeling results with CBA performance using Z-scores

Covariates:	Model 1	Model 2	Model 3
Cultural distance (IV Z-score)	−0.235	−0.353	−
	(0.231)	(0.373)	
Data = Survey	2.085**	3.333*	2.687**
	(0.760)	(1.488)	(0.976)
DV = Cumulative abnormal returns (CAR)	−0.071	−1.142	−0.057
	(0.774)	(2.959)	(0.845)
DV = Innovativeness	−0.196	−1.187	0.156
	(1.236)	(3.130)	(1.195)
DV = Manager's self-assessment	1.721	0.076	0.171
	(1.187)	(1.495)	(1.380)
DV = Other	1.177	−0.176	1.173
	(0.962)	(3.316)	(0.845)
CD = Hofstede	0.163	−1.029	−
	(0.769)	(3.110)	
CD = Kogut and Singh	0.381	−0.171	−
	(0.515)	(0.914)	
Home = Emerging markets	0.759	−0.118	
		(4.088)	(0.845)
Home = Europe		−2.288	−1.588
		(0.970)	(0.845)
Home = Global		−0.147	−0.108
		(1.222)	(0.690)
Home = OECD		1.488	2.310*
		(2.037)	(0.976)
Host = Global		1.458	0.871
		(1.840)	(0.975)
Host = OECD		NA	0.508
Adjusted R²	0.77	0.85	0.85
Sample 1	33	33	33
Train/test partition	50/50	50/50	50/50

* is p < .05. ** is p < .01.

studies with survey data displaying a positive and significant relationship with CBA performance. In Model 2, we added information about host and home countries. If a country-of-origin effect influences CBA performance, then the influence of home country would provide more explanatory power than CD.

The influence of cultural distance from the inclusion of the home and host country variables is minimal for the reported results for Model 2. However, our results were not stable across different partitions and seeds, and results suggest some randomness on the sign of CD after host and home countries are included as controls. The use of survey data is the only factor that comes out as consistently important with the same sign, size, and significance across different partitions and seeds. This finding

Cross-border acquisition performance insights   163

is consistent with other organizational research (Junni, Sarala, Taras, & Tarba, 2013), and it is consistent with potential concerns with common method bias (Podsakoff & Organ, 1986). Additionally, home country of Europe is negative and close to being partially significant (p < 0.12). This suggests there is some country-of-origin effect with acquirers from Europe more likely to experience lower CBA performance.

Model 3 excludes the CD construct, allowing comparison of the relative performance of the model, when keeping the information about host and home countries. Excluding cultural distance has a limited impact on overall explanatory power of the model (R^2). There is an important, positive and significant influence of the country of origin being the OECD on CBA performance when CD is excluded, but a negative impact for "acquirer from Europe". This result is consistent with the findings of von Eije and Wiegenrinck (2010), who find that private acquisitions by European firms from civil law legal systems generate smaller bidder returns, while private acquisitions by common law firms from the UK and Ireland increase such returns for acquisitions in the US. In considering cultural distance, home country effects may be stronger than host country effects for CBA (Marano et al., 2016).

Sample 2: Categorical T-stat as dependent variable, predictive model

A nonlinear classifier approach demonstrates the full advantages of using prediction modeling to aggregate research results. The initial exploratory model rendered a maximum accuracy (model explanatory power) of around 32 percent and it used 20 variables. The three most important variables were all related to methodological factors of sample balance (n/p, sample size divided by the number of controls), number of controls (p), and sample size (n). Home and host country factors were moderately important with Home = Anglo-Saxon countries ranked tenth in importance.

We next applied machine learning to render a better model using the classification shown in Table 7.2 with home and host country. We used recursive feature elimination to select the most important features or predictors of the effect size. We asked the machine learning algorithm to identify the optimal model by implementing a ten-fold cross-validation repeated five times that is sufficient for our modest sample size. Using our total sample of 93 observations (with 48 observations for training and 45 observations for testing in the reported results), we are able to generate a stable model, suggesting robustness and external validity (e.g., the model applies to samples outside the data used to generate the model). Figure 7.1 reports a representative decision tree.[1]

---

1 While the importance plot is stable for different partitions and seeds, the representative decision trees that we are able to draw may vary across seeds, or the first paper classified by the algorithm. Therefore, we went through all possible seeds and drew a 'representative' decision trees (48 x 500 = 24,000 trees) to derive the partial influence of the predictors upon the relationship between CBA performance and cultural distance, see Figure 7.1.

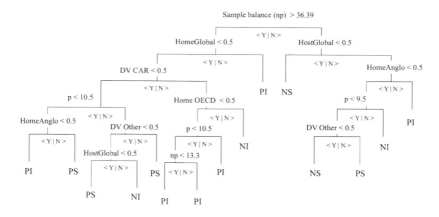

Figure 7.1 Representative decision tree resulting from predictive modeling.

Note: The interpretation of the tree is that the right daughter node statement is false, and the left daughter is true. For example, at the first node, we split the sample in papers with a sample balance above the number 36.39 (papers that had more than 36 observations per predictor) on the right daughter and below the number (papers that had less than 36 observations per predictor) on the left daughter.

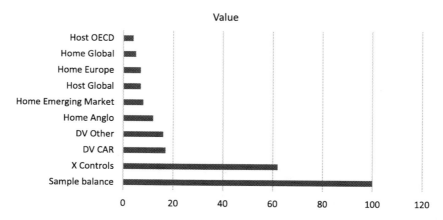

Figure 7.2 Variable importance plot for categorical T-statistic predictive model.

We also report variables using an importance plot (see Figure 7.2) where variable importance score is calculated as the sum of the decrease in the prediction error when that particular variable is used in the sample splitting exercise. The relative importance is then the variable importance divided by the highest variable importance value, so that all values are bounded between 0 and 1 (see Louppe and colleagues, 2013). A resulting importance plot allows us to systematically summarize the findings of our nonlinear predictive modeling. The most important factor across the papers were study factors such as sample size and number of control factors. Specifically, the most salient predictor is *sample balancing*, or the number of observations n relative to the number of predictors p. We observe that smaller samples are more likely to find significant results. For example, studies with a sample balance below 36 (e.g., 36 observations per predictor) are associated with significant results and a sample balance above 36 findings was more likely to result in an insignificant T-stat for the CD variable. This suggests that significant research can result from the sampling error from studies with a smaller sample balance being less heterogenous (Murphy and Myors, 2004). Additionally, we find that studies including several control factors (to account for heterogeneity in large samples with diverse countries), but not too many in view to sample balance (excessive control factors in small samples worsen the problems associated with multicollinearity) were more likely to generate significant results.

The second set of factors concern the dependent variables used in the sampled papers. Here we find that papers using CAR as a dependent variable were more likely to give insignificant results, and that studies using survey were more likely to find significant results. This result is similar to our results using Z-scores and a linear model. Also consistent with our linear model, Home = Anglo-Saxon was identified as the most important predictor among the home country variables, and we find there is an 'average' result that is positive for an Anglo-Saxon home country. A potential explanation is that a strong positive effect from the purely Anglo-Saxon samples may reflect that more heterogeneous global samples are less likely to identify significant results. However, our earlier results using a linear model found that there was a negative home country effect from European acquirers (excluding the UK), but there was a positive home country effect from OECD acquirers. This comparative evidence suggests that the Anglo-Saxon home country effect is real rather than a reflection of sampling.

Overall, we believe that our study has predictive and significant results. If studies are carefully sampled, controlled, and crafted our results suggest that cultural distance has a positive and significant effect on CBA performance. However, some home country acquirers may have advantages due to historical and institutional factors including culture, experience, and language. Further, home country effects may dominate cultural distance in predicting CBA performance. As a result, future research needs to include sufficient control variables such as fixed effects for different host and home countries.

Discussion

Predicting performance effects of acquisitions represents an area of continued study (Das & Kapil, 2012), and our comparison of linear and predictive modeling reviews the usefulness of cultural distance in

166 *Camilla Jensen et al.*

comparison to country effects in predicting CBA performance. While the linear predictive model shows a positive impact of cultural distance on CBA performance, nonlinear predictive modeling (decision tree) identifies this may depend on home and host country effects. With the caveat that CBA performance research often relies on limited samples of home and host countries to examine the impact of cultural distance, our analysis suggests that home country effects (vs. cultural distance) may have a dominant effect on CBA performance. This offers an alternate explanation for observed differences for cultural distance. Additional research implications, and limitations and opportunities for future research are discussed next.

Research implications

Our results validate a renewed interest in applying institutional theory to examine CBA performance (Bauer et al., 2018; Bhaumik, Owolabi, & Pal, 2018; Levine, Lin, & Shen, 2020). For example, regulatory history has proven relevant, especially during the golden age of globalization from 1985 to 2008, when national mergers experienced greater regulation than CBA (Buch & DeLong, 2004; Clougherty, 2005). Another reason formal institutional differences matter relates to continuing asymmetries in the regulatory practices of developed and emerging economies (Bauer et al., 2018; Karolyi & Taboada, 2015). The differential impact of institutional differences still needs further development, as until recently research simply assumed that the distance between two countries is the same in both directions (Hernández & Nieto, 2015; Weber et al., 2009). However, it may be more difficult for one country to acquire in another due to institutional differences. For example, a developed economy will be more likely to have available infrastructure to complete a deal, including legal frameworks and banking institutions. As a result, formal institutions are increasingly important in explaining CBA performance, with specific aspects such as labor market flexibility and efficiency (Bauer et al., 2018), economic freedom (Liou & Rao-Nicholson, 2019), intellectual property rights (Zhu & Qian, 2015), and shareholder orientation (Zhu et al., 2019).

Relatedly, acquisitions by developed Anglo-Saxon countries appear to experience higher performance. This has different possible interpretations. On one hand, Anglo-Saxon acquirers may have an advantage from an institutional foundation based on common law (von Eije & Wiegenrinck, 2010), a longer history of using acquisitions, or cultural differences. On the other hand, it may reflect an artifact of research. For example, acquisition research is biased to a North American (Meglio & Risberg, 2010) or an Anglo-Saxon context that may mask other factors of home country factors such as language (Kedia & Reddy, 2016). Additional research is needed to confirm an Anglo-Saxon advantage for CBA performance and to determine whether it results from institutional or cultural differences.

Still, our analysis reinforces limitations and criticism of cultural distance in general (Beugelsdijk et al., 2018; Hutzschenreuter, Kleindienst, & Lange, 2016; Konara & Mohr, 2019), and its use in CBA research specifically. In our review, cultural distance is included in 46 out of 59 papers, while administrative distance is used by 24 papers, geographic distance by nine papers, and economic distance in six papers (Ghemawat, 2001). Harzing and Pudelko (2016, p. 7) identified that only 7 out of 92 studies included both multiple home and multiple host countries. Our sample shows some improvement with 19 of 59 studies including multiple home and host countries. In our analysis, the impact of acquirer home nation appears to dominate the impact of host country characteristics. This suggests that acquirer country conditions provide important context for CBA. This finding is consistent with institutional theory (Gregory and Stuart, 2004; North, 1990) that has begun to be applied to CBA research (Bauer et al., 2018; He & Zhang, 2018; Levine et al., 2020). While our results are not definitive, they suggest future research needs to include multiple home and host countries, and to include formal institutional country factors along with cultural distance.

Our findings also show an impact of other methodological choices. Specifically, results were more significant for survey than archival research, suggesting cross-sectional survey designs are either susceptible to common method bias (Podsakoff & Organ, 1986), or they are better designed to focus on variables of interest. Junni and colleagues (2013) also observe higher significance of survey research in a meta-analysis of organizational ambidexterity, and they conclude that observed relationships may be too complex for archival measures alone. As a result, CBA performance research can benefit from using multiple methods and measures. There is also a need for better controls to avoid model misspecification that can bias results (Busenbark et al., 2016; King, Dalton, Daily, & Covin, 2004).

Managerial implications

Beyond questions about differences in CBA performance, there remain questions on how to manage them (Teerikangas & Very, 2006), and how home and host country institutions affect post-merger integration (Bauer et al., 2018; Kwok, Meschi, & Bertrand, 2020). Our findings suggest a greater effect of an acquirer's home country in CBA. However, this may be skewed by research focusing on developed nation acquisitions. Still, a positive impact of Anglo-Saxon acquirers suggests that either greater institutional development, settings with greater acquisition experience, or a common law tradition facilitates acquisitions and their subsequent performance. Research currently offers limited insights for managing CBA, and managers need to approach them with suitable caution and planning to consider country-level differences and the human side of CBA (Sarala, Vaara, & Junni, 2019) such as CEO motivations and biases (Lewellyn, 2018).

168 *Camilla Jensen et al.*

Limitations and future research

Like all research projects, trade-offs in our research design led to limitations that provide opportunities for future research. Primarily, we compare predictive modeling on a very specific setting (CBA) and relationships (e.g., cultural distance and performance). While this enabled examination of an important question where research exists in adequate quantities to aggregate, as well as conflicting findings with the potential alternate explanations, our observed differences between linear and nonlinear predictive modeling may not hold in other settings. Still, we demonstrate that predictive modeling enables considering effects not traditionally captured by meta-analysis that can offer different interpretations of available research than meta-analysis alone. For example, we find country effects have explanatory power that are stronger for home country than host country. Still, this observation rests on a limited sample of home and host country pairings and studies using multiple countries in the same dataset. As a result, the impact of home and host countries requires additional research to build evidence for a more heterogeneous composition of studies to aggregate results. This reinforces a prior call for "moving beyond the home country reference point" in research on cultural distance (Hutzschenreuter et al., 2016, p. 172). Further, future research needs to include control for both formal institutional and cultural distance to enable direct comparison of the variance they can explain in CBA research. In closing, our results underscore the importance of CBA performance research, and more broadly the use of multiple methods and measures to establish knowledge and to synthesize and aggregate research findings.

References

Aybar, B., & Ficici, A. (2009). Cross-border acquisitions and firm value: An analysis of emerging-market multinationals. *Journal of International Business Studies, 40*(8), 1317–1338.

Basuil, D., & Datta, D. (2015). Effects of industry-and region-specific acquisition experience on value creation in cross-border acquisitions: The moderating role of cultural similarity. *Journal of Management Studies, 52*(6), 766–795.

Bauer, F., Schriber, S., Degischer, D., & King, D. (2018). Contextualizing speed and cross-border acquisition performance: Labor market flexibility and efficiency effects. *Journal of World Business, 53*(2), 290–301.

Bergh, D., Aguinis, H., Heavey, C., Ketchen, D., Boyd, B., Su, P., Lau, C., & Joo, H (2016). Using meta-analytic structural equation modeling to advance strategic management research: Guidelines and an empirical illustration via the strategic leadership-performance relationship. *Strategic Management Journal, 37*(3), 477–497.

Beugelsdijk, S., Kostova, T., Kunst, V., Spadafora, E., & van Essen, M. (2018). Cultural distance and firm internationalization: A meta-analytical review and theoretical implications. *Journal of Management, 44*(1), 89–130.

Cross-border acquisition performance insights 169

Bhagat, S., Malhotra, S., & Zhu, P. (2011). Emerging country cross-border acquisitions: Characteristics, acquirer returns and cross-sectional determinants. Emerging *Markets Review, 12*(3), 250–271.

Bhaumik, S., Owolabi, O., & Pal, S. (2018). "Private information, institutional distance, and the failure of cross-border acquisitions: Evidence from the banking sector in Central and Eastern Europe". *Journal of World Business, 53*(4), 504–513.

Breiman, L., Friedman, J., Stone, C., & Olshen, R. (1984). *Classification and regression trees.* Boca Raton, FL: CRC press.

Buch, C., & DeLong, G. (2004). Cross-border bank mergers: What lures the rare animal? *Journal of Banking & Finance, 28*(9), 2077–2102.

Busenbark, J., Krause, R., Boivie, S., & Graffin, S. (2016). Toward a configurational perspective on the CEO: A review and synthesis of the management literature. *Journal of Management, 42*(1), 234–268.

Chakrabarti, R., Gupta-Mukherjee, S., & Jayaraman, N. (2009). Mars–Venus marriages: Culture and cross-border M&A. *Journal of International Business Studies, 40*(2), 216–236.

Chan, W., & Emanuel, D. (2011). Board governance and acquirers' returns: A study of Australian acquisitions. *Australian Journal of Management, 36*(2), 174–199.

Cheng, C., & Yang, M. (2017). Enhancing performance of cross-border mergers and acquisitions in developed markets: The role of business ties and technological innovation capability. *Journal of Business Research, 81*, 107–117.

Cho, H., & Ahn, H. (2017). Stock payment and the effects of institutional and cultural differences: A study of shareholder value creation in cross-border M&As. *International Business Review, 26*(3), 461–475.

Cloodt, M., Hagedoorn, J., & Van Kranenburg, H. (2006). Mergers and acquisitions: Their effect on the innovative performance of companies in high-tech industries. *Research Policy, 35*(5), 642–654.

Clougherty, J. (2005). Antitrust holdup source, cross-national institutional variation, and corporate political strategy implications for domestic mergers in a global context. *Strategic Management Journal, 26*(8), 769–790.

Cording, M., Christmann, P., & Weigelt, C. (2010). Measuring theoretically complex constructs: The case of acquisition performance. *Strategic Organization, 8*(1), 11–41.

Cummings, P. (2011). Arguments for and against standardised mean differences (effect sizes). Archives of Pediatrics *& Adolescent Medicine, 165*(7), 592–596.

Das, A., & Kapil, S. (2012). Explaining M&A performance: A review of empirical research. *Journal of Strategy and Management, 5*(3), 284–330.

Dikova, D., & Sahib, P. (2013). Is cultural distance a bane or a boon for cross-border acquisition performance? *Journal of World Business, 48*(1), 77–86.

Du, M., & Boateng, A. (2015). State ownership, institutional effects and value creation in cross-border mergers & acquisitions by Chinese firms. *International Business Review, 24*(3), 430–442.

Feld, L., & Heckemeyer, J. (2011). FDI and taxation: A meta-study. *Journal of Economic Surveys, 25*(2), 233–272.

Gaur, A., & Kumar, M. (2018). A systematic approach to conducting review studies: An assessment of content analysis in 25 years of IB research. *Journal of World Business, 53*(2), 280–289.

Ghemawat, P. (2001). Distance still matters. *Harvard Business Review, 79*(8), 137–147.

Gregory, P., & Stuart, R. (2004). *Comparing economic systems in the twenty-first century.* New York: Houghton Mifflin.

Gubbi, S., Aulakh, P., Ray, S., Sarkar, M., & Chittoor, R. (2010). Do international acquisitions by emerging-economy firms create shareholder value? The case of Indian firms. *Journal of International Business Studies, 41*(3), 397–418.

Harzing, A., & Pudelko, M. (2016). Do we need to distance ourselves from the distance concept? Home and host country context might matter more than (cultural) distance. *Management International Review, 56*(1), 1–34.

He, X., & Zhang, J. (2018). Emerging market MNCs' cross-border acquisition completion: Institutional image and strategies. *Journal of Business Research, 93*, 139–150.

Hernández, V., & Nieto, M. (2015). The effect of the magnitude and direction of institutional distance on the choice of international entry modes. *Journal of World Business, 50*(1), 122–132.

Holmes Jr, R., Miller, T., Hitt, M., & Salmador, M. (2013). "The interrelationships among informal institutions, formal institutions, and inward foreign direct investment". *Journal of Management, 39*(2), 531–566.

Huang, Z., Zhu, H., & Brass, D. (2017). Cross-border acquisitions and the asymmetric effect of power distance value difference on long-term post-acquisition performance. *Strategic Management Journal, 38*(4), 972–991.

Hutzschenreuter, T., Kleindienst, I., & Lange, S. (2016). The concept of distance in international business research: A review and research agenda. *International Journal of Management Reviews, 18*(2), 160–179.

Jak, S. (2015). *Meta-analytic structural equation modelling.* Dordrecht, NL: Springer.

James, G., Witten, D., Hastie, T., & Tibshirani, R. (2013). *An introduction to statistical learning.* New York: Springer.

Junni, P., Sarala, R., Taras, V., & Tarba, S. (2013). Organizational ambidexterity and performance: A meta-analysis. *Academy of Management Perspectives, 27*(4), 299–312.

Karolyi, G., & Taboada, A. (2015). Regulatory arbitrage and cross-border bank acquisitions. *Journal of Finance, 70*(6), 2395–2450.

Kedia, B., & Reddy, R. (2016). Language and cross-border acquisitions: An exploratory study. *International Business Review, 25*(6), 1321–1332.

King, D., Dalton, D., Daily, C., & Covin, J. (2004). Meta-analyses of post-acquisition performance: Indications of unidentified moderators. *Strategic Management Journal, 25*(2), 187–200.

King, D., Wang, G., Samimi, M., & Cortes, A. (2021). A meta-analytic integration of acquisition performance prediction. *Journal of Management Studies, 58*(5), 1198–1236.

Kogut, B., & Singh, H. (1988). The effect of national culture on the choice of entry mode. *Journal of International Business Studies, 19*(3), 411–432.

Konara, P., & Mohr, A. (2019). Why we should stop using the Kogut and Singh index. *Management International Review, 59*(3), 1–20.

Kwok, D., Meschi, P., & Bertrand, O. (2020). In CEOs we trust: When religion matters in cross-border acquisitions. The case of a multifaith country. *International Business Review, 29*(4), 912.

Lewellyn, K. (2018). Gold for now and the golden years. *Journal of Strategy and Management*, *11*(3), 306–327.

Levine, R., Lin, C., & Shen, B. (2020). Cross-border acquisitions: Do labor regulations affect acquirer returns. *Journal of International Business Studies*, *51*(2), 194–217.

Liaw, A., & Wiener, M. (2002). Classification and regression by randomForest. *R News*, *2*(3), 18–22.

Liou, R., & Rao-Nicholson, R. (2019). Age matters: The contingency of economic distance and economic freedom in emerging market firm's cross-border M&A performance. *Management International Review*, *59*(3), 355–386.

Lipsey, M., & Wilson, D. (2001). *Practical meta-analysis*. Thousand Oaks, CA: Sage.

Louppe, G., Wehenkel, L., Sutera, A., & Geurts, P. (2013). Understanding variable importances in forests of randomized trees. In *Advances in neural information processing systems* (pp. 431–439). Bingley: Emerald.

Marano, V., Arregle, J., Hitt, M., Spadafora, E., & van Essen, M. (2016). Home country institutions and the internationalization-performance relationship: A meta-analytic review. *Journal of Management*, *42*(5), 1075–1110.

Meglio, O., & Risberg, A. (2010). Mergers and acquisitions—Time for a methodological rejuvenation of the field? *Scandinavian Journal of Management*, *26*(1), 87–95.

Morosini, P., Shane, S., & Singh, H. (1998). National cultural distance and cross-border acquisition performance. *Journal of International Business Studies*, *29*(1), 137–158.

Murphy, K., & Myors, B. (2004). *Statistical power analysis: A simple and general model for traditional and modern hypothesis tests* (2nd ed.). London: Lawrence Erlbaum Associates.

Nicholson, R., & Salaber, J. (2013). The motives and performance of cross-border acquirers from emerging economies: Comparison between Chinese and Indian firms. *International Business Review*, *22*(6), 963–980.

North, D. (1990). *Institutions, institutional change, and economic performance*. New York: Norton.

Nowiński, W. (2017). International acquisitions by Polish MNEs. Value creation or destruction?. *European Business Review*, *29*(2), 205–218.

Park, B., & Ghauri, P. (2011). Key factors affecting acquisition of technological capabilities from foreign acquiring firms by small and medium sized local firms. *Journal of World Business*, *46*(1), 116–125.

Patel, P., & King, D. (2016). Interaction of cultural and technological distance in cross-border, high-technology acquisitions. In Finkelstein, S., and Cooper, C. (eds.) *Advances in mergers and acquisitions* (Vol. 15, pp. 115–144). Bingley: Emerald Group Publishing.

Podsakoff, P., & Organ, D. (1986). Self-reports in organizational research: Problems and prospects. *Journal of Management*, *12*(4), 531–544.

Popli, M., Akbar, M., Kumar, V., & Gaur, A. (2016). Reconceptualizing cultural distance: The role of cultural experience reserve in cross-border acquisitions. *Journal of World Business*, *51*(3), 404–412.

Putka, D., Beatty, A., & Reeder, M. (2018). Modern prediction methods: New perspectives on a common problem. *Organizational Research Methods*, *21*(3), 689–732.

172 *Camilla Jensen et al.*

Reuer, J. (2001). From hybrids to hierarchies: Shareholder wealth effects of joint venture partner buyouts. *Strategic Management Journal, 22*(1), 27–44.

Reus, T., & Lamont, B. (2009). The double-edged sword of cultural distance in international acquisitions. *Journal of International Business Studies, 40*(8), 1298–1316.

Rottig, D. (2017). Meta-analyses of culture's consequences for acquisition performance: An examination of statistical artifacts, methodological moderators and the context of emerging markets. *International Journal of Emerging Markets, 12*(1), 8–37.

Sarala, R., Vaara, E., & Junni, P. (2019). Beyond merger syndrome and cultural differences: New avenues for research on the "human side" of global mergers and acquisitions (M&As). *Journal of World Business, 54*(4), 307–321.

Schriber, S., King, D., & Bauer, F. (2018). Acquisition integration flexibility: Toward a conceptual framework. *Journal of Strategy and Management, 11*(4), 759–796.

Shaikhina, T., Lowe, D., Daga, S., Briggs, D., Higgins, R., & Khovanova, N. (2019). Decision tree and random forest models for outcome prediction in antibody incompatible kidney transplantation. *Biomedical Signal Processing and Control, 52*, 456–462.

Shimizu, K., Hitt, M.A., Vaidyanath, D., & Pisano, V. (2004). Theoretical foundations of cross- border mergers and acquisitions: A review of current research and recommendations for the future. *Journal of International Management, 10*(3), 307–353.

Simonsson, M., & Holm, C. (2011). *Cultural distance and cross-border M&A's- An event study on the announcement effect of Swedish cross-border M&A's between 1996–2009* (Master's thesis). Lund, Sweden: Lund University.

Stahl, G., & Voigt, A. (2008). Do cultural differences matter in mergers and acquisitions? A tentative model and examination. *Organization Science, 19*(1), 160–176.

Steigner, T., & Sutton, N. (2011). How does national culture impact internalization benefits in cross-border mergers and acquisitions? *Financial Review, 46*(1), 103–125.

Steigner, T., & Sutton, N. (2015). Worth waiting for–evidence of late-mover benefits in cross-border mergers and acquisitions. *Quarterly Journal of Finance & Accounting, 53*(3), 113–146.

Suddaby, R. (2010). Editor's comments: Construct clarity in theories of management and organization. *Academy of Management Review, 35*(3), 346–357.

Teerikangas, S., & Very, P. (2006). The culture–performance relationship in M&A: From yes/no to how. *British Journal of Management, 17*(S1), S31–S48.

Tonidandel, S., King, E., & Cortina, J. (2018). Big data methods: Leveraging modern data analytic techniques to build organizational science. *Organizational Research Methods, 21*(3), 525–547.

Uhlenbruck, K., & Castro, J. (2000). Foreign acquisitions in Central and Eastern Europe: Outcomes of privatization in transitional economies. *Academy of Management Journal, 43*(3), 381–402.

Vaara, E., Sarala, R., Stahl, G., & Björkman, I. (2012). The impact of organizational and national cultural differences on social conflict and knowledge transfer in international acquisitions. *Journal of Management Studies, 49*(1), 1–27.

Verbeke, A. (2019). The JIBS 2018 decade award: Comparing capitalisms: Understanding institutional diversity and its implications for international business. *Journal of International Business Studies*, 50(1), 1–3.

Viechtbauer, W. (2010). Conducting meta-analyses in R with the metafor package. *Journal of Statistical Software*, 36(3), 1–48.

von Eije, H., & Wiegerinck, H. (2010). Shareholders' reactions to announcements of acquisitions of private firms: Do target and bidder markets make a difference? *International Business Review*, 19(4), 360–377.

Weber, Y., Tarba, S., & Reichel, A. (2009). International mergers and acquisitions performance revisited–The role of cultural distance and post. In Finkelstein, S., and Cooper, C. (eds.) *Advances in mergers and acquisitions* (pp. 1–17). Bingley: Emerald Group Publishing.

Zhu, H. (2012). *Institutions and cross-border mergers and acquisitions (M&A) value creation* (Doctoral dissertation). College Station, TX: Texas A&M University.

Zhu, H., & Qian, G. (2015). High-tech firms' international acquisition performance: The influence of host country property rights protection. *International Business Review*, 24(4), 556–566.

Zhu, H., Ma, X., Sauerwald, S., & Peng, M. (2019). Home country institutions behind cross-border acquisition performance. *Journal of Management*, 45(4), 1315–1342.

Appendix 7.1 Overview of the 59 reviewed studies by home country and main theoretical perspective

Home/theory	Org. learning	Eclectic (empirical)	RBV	Institutional	TCE	Governance	Other	TOTAL
Global	6	3	2	1	2	1	2	17
US	6	2	3	0	1	0	3	15
UK	2	0	0	0	0	0	1	3
Australia	0	0	0	0	0	1	0	1
Anglo	8	2	3	0	1	1	4	19
EU15	0	1	0	0	0	0	0	1
Finland	4	0	0	0	0	0	0	4
Sweden	0	1	0	0	0	0	0	1
Netherlands	1	1	0	0	0	0	0	2
Europe	5	3	0	0	0	0	0	8
OECD	0	2	2	0	0	0	0	4
OECD	13	7	5	0	1	1	4	31
Poland	0	1	0	0	0	0	0	1
China	1	1	1	1	0	0	0	4
India	0	2	0	0	0	0	0	2
South Africa	0	0	0	1	0	0	0	1
Lat. America	0	1	0	0	0	0	0	1
Emerg. Mkts	0	1	0	0	0	1	0	2
EMs	1	6	1	2	0	1	0	11
TOTAL	20	16	8	3	3	3	6	59

Note: The rows in bold were used as categories in our analysis of home country effects. The category of Anglo (Anglo-Saxon countries—the sum of US, UK, and Australia) was created by us and not used in this form in any of the 59 studies. Eclectic implies an atheoretical, empirical focus, RBV stands for the resource-based view, and TCE stands for transaction cost economics.

Cross-border acquisition performance insights   175

Appendix 7.2 Studies with host or home country effect

Study	Home country effect	Host country effect
Basuil and Datta (2015)		Host country GDP growth Host country political risk
Chakrabarty and Gupta-Mukherjee (2009)		Target-country fixed effects
Dikova and Sahib (2013)		Target nation diversity index
Cloodt, Hagedoorn, and Van Kranenburg (2006)	Dummies for North America, Asia, Europe	
Aybar and Ficici (2009)	Dummies for Asian and Latin American acquirers; Panels for Asian, Latin American and Other = South Africa/Hungary home	Host is OECD (Czech Republic and South Korea excluded) World Economic Freedom Index of host
Bhagat, Malhotra, and Zhu (2011)		Target GDP growth USA targets Target anti-director rights Target French legal origin Target English legal origin
Steigner and Sutton (2011)		Target civil law country Target's government corruption Target's use of English as primary language
Reuer (2001)		Host market size Host market growth Host cultural clusters (Far East, Germanic, Latin American, Latin European, Japan, other non-Anglo)
Huang et al. (2017)	Acquirer country GDP	Target country GDP
Nicholson and Salaber (2013)	Home-China Home-India Separate panels	Host Developed (Developed = OECD or indicated as developed by IMF)
Du and Boateng (2015)		Host North America, Europe, Asia
Steigner and Sutton (2015)		Host a Common vs Civil law country Host English speaking

Study	Home country effect	Host country effect
Uhlenbruck and De Castro (2000)	Dummy for Western Europe as an indication of low distance from CEE	Host country risk (based on Institutional Investor measure)
Nowinski (2017)		Target developed vs emerging
Simonsson and Holm (2011)	Dummy for the EU as home country	
Zhu (2012)	Home institutions (regulatory, economic, political, physical infrastructure)	Host physical institutions
Total	7	**14**

Section III

What are persistent acquisition research issues?

David R. King

Acquisitions are not stand-alone events, as the impacts to a firm and its stakeholders (e.g., employees, customer, suppliers, and competitors) can be felt for years. For example, a study of two banks that merged concluded the effects spanned 25 years (Lu, 2014), or the initial architects of a deal were likely gone and many of the customers when integration was completed had only interacted with the combined firm. Meanwhile, the majority of acquisition research is cross-sectional and this reflects better data availability. However, studying a known multi-year phenomenon by taking a snapshot is analogous to trying to understand humanity by taking a single photo of many individuals on the same day. While easier than a longitudinal design, what can be learned about people's lives from a cross-sectional snapshot is limited, as it requires an observer inferring meaning from their own experience with the risk that experience is not relevant to what is viewed.

In Chapter 8, Olimpia Meglio reprises her review of acquisition performance (mis)measurement (Meglio & Risberg, 2011) that focuses on assumptions commonly made in acquisition research. Since her prior review, samples used in research have diversified outside the US; however, research largely remains restricted to a Western context with studies largely only extending to Europe. There is also progress in acquisition research using a variety of performance measures that is consistent with recognition that acquisition performance is multidimensional. However, research continues to focus on an acquiring firm's shareholders as the primary stakeholder. Broadening the consideration of other stakeholders offers the opportunity to improve performance for shareholders, as well as other impacted groups. This reflects a constraint that scholars have largely adopted themselves. The result is that there are multiple opportunities to expand acquisition research that will enable developing a better understanding of this important phenomenon.

DOI: 10.4324/9781003188308-11

178 *David R. King*

Performance variable selection can also drive theoretical sampling to control for context (Bower, 2001); however, the choice for study variables may, in turn, result in endogeneity problems that must be addressed. Still, corrections to address associated issues are possible, and methodological choices in designing acquisition research are the subject of Chapter 9 by Gonzalo Molina Sieiro. In the chapter, he discusses the main problems from endogeneity and potential solutions. Specifically, he highlights the importance of thoroughly understanding the acquisition context in order to facilitate the needed improvements in research design. In addition to his insights for addressing endogeneity, I would argue that research on acquisitions is important, given the annual dollar value of the phenomenon, and that understanding the implications for firms that decide to make acquisitions can justify their separate study.

In Chapter 10, Satu Teerikangas and Melanie Hassett review prior research on the cultural dynamics in domestic and cross-border acquisitions. While begun with optimism, cross-border acquisitions often experience difficulty due to cultural differences. Recognizing the intensity of attention paid to the empirical study and theoretical review of research on the culture-performance relationship, the authors review prior research on the cultural dynamics in acquisitions. Beginning with a discussion of how culture is conceptualized in acquisitions research, they then assess research on cultural distance and fit for insights on managing cultural change in acquisitions. The chapter provides relevant insights for managing acquisitions, as well as identifies research gaps and opportunities.

References

Bower, J. (2001). Not all M&As are alike – and that matters. *Harvard Business Review*, 79(3), 92–101.

Certo, S., Busenbark, J., Woo, H., & Semadeni, M. (2016). Sample selection bias and Heckman models in strategic management research. *Strategic Management Journal*, 37(13), 2639–2657.

Larcker, D., & Rusticus, T. (2010). On the use of instrumental variables in accounting research. *Journal of Accounting and Economics*, 49(3), 186–205.

Lu, Q. (2014). Is the speed of post-acquisition integration manageable? Case study: Post-acquisition integration of HSBC with the Mercantile Bank, 1959–84. *Business History*, 56(8), 1262–1280.

Meglio, O., & Risberg, A. (2011). The (mis) measurement of M&A performance: A systematic narrative literature review. *Scandinavian Journal of Management*, 27(4), 418–433.

8 A reconceptualization

The mis(measurement) of acquisition performance ten years later

Olimpia Meglio

Introduction

Acquisition performance plays a central role in acquisition research. Indeed, a huge number of studies, especially in the strategic management field, aim to either predict how acquisition perform or identify mechanisms for acquisition success (Bruner, 2002; King, Dalton, Daily, & Covin, 2004, King, Wang, Samimi, & Cortes, 2021). Over time, inconsistency and fragmentation in research findings have led acquisition scholars to develop increasingly complex or integrative models (Larsson & Finkelstein, 1999) to predict acquisition performance and dig deeper into acquisition processes to understand formula for success or reasons behind failure. Today, we have a broad repertoire of variables, such as relatedness (Datta, 1991), speed (Bauer & Matzler, 2014), integration (Teerikangas & Thanos, 2018), integration models (Angwin & Meadows, 2015) or mechanisms (Meglio, King, & Risberg, 2015), employed in empirical research that testify to the scholarly effort on understanding this complex and ambiguous phenomenon (see Graebner, Heimeriks, Huy, & Vaara, 2017; Haleblian, Devers, McNamara, Carpenter, & Davison, 2009; Welch, Pavićević, Keil, & Laamanen, 2020 for systematic reviews).

Looking back and reflecting upon the evolution of the field, we can conclude that from the first study about acquisitions (Dewing, 1921) onward, a consistent body of knowledge on acquisition performance has been accumulated. Existing research has been summarized through reviews (Meglio & Risberg, 2011; Schoenberg, 2006; Zollo & Meier, 2008) and meta-analyses (Datta, Pinches, & Narayanan, 1992; King et al., 2004, 2021). Still, scholars have not provided conclusive and unambiguous results about how acquisitions perform, typically concluding that the majority of acquisitions fail (Bauer & Matzler, 2014) and that acquisition performance is contingent upon a range of internal and external conditions (Risberg, King, & Meglio, 2015). As consequence, scholars are increasingly aware that acquisition performance should not be seen as a holy grail (Very, 2011) and that pursuing a grand, general, theory about acquisition performance is too ambitious. Instead, "given the complexity of acquisitions, there is a need for greater acceptance of

DOI: 10.4324/9781003188308-12

180 *Olimpia Meglio*

multiple perspectives and interplay of paradigms to appreciate underlying nuances" (Risberg, King, & Meglio, 2015, p. 2). Seen in this light, different acquisition performance measures tell a different story about, and provide a partial depiction of, this complex phenomenon (Meglio & Risberg, 2011).

In parallel with substantive research into acquisition performance, scholars have debated about how to best measure it. The debate has revolved around three primary issues: (1) whether the construct should be uni- or multidimensional (Papadakis & Thanos, 2010); (2) what the appropriate time interval of measurement is (Lubatkin & Shrieves, 1986); and (3) whether different measures converge or diverge (Zollo & Meier, 2008). This state of affairs led me and Annette Risberg, ten years ago, to review 101 empirical articles published in top-tier journals to understand what was that acquisition scholars measured under the label "acquisition performance" (Meglio & Risberg, 2011). The review was driven by a general interest in construct measurement and the assumption, at least from my side, that acquisition performance suffered from measurement flaws. As Annette Risberg and I progressed in reading the reviewed articles, we realized that while all scholars seemed to talk about acquisition performance as a unitary, objective construct, the ways it was actually measured varied a great deal. We noticed that the major preoccupation of acquisition scholars was how to best operationalize this construct, often taking for granted its conceptualization. Our findings highlighted that, while talked in singular, acquisition performance stood actually for a broad variety of meanings (either explicitly or implicitly subsumed), covering different domains, from the economic/financial to the innovation or the operational. The heterogeneity of performance measures extended to objective or perceptual measures and also referred to the time interval of measurement, typically ranging from a short event window around the announcement data up to two or three years after the deal is signed (Meglio & Risberg, 2011).

By looking at the big picture arising from the review, our findings surfaced two distinct, seemingly conflicting, yet complementary, patterns. On one hand, they showed a polarization towards conceiving acquisition performance as the financial market's reaction, typically measured within a short event window around the announcement date, to avoid confounding effects (Lubatkin & Shrieves, 1986). On the other hand, the review also displayed a repertoire of alternative measures, from accounting performance, either objective or perceptual, to survival or innovative performance, this latter typically measured as the number of patents after a deal (Ahuja & Katila, 2001; Hagedoorn & Duysters, 2002). Findings from the review suggested that the notion of acquisition performance had progressively expanded over time to encompass new connotations and reflect the typologies under investigation and the availability of data. For instance, for high tech deals, acquisition performance is often measured as innovative performance such as the number of patents (Cloodt, Hagedoorn, & Van Kranenburg, 2006). Also, when deals involve privately held companies, or financial market reaction is not available, accounting performance measures (Zollo & Singh, 2004) or perceptual measures are used (see for instance Bauer & Matzler, 2014).

The coexistence of these seemingly contradictory patterns—a polarization towards financial performance and a variety of alternative measures, all labeled as acquisition performance—may be understood as unavoidable for a broad and ambiguous construct such as acquisition performance. Indeed, seeing acquisition performance as an umbrella construct recognizes that acquisition performance may change during its travel, within and outside the academic community (Meglio & Schriber, 2020). More specifically, within the academic community, it is possible to discern both replication and variation patterns. Replication of acquisition performance is visible in the adoption of financial market reaction to a deal announcement that dominates acquisition research (King et al., 2021; Meglio & Risberg, 2011). Replicating previous studies' key construct measures is an established publishing strategy that helps prospective authors to position their contribution and ensure accumulation of knowledge in a given field (MacDonald & Kam, 2007). In contrast, variation is visible in the way acquisition performance has evolved in connection to the phenomenon it aims to capture. By way of example, the emergence of high-technology deals has favored the adoption of measures that account for innovative output an acquiring company experiences after a deal (Meglio, 2009). A variety of measures provides an alternative explanation to the frequently evoked fragmentation and inconsistency of research findings, which are simply not comparable (Meglio & Risberg, 2011).

Has anything changed ten years later? Did acquisition scholars make any progress towards acquisition performance construct clarity? Are there still blind-spots in existing studies? To answer these questions, in this chapter, I update the analysis published in 2011. However, instead of merely replicating the review that Annette Risberg and I carried out in 2011, I draw inspiration from what Alvesson and Sandberg (2020) refer to as 'problematizing review'. This review challenges the ambition of systematic reviews to cover each and every study in a broad field and proposes to focus on a narrow set of articles for a critical scrutiny, as the review does not take the review domain as given (Alvesson & Sandberg, 2020). This type of review is particularly suitable to get fresh perspectives. Accordingly, my aim here is to disentangle hidden assumptions in acquisition performance research as a means to draw inspiration from sister fields and foster a renewed research agenda.

Method

A problematizing review does not aim to systematize a crowded field of study to make sense what is already published; rather it generates

182   *Olimpia Meglio*

fresh perspectives or envisions new and unchartered areas of investigation (Alvesson & Sandberg, 2020). Acquisition performance research has been extensively reviewed through narrative (Meglio & Risberg, 2011), systematic syntheses (Zollo & Meier, 2008), and meta-analyses (King et al, 2004, 2021). By offering a critical reflection on how we as a scholarly community have dealt with this important construct, I complement existing extensive treatments of the topic (Feldman & Hernandez, 2020; King, Meglio, Gomez-Mejia, Bauer, & De Massis, 20222).

A problematizing review, Alvesson and Sandberg (2020) contend, is inspired by four core principles: (1) the ideal of reflexivity, (2) reading more broadly but selectively, (3) not accumulating but problematizing, and (4) the concept of 'less is more'. In line with the idea of reading selectively but in greater depth, Alvesson and Sandberg (2020) suggest to identify ten influential articles in a given field. The analysis should aim to disentangle hidden assumptions. Then, scholars are suggested to borrow ideas or fresh perspectives from adjacent fields. An underlying assumption is that scholars are not neutral agents and through their choices (what to include, leave outside or get inspiration from) actively contribute to build their interpretation of the phenomenon of interest (Pettigrew, 2012).

In line with these guidelines, the starting point of this review are ten papers that, in my view, offer ground for a critical analysis. This is a distinguishing feature of problematizing reviews that abandon both the ambition of comprehensiveness and the assumption of neutrality of the researcher. I identified these papers by looking into management and strategy top tier journals, published in the last ten years and dealing with performance, as I am interested to look into these academic domains. They represent a purposeful sample of studies published by prominent acquisition scholars and published in top tier journals. As such, they can be considered representative of cutting-edge research in the acquisition field.

I have first reviewed these papers using a coding scheme that builds upon and integrates the scheme used in the 2011 article (Meglio & Risberg, 2011). The coding scheme contains the following information: (a) authors; (b) journal and year of publication; (c) the research setting under investigation; (d) the notional definition of value used in the paper; (e) the operational definition of the value used in the paper; (f) hidden assumptions inspiring the notion of value used in the study; and (g) a summary of major findings.

Following the ideal of reflexivity, I next critically engage with the hidden assumptions inspiring the most prominent studies, and I contrast them with alternative interpretations (Alvesson & Sandberg, 2013). To achieve this aim, I dig deeper in the acquisition field, as well as borrowed from other disciplinary domains to identify similarities and anomalies (Hoon & Baluch, 2020) that taken together offer complementary perspectives. By looking into similarities, I detect common and dominant assumptions

Revisiting acquisition performance measurement   183

in acquisition research. Meanwhile, by acknowledging anomalies, I provide ground for broadening the repertoire of different notions attached to acquisition performance in acquisitions.

Findings

What acquisition performance research looks like today

I start by summarizing patterns emerging from the ten articles that were purposefully selected to illustrate the current status of the acquisition performance research. Appendix 8.1 provides a synopsis of article coding.

The sample of studies involve US (Bettinazzi & Zollo, 2017) and European companies, especially German speaking (Bauer & Matzler, 2014) or Finnish ones (Vaara, Junni, Sarala, Ehrnrooth, & Koveshnikov, 2014) operating in manufacturing and service industries, as well as high tech ones such as software (Laamanen, Brauer, & Junna, 2014). Companies under investigation are predominantly public companies (Zorn, Sexton, Bhussar, & Lamont, 2019) that also perform cross-border acquisitions (CBA) (Basuil & Datta, 2015). As compared with Meglio and Risberg (2011), there is budding attention to service and high-technology industries that reflects recent trends in acquisition waves. There is also mounting interest in CBA and acquisition programs, again in line with an increasing reliance on multiple acquisitions to support internationalization processes (Park, Meglio, Bauer, & Tarba, 2018).

In line with Meglio and Risberg (2011) acquisition performance remains an important dependent variable, the gauge against which scholars assess acquisition success. This is consistent with the strategic management tradition to identify variables that explain or predict performance (Bracker, 1980; Schendel & Hofer, 1979). In my sample this happens in nine out of ten articles. The only exception is represented by Devers, McNamara, Haleblian, and Yoder (2013) where acquisition performance is an independent variable.

All studies are quantitative and are based either on secondary data or primary data collected through surveys (Bauer & Matzler, 2014). Again, this is a finding consistent with Meglio and Risberg (2011), who find only a few qualitative studies in their sample. Some of the studies are longitudinal, meaning that cross-sectional research designs are increasingly augmented by research approaches better suited to grasp the processual nature of acquisitions (Jemison & Sitkin, 1986; Meglio & Risberg, 2010). This represents an important sign of change, which I hope will eventually result into a clearer discontinuity.

Moving to the notional definitions of performance, in line with Meglio and Risberg (2011), acquisition performance remains an umbrella construct (Meglio & Schriber, 2020) as it still encompasses a variety of definitions, including none. When defined, the acquisition performance typically overlaps with the operational measure using either an

184 *Olimpia Meglio*

objective (i.e., financial) or a subjective (i.e., manager) assessment of acquisition performance. However, a focus on acquisition performance is not universal with some research referring to shareholder value creation (Basuil & Datta, 2015) or to value creation (Cuypers, Cuypers, & Martin, 2017) or acquisition announcement market performance (Devers et al., 2013). Interestingly, my review also finds references to acquisition success (Bauer & Matzler, 2014; Trichterborn, Knyphausen-Aufseß, & Schweizer, 2016) or outcomes (Cuypers et al., 2017; Vaara et al., 2014), suggesting acquisition performance, success, and outcomes are intertwined. Moreover, shifting from performance in singular to outcomes in plural highlights that there is an increasing awareness that the financial dimension of performance does not exhaust all possible "performances" arising from a combination of two companies and recognizes that acquisitions typically produce multiple effects. In a similar vein, Zorn et al. (2019) use Tobin's Q as a measure for acquisition performance as it captures both accounting and market performance. More specifically, it is a ratio of a firm's market value (stock valuation) to book value (King, Bauer, & Schriber, 2018). As a result, it combines historical accounting information with forward looking information from the stock market.

The time interval used to measure performance also varies a great deal. One study uses a '–3 +3' event window that is most common (King et al., 2021), but it does not report the estimation window (Devers et al., 2013), and another (Laamanen et al., 2014) reports the estimation window, but not the event window. The estimation window uses historical information to predict the expected or normal return during the event window to identify any abnormal return. To replicate a research study, both the estimation and event windows need to be reported. Meanwhile, the balance of reviewed research emphasizes the importance of measuring the long-term performance with time frames ranging from 12 months (Vaara et al., 2014) to 36 months (Bettinazzi & Zollo, 2017). This is a particularly important variation in more recent studies vis-à-vis previous ones, as it reflects the recognition that acquisitions take time and acquisition performance should incorporate the processual nature in the time interval scholars choose when they measure performance. However, the use of different time intervals paired with different notional definitions and measurement methods reproduce the incomparability of findings observed by Meglio and Risberg (2011).

To summarize, while I did not conduct a systematic search and review of studies dealing with acquisition performance in the last decade, findings from the ten studies examined here confirm that acquisition performance is typically conceived as shareholder value, even though it is increasing acknowledged that it should be measured over a longer time interval (as compared with the very short interval generally used in event studies). There is also rising awareness that performance is multidimensional and should reflect multiple dimensions.

Engaging with hidden assumptions

After describing the big picture emerging from the review, I now provide a critical reflection intended to reveal important assumptions permeating acquisition performance research. While I acknowledge that there are many, here I will focus on two that appear important to acquisition performance measurement: (1) a shareholder-centric view of acquisition performance (Meglio, 2015), and (2) a financial market efficiency assumption (Fama, 1970). Taken together, these assumptions portray acquisitions as revolving around two stakeholders: shareholders and top management. However, a shareholder-centric view of acquisition performance puts acquiring company's shareholders at the center of the scene and describes acquisitions as shareholder-value maximizing strategies. Indeed, efforts to measure acquisition performance reflect the idea that acquisitions should serve acquiring company shareholders' interest and is compelling to understand whether they are beneficial or detrimental towards this goal.

A shareholder-centric view stipulates that shareholders are residual claimants and this implies that satisfying them is only possible if all of the other constituencies have been satisfied (Friedman, 1970). According to Friedman (1970), maximizing shareholder value is also an effective means to maximize societal wealth. In this light, the only social responsibility of business is to use its resources and engage in activities that increase its profits that assigns an important role to managers. Bounded by fiduciary duties, managers are expected to act as stewards of the firm's shareholders by striving for maximum shareholder value (Maas, Heugens, & Reus, 2019). As part of their duties, they are expected to identify suitable acquisition targets that offer synergies to the acquirer and increase shareholders' wealth. However, 'principal-agent' conflicts (Jensen & Meckling, 1976) may arise when managers deviate from their duties and maximize their own interest at the expense of shareholders' wealth (Jarrell, Brickley, & Netter, 1988). The extent of the principal-agent problem depends on the accountability of managers towards shareholders, and the existence of legal institutions, including an effective market for corporate control (Roll, 1986) that governs this process by making poorly performing managers accountable to shareholders (Guillén & Capron, 2016).

Assumptions of market efficiency (Fama, 1970) are also pervasive in acquisition performance construct measurement. It postulates that financial markets are efficient and transparent and as such they are capable to reflect whether the value creates or destroys value in a very short event window around the announcement date (usually –/+3 days). While its popularity has not been undermined, over time, there has been criticism on the suitability of this measure (Harrison & Schijven, 2015). Additionally, identifying abnormal returns depends on an estimation window, and my review suggests that research stops short of reporting both the event and estimation windows. Still, Oler and colleagues (2008) contend that, given the complexity of acquisitions, empirical results

186 Olimpia Meglio

from short-window event studies of acquisitions may foster incorrect inferences. For example, positive stock market reactions at acquisition announcement become negative for event windows longer than one week (King et al., 2004, p. 192). Further, in a comparison of event windows, Sirower (1997) suggests that researchers pick event windows that support hypothesized results.

Taken together these assumptions emphasize public companies at the expense of privately held or family firms, often of small size, who actively contribute to the market for corporate control (King et al., 20222). One of the primary reasons is accessibility of secondary data about public companies paired with a lack of data about privately held ones. As a consequence, we do not account for non-economic goals that play a role in the heterogeneous universe of non-public firms, with the consequence of failing to account for a huge proportion of the variance in acquisition behaviors and performance (King et al., 2022).

Discussing measurement practices

The dominating financial connotation of acquisition performance also rests on scholarly measurement practices in published research. This is particularly important to understand the replication pattern, where scholars rely on previous studies to highlight that there is a consolidated tendency to use a certain measurement method that has passed the test of peer review and has become accepted within a community (Meglio & Risberg, 2011). Citations represent an important trait of scientific knowledge (Golden-Biddle, Locke, & Reay, 2006), and my aim here is not to criticize it, rather to observe that citing previous research and conforming to publishing norms increase the chances of getting a paper accepted in target journals (Patriotta, 2017). As a result, scholars are not neutral agents, and they jointly make up the appreciative system of scholarly inquiry that influences what topics are studied and how scholars study them (Pettigrew, 2012). The above factors explain the convergence towards certain measure in a given period of time. Although the sample of studies is selective and not statistically significant, I still identify a more pronounced discontinuity vis-à-vis previous studies, with more attention paid to the time interval of measurement and the importance of adapting to the specific characteristics of the deals under investigation. In the reviewed sample, Basuil and Datta (2015) contextualize the performance measure within the context of CBA, signaling an appreciation for contextual conditions. Another example is offered by Zorn and colleagues (2019) who consider the effects of prior target firm acquisitions on the performance of subsequent acquisitions.

To summarize, acquisition performance research is socially constructed (Astley, 1985). A primary role is played by acquisition scholars which reflects a current emphasis on financial outcomes at the expense of other considerations. This happens as scholarly research is shaped by several constraints that have, over time, consolidated certain measurement methods. Accessibility of data together with publishing strategies also explains why certain measures dominate the acquisition performance research.

Onwards and upwards: Ideas for future research

A critical review of acquisition performance research published in the last decade confirms that acquisition performance represents an umbrella construct. A unitary label masks a variety of different conceptualizations and measures for acquisition performance (Meglio & Schriber, 2020), allowing for replication and variation patterns across time. I do not see this as problematic, as long as acquisition scholars acknowledge the umbrella nature of acquisition performance and clearly define the construct in their studies. Referring to previous studies, although important to position a contribution within a certain tradition and join a specific conversation (Golden-Biddle et al., 2006), it may not be enough to achieve needed construct clarity (Suddaby, 2010). However, the solution is not building a repertoire of universal measures acquisition scholars uniformly and consistently apply in empirical and theoretical research, as organizational scholars recommended in the 1990s (Osigweh, 1989; Warriner, Hall, & McKelvey, 1981). That solution would be too simplistic and reductionist (Astley, 1985). Acquisitions remain complex and ambiguous phenomena and constructs, including performance, should reflect and capture the heterogeneity of actual deals. In measuring acquisition performance, scholars should account for the heterogeneity of the phenomenon and be cognizant of the importance of clearly defining this construct (Suddaby, 2010).

Heterogeneity of acquisitions

Acquisitions vary over time and initial typologies built around clearly demarcated boundaries between industries no longer capture the spectrum of possible combinations among companies (Bower, 2001) or integration models (see Angwin & Meadows, 2015 or Zaheer, Castañer, & Souder, 2013). By a way of example, Pagani and colleagues (2021) analyze the acquisition behaviors of digital platform such as Uber or Airbnb and propose an octopus model to describe deals involving platform companies growing tentacles through acquisitions in other markets, broadening the field throughout their development, with an impressive number of acquisitions in different sectors. The octopus model builds on the traditional related/unrelated dichotomy inspiring the Federal Trade Commission (FTC) Large Merger Series database (1948–1979) classifications that provided a foundation for research (see Lubatkin, 1983). Since the 1990s, research has often relied on the SDC platinum financial transactions database.

188   Olimpia Meglio

Another important and frequently overlooked source of variance in acquisitive behaviors arises when one considers that not all companies are public and therefore only studying public companies does not represent all acquirers and potential targets. Family firms do actively contribute to the market for corporate control and they are driven by economic and, most importantly, non-economic goals that drive an acquisition choice and reflect in the way acquisition performance should be assessed (King et al., 2022; Meglio & King, 2019). These considerations are just illustrative of an increasing complexity surrounding current deals. In light of such complexity, my aim here is not to provide a new performance construct measure, rather a list of issues to reflect upon while measuring acquisition performance to best capture the heterogeneity of the phenomenon.

Clearly define the construct

An important condition for clarity is to specify whether performance is narrowly defined as financial performance or more broadly as social performance. Financial performance and corporate social performance are typically seen as dichotomous and the major concern among management scholars is to find ways to reconcile the two (Waddock & Graves, 1997). Based on the considerations developed earlier, my point is not to suggest that financial performance no longer matters or that it should be replaced by corporate social performance. Instead, I offer a more modest proposal of abandoning shareholders as the only or predominant stakeholder in acquisitions (Bettinazzi & Zollo, 2017) and trying to account for different outcomes that acquisitions may bring to additional stakeholders.

Adopting broader stakeholder interests in future research requires integrative frameworks that combine acquisition and business and society fields. So far, there have been only a few attempts from business and society scholars to measure the impact acquisition may have upon stakeholder practices (Waddock & Graves, 2006). More recently, Chiu and Sabz (2021) propose that corporate divestiture may have a positive impact upon corporate social performance. The acquisition field seems to be entrenched into a primacy of financial performance with socially or environmentally responsible choices being relevant as long as they produce a positive impact upon financial performance, thus reemphasizing a shareholder-centric view of acquisitions. Put differently, more can be done to explore what are the outcomes that acquisitions produce upon different stakeholders. Relatedly, it is important to clarify whether performance entails single or multiple dimensions (Papadakis & Thanos, 2010). However, by itself, I am afraid this simplifies a more profound and broader issue in acquisition research and reproduces one of the hidden assumptions discussed earlier, that is that acquisitions should serve a narrow group of actors, namely shareholders or top managers.

Revisiting acquisition performance measurement 189

Within the acquisition scholarly community there has been an increasing recognition that a stakeholder perspective is needed to better understand acquisitions dynamics (Anderson, Havila, & Nilsson, 2013; Bettinazzi & Zollo, 2017; Cording, Harrison, Hoskisson, & Jonsen, 2014; Hitt, Harrison, & Ireland, 2001). However, from an instrumental view, attending to stakeholders' interests remains important, as it is still frequently assumed that considering other stakeholders still pays off in terms of shareholder value. A fresh perspective to acquisitions and acquisition performance should abandon the instrumental view of stakeholders in acquisitions conceive them as potentially bringing benefits and harms to multiple actors, and even the environment. Therefore, it is not simply a matter of choosing what are the most relevant dimensions in acquisition performance, but also querying the stakes that the acquisitions under investigation affect and are affected by. The issue is not simply to assess who gains or loses a deal but also what is it that actors gain or lose over different time horizons. For example, actors considered need to expand to include employees, business to business and end customers, competitors, suppliers, local communities, and the environment. A careful scrutiny of costs and benefits upon individuals (being them companies or citizens) is a way to acknowledge that acquisitions are not simply strategic moves, but also a powerful tool to improve or impoverish individuals' living conditions.

The time interval of measurement also represents a fundamental issue in acquisition performance. The choice of looking at financial market reactions around a short time interval is typically justified by the importance of ruling out any possible confounding effects (McWilliams, Siegel, & Teoh, 1999). Yet, acquisitions take time to unfold and benefits arising from the combination also require time and efforts (costs) from the acquiring company. Typically, when a longer time interval is considered, it ranges between one to three years to reflect the time necessary to reap benefits (Zollo & Meier, 2008). Yet, these time intervals are based on research convention, and they do not reflect the heterogeneity of deals and the different integration approaches referred above. Different integration choices may have different implications for the costs and benefits in the short, medium, or long run, but the real problem is that they are difficult to anticipate even when due diligence is carefully performed. Additionally, regardless of the measures selected, research needs to report sufficient information to enable replication.

Conclusion

Acquisition performance represents a central construct in acquisition research. While it is typically considered as an objective entity, it is actually socially constructed by acquisition scholars and shaped by assumptions and constraints. In this chapter, I have critically reflected on how hidden assumptions related to acquisition performance measurement influence

190   *Olimpia Meglio*

the way we look at acquisitions. Broadening the actors and stakes playing a role in acquisitions may offer an important turning point to change the way we investigate acquisitions and measure their outcomes.

References (* studies included in the review)

Ahuja, G., & Katila, R. (2001). Technological acquisitions and the innovation performance of acquiring firms: A longitudinal study. *Strategic Management Journal, 22*(3), 197–220.

Alvesson, M., & Sandberg, J. (2013). Has management studies lost its way? Ideas for more imaginative and innovative research. *Journal of Management Studies, 50*(1), 128–152.

Alvesson, M., & Sandberg, J. (2020). The problematizing review: A counterpoint to Elsbach and Van Knippenberg's argument for integrative reviews. *Journal of Management Studies, 57*(6), 1290–1304.

Anderson, H., Havila, V., & Nilsson, F. (Eds.). (2013). *Mergers and acquisitions: The critical role of stakeholders* (Vol. 52). Oxon: Routledge.

Angwin, D.N., & Meadows, M. (2015). New integration strategies for post-acquisition management. *Long Range Planning, 48*(4), 235–251.

Astley, W. (1985). Administrative science as socially constructed truth. *Administrative Science Quarterly, 30*(4), 497–513.

*Basuil, D., & Datta, D. (2015). Effects of industry-and region-specific acquisition experience on value creation in cross-border acquisitions: The moderating role of cultural similarity. *Journal of Management Studies, 52*(6), 766–795.

*Bauer, F., & Matzler, K. (2014). Antecedents of M&A success: The role of strategic complementarity, cultural fit, and degree and speed of integration. *Strategic Management Journal, 35*(2), 269–291.

*Bettinazzi, E., & Zollo, M. (2017). Stakeholder orientation and acquisition performance. *Strategic Management Journal, 38*(12), 2465–2485.

Bower, J. (2001). Not all M&As are alike: And that matters. *Harvard Business Review, 79*(3), 93–101.

Bracker, J. (1980). The historical development of the strategic management concept. *Academy of Management Review, 5*(2), 219–224.

Bruner, R. (2002). Does M&A pay? A survey of evidence for the decision-maker. *Journal of Applied Finance, 12*(1), 48–68.

Chiu, S., & Sabz, A. (2021). Can corporate divestiture activities lead to better corporate social performance? *Journal of Business Ethics*, 1–18. https://doi.org/10.1007/s10551-021-04869-2

Cloodt, M., Hagedoorn, J., & Van Kranenburg, H. (2006). Mergers and acquisitions: Their effect on the innovative performance of companies in high-tech industries. *Research Policy, 35*(5), 642–654.

Cording, M., Harrison, J.S., Hoskisson, R., & Jonsen, K. (2014). Walking the talk: A multistakeholder exploration of organizational authenticity, employee productivity, and post-merger performance. *Academy of Management Perspectives, 28*(1), 38–56.

*Cuypers, I., Cuypers, Y., & Martin, X. (2017). When the target may know better: Effects of experience and information asymmetries on value from mergers and acquisitions. *Strategic Management Journal, 38*(3), 609–625.

Datta, D. (1991). Organizational fit and acquisition performance: Effects of post-acquisition integration. *Strategic Management Journal, 12*(4), 281–297.

Datta, D., Pinches, G., & Narayanan, V. (1992). Factors influencing wealth creation from mergers and acquisitions: A meta-analysis. *Strategic Management Journal*, 13(1), 67–84.

*Devers, C., McNamara, G., Haleblian, J., & Yoder, M. (2013). Do they walk the talk? Gauging acquiring CEO and director confidence in the value creation potential of announced acquisitions. *Academy of Management Journal*, 56(6), 1679–1702.

Dewing, A. (1921). A statistical test of the success of consolidations. *Journal of Economics*, 36(1), 84–101.

Fama, E. (1970). Efficient market: A review of theory and empirical work. *Journal of Finance*, 25(2), 383–417.

Feldman, E., & Hernandez, E. (2020). Synergy in mergers and acquisitions: Typology, lifecycles, and value. *Academy of Management Review*. https://doi.org/10.5465/amr.2018.0345

Friedman, M. (1970). The social responsibility of business is to increase its profits. *New York Times Magazine*, September 13.

Golden-Biddle, K., Locke, K., & Reay, T. (2006). Using knowledge in management studies: An investigation of how we cite prior work. *Journal of Management Inquiry*, 15(3), 237–254.

Graebner, M., Heimeriks, K., Huy, Q., & Vaara, E. (2017). The process of postmerger integration: A review and agenda for future research. *Academy of Management Annals*, 11(1), 1–32.

Guillén, M., & Capron, L. (2016). State capacity, minority shareholder protections, and stock market development. *Administrative Science Quarterly*, 61(1), 125–160.

Hagedoorn, J., & Duysters, G. (2002). The effect of mergers and acquisitions on the technological performance of companies in a high-tech environment. *Technology Analysis & Strategic Management*, 14(1), 67–85.

Haleblian, J., Devers, C., McNamara, G., Carpenter, M., & Davison, R. (2009). Taking stock of what we know about mergers and acquisitions: A review and research agenda. *Journal of Management*, 35(3), 469–502.

Harrison, J., & Schijven, M. (2015). Event-study methodology in the context of M&As. In Risberg A., King D., & Meglio O. (Eds.), *The Routledge companion to mergers and acquisitions* (pp. 245–265). Oxford: Routledge, Taylor & Francis Group.

Hitt, M., Harrison, J., & Ireland, R. (2001). *Mergers & acquisitions: A guide to creating value for stakeholders*. Oxford: Oxford University Press.

Hoon, C., & Baluch, A. (2020). The role of dialectical interrogation in review studies: Theorizing from what we see rather than what we have already seen. *Journal of Management Studies*, 57(6), 1246–1271.

Jarrell, G., Brickley, J., & Netter, J. (1988). The market for corporate control: The empirical evidence since 1980. *Journal of Economic Perspectives*, 2(1), 49–68.

Jemison, D., & Sitkin, S. (1986). Corporate acquisitions: A process perspective. *Academy of Management Review*, 11(1), 145–163.

Jensen, M., & Meckling, W. (1976). Theory of the firm: Managerial behavior, agency costs and ownership structure. *Journal of Financial Economics*, 3(4), 305–360.

King, D., Dalton, D., Daily, C., & Covin, J. G. (2004). Meta-analyses of post-acquisition performance: Indications of unidentified moderators. *Strategic Management Journal*, 25(2), 187–200.

192 Olimpia Meglio

King, D., Meglio, O., Gomez-Mejia, L., Bauer, F., & De Massis, A. (2022). Family business restructuring: A review and research agenda. *Journal of Management Studies*, 59(1): 197–235.

King, D., Wang, G., Samimi, M., & Cortes, A. (2021). A meta-analytic integration of acquisition performance prediction. *Journal of Management Studies*, 58(5), 1198–1236.

King, D.R., Bauer, F., & Schriber, S. (2018). *Mergers & acquisitions: a research overview*. Oxford, UK: Routledge.

*Laamanen, T., Brauer, M., & Junna, O. (2014). Performance of acquirers of divested assets: Evidence from the US software industry. *Strategic Management Journal*, 35(6), 914–925.

Larsson, R., & Finkelstein, S. (1999). Integrating strategic, organizational, and human resource perspectives on mergers and acquisitions: A case survey of synergy realization. *Organization Science*, 10(1), 1–26.

Lubatkin, M. (1983). Mergers and the performance of the acquiring firm. *Academy of Management Review*, 8(2), 218–225.

Lubatkin, M., & Shrieves, R. (1986). Towards reconciliation of market performance measures to strategic management research. *Academy of Management Review*, 11(3), 497–512.

Maas, A., Heugens, P., & Reus, T. (2019). Viceroys or emperors? An institution-based perspective on merger and acquisition prevalence and shareholder value. *Journal of Management Studies*, 56(1), 234–269.

Macdonald, S., & Kam, J. (2007). Ring a ring o'roses: Quality journals and gamesmanship in management studies. *Journal of Management Studies*, 44(4), 640–655.

McWilliams, A., Siegel, D., & Teoh, S. (1999). Issues in the use of the event study methodology: A critical analysis of corporate social responsibility studies. *Organizational Research Methods*, 2(4), 340–365.

Meglio, O. (2009). Measuring performance in technology-driven M&As: Insights from a literature review. In Cooper C.L., & Finkelstein S. (Eds.), *Advances in mergers and acquisitions* (Vol. 8, pp. 103–118).

Meglio, O. (2015). The acquisition performance game: A stakeholder approach. In Risberg A., King D., Meglio O. (Eds.), *The Routledge companion to mergers and acquisitions* (pp. 163–176). Oxford: Routledge, Taylor & Francis Group.

Meglio, O., & King, D. (2019). Family businesses: Building a merger and acquisition research agenda. In Cooper C., & Finkelstein S. (Eds.), *Advances in mergers and acquisitions* (Vol. 18, pp. 83–98). Bingley: Emerald.

Meglio, O. (2009). Measuring performance in technology-driven M&As: Insights from a literature review. In Cooper C., & Finkelstein S. (Eds.), *Advances in Mergers and Acquisitions*. (Vol 8, 103–118). Bingley: Emerald.

Meglio, O., & Risberg, A. (2010). Mergers and acquisitions—Time for a methodological rejuvenation of the field? *Scandinavian Journal of Management*, 26(1), 87–95.

Meglio, O., & Risberg, A. (2011). The (mis) measurement of M&A performance—A systematic narrative literature review. *Scandinavian Journal of Management*, 27(4), 418–433.

Meglio, O., King, D., & Risberg, A. (2015). Improving acquisition outcomes with contextual ambidexterity. *Human Resource Management*, 54(S1), s29–s43.

Meglio, O., & Schriber, S. (2020). *Mergers and acquisitions: Rethinking key umbrella constructs*. New York: Springer Nature.

Oler, D., Harrison, J., & Allen, M. (2008). The danger of misinterpreting short-window event study findings in strategic management research: An empirical illustration using horizontal acquisitions. *Strategic Organization*, 6(2), 151–184.

Osigweh, C. (1989). Concept fallibility in organizational science. *Academy of Management Review*, 14(4), 579–594.

Pagani, M., Miric, M., & El Sawi, O. (2021). The octopus effect: When and who platform companies acquire. https://blogs.lse.ac.uk/businessreview/2021/06/24/the-octopus-effect-when-and-who-platform-companies-acquire/ (Retrieved June 27 2021).

Papadakis, V., & Thanos, I.C. (2010). Measuring the performance of acquisitions: An empirical investigation using multiple criteria. *British Journal of Management*, 21(4), 859–873.

Park, K., Meglio, O., Bauer, F., & Tarba, S. (2018). Managing patterns of internationalization, integration, and identity transformation: The post-acquisition metamorphosis of an Arabian Gulf EMNC. *Journal of Business Research*, 93, 122–138.

Patriotta, G. (2017). Crafting papers for publication: Novelty and convention in academic writing. *Journal of Management Studies*, 54(5), 747–759.

Pettigrew, A. (2012). Context and action in the transformation of the firm: A reprise. *Journal of Management Studies*, 49(7), 1304–1328.

Risberg, A., King, D., & Meglio, O. (Eds.). (2015). *The Routledge companion to mergers and acquisitions*. Oxford: Routledge, Taylor & Francis Group.

Roll, R. (1986). The hubris hypothesis of corporate takeovers. *Journal of Business*, 59(2), 197–216.

Schendel, D., & Hofer, C. (1979). *Strategic management*. Boston: Little, Brown.

Schoenberg, R. (2006). Measuring the performance of corporate acquisitions: An empirical comparison of alternative metrics. *British Journal of Management*, 17(4), 361–370.

Sirower, M. (1997). *The synergy trap: How companies lose the acquisition game*. New York: Simon and Schuster.

Suddaby, R. (2010). Editor's comments: Construct clarity in theories of management and organization. *Academy of Management Review*, 35(3), 346.

Teerikangas, S., & Thanos, I.C. (2018). Looking into the 'black box'–Unlocking the effect of integration on acquisition performance. *European Management Journal*, 36(3), 366–380.

*Trichterborn, A., Knyphausen-Aufseß, Z., & Schweizer, L. (2016). How to improve acquisition performance: The role of a dedicated M&A function, M&A learning process, and M&A capability. *Strategic Management Journal*, 37, 763–773.

*Vaara, E., Junni, P., Sarala, R.M., Ehrnrooth, M., Koveshnikov, A. (2014). Attributional tendencies in cultural explanations of M&A performance. *Strategic Management Journal*, 35(9), 1302–1317.

Very, P. (2011). Acquisition performance and the "Quest for the Holy Grail". *Scandinavian Journal of Management*, 27(4), 434–437.

Waddock, S., & Graves, S. (1997). The corporate social performance–financial performance link. *Strategic Management Journal*, 18(4), 303–319.

Waddock, S., & Graves, S.B. (2006). The impact of mergers and acquisitions on corporate stakeholder practices. *Journal of Corporate Citizenship*, 22, 91–109.

Warriner, C.K., Hall, R.H., & McKelvey, B. (1981). The comparative description of organizations: A research note and invitation. *Organization Studies, 2*(2), 173–175.

Welch, X., Pavićević, S., Keil, T., & Laamanen, T. (2020). The pre-deal phase of mergers and acquisitions: A review and research agenda. *Journal of Management, 46*(6), 843–878.

Zaheer, A., Castañer, X., & Souder, D. (2013). Synergy sources, Target autonomy, and integration in acquisitions. *Journal of Management, 39*(3), 604–632.

*Zhu, H., Ma, X., Sauerwald, S., & Peng, M. (2019) Home country institutions behind cross-border acquisition performance. *Journal of Management, 45*(4), 1315–1342.

Zollo, M., & Meier, D. (2008). What is M&A performance? *Academy of Management Perspectives, 22*(3), 55–77.

Zollo, M., & Singh, H. (2004). Deliberate learning in corporate acquisitions: Post-acquisition strategies and integration capability in US bank mergers. *Strategic Management Journal, 25*(13), 1233–1256.

*Zorn, M., Sexton, J., Bhussar, M., & Lamont, B. (2019). Unfinished business: Nested acquisitions, managerial capacity, and firm performance. *Journal of Management, 45*(4), 1488–1516.

Appendix 8.1 Coding of ten influential studies of acquisition performance

Authors	Research Questions	Research setting	Notional definition	Independent/ Dependent/ Mediating/ Moderating	Operational measure	Assumptions	Major findings
Basuil and Datta (2015)	Examines the effects of acquiring firms' prior cross-border acquisition (CBA) experience in the same industry and geographic region as the acquired firm on shareholder value creation.	222 CBA by US firms in the service Sector	Shareholder value creation	Dependent	BHAR (buy-and-hold abnormal returns) methodology. assessing abnormal returns over a longer time horizon (one year in our study) to overcome limitations associated with narrow windows around the announcement date (event study).	Acquisition performance is captured by financial markets reactions. This method responds to the need to extend the measurement on a longer time horizon. However, the time interval of measurement is one year.	The effects of industry-specific acquisition experience on acquisition performance are contingent on the level of cultural similarity between the acquiring and acquired firm countries, with the benefits of prior experience being greater in acquisitions undertaken in culturally similar countries.

(continued)

Authors	Research Questions	Research setting	Notional definition	Independent/ Dependent Mediating/ Moderating	Operational measure	Assumptions	Major findings
Bauer and Matzler (2014)	Studies the impact of an integrative framework on acquisition success	106 SME transactions in the machinery, electronic, and logistic industries in the German-speaking part of Central Europe	Managerial assessment or perceptual measure	Dependent	Success is assessed by using the measurement model developed by Becker consisting of the two dimensions that are each measured with four items	Managerial bias Managers as knowledgeable informants	Success is a function of strategic complementarity, cultural fit, and the degree of integration. The degree of integration is positively related to speed of integration.
Bettinazzi and Zollo (2017)	Studies how a firm's stakeholder orientation affects the performance of its corporate acquisitions	A sample of US 1884 acquisitions between 2002 and 2010	Long term performance	Dependent	Acquiring firm's Cumulative Abnormal Returns (CAR) over the 36 months following the acquisition	Instrumental stakeholder orientation Limited set of stakeholders: Employees Customers Local communities Suppliers	Positive association between acquirers' stakeholder orientation and acquisition performance- Positive moderation of business relatedness on the performance impacts of stakeholder orientation. Structural integration has a similarly positive moderation effect only for some of the stakeholder categories.

Cuypers et al. (2017)	Examines how the differential in prior acquisition experience between the target and the acquirer affects the value they, respectively, obtain when the acquirer takes over the target.	1,241 deals over a 30-year period	Value creation and how it is distributed between the two parties that talk about outcomes	Dependent	CAR event study methodology with market model using a 250-day estimation window and a 21-day event window centered on the event date. This is consistent	Acquiring and target shareholders	The findings support that value obtained is an outcome of a distributive process where both an acquirer and target play an active role, such that differential experience is a key determinant of which one obtains how much value. The impact of this experience advantage is contingent on the level of information asymmetry imposed by the target's scope, and on whether the parties reach a friendly agreement.
Devers et al. (2013)	Explores whether acquiring CEOs and directors act consistently with the idea that their newly announced acquisitions will increase long-term value	2,069 public firms listed in ExecuComp between 1996 and 2007. No further information about the research setting. Availability of data is key.	Acquisition announcement market performance	Independent	CAR event window −3+3 days around the announcement date. Estimation window not defined.	Financial markets' expectations reflect the value of the combined firms	Directors tend to grant their acquiring CEOs stock options, after acquisition announcement, to align CEO-shareholder interests. When

(continued)

Authors	Research Questions	Research setting	Notional definition	Independent/ Dependent/ Mediating/ Moderating	Operational measure	Assumptions	Major findings
							CEOs and directors manage acquiring CEOs' equity-based holdings, they do not appear to anticipate long-term value creation from acquisitions.
Laamanen et al. (2014)	Compares acquirer returns in acquisitions of public firms, private firms, and divested assets.	5,079 acquisitions by US software industry firms during 1988–2008	A notional definition is lacking Reference to previous studies, and CAR	Dependent	CAR event study methodology. Estimation window measured from 295 to 45 days before each event, but event window not defined.	Market efficiency hypothesis Bargaining power explanation	Acquisitions of divested assets outperform those of privately held firms, which in turn outperform those of publicly held firms. While the higher returns for acquisitions of divested assets relative to stand-alone acquisition targets can be explained by market efficiency arguments, seller distress and improved asset fit

Revisiting acquisition performance measurement   199

					further enhance the positive returns of acquirers of divested assets consistent with the relative bargaining power explanation.		
Trichterborn et al. (2016)	Analyzes the relationship between an M&A function, capability, and performance	751 German firms that had acquired at least one German firm between 2003 and 2006.	A notional definition is missing. There is reference to previous studies.	Dependent	Subjective evaluation of development of sales, market shares, operating margin, synergy realization, and overall satisfaction relative to the primary expectations on a five-point Likert scale	Managerial bias Managers as knowledgeable informants	Acquisition experience has a positive impact on performance through the development of a M&A capability. When M&A capability acts as mediator, the indirect effect of acquisition experience on performance is significant.

(continued)

Authors	Research Questions	Research setting	Notional definition	Independent/ Dependent/ Mediating/ Moderating	Operational measure	Assumptions	Major findings
Vaara et al. (2014)	Focuses on managers' attributions of performance.	Finnish acquirers between 2001 and 2004	Performance consists of four items that measured the outcome of the acquisition and the integration process using managerial evaluation of acquisition performance.	Dependent	Subjective assessment of performances compared with objective performance, measured as the acquirer's ROI after the acquisition (in 2005). The two measures correlated positively and significantly	Managerial bias	There is a linear association between performance and attributions to cultural differences, which is moderated by prior experience. Furthermore, there is a curvilinear association between performance and attributions to managers' actions, no support for the moderating effect of experience for this association.
Zhu, Ma, Sauerwald, and Peng (2019)	Examines how home country institutions influence CBA performance	A sample of 12,021 CBA involving 43 home and target countries between 1995 and 2003	No notional definition of performance. Reference to previous studies.	Dependent	CBA performance is measured by using acquirers' return on sales (ROS) three years after CBA announcements.	Because ROS includes two flow measures (pretax income and net sales), it is less influenced by inflation and accounting standards than return on assets.	While collectivism and humane orientation (two major informal institutions) can facilitate post-acquisition integration and firm performance, shareholder orientation and

Revisiting acquisition performance measurement 201

property rights protection (two formal institutions) constrain post-acquisition integration and firm performance.

Nested acquisitions and all four dimensions of nested acquisition complexity were found to negatively affect acquirer performance.

| Zorn et al. (2019) | Examines nested acquisitions that likely tax the capacity of acquiring and acquired firm managers due to heightened integration challenges | US acquirers listed in the SDC Platinum database from 2000 to 2014. Only completed acquisitions of public companies where firms purchased at least 50% of the target firm resulting in 1,242 public nested acquisitions. | Tobin's q, a commonly used measures of performance and captures both accounting and market performance. | Dependent | Tobin's q is measured in the year following the acquisition $(t + 1)$. | It is a forward-looking measure that prior research suggests adequately captures the current financial position of the firm and shareholders' beliefs about future profitability. |

9 Improving acquisition research methods
Addressing endogeneity

Gonzalo Molina-Sieiro

Introduction

Acquisitions are one of the main ways a firm's leadership has to implement corporate strategy. Acquisitions also represent one of the largest uses of cash for corporations; yet research on them has failed to coalesce onto consistent methodological techniques and approaches. Moreover, the literature has not consistently applied research variables across studies (King, Dalton, Daily, & Covin, 2004; King, Wang, Samimi, & Cortes, 2021) leading to criticisms that acquisition research has become fragmented (King et al., 2021). An additional implication is methodological fragmentation with best practices inconsistently applied. As such, it is critical that researchers get a better understanding of acquisitions and how to study them.

Importantly, acquisitions are the result of many endogenous processes that are for the most part unobserved. As such, there are innumerable factors associated with acquisitions that may confound the effect from an independent variable to a dependent variable. For example, there are cognitive and behavioral elements in firm leadership (Nadolska & Barkema, 2014), differences in country characteristics (Dikova, Sahib, & Van Witteloostuijn, 2010; Gubbi, Aulakh, Ray, Sarkar, & Chittoor, 2010; Li, Arikan, Shenkar, & Arikan, 2020), and temporal, cross-sectional, and distributional issues (Bauer, Dao, Matzler, & Tarba, 2017; King et al., 2021) that influence acquisitions and may confound predicted $x \rightarrow y$ relationships. Yet, scholars have addressed these issues in idiosyncratic ways instead of utilizing a consistent approach that can be deployed to different scenarios. The fundamental problem of causal inference is that researchers can never know what would have happened had a different value of the independent variable been observed for any given unit (Holland, 1986; Rubin, 1974). Acquisitions present a particular problem for causal inference since they are hard to reverse; each deal has unobserved particularities that other deals might not serve as good counterfactuals, and engaging in them is inherently endogenous.

This chapter proposes a consistent way of framing causal inference in acquisition research. As such, I borrow from several disciplines to

DOI: 10.4324/9781003188308-13

Improving acquisition research methods 203

bring an eclectic approach that combines structural approaches to causal inference (Pearl, 2009) and potential outcome approaches (Rubin, 2005; Imbens & Rubin, 2015), as well as instrumental variable approaches (Heckman, 1979; Angrist, Imbens, & Rubin, 1996; Angrist & Pischke, 2008; Wooldridge, 2010). As such, I emphasize the structural approaches to choosing and identifying variables to account for and which variables to leave out. I use figures to illustrate concepts that are important to understand; yet the underlying math is complex and might mask the problem. I then discuss different design implementations to prevent sources of bias with an emphasis on confounding bias. This research does not intend to be a fully methodological paper or replace more detailed sources for methodological issues, but rather present certain ideas from other fields that researchers can find useful and serve as a starting point for accounting for biases in acquisitions.

Contextual issues

There are many ways how the acquisition context presents particular challenges to accounting for biases. Firms included in research frequently include only firms that made acquisitions, and firms making acquisitions can display important differences from firms that do not make acquisitions. For example, acquiring firms often spend significantly less on research and development (King, Slotegraaf, & Kesner, 2008). In other words, acquisition research often displays selection bias, or self-selection (Heckman, 1979). Moreover, there are multiple variables that should predict both the predictor and the outcome of interest, as similar unobserved issues predict multiple characteristics of acquisitions. For example, announcement CAR, deal premium, relatedness, integration success, and other characteristics depend on unobservable issues from acquisition expertise to managerial cognitive preferences. The result is that firms making acquisitions are not random across the broader population of firms, or the acquisition process is confounded between predictor and outcome variables. The combined result is potential bias for estimates of the influence of independent variables that inflate model fit.

As such, I enumerate some of the approaches to account for such potential biases and how they are related to one another. I put a special focus on addressing omitted variable bias, since acquisition research is prone to have many unobserved factors that can bias a researcher's findings. Nevertheless, I discuss how omitted variable bias relates to other kinds of bias from the exclusion or inclusion of control variables. Thus, I contextualize how findings might be biased from each type of variables in the data generating structure of the dependent variable, either from their inclusion or exclusion. For this, I take a structural approach to delineating which variables should be included or excluded (Cunningham, 2021; Pearl, 2009) for a research question. Most claims in this manuscript have

204   Gonzalo Molina-Sieiro

been verified with Monte Carlo simulations, and the code in R is available upon request.

The simplest way to prevent endogeneity from an omitted variable is to control for the confounding variable statistically. In an effort to prevent this bias, researchers include many control variables in their statistical models. However, researchers should identify certain controls that fit a general causal structure of the outcome of interest. Including a variable that is not a confounder can introduce bias, not just prevent said bias. As such, scholars should try to assess how the independent variable of interest fits into the overall causal structure of the dependent variable in order to identify which variables to include and which variables to leave out. Moreover, often times the source of confounding bias is unobserved, making statistically controlling for it challenging. In those cases, there are several approaches researchers can use to recover a treatment effect or at least provide assurances to the validity of the finding. I summarize three types of variables that influence how we estimate the relationship $x \to y$.

First, there are potential mediators where $x \to m \to y$. Researchers may control for mediators to prevent alternative explanations for the relationship $x \to y$ that are not hypothesized. This is because an uncontrolled mediator casts doubt, since x might influence y through the hypothesized mechanism, or it might influence it through the uncontrolled mediator. Uncontrolled mediators do not introduce systematic bias into the estimated coefficients, but the resulting coefficients might include the indirect effect through the uncontrolled mediator, not just through the hypothesized mechanism. As such, one should control for mediators if it is important to disentangle the effect of $x \to y$ from the effect of $x \to m \to y$, but not controlling for m does not introduce omitted variable bias. Importantly, one should not control for a mediator that is part of the hypothesized relationship $x \to y$ instead of controlling for an alternative explanation. An improperly controlled mediator can end up shutting down the path of interest in research and incorrectly conclude that there is no effect. In short, controlling for mediators is fine, but it should be done carefully, since the causal structure of the controlled mediator should be considered. This will be explained more below.

Second, there are potential variables to include that are outcome variables of both x and y. These variables are known as colliders (Bollen & Pearl, 2013; Cunningham, 2021; Pearl, 1998, 2009). Researchers should not control for these variables, since they introduce systematic bias. A collider is illustrated in Figure 9.1. It is in these cases that controlling for these variables is worse than not controlling for them. This is sometimes referred to as collider bias. The bias they introduce is substantial and can turn significant findings not significant estimated effects, positive effects into negative estimated effects, and non-existent effects into significant estimated effects.

Moreover, including any post-treatment variable (including mediators) may potentially introduce bias, as long as they are endogenous with y

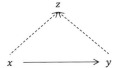

Figure 9.1 Collider variables that introduce bias as a control.

Figure 9.2 Collider bias from an endogenous control.

(see Figure 9.2). In Figure 9.2, there is a hidden collider bias that is harder to spot, and a researcher controlling for z opens up the endogenous paths through the unobserved variable ψ, therefore introducing bias. In that setup, z is a collider for x and ψ, whereas ψ is a confounder for z and y. This example serves to illustrate that a seemingly innocuous control variable might introduce systematic bias. Hence, researchers should focus on controlling for pre-treatment covariates (i.e., variables that influence the independent variable). Specifically, only pre-treatment covariates potentially confound the effect of $x \rightarrow y$ (i.e., omitted variable bias), and pre-treatment covariates cannot act as colliders, making them variables that is safe to control for. When controlling for post-treatment variables, there is always the possibility that collider bias is introduced if these are confounded with y. Researchers should be as concerned about collider bias as we are concerned about omitted variable bias. Both introduce systematic bias, yet in different ways. The inclusion of a collider introduces bias, while the exclusion of a confounder introduces bias. Moreover, including a collider variable in a regression can introduce bias in either direction, leading to potential false positives and false negatives.

Third, there are potential variables that are confounders that predict both x and y, and these variables should be controlled for. Confounders are illustrated in Figure 9.3. If researchers do not control for confounders, systematic bias is introduced creating a threat to internal validity. That is because the estimated effect $x \rightarrow y$ might be the result of the effect of $z \rightarrow x$ and $z \rightarrow y$, rather than the existence of a true $x \rightarrow y$ effect. Hence, the estimated $x \rightarrow y$ effect is due to the common cause of z, rather than a true existing relationship. Confounders can bias results both positively or negatively, so their exclusion from the regression can create both false positives and false negatives. This is known as either confounder bias or omitted variable bias. Omitted variable bias is also the most common

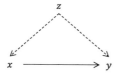

Figure 9.3 Excluding confounder variables introduces bias.

form of endogeneity and the most concerning. As such, it will be the focus for most of this piece.

The problem for scholars is that most confounding effects are unobserved, so controlling for them is challenging. For this reason, several techniques have been developed to recover the true $x \to y$ effect. Ideally, researchers could perform an experiment and directly control the level of the independent variable by random assignment. By doing this, researchers avoid the possibility that the path $z \to x$ exists since the values of x are due to the random assignment by researchers. However, acquisition researchers are unable to randomly assign firms into different treatment conditions because of the nature of the phenomenon. The most researchers can do in terms of experimental evidence is to test some of the underlying mechanisms in an experimental setting that may give credence to a mechanism in an observed acquisition sample without directly performing an experiment. For example, researchers examining cognitive influences on decision-making might run an experiment for that cognitive influence on an intermediate outcome that should be also present in the decision making during an acquisition. Some scholars have argued for the use of field experiments in strategy research (Bettis, Gambardella, & Helfat, 2014; Chatterji, Findley, Jensen, Meier, & Nielson, 2016). However, acquisitions differ from other phenomena where field experiments are possible (Bloom, Eifert, Mahajan, McKenzie, & Roberts, 2013), as an acquisition (unlike other treatments) cannot be reversed, so randomly assigning firms to making an acquisition is untenable.

Nevertheless, valuable counterfactuals can be used when creating acquisition research designs and data collection. The strength of experimental evidence is the inclusion of almost perfect counterfactuals, since the control group is the result of random assignment. This is consistent with the potential outcomes view from the Rubin Causal Model (Holland, 1986; Rubin, 1974, 2005). Researchers should design a study so the question of "what if" can be plausibly answered from other observed data. What if the firm had not done such deal? What if the firm had invested fewer resources in lobbying? Would the firm have made bad acquisitions had their CEO not being narcissistic or less narcissistic? What if the firm with x did not have x? These questions are answered in an experiment through random assignment, but researchers can still look for valuable comparisons. Still, this presents challenges because assignment into the

Improving acquisition research methods 207

comparison might be endogenous and subject to omitted variable bias. However, there are several ways to present evidence for this counterfactual, and I discuss four.

First, a researcher could create a setup where it exploits seemingly insignificant differences in the observations to find lack of support for the hypotheses. Sometimes known as placebo tests, the goal is to provide evidence that results found are due to important and interesting sources of variation, rather than irrelevant differences. These tests have become somewhat common in disciplines with similar confounding issues like finance (Agarwal, Mullally, Tang, & Yang, 2015; Bernile et al., 2017; Bernstein, 2015; Dimmock, Gerken, & Graham, 2018; Garmaise & Moskowitz, 2006). For example, the values for an independent variable x should predict the investor reaction to an acquisition in the focal announcement date, but not the same date the previous year, so if x predicts both abnormal returns in the focal date and other dates chosen at random (or a systematic way), it indicates that your results might be due to chance or some other reason not hypothesized. There are a multitude of ways in which these tests can be set up, depending on the issue researchers want to guard against. A placebo test cannot provide evidence for a hypothesis, but rather against an alternative explanation. As such, one can design such a test that gives evidence that it is not unobserved firm-level factors driving results, but the variable of interest.

Second, researchers might find a natural experiment where an exogenous event in the environment influences some (but not all) firms to display different values for an independent variable. Some researchers have already started exploiting these sources of variation (Gormley, Matsa, & Milbourn, 2013; Younge, Tong, & Fleming, 2015). Here, researchers can avoid the possibility that $z \rightarrow x$, because values in x are due to the exogenous change. Examples of these experiments would be a hurricane that influenced firms in one area, but not in other areas. While it may sound simple to use exogenous events to craft natural experiments, several conditions must be met. For example, one needs a comparison group that was not affected by the exogenous event. Firms in that comparison group must then be as similar as possible to firms that were affected by that exogenous event. Moreover, because natural experiments are normally used as an instrumental variable, it should satisfy other assumptions of instrumental variables beyond exogeneity. Nevertheless, natural experiments or exogenous changes in the environment should be incorporated more broadly in acquisition research. For example, changes in laws in different countries or jurisdictions might have an influence on whether firms engage in acquisition (Martynova & Renneboog, 2008). In this case, we can isolate those firms that chose to pursue acquisitions as a result of legislation changes, rather than endogenous firm strategic choices.

Third, researchers can use research designs that are somewhat robust to these violations, like regression discontinuities or

208   *Gonzalo Molina-Sieiro*

difference-in-differences. Some acquisition research in the finance and strategy has already implemented regression discontinuities (Becht, Polo, & Rossi, 2016; Chemmanur & Tian, 2018) or difference-in-difference (Shi, Hoskisson, & Zhang, 2017). In particular, differences-in-difference designs might be useful in certain situations in research. This is because it entails a comparison of pre-treatment differences with post-treatment differences, where researchers can construe the focal acquisition as the treatment. An important issue to consider is that acquisitions are different from each other, so the treatment is not homogenous, making implementation challenging and researchers should pay attention to these issues. Moreover, proving the parallel trends assumption in a difference-in-difference design is often challenging. Nevertheless, the robustness of a design to isolate an effect by accounting for pre-treatment differences requires a well-chosen control group when comparing post-treatment differences.

Lastly, researchers can correct statistically for endogeneity concerns, including omitted variable bias. This is normally done through either selection on observables (e.g., sample rebalancing methods like matching) or through selection on unobservables (e.g., instrumental variables implemented through a variety of methods). It is important to note that a few of the previous solutions might be implemented as instrumental variables, and sample rebalancing might be part of how research designs are executed.

Selection on observables

Again, firms that engage in acquisitions can present different choices, and here I outline sample rebalancing, matching and weighting considerations for acquisition research.

Sample rebalancing

The goal of sample rebalancing methods is to achieve balance between treated observations and untreated observations on other covariates of interest. These methods seek that by achieving balance on covariates between treated and untreated observations, the estimated effect $x \rightarrow y$ is unconfounded to these covariates. Balance means that treated and untreated observations do not differ along dimensions of interest. For example, before correcting it could be that treated observations have higher revenue, which could explain $x \rightarrow y$. After implementing any of these methods, one should find that treated and untreated observations have similar revenues. There are two main ways to implement these methods: matching and reweighting. As such, the adequateness of the matching or reweighting method is determined by whether the researchers achieved balance after adjusting the sample. Are treated observations similar to untreated observations after the adjustment, either on the matched sample or on the weighed sample?

Improving acquisition research methods 209

This follows from the tradition of potential outcomes in experimental settings. Rosenbaum and Rubin (1985) develop the method to describe how a randomized control trials experiment achieves balance on covariates, then develops how using propensity scores can achieve balance on observable covariates, but not unobservable covariates like a randomized control trial. The purpose of these methods is to accomplish ignorability (unconfoundedness) on observable covariates. This means that the characteristics of the treatment assignment can be ignored based on the covariates used on the first stage.

Sample matching

For matching, researchers should seek to find the best paired matches among the control units. That is, what are the untreated observations that most resemble the treated observations? There are many ways to achieve this. In a way, we can think of matching as systematically discarding the untreated observations that least resemble the treated observations. By doing so they prevent that these discarded observations influence the estimated effects. Importantly, researchers should only match treated and untreated observation on pre-treatment covariates.

There are several ways of matching observations. The most straightforward method is to use exact matching where observations are matched based on sharing certain characteristics with the treated observations. For example, if all treated firms in my sample are in either New York and California in a study where locational issues might be confounding, discarding untreated observations that are not located in New York and California is reasonable and this is what exact matching does. Ideally, there might be a sample adjustment, since we would want the same number of observations in each "bin" between treated and untreated observations to prevent variance being weighed in such a way that introduces imbalance. However, there can still be problems with balancing if treated observations in our sample are 90 percent in New York and 10 percent in California, and matching untreated observations are 90 percent in California and 10 percent in New York. Hence, focusing on the same states can still be imbalanced if there are unobserved differences between New York and California. One of the main challenges with exact matching is multidimensionality, or finding firms that share all characteristics across many dimensions with the treated observations might be challenging.

The most common type of matching is nearest neighbor matching, either Mahalanobis distance matching or propensity score matching. The main advantages these methods provide are that a researcher can match on a continuous covariate, since the goal is to find the untreated observations that most closely resemble the treated observations by estimating a multidimensional distance score. Mahalanobis matching finds a matched observation for each treated observation that is closest across multiple dimensions using a mahalanobis distance score. Normally, mahalanobis distance finds matches from yet unmatched untreated observations. Propensity score matching estimates the probability of being treated (i.e., the propensity score) and then for each treated observation finds the closest untreated observation with the most similar propensity score. As such, it resembles ranking treated and untreated observations by the propensity score, and it keeps untreated observations with the highest propensity scores, and it discards untreated observations with the lowest propensity score. The main advantage of propensity score matching is that it reduces the multidimensionality problem to just one number for matching, the propensity score. However, it does not guarantee that there will be good balance across all dimensions. This is because across two dimensions with similar influence on the propensity score, the method might match a treated observation high on first dimension (e.g., sales), yet low on the second dimension (e.g., R&D), with an untreated observation high on the second dimension (e.g., R&D), yet low on the first dimension (e.g., sales). Mahalanobis distance would not match such observation pair, but it has trouble finding good matches when matching across a large number of dimensions. For this reason, it is good to assess balance across all dimensions when choosing the matching method. As long as there is a good balance between treated and untreated observations the mahalanobis versus propensity score issue is not important since they share a goal that can be assessed from looking at whether the untreated observations that are retained resemble the treated observations across all matching dimensions. As such, researchers might even use mahalanobis distance with one of the dimensions being a function of the propensity score, while other dimensions represent those that are really important to balance.

The last important matching method is coarsened exact matching (CEM). This method was first developed by Iacus, King, and Porro (2012), as a way to introduce exact matching techniques on continuous covariates. Importantly, there is no need to check for balance across covariates in CEM because the researcher can specify the acceptable level of imbalance before matching. The technique consists of first coarsening the continuous covariates into different set of "bins", before performing exact matching within those bins. Importantly, it also estimates weights to use in the second stage regression so that treated and untreated observations in each bin have the same weight. For example, if one of the covariates used to match is the age of the CEO, then researchers could coarsen the variable into age groups: 20–30 year old, 30–40 year old, and so on. However, a researcher controls how much imbalance is acceptable, as smaller bins (30–35 year old, 35–40 year old, and so on) result in better balance than wider bins (30–50 year old, 50–70 year old, and so on). It involves a trade-off as smaller bins make finding matches harder, but better matches are possible. This is relevant, because only matched

Improving acquisition research methods 211

observations are included in the final sample. If a treated observation does not have a good untreated match, it will be discarded.

Additional matching methods include parametric and non-parametric options. An example of parametric options for optimal balance finds untreated observations that have balance with the treated observations versus a nearest neighbor. Non-parametric options perform genetic matching (Diamond & Sekhon, 2013) (starting from a matched sample, calculate scores for balance, then algorithmically improves balance) or entropy balance (Hainmuller, 2012). Entropy balance calculates weights for untreated observations that algorithmically make the untreated sample equal on the first (mean) and second (standard deviation) moments as the treated observations, but it can be modified to achieve balance on higher moments. This topic is a large and ongoing literature in statistics and other disciplines, so this list is not meant to be exhaustive.

Matching methods can be implemented quite easily in many statistical languages and packages. The best distribution to implement a variety of matching methods is MatchIt that has implementations in R and Stata (Stuart, King, Imai, & Ho, 2011). Besides simply creating a matched sample, matching methods can be useful as part of a broader research design for causal inference. For example, matching can help find untreated observations with parallel trends to use in a difference-in-difference design (Shi, Hoskisson, & Zhang, 2017). Matching can be used to find firms that did not engage in an acquisition that are very similar to those firms that did in order to estimate other effects of interest. One could either prove parallel trends, or if one does not have multi-period longitudinal data one can at least match observations pre-treatment to calculate outcome differences pre-treatment and post-treatment with a simplified difference-in-differences design. This could be as simple as matching observations that are very similar on pre-treatment outcome levels as well as several other dimensions to enable assessing the differences on the outcome of interest post-treatment. The treatment can take the form of an acquisition, but it could take other forms depending on the theory of interest. Without showing parallel trends it is not strictly a difference-in-difference design, but such design would approximate one.

Sample weighting

There are many ways to create weights to rebalance the sample. However, the most common way is to create weight such that treated observations that were unlikely to be treated and untreated observations that were likely to be treated are those with the highest weights in the sample (Glynn & Quinn, 2010). This type of procedure is known by several names, like Inverse Propensity Score Weights (IPSW), Inverse Probability of Treatment Weights (IPTW), and a few others. There are several ways to actually calculate the resulting weights, where some weights try to

212 Gonzalo Molina-Sieiro

estimate an Average Treatment Effect (ATE) while others try to estimate an Average Treatment Effect for the Treated (ATT). An example for a basic formula for these weights is such that the weight is provided by:

$$\eta_i = \left(\psi_i^t \left(1 - \psi_i \right)^{\{1-t\}} \right)^{-1}$$

Where η_i are the estimated weights for observation i; ψ_i is the estimated probability that observation i is treated, and t is the treatment indicator. It is important to note that these are just one of many variations of weights to use in this type of adjustment. Again, balance should be assessed by differences between treated and untreated observations without weighing the sample and those differences after weighing the sample.

Moreover, weighting opens the option to create weights to rebalance the sample when researchers are faced with continuous treatments. Covariate Balancing Propensity Score (CBPS) has been adapted to create weights to rebalance for a continuous treatment variable (Fong, Hazlett, & Imai, 2018). In this instance, balance is assessed by comparing pre-weighting correlations with the treatment variable with post-weighting correlations with the treatment variable.

Sample reweighing methods are doubly robust, which means that an effect is well estimated as long as either of the two stages is appropriate. However, it might lead to poor estimates of the standard error. Ideally, when using sample rebalancing through reweighting, researchers should estimate both stages in a bootstrap procedure since variance estimates might not be consistent. This is particularly important if a few observations have an outsized weight (e.g., if their resulting weight is over 100 in a sample of just a 1,000 observations). Alternatively, researchers can trim the weights to a pre-defined maximum to avoid just a couple of observations driving the results since they might be overweighted and use robust standard errors based on HC3, rather than the default HC1 since HC3 better account for influential observations (Hayes & Cai, 2000; Long & Ervin, 2000).

There are many benefits to the methods of sample rebalancing, since they rely on fewer assumptions than instrumental variable methods. For example, they do not assume that the covariates used in the first stage are exogenous. Instead, the goal is to improve the balance between treated and untreated observations. Nevertheless, the main drawback is that they do not fully prevent unobserved variables from influencing the $x \rightarrow y$ effect. They only prevent this insofar as the observed covariates included in the first stage estimation are related to the unobserved factors. For this reason, Stuart (2010) suggests that as many covariates as possible be included in the first stage, since the main drawback from including these is that they may not predict the probability of treatment in which case they only have negligible influence on the estimated propensity

Improving acquisition research methods 213

score. Using more predictors to calculate the propensity score also has the advantage that it increases the chances that unobservable covariates correlate with the observables included. When choosing variables for the first stage, priority should be given to variables that would predict both the treatment and the outcome (Stuart, 2010), as well as avoiding the selection post-treatment variables.

The goal of propensity score methods (and others sample balancing methods) is to replicate the conditions of a controlled experiment with random assignment based on observable covariates. However, random assignment controls for both observable and unobservable characteristics. The extent of how well this method achieves that is based on the covariates included in the first stage (how well they predict treatment and how much they correlate with unobservable covariates) and on the quality of the adjustment made to the second stage that estimates the causal effect. Both of these are untestable, but a good faith judgment must be made regarding them that makes the claims of causality and endogeneity adjustment believable.

Instrumental variables

Scholars can also use instrumental variable techniques to identify the endogenous $x \to y$ effect. These methods are the commonly used in strategic management and related disciplines like economics, but rarely used in behavioral disciplines like psychology. However, it is important to note that the potential for abuse of these methods can lead to incorrect inferences when implemented inappropriately (Semadeni, Withers, & Certo, 2014).

For this reason, I would like to separate the discussion of instrumental variables implementation into two parts: (1) the appropriateness of the instrumental variables chosen, and (2) the method of estimation. This is important because if an appropriate instrument is found, implementation of an estimation method is quite simple. Still, researchers often confuse the estimation method with a solution for endogeneity. I want to say that whether endogeneity is addressed depends on the validity of the instrumental variables used, and not on the statistical estimation method. Using two stages least squares only means that the estimation took two stages, and the second stage predictor variable takes the form of the predicted values from the first stage. A similar argument can be made for control functions, generalized method of moments (GMM), and other estimators. Whether endogeneity is addressed by these methods depends on the appropriateness of the instrumental variables used in the first stage. This contributes to what makes adequately addressing endogeneity challenging.

Instrumental variables can address endogeneity, because they can block the path $z \to x$ as shown in Figure 9.4. This is because while z predicts x, it does not predict $\hat{x}$, since that is predicted by a valid instrumental

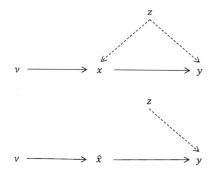

Figure 9.4 Instrumental variable estimation.

variable. To adequately address endogeneity, a good instrumental variable requires meeting several assumptions described below. In discussing these assumptions, figures will be used when appropriate.

First, an instrumental variable needs to be an important predictor of the endogenous variable of interest. This might be achievable if not for assumption number II, III, and IV (i.e., exogeneity, monotonicity, and the exclusion restriction). In Figure 9.4, this would mean that the $v \rightarrow x$ relationship exists, and it explains an important portion of x. This is because instrumental variables explain a Local Average Treatment Effect (LATE) where only the effect for those observations where v led to x is identified (Imbens & Rubin, 2015). This is important because it stresses the fact that the instrument v may have an influence on the level of x for some firms, but not others which are sometimes referred to as non-compliers. Compliance versus non-compliance may be endogenous in itself, so an instrumental variable v only identifies an effect for compliers (Angrist, Imbens, & Rubin, 1996). For example, if the researcher was interested in estimating the effects of arriving to work one hour early on job satisfaction, the researcher could randomly assign people to conditions, somehow incentivize them to arrive early with a bonus, and then estimate the effects on job satisfaction. However, random assignment happens at the incentive stage not at the time of arrival stage, but the variable of interest is time of arrival. The researcher can use the randomly assigned incentive as an instrumental variable of whether the employee actually arrived early, and this should meet all assumptions behind instrumental variables. However, there are people that no matter the incentive will not arrive early (never-early), and others that even without the incentive would arrive early (always-early). It is unlikely that the people who never arrive early are comparable to the people who always do. In other words, each group contains people that responded to the incentive and changed their behavior as a result, as well as people that did not alter their behavior as a result of the incentive. Using such an instrument can

Improving acquisition research methods 215

then only identify an effect for those people that arrived early as a result of the incentive.

Second, to assess whether the instrument conforms to the non-zero causal effect on the endogenous predictor, researchers should provide evidence of the strength of the relationship between the instrument v and the independent variable x. Researchers should perform a weak instruments test that can be as simple as an F-test on the first stage on whether including versus excluding the set of instrumental variables predict the variance in the endogenous independent variable x, which should be significant and greater than a cutoff, usually $F > 10$ (Steiger & Stock, 1997; Andrews, Stock, & Sun, 2019). However, Stock and Yogo (2005) argue that $F > 16.4$ is more appropriate and there are scholars who suggest even larger cutoffs in recent working papers, including $F > 50$ (Keane & Neal, 2021) or $F > 104.7$ (Lee, McCrary, Moreira, & Porter, 2020). There are also other tests that in some cases may be more appropriate than a simple F-test (Olea & Pflueger, 2013), and researchers should pay attention to potential violations. It is clear from simulations that weak instruments might cause more problems than they solve (Semadeni, Withers, & Certo, 2014), so scholars should be mindful of the impact their instrumental variables have on the endogenous regressor and report a weak instruments test for the first stage.

Third, the instrumental variable can only affect observations of the endogenous variable in one direction (monotonicity). It cannot have a positive impact on some and a negative impact on others. This is best aided by theory or research design. When using the example of the experiment examining the relationship of arriving early to work on job satisfaction, the bonus for an early arrival (i.e., instrumental variable) should only make it more likely that an individual arrives early to work. It should not decrease the chances of anybody arriving early. In observational studies, this assumption is hard to test, but scholars should make a good faith effort to explain why the relationship of $v \to x$ is monotonous. This is also sometimes referred to as the absence of defiers. Defiers are those people that act in opposition to the assignment in the instrumental variable. In the example about the incentives for arriving early, a defier would be a person that, in response to being offered an incentive for arriving early to work, chooses to arrive late. This differs from non-compliance in that non-compliers are people that would never arrive early whether there is an incentive or not. In comparison, defiers are people that arrive late in response to being offered an incentive to arrive early. In our example, defiance is clear, but in applications to acquisitions may be hard to identify. Defiers in acquisitions are a subtle issue that would be linked to untestable and complex relationships between the instrumental variable and the predictor of interest. For example, if a change in legislation is used as an instrumental variable predicting whether a firm attempts an acquisition, it is difficult to know ex-ante whether a legislation change pushes firms to make more or fewer acquisitions. As a result, identifying the issue of defiance is difficult in acquisitions research.

Fourth, there needs to be an exclusion restriction. The instrumental variable can only predict the outcome variable through its effects on the endogenous variable, so that it is uncorrelated with the error term in the second stage. There exists a test to assess whether it is uncorrelated with the error term, but it requires the first stage to be overidentified (more than one valid instrument per endogenous variable) and the existence of a second instrument that is valid (which cannot be tested) (Larcker et al, 2010). This is complicated because, as researchers, we are forced to make the assumption that the only way v has an effect on y is through the $v \to x \to y$ path. That means that there is no variable ζ where the path $v \to \zeta \to y$ exists. By implication, this means that the path $v \to y$ also does not exist. A violation of this assumption is illustrated in Figure 9.5. In the example about paying incentives to arrive early to work, one can assume that the incentive should only increase job satisfaction through its influence on arriving early since only those who arrive early receive such bonus. In acquisitions, this is challenging as researchers have to assume that the chosen instrumental variable can only influence the dependent variable through its influence on the independent variable. In the case of a legislation change that may predict acquisitions, legislation changes may also influence a variety of behavior by firms that, in turn, may influence the dependent variable to potentially make an instrumental variable invalid. As such, the instrumental variable (e.g., legislation change) should address issues that are as closely tied to the independent variable as possible to make this assumption tenable. For example, a legislation that introduces quotas for women on boards may serve as an instrument for the observed share of women on individual boards, since any effects of the new legislation on any dependent variable can be thought to only be related to the changes brought about by adding women on boards.

Fifth, there needs to be exogeneity, or the instrumental variable needs to be exogenously generated. Ideally, it is the result of random assignment or some other random process. In acquisitions, this is the hardest assumption to satisfy since the phenomenon depends on each other. While it is not necessary that a completely randomly generated variable be used, an instrument v cannot be predicted by an unobservable factor z such that $z \to v$ does not exist for all z with an existent $z \to y$ path. In this

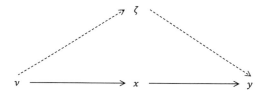

Figure 9.5 Exclusion restriction violation.

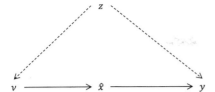

Figure 9.6 Exogeneity assumption violation.

case, natural experiments are useful since it is unlikely that $z \to v$ exists. A violation of this assumption is illustrated in Figure 9.6. In the case of the example where incentives are paid to arrive early, the assumption would be satisfied since the researchers would control who gets access to the incentive through random assignment, which prevents the possibility that $z \to v$ exists. In the case of a legislation change predicting the engagement in acquisitions, this is satisfied since it is unlikely that legislators responded to a factor that also influences the dependent variable of interest.

Sixth, after an appropriate instrument has been identified, researchers can utilize it statistically through a variety of methods. The most common one is through two-stage least squares (2SLS) where the instrumental variable v predicts the independent variable x, and the predicted values from the first stage $\hat{x}$ are used as the independent variable in the second stage. Two other common methods to implement instrumental variables are GMM and limited-information maximum likelihood (LIML). These three estimators can be used with the *ivregress* command in Stata or through a variety of packages in R. Instrumental variables can also be utilized in other methods, including structural equation modeling (SEM). To apply an instrumental variable method in SEM, researchers need to freely estimate the covariance term of the errors of x and y. The issue with implementing in SEM is that it might be challenging to achieve convergence when estimating the covariance between x and y in small samples. As such, unless the measurement stage is important for the research setting and sample, more traditional instrumental variables methods are preferred. A third way to implement instrumental variables is through a control function where researchers include the residuals of the first stage as a control variable in the second stage. A control function is especially useful when researchers include the endogenous independent variable x in multiple polynomial terms in the second stage model such as quadratic terms for testing curvilinear effects or interaction terms for testing moderation effects (Wooldridge, 2010). This is because those polynomial terms would also be endogenous, but researchers may only have one valid instrumental variable. Importantly, both stages should be estimated together or bootstrap both stages concurrently. This is because

218 *Gonzalo Molina-Sieiro*

standard errors might not have a normal distribution across two stages when estimating two stages separately.

Sample selection bias

An effect can also be confounded because of sample selection bias with sources of bias possible from both confounding and collider bias. In this case, bias comes from a confounder that can predict both the independent variable x and the probability of observing the dependent variable y in the sample. This results in sample selection bias, since the selection into observing y is endogenous. For example, researchers only observe firms that attempt acquisitions (Welch et al., 2020), and this can be endogenous since firm characteristics can predict independent variables of interest and also explain whether a firm attempts an acquisition. Since any deal-level dependent variable can only be observed for firms that attempt an acquisition, scholars should attempt to address omitted variable bias. Similarly, sample inclusion can be dependent on y and z, so that higher levels of y are more likely to be observed and included in the sample. As such, sample inclusion can be both an antecedent or descendant from y, and possible solutions differ. For acquisitions, it is important to note that some indicators are not limited to firms that engage in an acquisition. For example, scholars can estimate cumulative abnormal returns (CAR) for firms that did not engage in an acquisition around the same date. In that way, one could match firms that resemble the acquiring firm and then calculate a CAR for a firm engaging in an acquisition matched with a non-acquiring firm.

There are many ways to address confounding sample selection bias. It is important to note that other solutions to the endogeneity in x should also address this if inclusion into the sample is an ancestor to y (i.e., inclusion does not depend on y, but is also confounded with x and y). This is because, when using other instrumental variables methods, x would be predicted by the instrumental variables or corrected through other methods, therefore not endogenous to the confounder with selection in y. This is because the confounder predicts x, but it should not predict $\hat{x}$, thus instrumental variables would also unconfound the effect. If the researcher has a valid instrument for x using such instrument should be preferred because it blocks the path from the confounder on the probability of inclusion, but other potential confounders as well. Alternatively, researchers can implement what is normally called a Heckman correction (Heckman, 1979). In simulations, a Heckman correction seems to perform better, when inclusion is a descendent of y (i.e., sample inclusion depends on the values of y, such as levels of y above a threshold are not observed). In this correction, researchers use a broader sample with instrumental variables to predict whether y is observed, then create an inverse mills ratio that can be included as a control in the model. Ideally, the whole procedure should be performed as a system of equations or

Improving acquisition research methods 219

bootstrapped. In other words, scholars can block the confounding path by blocking the confounder's path to x by correcting for omitted variable bias, or researchers can block the path from the confounder to y by controlling for the predicted probability of inclusions through an inverse Mills ratio.

Sample selection bias can also occur because of collider bias from conditioning on inclusion. In this case, we have a case where a firm engages in an acquisition because of either x or y. That is because by using a selected sample, one is conditioning on whether an acquirer is a collider. Even though x and y might have no relationship, if one uses a conditioned sample of acquisitions, researchers will find a negative relationship between x and y. This is because some firms will perform acquisitions because of x and other firms will perform acquisitions because of y. As such, within a conditioned sample of acquisitions, x and y will be negatively related, since some will be high on y while others will be high on x. In this case, a Heckman correction or another inverse propensity weighing mechanism would help by giving more weight to observations that were least likely to be included in the sample (i.e., firms less likely to use acquisitions). However, in simulations, no method of addressing conditioned samples completely did away with bias. As other issues, this is a difficult issue to resolve, but it is present in many research settings. For example, if a researcher is studying the effect of extraversion on job satisfaction from a sample drawn from an optional social work event, one could find that extraversion is negatively related to job satisfaction. That is because extraverted individuals like social settings, so it increases their chances of participating in a social event. Likewise, people who like their jobs (independent of their extraversion) would tend to participate on a work-organized social event. As such, some employees would participate because they are extraverted, while others would participate because they like their job. Thus, they would exhibit a negative correlation in that specific sample. When dealing with sample selection bias, researchers should carefully consider sample selection and its influence, as solutions differ across sources of inclusion bias.

What should scholars do?

In considering the preceding summary of concerns and potential remedies, I now offer advice for designing acquisition research.

Start with causal inferences in mind

Acquisition research design needs to be planned with the adequate causal inference issues in mind (Cording, Christmann, & Weigelt, 2010). As scholars, we should ask what the main threats are for valid inference of $x \rightarrow y$ effect, and then try to control for confounders. If there is a potential confounder that is unobserved, a plausible and defensible

220   *Gonzalo Molina-Sieiro*

identification strategy should be planned before data collection. It is oftentimes much easier to start a research project with an identification strategy in mind, than to try to figure out a valid identification strategy for a project that is already under way. Moreover, it is preferable to do so early, since endogeneity solutions that are planned in advance of data collection tend to be more robust.

This means that researchers should understand what the main antecedents for their outcome of interest are and try to understand how their predictor of interest fits into that causal structure. Further, it means that when predicting acquisition performance, a researcher should anticipate what are the antecedents of acquisition performance. This is because, if an antecedent of acquisition performance could also explain the predictor of interest, researchers should make a plan to control for potential confounding. Most simply, researchers can make these confounders part of their data collection efforts to avoid corrections that make further assumptions. Relying on variables included in meta-analysis is a good start (King et al., 2021). Nevertheless, researchers should take care to avoid including colliders in their regression models, so a thoughtful exercise in distinguishing effects from causes is needed when choosing variables to include in a research model. In other words, scholars should not control for factors that may be predicted by acquisition performance.

At a minimum, scholars should understand the main causal structure of the main phenomena under study in acquisition research. This should help scholars control for a consistent set of control variables that are highly relevant and potential confounders, while saving time and effort by not controlling for a battery of other controls that may be irrelevant. Since acquisitions tend to have similar antecedents, outcomes, and measurement across different industries and contexts (e.g., announcement precedes closure or payment method precedes announcement returns), this should help create a consistent set of important control variables that scholars should control for. While these might not be confounders in certain research questions, they are potential irrelevant mediators that pose important alternative explanations that are not of interest to researchers. For instance, if an independent variable x influences payment method such that an acquisition dilutes shareholder ownership, then it is not unreasonable that x may seem to damage announcement returns (Blackburn, Dark, & Hanson, 1997) unless scholars account for the dilution from paying with stock. A good practice is to control for variables that might predict the independent variable x, since these cannot be colliders or mediators, but they could be confounders, with particular attention to variables that could also predict the dependent variable y.

Know the phenomenon being studied

Scholars should also scour acquisition cases to identify effects that can serve as instrumental variables. An important thing to mention is that an instrumental variable that can identify an effect for $x \rightarrow y_1$ can also identify an effect for $x \rightarrow y_2$ as long as the instrument v also satisfies the exogeneity and exclusion restriction for y_2. This means that while search costs for a valid instrument γ are high, the payoff is such that it can be applied when trying to explain many effects of x. Ideally, other scholars should pay note of valid instruments used in the literature and mimic the best instruments in the literature across different research projects. This would let researchers that identify good instruments to have an influential paper that can inform other research, creating a virtuous circle that improves research.

Hence, researchers should get to know acquisition phenomena more closely. As scholars, we should know what is happening in acquisition practice. Acquisition activity evolves quickly, and each merger wave tends to have new characteristics worthy of study (Martynova & Renneboog, 2008). Beyond that, understanding deals at a more qualitative level should help scholars identify appropriate instrumental variables, as well as situations that can be exploited for answering important yet lingering research questions. Moreover, knowing the phenomena inside and out should help researchers identify ways to improve their research design. In some cases, researchers already know the phenomena quite well, but the goal is to bridge the gap and bring that knowledge into our research.

In closing, the frequency and value of acquisition activity requires more careful research design to facilitate a better understanding of this important phenomenon. The nature of the acquisition phenomenon makes some canonical designs impossible (e.g., randomized controlled experiments), makes confounding variables more likely, and it impairs the ability of researchers to identify an effect. Nevertheless, researchers should address these issues, and this chapter provides a framework for identifying causal effects in acquisitions. I argue that researchers should strive for the best potential alternative and take care in drawing conclusions from their chosen methodology. I show that haphazardly including controls is as likely to contribute to bias as omitting a needed control, depending on the causal structure of the problem. As such, researchers should pay close attention to the research design phase when starting work on their research projects, as opposed to scrambling to satisfy reviewer concerns after data collection and analysis is complete.

References

Agarwal, V., Mullally, K., Tang, Y., & Yang, B. (2015). Mandatory portfolio disclosure, stock liquidity, and mutual fund performance. *Journal of Finance*, 70(6), 2733–2776.

Andrews, I., Stock, J., & Sun, L. (2019). Weak instruments in instrumental variables regression: Theory and practice. *Annual Review of Economics*, 11, 727–753.

Angrist, J., & Pischke, J. (2008). *Mostly harmless econometrics: An empiricist's companion*. Princeton, NJ: Princeton University Press.

Angrist, J., Imbens, G., & Rubin, D. (1996). Identification of causal effects using instrumental variables. *Journal of the American Statistical Association*, 91(434), 444–455.

Bauer, F., Dao, M., Matzler, K., & Tarba, S. (2017). How industry lifecycle sets boundary conditions for M&A integration. *Long Range Planning*, 50(4), 501–517.

Becht, M., Polo, A., & Rossi, S. (2016). Does mandatory shareholder voting prevent bad acquisitions? *Review of Financial Studies*, 29(11), 3035–3067.

Bernile, G., Bhagwat, V., & Rau, P. (2017). What doesn't kill you will only make you more risk-loving: Early-life disasters and CEO behavior. *Journal of Finance*, 72(1), 167–206.

Bernstein, S. (2015). Does going public affect innovation? *Journal of Finance*, 70(4), 1365–1403.

Bettis, R., Gambardella, A., Helfat, C., & Mitchell, W. (2014). Quantitative empirical analysis in strategic management. *Strategic Management Journal*, 25(7), 949–953.

Blackburn, V., Dark, F., & Hanson, R. (1997). Mergers, method of payment and returns to manager-and owner-controlled firms. *Financial Review*, 32(3), 569–589

Bloom, N., Eifert, B., Mahajan, A., McKenzie, D., & Roberts, J. (2013). Does management matter? Evidence from India. *Quarterly Journal of Economics*, 128(1), 1–51.

Bollen, K., & Pearl, J. (2013). Eight myths about causality and structural equation models. In Morgan, S. (ed.) *Handbook of causal analysis for social research* (pp. 301–328). Springer, Dordrecht.

Chatterji, A., Findley, M., Jensen, N., Meier, S., & Nielson, D. (2016). Field experiments in strategy research. *Strategic Management Journal*, 37(1), 116–132.

Chemmanur, T., & Tian, X. (2018). Do antitakeover provisions spur corporate innovation? A regression discontinuity analysis. *Journal of Financial and Quantitative Analysis*, 53(3), 1163–1194.

Cording, M., Christmann, P., & Weigelt, C. (2010). Measuring theoretically complex constructs: The case of acquisition performance. *Strategic Organization*, 8(1), 11–41

Cunningham, S. (2021). *Causal inference: The mixtape*. New Haven, CT: Yale University Press.

Diamond, A., & Sekhon, J. (2013). Genetic matching for estimating causal effects: A general multivariate matching method for achieving balance in observational studies. *Review of Economics and Statistics*, 95(3), 932–945.

Dikova, D., Sahib, P., & Van Witteloostuijn, A. (2010). Cross-border acquisition abandonment and completion: The effect of institutional differences and organizational learning in the international business service industry, 1981–2001. *Journal of International Business Studies*, 41(2), 223–245.

Dimmock, S., Gerken, W., & Graham, N. (2018). Is fraud contagious? Coworker influence on misconduct by financial advisors. *Journal of Finance*, 73(3), 1417–1450.

Fong, C., Hazlett, C., & Imai, K. (2018). Covariate balancing propensity score for a continuous treatment: application to the efficacy of political advertisements. *Annals of Applied Statistics*, 12(1), 156–177.

Garmaise, M., & Moskowitz, T. (2006). Bank mergers and crime: The real and social effects of credit market competition. *Journal of Finance*, 61(2), 495–538.

Glynn, A., & Quinn, K. (2010). An introduction to the augmented inverse propensity weighted estimator. *Political Analysis*, 18(1), 36–56.

Gormley, T., Matsa, D., & Milbourn, T. (2013). CEO compensation and corporate risk: Evidence from a natural experiment. *Journal of Accounting and Economics*, 56(2–3), 79–101.

Gubbi, S., Aulakh, P., Ray, S., Sarkar, M., & Chittoor, R. (2010). Do international acquisitions by emerging-economy firms create shareholder value? The case of Indian firms. *Journal of International Business Studies*, 41(3), 397–418.

Hayes, A., & Cai, L. (2007). Using heteroskedasticity-consistent standard error estimators in OLS regression: An introduction and software implementation. *Behavior Research Methods*, 39(4), 709–722.

Heckman, J. (1979). Sample selection bias as a specification error. *Econometrica: Journal of the Econometric Society*, 47(1), 153–161.

Holland, P. (1986). Statistics and causal inference. *Journal of the American Statistical Association*, 81(396), 945–960.

Iacus, S., King, G., & Porro, G. (2012). Causal inference without balance checking: Coarsened exact matching. *Political Analysis*, 20(1), 1–24.

Imbens, G., & Rubin, D. (2015). *Causal inference in statistics, social, and biomedical sciences*. Cambridge: Cambridge University Press.

Keane, M., & Neal, T. (2021). A new perspective on weak instruments. *UNSW Economics Working Paper No. 2021-05*. Available at: https://papers.ssrn.com/sol3/papers.cfm?abstract_id=3846841

King, D., Dalton, D.., Daily, C. M., & Covin, J. (2004). Meta-analyses of post-acquisition performance: Indications of unidentified moderators. *Strategic Management Journal*, 25(2), 187–200.

King, D. R., Slotegraaf, R. J., & Kesner, I. (2008). Performance implications of firm resource interactions in the acquisition of R&D-intensive firms. *Organization science*, 19(2), 327–340.

King, D., Wang, G., Samimi, M., & Cortes, A. (2021). A meta-analytic integration of acquisition performance prediction. *Journal of Management Studies*, 58(5), 1198–1236.

Larcker, D. F., & Rusticus, T. O. (2010). On the use of instrumental variables in accounting research. *Journal of Accounting and Economics*, 49(3), 186–205.

Lee, D., McCrary, J., Moreira, M., & Porter, J. (2020). Valid t-ratio inference for IV. National Bureau of Economic research. *arXiv preprint arXiv:2010.05058*. www.nber.org/papers/w29124.

Li, C., Arikan, I., Shenkar, O., & Arikan, A. (2020). The impact of country-dyadic military conflicts on market reaction to cross-border acquisitions. *Journal of International Business Studies*, 51(3), 299–325.

Long, J., & Ervin, L. (2000). Using heteroscedasticity consistent standard errors in the linear regression model. *American Statistician*, 54(3), 217–224.

Martynova, M., & Renneboog, L. (2008). A century of corporate takeovers: What have we learned and where do we stand? *Journal of Banking & Finance*, 32(10), 2148–2177.

Nadolska, A., & Barkema, H. (2014). Good learners: How top management teams affect the success and frequency of acquisitions. *Strategic Management Journal*, 35(10), 1483–1507.

Olea, J., & Pflueger, C. (2013). A robust test for weak instruments. *Journal of Business & Economic Statistics*, 31(3), 358–369.

Pearl, J. (1998). Graphs, causality, and structural equation models. *Sociological Methods & Research*, 27(2), 226–284.

Pearl, J. (2009). *Causality*. Cambridge: Cambridge University Press.

Rosenbaum, P. R., & Rubin, D. B. (1985). Constructing a control group using multivariate matched sampling methods that incorporate the propensity score. *The American Statistician*, 39(1), 33–38.

Rubin, D. (1974). Estimating causal effects of treatments in randomized and nonrandomized studies. *Journal of Educational Psychology*, 66(5), 688.

Rubin, D. (2005). Causal inference using potential outcomes: Design, modeling, decisions. *Journal of the American Statistical Association*, 100(469), 322–331.

Semadeni, M., Withers, M., & Certo, T. (2014). The perils of endogeneity and instrumental variables in strategy research: Understanding through simulations. *Strategic Management Journal*, 35(7), 1070–1079.

Shi, W., Hoskisson, R., & Zhang, Y. (2017). Independent director death and CEO acquisitiveness: Build an empire or pursue a quiet life? *Strategic Management Journal*, 38(3), 780–792.

Stock, J., & Yogo, M. (2005). Testing for weak instruments in linear IV regression. In Andrews, D., and Stock, J (eds.) Identification and inference for econometric models: Essays in honor of Thomas Rothenberg, (Vol. 1, p. 80).

Stuart, E. A. (2010). Matching methods for causal inference: A review and a look forward. *Statistical Science: A Review Journal of the Institute of Mathematical Statistics*, 25(1), 1.

Stuart, E., King, G., Imai, K., & Ho, D. (2011). MatchIt: nonparametric preprocessing for parametric causal inference. *Journal of Statistical Software*. 42(8), 1–28.

Welch, X., Pavićević, S., Keil, T., & Laamanen, T. (2020). The pre-deal phase of mergers and acquisitions: A review and research agenda. *Journal of Management*, 46(6), 843–878.

Wooldridge, J. (2010). *Econometric analysis of cross section and panel data*. MIT Press.

Younge, K., Tong, T., & Fleming, L. (2015). How anticipated employee mobility affects acquisition likelihood: Evidence from a natural experiment. *Strategic Management Journal*, 36(5), 686–708.

10 Cultural dynamics in acquisitions

Satu Teerikangas and Melanie Hassett

Introduction

Despite ongoing acquisition activity and research, reviews of the field point to advances and a continuing inability to tap into what happens when two formerly distinct organizations combine (Graebner, Heimeriks, Huy, & Vaara, 2017; Schweiger & Goulet, 2000). Still, there is agreement that acquisition integration determines acquisition performance (Ashkenas, DeMonaco, & Francis, 1998; Larsson & Finkelstein, 1999). Zooming closer, it has been argued that socio-cultural issues (for a review, see Stahl et al., 2013) explain many of the challenges experienced in integration (Gunkel, Schlaegel, Rossteutscher, & Wolff, 2015; Kusstatscher & Cooper, 2005; Sarala, Vaara, & Junni, 2019; Stahl & Voigt, 2008).

As a result, acquisition scholars have worked to unravel how culture affects acquisitions, making it among the most important streams of research on acquisition performance (Rottig & Reus, 2018). Several efforts have been made to review knowledge on the culture-performance relationship (Rottig, 2017; Rottig & Reus, 2018; Rottig, Reus, & Tarba, 2014; Stahl & Voigt, 2008; Teerikangas, 2007; Teerikangas & Very, 2006, 2012). While the results remain largely mixed and depend on the measures used (Teerikangas & Very, 2012), culture can represent a double-edged sword in acquisitions (Stahl & Voigt, 2008). Recognizing that prior reviews have given prominence to the culture-performance relationship following acquisitions, we review prior research on the cultural dynamics occurring in acquisitions.

We have structured our review along the following topics: (1) conceptualization of culture in acquisitions research, (2) assessment of cultural distance and cultural fit, (3) cultural change, and (4) impact and management of national cultures in CBA. Conclusions and pointers toward future research end the chapter. For further reading, we recommend conceptual frameworks of culture in acquisitions (Lakshman, 2011; Mignerat & Marmenout, 2017; Viegas-Pires, 2013) and reviews of the cultural challenge in acquisitions in geographic contexts such as the Asia-Pacific region (Kar & Kar, 2017).

DOI: 10.4324/9781003188308-14

226 Satu Teerikangas and Melanie Hassett

Conceptualizing culture in acquisition research

A historical tour of research on culture in acquisitions points to the conceptualization of culture as differing over time. From an early focus on organizational culture in domestic deals (Buono & Bowditch, 1989), the field started studying national cultures in CBA (Morosini, 1998), and the simultaneous effects of organizational and national cultures particularly as regards acquisition performance (Very, Lubatkin, & Calori, 1996; Weber, Shenkar, & Raveh, 1996). In other words, the "cultural challenge" at stake can range from a clash of organizational cultures in domestic deals, to a clash of both organizational and national cultures in cross-border transactions. To complicate matters still, Kogut and Singh (1988) identify the need to account for professional cultures, while Chatterjee et al. (1992) refer to the diversity of subcultures in the workplace. Moving beyond the organizational boundaries, Pioch (2007) points to the impact of the underlying industry culture in a given sector, while Teerikangas (2006) finds that within-country regional cultures matter in addition to national cultures (McSweeney, 2009).

In synthesis, this leads us to conclude that cultural diversity in acquisitions exists at the subcultural, functional, organizational, and industrial levels of analysis, in addition to regional and national cultures in the case of cross-border transactions. Yet, while the trend in sociological and organization research has been toward a multi-level view of culture, extant research in acquisitions has continued to retain a more traditional outlook, focusing on one, at maximum two levels of culture simultaneously (see Viegas-Pires, 2013 for a conceptual framework). What is more, the paradigm of a 'unitary' corporate culture has prevailed, omitting that organizations might consist of fragmented cultures (Vaara, 1999). Looking forward, the field could gain from multi-level perspectives to the study of culture.

All the while, authors have adopted critical views regarding the way that culture is conceptualized in acquisitions research. In a conceptual paper, Risberg (1997) argues for an 'ambiguity' perspective to CBA. She sees that an 'integration' perspective to culture prevails (i.e., seeking to merge the acquired firm's culture into the acquiring firm). Alternatively, a 'differentiation' perspective can be adopted where both firms' cultures coexist. Risberg (1997), in turn, calls for an 'ambiguity' perspective where differences and resulting ambiguities are acknowledged. The acquired firm is then not forced culturally into the buying firm's regime, and potential areas of differences and ambiguity are negotiated via two-way communication. Yet, such an approach also lends itself to critique. Based on ethnographic research, Riad (2007) criticizes existing acquisition research for forcing a binary opposition between coherence versus pluralism of cultures. She argues that this is not an either/or issue, as employees can be simultaneously united and divided in their cultural allegiance. A cohesive culture might not exist; yet it can be socially constructed during an

Cultural dynamics in acquisitions 227

acquisition. Riad cautions against the tradition to categorize cultures into certain types, or focusing only on differences between cultures. She asks, whether cultures and their potential differences could be embraced, as they are in multicultural societies?

As another critique, extant research tends to approach culture as 'something an organization has', rather than 'something an organization is' (Vaara, 1999). Vaara therefore takes an ontological position, and he argues that most studies on culture in acquisitions research adopt a realist approach to culture, treating culture as a given that 'can be managed'. Following the constructionist tradition where culture is seen as the continuous interpretations of its members, Vaara (2000) uncovers the sense-making processes in cross-border mergers. In addition to the traditional cultural sense-making process, he also identifies new ones as regards the manipulation of cultural conceptions and the suppressed emotional identification with one of the merger sides. This suggests that the culture shock experienced by people participating in acquisitions is possibly more complex than traditional research suggests. The realistic and positivist approach to culture needs to be complemented by interpretive and critical approaches, to offer nuanced perspectives (Vaara, 2000). Since the end of the 1990s, a stream of research has adopted a constructionist approach to CBA (Gertsen, Söderberg, & Torp, 1998). Associated research looks at how cultural differences are constructed through the involved actors' interpretations and sense-making processes (Söderberg & Vaara, 2003; Vaara, 1999, 2000), the process of social identity construction (Kleppesto, 1993, 1998), and the role of metaphors therein (Vaara, Tienari, & Säntti, 2003).

It also deserves mention that a cultural view to acquisitions is not without problems. In a critical analysis of the field, Riad (2005) finds that the 'culture' discourse has become so prevalent that it has become 'naturalized' as part of conversations on acquisitions. The term itself has become normative and quasi-institutionalized. Subsequently, critical voices regarding the role of culture in acquisitions become discounted. Riad (2005) calls for scholars to become aware of their role in producing this discourse.

In synthesis, there is need for a more complex and multi-layered view to the cultural encounter taking place in acquisitions. Such a perspective would account for ambiguities, how culture carriers construct cultures, the possibility that employees maintain plurality in their cultural allegiances, and recognize that culture can bear both positive and negative effects. Going forward, the next section furthers our analysis by discussing how cultural differences are assessed in acquisitions research.

Assessing cultural distance and fit

The role of culture in mergers and acquisitions is often defined in terms of 'compatibility', 'fit', or 'distance' between 'units' of national culture

228 *Satu Teerikangas and Melanie Hassett*

(Moore, 2021). In order to appreciate the extent of cultural differences between merging parties, the notions of cultural distance and/or cultural fit (Vaara Sarala, Stahl, & Björkman, 2012) have become prevalent. In this section, we focus on these two key concepts.

Cultural distance

Cultural distance is one of the most used measures in research on foreign expansion. Indeed, cultural distance represents one of the most popular constructs in research focusing on foreign direct investments, which is mainly composed of CBA (Shenkar, 2001; Yildiz, 2014). Cultural distance has dominated studies on the implications of pre-merger similarities/differences between the merging organizations (Yildiz, 2014).

In research focusing on similarities and differences between national cultures, two related and partly overlapping concepts are used: cultural distance and psychic distance. Beckerman (1956) defines psychic distance as a country being 'nearer' in a psychic evaluation. In the context of the internationalization of the firm, psychic distance has been referred to as "the sum of factors preventing or disturbing the flows of information between firms and markets" (Johansson & Wiedersheim-Paul, 1975, p. 308).

The terms cultural distance and psychic distance are often used interchangeably (Sousa & Bradley, 2006). This can contribute to the conceptual confusion. Psychic distance is evaluated at the individual level (i.e., based on respondents' subjective perceptions), while cultural distance is an organizational-level construct which refers to the differences between cultural values in different countries (Sousa & Bradley, 2006). Cultural distance has been defined as "the sum of factors creating, on the one hand, a need for knowledge, and on the other hand, barriers to the knowledge flow and hence also for other flows between the home and the target countries" (Luostarinen, 1979, pp. 131–132). While cultural distance and psychic distance are distinct concepts, they have been measured with the same indicators, often based on Hofstede's (1980) index of cultural dimensions and Kogut and Singh's (1988) index modified from Hofstede's (1980) four dimensions of culture. This established measure has been criticized for its assumption of linearity, the lack of cognitive dimensions, for not viewing culture as bearing potential for both synergy and disruption (Shenkar, 2001), and for assuming that one can measure the cultural traits of nations, or calculate the differences between cultures via a quantitative measure (Moore, 2021). Recently, research has attempted to further theorize on cultural distance by shedding light on the illusion of symmetry and discordance (Yildiz, 2014) or focusing on the positive role national culture can play in acquisitions (Moore, 2021).

Traditionally, both geographical and physic distance are perceived to be negative factors in CBA (Johnson, Lenartowicz, & Apud, 2006). However, perceived similarity can prevent executives from acknowledging

Cultural dynamics in acquisitions   229

sometimes small but crucial differences which can lead to failure (Angwin & Savill, 1997; Fang, Camilla, & Schultzberg, 2004; O'Grady & Lane, 1996). Still, cultural clashes may result not only from cultural distance but also from a lack of cultural fit between the organizations (Nummela & Raukko, 2012). Recent studies also suggest a more nuanced approach to cultural distance by considering the closest previous target information and prior experience, or the 'added cultural distance' (Hutzschenreuter & Voll, 2008), referring to the additional distance covered by the firm in a given time interval (Kim, Gaur, & Mukherjee, 2020). Similarly, Moore (2021) suggests that national cultures can be treated as a potential integration agent, not just a source of distance or friction.

Cultural Fit

Cultural fit is discussed in literature under labels of cultural differences and cultural clashes (Cartwright & Cooper, 1993; Datta, 1991; Moore, 2021; Nummela & Raukko, 2011; Weber, 1996). There is oftentimes a conceptual overlap between the concepts of organizational fit and cultural fit (Jemison & Sitkin, 1986; Rottig & Reus, 2018). While Rottig and Reus (2018) suggest that cultural fit would be part of the broader literature on organizational fit, cultural fit encompasses national and organizational cultural differences.

There is an underlying assumption that the greater the dissimilarity between organizational culture types, the more problematic and the longer the integration phase (Cartwright & Cooper, 1993). Yet, it is acknowledged that cultural differences per se do not necessarily lead to cultural clashes and in some cases cultural similarity may even be an impediment to successful integration (Moore, 2021). Nonetheless, Moore (2021) argues that national culture can have a positive role in acquisitions. National culture can also be a source of symbolic discourse incorporating good and bad aspects, which enables managers to shape their reality and integrate the new organization's culture (Moore, 2021).

The degree of compatibility, or cultural fit, between the two merging organizations has been acknowledged as one of the reasons for high failure rates in acquisitions (Buono & Bowditch, 1989; Cartwright & Cooper, 1993; Rottig & Reus, 2018). Nevertheless, the construct is ill-defined (Cartwright & Cooper, 1993; Teerikangas & Very, 2006; Weber, 1996). Due to the lack of measures of cultural compatibility, it has been argued that understanding the relationship between cultural fit and acquisition outcomes remains limited, while studies with meaningful cross-cultural comparisons across organizations and nations are scarce (Veiga, Lubatkin, Calori, & Very, 2000; Weber et al., 1996). Cultural compatibility or fit only becomes valuable through understanding; thus some degree of cultural awareness is called for (Risberg, 2001).

In sum, research on cultural distance and fit is gradually moving from a purely positivistic approach, where these constructs have been viewed

230 *Satu Teerikangas and Melanie Hassett*

as something that can be measured, toward also involving subjective approaches. Research suggests that culture-related problems intensify in international settings. Therefore, cultural fit is a requisite for acquisition success (Rottig & Reus, 2018). Critically speaking, research has adopted a narrow view on cultural distance (Rottig & Reus, 2018; Shenkar, 2001). Nonetheless, more fine-tuned approaches are emerging, which consider the role of previous experience on perceived cultural distance, as well as cultural awareness (Moore, 2021; Yildiz, 2014). From an appreciation of cultural differences, our attention shifts in the next section to cultural change.

Cultural change in acquisitions

The management of post-acquisition cultural change was initially addressed in domestic deals (Buono, Bowditch, & Lewis, 1985; Sales & Mirvis, 1984), while an appreciation of the dynamics of cultural change in CBA is increasing (Denison, Adkins, & Guidroz, 2011; Teerikangas & Irrmann, 2016). The main themes addressed in this largely qualitative body of research relate to (1) the strategies and phases of cultural change, (2) cultural change dynamics in CBA, (3) employee reactions and the complexities of cultural change, as well as (4) cultural change taking place via post-acquisition integration activity.

Strategies and phases of cultural change

To begin, different types of cultural integration strategies have been identified, depending on the buying firm's aim with regard to cultural integration and the type of acquisition (David & Singh, 1994; Forstmann, 1998; Olie, 1990; Schweiger, Csiszar, & Napier, 1993). The conceptual paper on acculturation by Nahavandi and Malekzhadeh (1988) marked a milestone in the study of cultural change strategies. The concept of acculturation, borrowed from cross-cultural psychology (Berry, 1983), represents the cultural adaptation process and alternative scenarios in the merging of two organizational cultures. The choice of the acculturative mode depends on acquired and acquiring companies. When an acculturative mode accepted by both companies is adopted, less acculturative stress is expected to occur. The acculturative mode will affect both cultures. The authors recognize different approaches and choices for cultural integration. Mirroring these acculturative modes, Buono, Bowditch, and Lewis (1989) also defined four modes of integrating cultures in acquisitions: cultural pluralism, cultural blending, cultural take-over, and cultural resistance. Later, Cartwright and Cooper (1996) identified four approaches to cultural change as aggressive, conciliative, corrosive, and indoctrinative. Subsequent work has found that the direction of cultural change dictates the ease of change, particularly if the change is paralleled with increased levels of openness (Cartwright & Cooper, 1992, 1993).

Cultural dynamics in acquisitions   231

Where existing beliefs are widely shared, cultural change is challenging (Buono & Bowditch, 1989).

Cultural change following acquisitions is considered to take place in phases (see Denison et al., 2011 for an overview) paralleling the acquisition process. To this end, amid the earliest works, Sales and Mirvis (1984) identify three phases of cultures coming into contact following acquisitions. Managing a culture in transition requires understanding the factors influencing acculturation. First, the existing culture perceives a threat to its culture. This phase can be managed by preparing strategically and emotionally for the change, rehearsing possible implications, and developing ground rules for cultural contact. Second, there is cultural contact between the two organizations. The management of this phase entails managing the processes of polarization, evaluation, and ethnocentrism as well as the conflicts resulting from cultural differences. Third, acculturation begins. This phase needs to be accompanied by a conscious scanning of culture and its re-examination.

A similar perspective is provided by Cartwright, Cartwright and Cooper (1996), who provide recommendations for a program of cultural change. Such a program begins with an understanding of both participating cultures. Next, it proceeds to unfreezing these cultures. Further, it presents the positive and realistic view of the future to both organizations. It ensures the wide-scale involvement of organizational members and adopts a realistic timescale for integration. Finally, it monitors the change process and takes corrective action where necessary. More recently, the phases of the cultural clash occurring in acquisitions have been conceptualized by Marks and Mirvis (2010) as occurring via the stages of: (1) perceiving, (2) magnifying differences, (3) stereotyping, and (4) the final phase where the other party is put down. In a subsequent publication, Marks and Mirvis (2011) offer a conceptual framework for human resource managers for managing cultural change following acquisitions, building on Lewin's (1947) three-stage model of change management as unfreezing, moving, and refreezing. In the pre-combination phase, the cultural end state needs to be defined. In the combination phase, cultural mindsets are 'unfrozen', while the organizations move toward the desired culture. Finally, in the post-combination stage the desired end culture is 'refrozen'.

Concurrently, means of enabling cultural change have been identified. Buono et al. (1989) identify factors influencing post-acquisition cultural change as: (1) changing the behavior of organizational members and justifying this change, (2) using cultural communication to facilitate the change, (3) hiring and socializing new recruits to speed up the change, and (4) removing deviants. The importance of attitudes (Deiser, 1994; Morosini, 1998; Napier, Schweiger, & Kosglow, 1993) when implementing cultural change is emphasized. Schraeder and Self (2003) argue that training, support, and socialization foster post-acquisition acculturation. In her study of cultural change across series of

232 *Satu Teerikangas and Melanie Hassett*

acquisitions with varying degrees of success, Bijlsma-Frankema (2001) concludes that mutual trust, shared norms and goals, dialogue, progress tracking, and rewarding mechanisms foster post-acquisition cultural change. Importantly, a culture promoting psychological safety allows for employees to raise their concerns, while the role of managers is critical in developing a new culture.

Cultural change in cross-border acquisitions

Paralleling the rise of cross-border transactions, research has shifted to studying cultural change in cross-border settings. The first such papers were by Olie (1990, 1994), who highlighted that both organizational and national cultures meet in cross-border mergers, the latter influencing the former. Olie (1990) argues that integration success depends on the degree of interaction and integration as well as the extent to which firms value their original cultures. In a later study, Olie (1994) found that the degree of compatibility of administrative practices, management styles, organizational structures and cultures, the kind and degree of post-merger consolidation, the extent parties value and want to retain their organizational integrity, and the nature of the relationship between the two organizations together contribute to explain the difficulties encountered during CBA.

Building on the work of Nahavandi and Malekzadeh (1988) in a cross-border setting, Larsson (1993) points out that national cultures create additional barriers to the development of joint corporate cultures. In a similar vein, Nahavandi and Malekzadeh (1998) discuss acculturation in CBA where double-layered acculturation (Barkema & Bell, 1996) or changes in national and organizational cultures occur. Quah and Young's (2005) phased approach points to the parallel impact of organizational and national cultures. Despite these advances, we note a relative scarcity of research on the dual impact of national and organizational cultures on cultural change during CBA, notwithstanding the paucity of research considering other levels of culture.

Employee reactions to cultural change

In parallel, research has studied employee reactions and considered the ensuing complexities toward the progress of cultural change. The power of cultural clashes occurring in domestic mergers was first highlighted by Marks (1982). Thereafter, Buono et al. (1985) introduced the concept of 'culture shock'. They defined culture shock as the distress when two corporate cultures merge, affecting the members by contributing to changing feelings and discomfort. Despite a rational understanding of the need to merge, culture shock impacts employees' willingness to view the deal positively. As culture provides a frame of life for its members, cultural changes are among the most difficult to cope with.

Cultural dynamics in acquisitions   233

In a similar vein, Nahavahdi and Malekzadeh (1988) consider that the concept of acculturative stress signals the emotional distress incurred (particularly) by the acquired company's members. They further observe that different sub-units within the company can experience different levels of acculturative stress. Studying cross-border mergers, Olie (1990) found that obstacles relate to the way people react. First, there is resistance to changing working methods and opposition against alienation from the national character of the environment. Second, there is a perceived threat to one's position in the company. A third issue concerns nationalism owing to the involved countries' historical backgrounds. More recently, Styhre, Börjesson, and Wickenberg (2006) point to the cultural anxieties that employees experience during cross-border mergers. Cultural change represents an emotionally painful process for organizational members, as they have to let go of their previous culture while developing an allegiance toward a new one.

Further, cultural change is experienced differently, depending on the level of hierarchy. Studying a CBA in the UK's retail sector, Pioch (2007) finds that while top management views post-acquisition cultural change from a company-wide integration perspective, employees experience a differentiation of cultures. Upon closer look, managers have had time to internalize the new organizational culture at the deeper level of assumptions (Schein, 1985), whereas the majority of employees have only experienced surface-level cultural changes. While the bulk of the cultural change literature focuses on organizational culture as a homogenous entity, the 12-year longitudinal study by Van Marrewijk (2016) illustrates how subcultures within a small, radical internet company purchased by a larger media and telecommunications company influence the progress of cultural change. Further, the study highlights the difficulty faced by incumbent firms in integrating acquisitions of technology-based start-ups, owing to the cultural discrepancy between the two organizational worlds. Instead of accepting cultural change, employees from the purchased company engage in cultural revitalization to recreate elements of their prior culture. Therefore, acculturation is not a unidirectional process; it is influenced by acquired firm employees. In the studied 12-year period, the acquiring firm completes cultural integration, yet alienating the radical innovators that were central to the initial purchase decision.

Cultural change embedded in post-acquisition activity

Taking a critical stance, literature on cultural change in acquisitions has tended to assume cultural change as stemming from cultural activity only. Further, research on post-acquisition cultural change tends to pocket this activity as paralleling post-acquisition integration. Recent findings contradict these assumptions.

Studying cultural change in CBA by global organizations, Teerikangas and Irrmann (2016) find that in the post-acquisition era, acquired firms

234 Satu Teerikangas and Melanie Hassett

cohabit a tension between shifting toward the acquiring firm's espoused versus practiced values. While acquirers' espoused values drive official cultural change initiatives, practiced values reflect the reality of post-acquisition integration. Therefore, post-acquisition cultural change is a dyadic, bipolar process; its direction and progress depend on both explicit cultural change initiatives and daily integration activity. While prior research has emphasized the former, the authors highlight the significance of post-acquisition integration toward cultural change. Notwithstanding, when an acquiring firm's espoused and practiced cultures are in alignment, cultural change progresses smoothly and unidirectionally.

Additionally, recent findings posit that cultural change is influenced by post-acquisition structural changes. To begin with, cultural change depends on passive and active structural changes (Teerikangas & Irrmann, 2016). Passive structural changes concern quasi-automatic changes introduced via a change in ownership (e.g., changes to firm size, international reach, governance structures, and unit status). Although not actively pursued, these incur changes in the targets' governance practices and mindsets. Active structural changes result from the acquirer's deliberate action to integrate the target (e.g., changes to the degree of global integration, organization structure and ways of working). Although not recognized, these incur changes to mindsets and management practices. What is more, the progress of cultural and structural change intertwine (Teerikangas & Laamanen, 2014), as cultural change begins only once structural integration progresses. Therefore, structural integration should start first; yet it needs to be implemented in a way that is appreciative of the acquired company's culture. Subsequently, cultural change is facilitated in an iterative manner over time by the new structure. If structural integration is implemented in disregard of the existing acquired firm's culture, cultural differences can impede structural integration.

Synthesis

In conclusion, existing research has highlighted alternative approaches to cultural change (Figure 10.1). To begin with, attention to the cultural integration strategy and the phases of cultural change is warranted. Best practices with regard to enabling cultural change revolve around attitudes conveying trust as well as communications, dialogue, clarity of goals, and employee rotation. Different employee groups can experience the acquisition differently, though this results in diverse and potentially conflictual subcultural or cultural differentiation dynamics. While early research viewed post-acquisition cultural change in silo, recent findings show that it is also enabled by post-acquisition structural change and integration activity. This calls for a systemic perspective toward cultural change and organizational culture as shaping and being shaped by the acquisition process.

Cultural dynamics in acquisitions 235

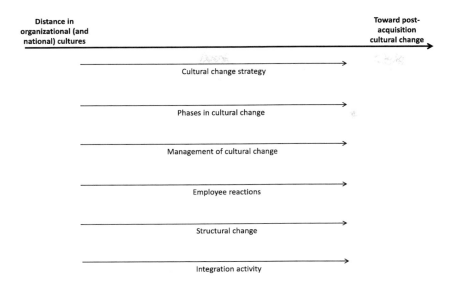

Figure 10.1 Factors affecting cultural change following acquisitions.

National culture

This section zooms into national culture in CBA. Research has looked at how firm behaviors are conditioned by national cultures, and how national cultures should be accounted for. We will review these streams next.

Impact of national culture

Some studies have explicitly focused on the impact of national culture on acquisitions. Morosini, Shane, and Singh (1998) argue that national cultures provide a competitive advantage to firms involved in an acquisition, as each national culture introduces particular new routines to the organization. Furthermore, many studies confirm that acquirers from different countries adopt specific kinds of due diligence (Angwin, 2000) and integration approaches (Calori, Lubatkin, & Véry, 1994; Child, Faulkner, & Pitkethly, 2001; Dunning, 1958; Faulkner, Child, & Pitkethly, 2003; Jaeger, 1983; Larsson & Lubatkin, 2001; Lubatkin, Calori, Very, & Veiga, 1998; Pitkethly, Faulkner, & Child, 2003). For example, earnout practices (Ewelt-Knauer, Gefken, Knauer, & Wiedemann, 2021) reflect an acquirer's national culture origin. Further, national cultural backgrounds constrain acquiring managers' emotional attending during integration (Reus, 2012). While some constants across acquirers have been found, organizations do not fully conform to their national cultural stereotype when acquiring (Faulkner, Pitkethly, & Child, 2012). Indeed, in studying

236 *Satu Teerikangas and Melanie Hassett*

international firms' acquisitions in Japan, Olcott (2008) observes there is not one approach that characterizes international firms' integration styles.

The Chinese government's "Go Global" policy, in 2000, resulted in a rise in Chinese CBA paralleled by increasing research on Chinese acquisitions. In particular, their distinctive integration approach has been reviewed (Chatzkel & Ng, 2013), suggesting a light-touch approach (Liu & Woywode, 2013). Chinese acquirers have also been compared to other acquirers from emerging markets, such as Russian (Panibratov, 2017) or Indian acquirers (Kale & Singh, 2012), while reverse acquisitions by Chinese acquirers in the Netherlands (Sun & Zhao, 2019) and Germany (Yang, Lütge, & Yan, 2019) have come under scrutiny. The cross-border challenge relates to national culture differences as well as differing institutional and regulatory environments. For example, Wu, Hoon, and Yuzhu (2011) study Chinese-American acquisitions, including challenging ones, such as Huawei's, and successful ones, such as Haier's deals.

In parallel, target firms prefer different kinds of integration approaches consistent with their home countries' national cultures (Cartwright & Price, 2003; Morosini, 1998). Nevertheless, acquisitions where target firms are involved in the integration fair best (Calori et al., 1994; Child et al., 2001; Larsson & Lubatkin, 2001). In both of the above research streams, the dimensions of uncertainty avoidance (Morosini, 1998; Schoenberg, 2000), risk orientation (Schoenberg, 2000), and individualism versus collectivism (Morosini, 1998) have received emphasis.

Only few studies focus on national cultures interacting during acquisitions. Studying the European EADS tri-party merger, Barmeyer and Mayrhofer (2008) found inter-cultural team-working to be negatively affected by the involved French, German, and Spanish parties' interpretations of teamwork, cooperation, leadership, and authority. Such differences complicate post-acquisition integration, as members operate with culturally dependent behavioral strategies. Studying the implementation of lean production into a Japanese-owned factory in Sweden, Oudhuis and Olsson (2015) find that cultural clashes relate to national cultures and different approaches to manufacturing. Similarly, Lee, Kim, and Park (2015) study how employees experience cultural differences in Sweden's Volvo's acquisition of South-Korean Samsung's business division. Adopting an 11-year interval, the authors find that a classic, positivistic conception of culture predicts culture-related problems, while a social constructivist perspective predicts whether such problems actually materialize. Finally, the trust-building practices of Chinese managers (Sachsenmaier & Guo, 2019; Sun & Zhao, 2019) and the roles of Chinese CEOs in managing individualist cultures when acquiring abroad have received attention (Zhu, Zhu & Ding, 2020).

Working across national cultures in acquisitions

Some studies have sought to understand how national cultures can be accounted for during CBA. First, culture needs to be considered during pre-acquisition target evaluation. For example, Datta (1991) found that organizational fit and pre-deal financial evaluation need to occur in tandem, arguing that differences in management styles cause difficulties. Similarly, Cartwright and Cooper (1993) observed that evaluation of cultural differences and similarities prior to entering a deal is an early means of assessing an acquisition's potential. While Denison and Ko (2016) examine domestic acquisitions, a framework to facilitate cultural due diligence for CBA is needed.

Second, post-acquisition integration strategy needs to be culturally sensitive. In a study on the human resource implications of acquisitions, Schweiger et al. (1993) highlighted that integration strategy guides post-acquisition change. Morosini and Singh (1994) suggested that acquirers adopt a national culture compatible post-acquisition strategy, coherent with the target country's culture. This matters, as characteristics influenced by national culture are difficult to change.

Third, interactive ties between combining organizations ease cultural differences. Studying the creation of the European Aeronautic Defence and Space Company (EADS) that combined French Aerospatiale Matra, German DASA, and Spanish CASA, Barmeyer and Mayrhofer (2008) describe how shared organization structures and organizational culture, or the EADS spirit, helped to develop inter-organizational ties. Progress was further facilitated by human resource management practices supporting team-working, cooperation, leadership, and career development.

Fourth, integration attitudes and intercultural sensitivity enable dealing with cultural differences. Chatterjee et al. (1992) found a tolerant attitude to ensure acquisition success. Napier et al. (1993), in turn, looked at how organizational diversity is managed in cross-border mergers from a human resource management perspective to find assertive tolerance offers a powerful integration tool. Further, in cross-border deals, intercultural skills are critical, including the notion of cultural intelligence from international business (Thomas & Inkson, 2005). The significance of intercultural sensitivity has paralleled the rise in CBA. Morosini et al. (1998) observe that pragmatic cross-cultural skills are required. Similarly, Ashkenas and Francis (2000) call for cultural intelligence when acquiring across borders. Combining insights from empirical studies across countries, Teerikangas and Birollo (2018) consider that managers' cultural sensitivity refers to openness toward differences and being able to talk through conflicting viewpoints. Further, interculturally sensitive managers adjust to the best of both sides, instead of force-fitting their views onto the other party.

Fifth, intercultural training offers a means of enhancing awareness of cultural differences (Thomas & Inkson, 2005). The underlying

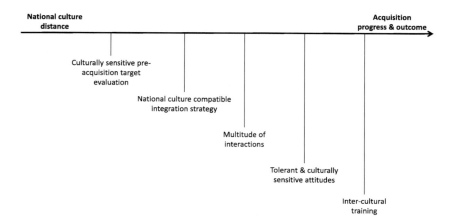

Figure 10.2 Working across national cultures in acquisitions.

assumption is that cultural differences can be learned, managed, or even manipulated (David & Singh, 1993). When testing the effect of deep versus surface-level cultural learning interventions on acquired firm employees' experiences, Schweiger and Goulet (2005) conclude that a positive experience is not about merging similar cultures, but rather about cultural learning. Consistent with their hypotheses, they found deep-level cultural learning interventions to result in intercultural awareness, understanding and communication, as well as cooperation-based attitudes. In contrast, misunderstandings flourished in units receiving no learning interventions. Yet, surface-level cultural interventions did not result in the partner being better accepted, potentially even furthering existing stereotypes. Studying the European merger that formed EADS, Barmeyer and Mayrhofer (2008) identified training practices that improved intercultural skills. The intercultural training program was part of the larger goal in the merger to create a 'Corporate Business Academy', which developed involved managers' leadership, change management, intercultural management, and business excellence skills.

In synthesis, we make the following observations. For one, the behaviors of both the buying and acquired parties are dependent on their national culture heritage. For another, differences in the merging partners' national cultures should be included in the management of the acquisition process, starting from evaluation, through strategy, and skills in integration, as summarized in Figure 10.2. Finally, intercultural awareness and training are needed.

Discussion and future research directions

Our aim has been to review how acquisition research has studied the cultural dynamics amid this inter-organizational change of ownership. In

Cultural dynamics in acquisitions 239

the following, we proceed to a critical analysis of our findings, continuing with implications for future research.

A critical analysis of the state of the art

First, one needs to appreciate the concept under study, namely culture. Our critical review demonstrates that definitions of culture remain narrow. To this end, there is little attention toward the layer of culture studied (e.g., artifacts, practices, values, norms, and/or assumptions). As an example, Sally Riad's research is among the few studies adopting a deeper perspective of culture via values. Similarly, Teerikangas and Irrmann (2016) distinguish between espoused and practiced organizational values. Going forward, a deeper understanding of culture, across its layers, is called for.

Second, the level of culture studied needs attention. In line with findings from across the social sciences, cultural encounters in acquisitions occur at the subcultural, functional, organizational, and industrial levels of analysis, in addition to regional and national cultures in CBA. As Table 10.1 shows, we find predominance in the use of the concepts of organizational and national culture to conceptualize the cultural challenge at stake in acquisitions. While other cultures are mentioned, including professional, regional, or industrial ones, the multi-level complexity of the cultural encounters in acquisitions remains unaddressed. Instead, research appears to stick to the dichotomy of organizational versus national cultures, which by themselves are messy, ambiguous, and mutually intertwined concepts. This brings us to a related future research direction: unearthing the multi-level complexity of cultural encounters, including cultural change, in times of acquisitions.

Table 10.1 Synthesis of the levels of analysis in the study of cultural challenges in acquisitions

Theme studied	*Cultural distance and fit*	*Cultural change*	*Impact and management of national cultures*
Level of analysis	Organizational culture	Organizational culture	
	National culture		National culture
	Organizational and national culture	Subcultures, organizational, national, and industrial culture	
Research paradigm	Realist	Largely realist with some interpretive research	Realist

240　*Satu Teerikangas and Melanie Hassett*

Third, the bulk of research on the cultural dynamics in acquisitions is ontologically positioned toward realism and an objective epistemology, coupled with a pragmatic touch (see Table 10.1). The realist ontology is observable in the assumptions that cultural distance, cultural change, and national culture can be 'managed'. While bearing practical relevance, such a perspective offers a mechanistic, linear, one-sided, and simplistic perspective to culture. This one-sided emphasis is mirrored in the literature not questioning the assumption of 'culture' as a monolith that an organization 'has', instead of seeing culture as something the organization 'is', 'lives', 'breathes', and is continually created. As another example, rather simplistic conceptualizations of organizational and national cultural distance and their dimensions are in use (cf. Shenkar, 2001). As regards national culture, the field's weakness as with other cross-border studies in the international management and strategy literatures is its over-reliance on existing frameworks of national culture, such as Hofstede's (1980) or House, Hanges, Javidan, Dorfman, and Gupta's (2004). The field takes national cultures and its particular dimensions for granted (for a critique, see McSweeney, 2002). The same holds for the way that organizational culture is conceptualized. We argue that research on the national and organizational culture dimensions affecting domestic and CBA is needed. Further, as the majority of the research adopts objectively measurable dimensions of culture, subjective approaches to culture considering values, experience, awareness, perceptions, or tensions and ambiguity are needed, as are more fine-grained, interpretive, and critical studies.

Fourth, in contrast to the lively body of work on the culture performance relationship, less attention has been placed on appreciating cultural change. This inquiry began in the 1980s–1990s. Thereafter, work on cultural dynamics in domestic acquisitions has been less vocal. This begs the question: has everything been found? Likewise, whereas studies on the cultural encounter in CBA exist, this stream is dwarfed by its importance and relevance. As a result, our understanding of the fine-tuned ways of how organizational and national cultures intertwine amid post-acquisition cultural change remains scarce. Further, work on cultural change views the latter in relative isolation from other changes occurring following acquisitions (e.g., integration, change processes, or identification). Critically speaking, the study of post-acquisition cultural change is amiss from mainstream top-tier academic journals. Going forward, there are opportunities to further our understanding of acquisitions through more in-depth qualitative ethnographic studies, large-scale interview studies, action research, or longitudinal, mixed-methods studies (Cartwright, Teerikangas, Rouzies, & Wilson-Evered, 2012). Clearly, there is a need for ethnographers and action researchers to study 21st-century CBA.

Future research directions

Our literature review incites us to highlight neglected questions, or gaps in our understanding of the cultural dynamics in acquisitions. To begin

Cultural dynamics in acquisitions   241

with, the field treats mergers and acquisitions as equal, inferring conceptual similarity and transferability of findings. Culturally speaking, the merger of two organizations represents a challenge different to that of acquiring another organization. We ask, what are the differences in the cultural encounter between these phenomena? Is it time to unveil their 'cultural' differences instead of assuming similarity?

Further, there is need to account for the cultural plurality organizations. The bulk of the research considers an acquisition to occur between two organizational culture monoliths. Yet, given that multinational firms have grown via acquisitions, they likely bear a plethora of organizational subcultures (Barkema & Schijven, 2008; Teerikangas, 2006, 2012). Acquisitions undertaken by such giants are likely to portray messier cultural dynamics than a monolithic assumption of organizational culture prevailing in current research assumes.

Another research gap relates to considering that cultural encounters are 'uniform' across the organization. It is often assumed that cultural reactions of employees are consistent across business units, departments, services, countries, etc., but there are chances that it is not true. Cultural issues and their management are likely to vary per degree of integration, per unit, per team, and per employee. Exploration in this direction is worthwhile. For example, at a sub-organizational level, are experiences of cultural distance, cultural shock, and cultural change similar across sites, functions, departments, or professions?

Further, research on the cultural dynamics in acquisitions largely entertains a within-stream and within-sub-literature debate. Whereas practitioners need to simultaneously deal with financial, strategic, cultural, and managerial issues in acquisitions, academics have the luxury of choosing our scope of work to focus on a particular lens. By so doing, we risk losing overall perspective. Future research on the cultural dynamics in acquisitions deserves to be linked to findings from other disciplines and also to those from other research streams on acquisitions (e.g., finance, strategy, integration, identity, or performance). This will enable a more holistic understanding of acquisitions and the role of culture therein.

As one example, research on cultural change in acquisitions research could connect with research on cultural change and change management in organizational and social sciences. Presently, Kurt Lewin's model of planned change is used as the theoretical backing of stage-based models of cultural change in acquisitions. Meanwhile, this model has been critiqued for its assumptions of linearity and manageability toward a seemingly stable state (Burnes, 1996; By, 2005) that may be less relevant to a 21st-century context (Tsoukas & Chia, 2002). We argue that the messy, turbulent facets of change that represent the contexts within which contemporary acquisitions are undertaken, deserve attention.

Another example relates to connecting research on cultural change with research on sociocultural integration. The concept of sociocultural integration (Birkinshaw, Bresman, & Håkansson, 2000; Stahl & Voigt, 2008) represents the human side of integration including employee motivation,

242 *Satu Teerikangas and Melanie Hassett*

cultural change, and identity formation. Findings from studies on sociocultural integration are not too different from those regarding cultural change (Harikkala-Lahinen et al., 2018 Łupina-Wegener, Schneider, & Van Dick, 2011; Rottig, Schappert, & Starkman, 2017). Going forward, there is potential for construct clarity between the concepts of cultural change, cultural integration, and sociocultural integration (Teerikangas, Rouzies, & Colman, 2015). While they all relate to post-acquisition cultural integration, there is deviation as regards the extent other concepts such as employee reactions, integration, and identity are included or considered as neighboring concepts. Further, these studies differ with respect to the levels of culture included.

Conclusion

Our reflection leads to the broader question on the interconnectedness between the various change processes taking place during acquisitions (e.g., operational, structural, cultural, sociocultural, identification). As illustrated in the integrative framework on post-acquisition integration by Teerikangas (2006, 2012), these are related, and together shape integration progress and outcomes (Larsson & Finkelstein, 1999; Teerikangas & Thanos, 2017). Therefore, studying any single process on its own bears the limitation of providing a reductionist perspective. Cultural change is shaped by post-acquisition integration, while it is also shaped by the involved organizations' cultural regimes and employee agency.

References

Angwin, D. (2000). Mergers and acquisitions across European borders: National Perspectives on pre-acquisition due diligence and the use of professional advisers. *Journal of World Business, 36*(1), 32–57.

Angwin, D., & Savill, B. (1997). Strategic perspectives on European cross-border acquisitions: A view from top European executives. *European Management Journal, 15*(4), 423–435.

Ashkenas, R., & Francis, S. C. (2000). Integration managers: Special leaders for special times. *Harvard Business Review, 78*(6), 108–116.

Ashkenas, R., DeMonaco, L., & Francis, S. (1998). Making the deal real: How GE capital integrates acquisitions. *Harvard Business Review, 76*(1), 165–178.

Barkema, H., & Bell, H. (1996). Foreign entry, cultural barriers, and learning. *Strategic Management Journal, 17*, 151–166.

Barkema, H., & Schijven, M. (2008). Toward unlocking the full potential of acquisitions: The role of organizational restructuring. *Academy of Management Journal, 51*(4), 696–722.

Barmeyer, C., & Mayerhofer, U. (2008). The contribution of intercultural management to the success of international mergers and acquisitions: An analysis of the EADS group. *International Business Review, 17*(1), 28–38.

Beckerman, W. (1956). Distance and the pattern of intra-European trade. *Review of Economics and Statistics, 38*(1), 31–40.

Cultural dynamics in acquisitions 243

Berry, J. W. (1983). Acculturation: A comparative analysis of alternative forms. In: R. Samuda & S. Woods (Eds.), *Perspectives in immigrant and minority education*. New York: University Press of America, pp. 65–78.

Bijlsma-Frankema, K. (2001). On managing cultural integration and cultural change processes in mergers and acquisitions. *Journal of European Industrial Training, 25*, 192–207.

Birkinshaw, J., Bresman, H., & Håkansson, L. (2000). Managing the post-acquisition integration process: How the human integration and task integration processes interact to foster value creation. *Journal of Management Studies, 37*(3), 395–425.

Buono, A., Bowditch, J., & Lewis, J. (1985). When cultures collide: The anatomy of a merger. *Human Relations, 38*(5), 477–500.

Buono, A., & Bowditch, J. (1989). *The human side of mergers and acquisitions: Managing collisions between people, cultures and organizations*. London: Jossey-Bass Inc.

Burnes, B. (1996). No such thing as … 'one best way' to manage organizational change. *Management Decision, 34*(10), 11–18.

By, R. (2005). Organizational change management: A critical review. *Journal of Change Management, 5*(4), 369–380.

Calori, R., Lubatkin, M., and Véry, P. (1994). Control mechanisms in cross-border acquisitions: An international comparison. *Organization Studies, 15*(3), 361–379.

Cartwright, S., Cartwright, S., & Cooper, C. L. (1996). *Managing mergers, acquisitions, and strategic alliances: Integrating people and cultures*. Routledge: New York.

Cartwright, S., & Cooper, C. (1992). *Managing mergers, acquisitions and strategic alliances: Integrating people and cultures*. Oxford: Butterworth-Heinemann.

Cartwright, S., & Cooper, C. (1993). The role of culture compatibility in successful organizational marriage. *Academy of Management Executive, 7*(2), 57–70.

Cartwright, S., & Price, F. (2003). Managerial preferences in international merger and acquisition partners revisited: How much are they influenced? In C. Cooper & A. Gregory (Eds.), *Advances in mergers and acquisitions*. Amsterdam: JAI Press, Vol. 1, pp. 81–95.

Cartwright, S., Teerikangas, S., Rouzies, A., & Wilson-Evered, E. (2012). Methods in M&A: A look at the past, and the future, to forge a path forward. *Scandinavian Journal of Management, 28*(2), 95–106.

Chatterjee, S., Lubatkin, M. H., Schweiger, D. M., & Weber, Y. (1992). Cultural differences and shareholder value in related mergers: Linking equity and human capital. *Strategic Management Journal, 13*(5), 319–334.

Chatzkel, J., & Ng, A. (2013). The emergence of contemporary Chinese enterprise: The heterogeneity of national culture, corporate controls and integration approaches in M&As. *Thunderbird International Business Review, 55*(5), 593–608.

Child, J., Faulkner, D., & Pitkethly, R. (2001). *The management of international acquisitions*. Oxford: Oxford University Press.

Datta, D. (1991). Organizational fit and acquisition performance: Effects on post-acquisition integration. *Strategic Management Journal, 12*(4), 281–297.

David, K., & Singh, H. (1993). Acquisition regimes: Managing cultural risk and relative deprivation in corporate acquisitions. In D. Hussey (Eds.),

International review of strategic management. New York: Wiley, Vol. 4, pp. 227–276.

David, K., & Singh, H. (1994). Sources of acquisition cultural risk. In G. von Krogh, A. Siknatra, & H. Singh (Eds.), *The management of corporate acquisitions*. London: The Macmillan Press, pp. 251–292.

Deiser, R. (1994). Post-acquisition management: A process of strategic and organisational learning. In G. Von Krogh, A. Siknatra & H. Singh (Eds.), *The management of corporate acquisitions*. London: The Macmillan Press, pp. 359–390.

Denison, D., Adkins B., & Guidroz A. (2011). Managing cultural integration in cross-border mergers and acquisitions. *Advances in Global Leadership, 6*, 95–115.

Denison, D., & Ko I. (2016). Cultural due diligence in mergers and acquisitions. *Advances in Mergers and Acquisitions, 15*, 53–72.

Dunning, J. (1958). *American Investment in British Manufacturing Industry*. London: Allen and Unwin.

Ewelt-Knauer, C., Gefken, J., Knauer, T., & Wiedemann, D. (2021). Acquirers' cultural background and the use of earnouts. *Journal of Accounting, Auditing & Finance, 36*(1), 30–55.

Fang, T., Camilla, C., & Schultzberg, S. (2004). Why did the Telia-Telenor merger fail? *International Business Review, 13*(5), 573–594.

Faulkner, D., Child, J., & Pitkethly, R. (2003). Organisational change processes in international acquisitions. In: C. Cooper and A. Gregory (Eds.), *Advances in mergers and acquisitions*, Vol. 1 (pp. 59–80). Amsterdam, JAI Press.

Faulkner. D., Pitkethly, R., & Child, J. (2012). Country cultural differences in acquisition management. In Faulkner, D., Teerikangas, S., & Joseph, R. (Eds.), *Handbook of mergers and acquisitions*. Oxford: Oxford University Press, pp. 431–453.

Forstmann, S. (1998). Managing cultural differences in cross-cultural mergers and acquisitions. In M. Gertsen, A. Söderberg, & J. Torp (Eds.), *Cultural dimensions of international mergers and acquisitions*. Berlin: De Gruyter, pp. 57–84.

Gertsen, M., Soderberg, A, & Torp, J. (1998). *Cultural dimensions of international mergers and acquisitions*. Berlin: De Gruyter.

Graebner, M., Heimeriks, K., Huy, Q., & Vaara, E. (2017). The process of postmerger integration: A review and agenda for future research. *Academy of Management Annals, 11*(1), 1–32.

Gunkel, M., Schlaegel, G., Rossteutscher, R., & Wolff, B. (2015). The human aspect of cross-border acquisition outcomes: The role of management practices, employee emotions, and national culture. *International Business Review, 24*(3), 394–408.

Harikkala-Lahinen, R., Hassett, M., Nummela, N., & Raitis, J. (2018). Dialogue as a source of positive emotions during cross-border post-acquisition socio-cultural integration. *Cross Cultural & Strategic Management, 25*(1), 183–208.

Hofstede, G. (1980). *Culture's consequences—International differences in work-related values*. California: Sage.

House, R., Hanges, P., Javidan, M., Dorfman, P., & Gupta, V. (2004). *Culture, leadership, and organizations: The GLOBE study of 62 societies*. Thousand Oaks, CA: Sage.

Cultural dynamics in acquisitions 245

Hutzschenreuter, T. & Voll, J.C. (2008). Performance effects of "added cultural distance" in the path of international expansion: The case of German multinational enterprises. *Journal of International Business Studies, 39*(1), 53–70

Jaeger, A. (1983). The transfer of organisational culture overseas: An approach to control in the multinational corporation. *Journal of International Business Studies, 14*(2), 91–114.

Jemison, D. B., & Sitkin, S. B. (1986). Corporate acquisitions: A process perspective. *Academy of Management Review, 11*(1), 145–163.

Johansson, V. & Wiedersheim-Paul, P. (1975). The internationalization of the firm: Four Swedish case studies. *Journal of Management Studies, 12*(3), 305–322.

Johnson, J., Lenartowicz, T. & Apud, S. (2006). Cross-cultural competence in international business: Toward a definition and a model. *Journal of International Business Studies, 37*(4), 525–543.

Kale, P. & Singh, H. (2012). Characteristics of emerging market mergers and acquisitions. In Faulkner, D., Teerikangas, S., & Joseph, R. (Eds.), *Handbook of mergers and acquisitions*. Oxford: Oxford University Press, pp. 545–565.

Kar, R., & Kar, M. (2017). Cross-cultural issues in M&As: Experiences and future agenda from Asia-Pacific deals. *Transnational Corporations Review, 9*(3), 140–149.

Kim, H., Gaur, A., & Mukherjee, D. (2020). Added cultural distance and ownership in cross-border acquisitions. *Cross Cultural & Strategic Management, 27*(3), 487–510.

Kleppesto, S. (1993). *Social Identitet vid Uppköp och Fusioner*. Lund: Lund University.

Kleppesto, S. (1998). A quest for social identity: The pragmatics of communication in mergers and acquisitions. In M. Gertsen, A-M. Söderberg & J. E. Torp (Eds.), *Cultural dimensions of international mergers and acquisitions*. Berlin: De Gruyter, pp. 147–166.

Kogut, B., & Singh, H. (1988). The effect of culture on the choice of entry mode. *Journal of International Business Studies, 19*(3), 411–432.

Kusstatscher, V., & Cooper, C. (2005). *Managing emotions in mergers and acquisitions*. Cheltenham: Edward Elgar Publishing Ltd.

Lakshman, C. (2011). Postacquisition cultural integration in mergers & acquisitions: A knowledge-based approach. *Human Resource Management, 50*(5), 605–623.

Larsson, R. (1993). Barriers to acculturation in mergers and acquisitions: Strategic human resource implications. *Journal of European Business Education, 2*(2), 1–18.

Larsson, R., & Finkelstein, S. (1999). Integrating strategic, organizational, and human resource perspectives on mergers and acquisitions: A case survey of synergy realization. *Organization Science, 10*(1), 1–26.

Larsson, R., & Lubatkin, M. (2001). Achieving acculturation in mergers and acquisitions: An international case study. *Human Relations, 54*(12), 1573–1607.

Lee, S. J., Kim, J., & Park, B. I. (2015). Culture clashes in cross-border mergers and acquisitions: A case study of Sweden's Volvo and South Korea's Samsung. *International Business Review, 24*(4), 580–593.

Lewin, K. (1947). *Change management model*. McGraw Hill: New York.

Liu, Y., & Woywode, M. (2013). Light-touch integration of Chinese cross-border M&A: The influences of culture and absorptive capacity. *Thunderbird International Business Review, 55*(4), 469–483.

246 Satu Teerikangas and Melanie Hassett

Lubatkin, M., Calori, R., Very, P., & Veiga, J. (1998). Managing mergers across borders: A two-nation exploration of a nationally bound administrative heritage. *Organisation Science*, 9(6), 670–684.

Luostarinen, R. (1979). *Internationalization of the firm*. Helsinki School of Economics: Helsinki.

Łupina-Wegener, A., Schneider, S., & Van Dick, R. (2011). Different experiences of socio-cultural integration: A European merger in Mexico. *Journal of Organizational Change Management*, 24(1), 65–89.

Marks, M. (1982). Merging human resources: A review of the literature. *Mergers and Acquisitions*, 17(2), 38–44.

Marks, M. L., & Mirvis, P. H. (2010). *Joining forces: Making one plus one equal three in mergers, acquisitions, and alliances*. John Wiley: New York.

Marks, M., & Mirvis, P. (2011). A framework for the human resources role in managing culture in mergers and acquisitions. *Human Resource Management*, 50(6), 859–877.

McSweeney, B. (2002). Hofstede's model of national cultural differences and their consequences: A triumph of faith—A failure of analysis. *Human Relations*, 55(1), 89–118.

McSweeney, B. (2009). Dynamic diversity: Variety and variation within countries. *Organization Studies*, 30(9), 933–957.

Mignerat, M., & Marmenout, K. (2017). Getting beyond culture clashes: A process model of post-merger order negotiation. *Advances in Mergers and Acquisitions*, 16, 165–181.

Moore, F. (2021). 'National culture' as an integrating agent in the post-acquisition organisation. *International Journal of Human Resource Management*, 32(13), 2783–2806.

Morosini, P. (1998). *Managing cultural differences: Effective strategy and execution across cultures in global corporate alliances*. Oxford: Pergamon.

Morosini, P., Shane, S., & Singh, H. (1998). National cultural distance and cross-border acquisition performance. *Journal of International Business Studies*, 19(1), 137–158.

Morosini, P., & Singh, H. (1994). Post-cross-border acquisitions: Implementing national culture-compatible strategies to improve performance. *European Management Journal*, 4, 390–400.

Nahavandi, A., & Malekzhadeh, A. (1988). Acculturation in mergers and acquisitions. *Academy of Management Review*, 13(1), 79–90.

Napier, N., Schweiger, D., & Kosglow, J. (1993). Managing organizational diversity: Observations from cross-border acquisitions. *Human Resource Management*, 32(4), 505–523.

Nummela, N. & Raukko, M. (2012). Analysing culture in a cross-border acquisition: An Indian-Finnish deal in focus. In M. Marinov & S. Marinova (Eds.), *Internationalization of emerging economies and firms*. London: Palgrave Macmillan, pp. 191–223.

O'Grady, S. & Lane, H. (1996). The psychic distance paradox. *Journal of International Business Studies*, 27(2), 309–333.

Olcott, G. (2008). The politics of institutionalization: The impact of foreign ownership and control on Japanese organizations. *International Journal of Human Resource Management*, 19(9), 1569–1587.

Olie, R. (1990). Culture and integration problems in international mergers and acquisitions. *European Management Journal*, 8(2), 206–215.

Olie, R. (1994). Shades of culture and institutions in international mergers. *Organization Studies, 15*(3), 381–405.

Oudhuis, M., & Olsson, A. (2015). Cultural clashes and reactions when implementing lean production in a Japanese-owned Swedish company. *Economic and Industrial Democracy, 36*(2), 259–282.

Panibratov, A. (2017). Cultural and organizational integration in cross-border M&A deals: The comparative study of acquisitions made by EMNEs from China and Russia. *Journal of Organizational Change Management, 30*(7), 1109–1135.

Pioch, E. (2007). Business as usual? Retail employee perceptions of organizational life following cross-border acquisition. *International Journal of Human Resource Management, 18*(2), 209–231.

Pitkethly, R., Faulkner, D., & Child, J. (2003). Integrating acquisitions. In C. Cooper & A. Gregory (Eds.). *Advances in mergers and acquisitions.* Amsterdam: JAI Press, pp. 27–58.

Quah, P., & Young, S. (2005). Post-acquisition management: A phases approach for cross-border M&A. *European Management Journal, 23*(1), 65–75.

Reus, T. (2012). Culture's consequences for emotional attending during cross-border acquisition implementation. *Journal of World Business, 47*(3), 342–351.

Riad, S. (2005). The power of 'organizational culture' as a discursive formation in merger integration. *Organization Studies, 26*(10), 1529–1554.

Riad, S. (2007). Of mergers and cultures: 'What happened to shared values and joint assumptions?' *Journal of Organizational Change Management, 20*(1), 26–43.

Risberg, A. (1997). Ambiguity and communication in cross-cultural acquisitions: Towards a conceptual framework. *Leadership and Organization Development Journal, 18*(5), 257–266.

Risberg, A. (2001). Employee experiences of acquisition processes. *Journal of World Business, 36*(1), 58–84.

Rottig, D. (2017). Meta-analyses of culture's consequences for acquisition performance: An examination of statistical artifacts, methodological moderators and the context of emerging markets. *International Journal of Emerging Markets, 12*(1), 8–37.

Rottig, D. & Reus, T. (2018). Research on culture and international acquisition performance: A critical evaluation and new directions. *International Studies of Management & Organization, 48*(1), 3–42.

Rottig, D., Reus, T., & Tarba, S. (2014). The impact of culture on mergers and acquisitions: A third of a century of research. *Advances in Mergers and Acquisitions, 12*, 135–172.

Rottig D., Schappert J. & Starkman E. (2017) Successfully managing the sociocultural integration process in international acquisitions: A qualitative analysis of canon's acquisition of océ. *Thunderbird International Business Review, 59*(2), 187–208.

Sachsenmaier, S., & Guo, Y. (2019). Building trust in cross-cultural integration: A study of Chinese mergers and acquisitions in Germany. *International Journal of Cross Cultural Management, 19*(2), 194–217.

Sales, A., & Mirvis, P. (1984). When cultures collide: Issues in acquisitions. In J. Kimberley & R. Quinn (Eds.), *New futures: The challenges of managing corporate transitions.* Homewood: Dow Jones-Irvin, pp. 107–133.

248 *Satu Teerikangas and Melanie Hassett*

Sarala, R., Vaara, E. & Junni, P. (2019). Beyond merger syndrome and cultural differences: New avenues for research on the "human side" of global mergers and acquisitions (M&As). *Journal of World Business, 54*(4), 307–321.

Schein, E. (1985). *Organizational culture and leadership: A dynamic view.* London: Jossey-Bass.

Schoenberg, R. (2000). The influence of cultural compatibility within cross-border acquisitions. In C. Cooper & A. Gregory (Eds.), *Advances in mergers and acquisitions.* Amsterdam: JAI Press, Vol. 1, pp. 43–60.

Schraeder, M., & Self, D. R. (2003). Enhancing the success of mergers and acquisitions: an organizational culture perspective. *Management Decision, 41*(5), 511–522.

Schweiger, D., Csiszar, E., & Napier, N. (1993). Implementing international mergers and acquisitions. *Human Resource Planning, 16*(1), 53–70.

Schweiger, D., & Goulet, P. (2000). Integrating mergers and acquisitions: An international research review. In C. Cooper & A. Gregory (Eds.), *Advances in mergers and acquisitions.* Amsterdam: JAI Press, Vol. 1, pp. 61–91.

Schweiger, D., & Goulet, P. (2005). Facilitating acquisition integration through deep-level cultural learning interventions: A longitudinal field experiment. *Organization Studies, 26*(10), 1477–1499.

Shenkar, O. (2001) Cultural distance revisited: Towards a more rigorous conceptualization and measurement of cultural differences. *Journal of International Business Studies, 32*(3), 519–535.

Sousa, C. & Bradley, F. (2006). Cultural distance and psychic distance: Two peas in a pod?. *Journal of International Marketing, 14*(1), 49–70.

Stahl, G., Angwin D., Very P., Gomes E., Weber Y., Tarba S., … & Yildiz H. (2013). Sociocultural integration in mergers and acquisitions: Unresolved paradoxes and directions for future research. *Thunderbird International Business Review, 55*(4), 333–356.

Stahl, G., & Voigt, A. (2008). Do cultural differences matter in mergers and acquisitions? A tentative model and examination. *Organization Science, 19*(1), 160–176.

Styhre, A., Börjesson, S., & Wickenberg, J. (2006). Managed by the other: Cultural anxieties in two Anglo-Americanized Swedish firms. *International Journal of Human Resource Management, 17*(7), 1293–1306.

Sun, Z., & Zhao, L. (2019). Chinese reverse M&As in the Netherlands: Chinese managers' trust building practices. *Chinese Management Studies, 25*(3), 69–91.

Söderberg, A, & Vaara, E. (2003). *Merging across borders.* Copenhagen: Copenhagen Business School Press.

Teerikangas, S. (2006). *Silent forces in cross-border acquisitions—An integrative perspective on post-acquisition integration* [Doctoral dissertation, Helsinki University of Technology].

Teerikangas, S. (2007). A comparative overview of the impact of cultural diversity on inter-organizational encounters. In C. Cooper & S. Finkelstein, S. (Eds.), *Advances in mergers and acquisitions.* Amsterdam: JAI Press, Vol. 6, pp. 37–76.

Teerikangas, S. (2012). Silent forces shaping the performance of cross-border acquisitions. In Faulkner, D., Teerikangas, S., & Joseph, R. (Eds.), *Handbook of mergers and acquisitions.* Oxford: Oxford University Press, pp. 517–544.

Cultural dynamics in acquisitions 249

Teerikangas, S. & Birollo, G. (2018). Leading M&As in a middle managerial role: A balancing act. In Raitis, J., Harikkala-Laihinen, R., Hassett, M., & Nummela, N. (Eds.), *Socio-cultural integration in mergers and acquisitions: The Nordic approach*. London: Palgrave Pivot Series.

Teerikangas, S., & Irrmann, O. (2016). Cultural change following international acquisitions: Co-habiting the tension between espoused and practiced cultures. *Management International Review*, 56(2), 195–226.

Teerikangas, S., & Laamanen, T. (2014). Structure first! Temporal dynamics of structural and cultural integration in cross-border acquisitions. *Advances in mergers and acquisitions*, 13, 109–152.

Teerikangas, S., & Thanos, I. C. (2018). Looking into the 'black box'—unlocking the effect of integration on acquisition performance. *European Management Journal*, 36(3), 366–380.

Teerikangas, S., Rouzies, R., & Colman, H. (2015). What actually is post-deal integration following M&A? Toward a synthesis and reconceptualization of the concept. Paper presented at the *Annual Meeting of the Academy of Management*, Vancouver.

Teerikangas, S., & Very, P. (2006). The culture-performance relationship in M&A: From yes/no to how. *British Journal of Management*, 17(1), 31–48.

Teerikangas, S., & Véry, P. (2012). Culture in mergers and acquisitions: A critical synthesis and steps forward. In Faulkner, D., Teerikangas, S., & Joseph, R. (Eds.), *Handbook of mergers & acquisitions*. Oxford: Oxford University Press, pp. 392–430.

Thomas, D., & Inkson, K. (2005). Cultivating your cultural intelligence. *Security Management*, 48(8), 30–32.

Tsoukas, H., & Chia, R. (2002). On organizational becoming. *Organization Science*, 13(5), 567–582.

Vaara, E. (1999). Cultural differences and post-merger problems: Misconceptions and cognitive simplifications. *Organisasjonsstudier*, 1(2), 59–88.

Vaara, E. (2000). Constructions of cultural differences in post-merger change processes: A sense-making perspective on Finnish-Swedish cases. *Management*, 3(3), 81–110.

Vaara, E., Sarala, R., Stahl, G., & Björkman, I. (2012). The impact of organizational and national cultural differences on social conflict and knowledge transfer in international acquisitions. *Journal of Management Studies*, 49(1), 1–27.

Vaara, E., Tienari, J., & Säntti, R. (2003). The international match: Metaphors as vehicles of social identity building in cross-border mergers. *Human Relations*, 56(4), 419–451.

Van Marrewijk A. (2016). Conflicting subcultures in mergers and acquisitions: A longitudinal study of integrating a radical internet firm into a bureaucratic telecoms firm. *British Journal of Management*, 27(2), 338–354.

Veiga, J., Lubatkin, M., Calori, R. & Very, P. (2000). Measuring organizational culture clashes: A two-nation post-hoc analysis of a cultural compatibility index. *Human Relations*, 53(4), 539–557.

Very, P., Lubatkin, M. & Calori, R. (1996). A cross-national assessment of acculturative stress in recent European mergers. *International Studies of Management and Organisation*, 26(1), 59–86.

Viegas-Pires, M. (2013) Multiple levels of culture and post M&A integration: A suggested theoretical framework. *Thunderbird International Business Review*, 55(4), 357–370.

250 *Satu Teerikangas and Melanie Hassett*

Weber, Y. (1996). Corporate cultural fit and performance in mergers and acquisitions. *Human Relations*, 49(9), 1181–1202.

Weber, Y., Shenkar, O. & Raveh, A. (1996). National and corporate fit in M&A: An explorative study. *Management Science*, 42(8), 1215–1227.

Wu, F., Hoon, L., & Yuzhu, Z. (2011). Dos and don'ts for Chinese companies investing in the United States: Lessons from Huawei and Haier. *Thunderbird International Business Review*, 53(4), 501–515.

Yang, Y., Lütge, C., & Yang, H. (2019). Organisational culture affecting post-merger integration: New insights from Chinese reverse M&As in Germany. *Review of International Business and Strategy*, 29(2), 139–154.

Yildiz, H. (2014). Not all differences are the same: Dual roles of status and cultural distance in sociocultural integration in cross-border M&As. *Journal of International Management*, 20(1), 25–37.

Zhu, H., Zhu, Q., & Ding, Z. (2020). The roles of Chinese CEOs in managing individualistic cultures in cross-border mergers and acquisitions. *Journal of Management Studies*, 57(3), 664–697.

Predictions for corporate restructuring research

David R. King

In studying acquisitions for over two decades, a consistent insight during that time is a constant reminder of how little we know about this complex, yet common phenomenon. Another insight involves gratitude to others that have also found the challenge of studying acquisitions interesting and worthwhile. I have benefited from working with others, interacting with people at conferences and other venues, and reading the research of others. In other words, I have been encouraged that my journey has not been solitary and that others continue to join their voice to the research conversations surrounding corporate restructuring.

My hope is that by capturing knowledge in this book that I will help others start further down the learning curve to be able to pursue relevant questions with better research designs, so we can advance our understanding of this important topic. Given the annual dollar value spent on acquisitions globally each year, even small improvement in acquisition outcomes would have significant social and economic benefits. To that end, this book addressed fundamental research questions:

1   How do acquisitions relate to other corporate strategy options;
2   What helps to predict acquisition performance; and
3   What are persistent acquisition research issues?

The associated sections and chapters of the book provide background and insights that can inform future research. Based on what is covered by the different contributors, I now turn my attention to areas where I think research can make advances. Below is a brief description of possible topics without a sense of priority.

First, research needs to go beyond the study of acquisitions to consider the broader topic of corporate restructuring and growth, and the different strategic options (e.g., acquisitions, alliances, divestment, and internal development) that facilitate firm goals. Research by Porrini (2004) and Chapter 1 by Shijaku, King, and Urtasun suggest that alliances can proceed and inform acquisitions. Chapter 2 by Amiri, King, and DeMarie summarizes research on divestment that often intersects with acquisitions. Further, Chapter 4 by Zhang and Clougherty suggests that FDI also

DOI: 10.4324/9781003188308-15

252 David R. King

substitutes for cross-border acquisitions. Understanding how the different strategic options for corporate restructuring interact with one another and the implications decisions to pursue different options represents an important area for research. For example, acquisitions may substitute for internal development (Heeley, King, & Covin, 2006; King, Slotegraaf & Kesner, 2008). Limited research exists on how firms use different corporate restructuring options together, but Chapter 3 by Kochura, Mirc, and Lacoste examine the intersection of acquisitions and divestiture. I am also aware of two papers that offer a guide (Achtenhagen, Brunninge, & Melin 2017; Barkema & Schijven, 2008). There is also a clear need to better understand how acquisitions and divestment interact during corporate restructuring.

Second, research needs better theory on the motives for acquisitions and then link them to performance outcomes. Existing research has largely relied on stock market measures of performance (Meglio & Risberg, 2010; King, Meglio, Gomez-Mejia, Bauer, & De Massis, 2022) that may be loosely linked to acquisition motives. Chapter 6 by Patel and King suggests a motive to reduce pollution in an industry that could be associated with avoiding additional regulation (Siegel, 2009). However, this cost avoidance may not be reflected in financial performance. There are other rational reasons for using acquisitions that may not lead to increased stock market performance. Increased use of mixed methods research using multiple measures of acquisition goals performance is needed (Cording, Christmann, & King, 2008; King et al., 2021). There is also a need to develop additional measures and use multiple measures to better reflect the complexity of studied constructs, as well as alternate explanations. For example, the influence of culture, as summarized by Teerikangas and Hassett in Chapter 10, needs to be refined. Further, significant effects of existing variables may depend on interactions or combinations, as well as the context surrounding an acquisition (Campbell, Sirmon, & Schijven, 2016; King et al., 2021). For example, family firms likely present important differences and not controlling for them can add unexpected heterogeneity (Meglio & King, 2019; King et al., 2022). There is also a need for more longitudinal research to identify relevant constructs and to better understand associated relationships. Overall, this reflects a general need for acquisition research to improve its methods, and this is covered in Chapter 9 by Molina-Sieiro.

Third, for over a decade, the majority of acquisitions have been cross-border. This opens new frontiers and complexity in acquisitions and their study. Early work focused on cultural differences. However, expectations for significant effects from research on Hofstede's dimensions have not proven significant, as shown by Stahl and Voigt (2008) and Chapter 7 by Jensen, Zámborský, and King. Expectations that cultural differences have a significant effect may relate to conflicting effects (Reus and Lamont,

Corporate restructuring research   253

2009), and Chapter 10 by Teerikangas and Hassett confirms that research also needs to recognize that culture has multiple dimensions (Ghemawat, 2001). There may also be alternate explanations, as geographic distance has been found to be a significant predictor of acquisition performance (Chakrabarti & Mitchell, 2013). Cultural dimensions of administrative (Bauer, Schriber, Degischer, & King, 2018) and economic (Chung & Luo, 2008) distance also receive less research attention. Consistent with observations above about better research designs and multiple measures of complex constructs, there is a need for cross-national studies to better understand national effects.

Fourth, there is a need to better understand acquisition experience. While simple counts of acquisition experience are not a significant predictor of stock performance, it does appear to help predict accounting performance and managerial surveys (King et al., 2021). How firms develop capabilities for acquisitions, the subject of Chapter 5 by Schriber, offers one area of focus. Others include seeing how experience between related processes of search, valuation, and so on across corporate strategic options of acquisitions, alliances, and divestment can develop capabilities if possible. Identifying limits of prior experience across different corporate strategy options or different types of acquisitions (e.g., cross-border, high-technology) is also needed.

Fifth, it is worth reinforcing that acquisition research needs better designs. Archival research that simply re-examine similar variables, because they are easy to measure, has limited utility. However, at the same time, simply examining novel variables without accounting for what existing research has examined also risks model misspecification that can contribute to spurious results (see Chapter 9). Obviously, a balance is needed, but broader samples of firms that pursue more than just acquisitions can help inform likely path dependence in firm decisions that lead to acquisitions. It is possible that a reliance on acquisitions may be a suboptimal strategy that can explain consistent observations that acquisitions (on average) do not improve acquisition performance.

Sixth, there is a need to consider additional stakeholders to acquisitions. Acquisition research predominantly takes the perspective of investors (Meglio & Risberg, 2010; King et al., 2021). However, other stakeholders can influence acquisition outcomes, and research has considered the impact of competitors (Keil et al., 2013; King & Schriber, 2016), customers (Rogan, 2014), employees (Bansal & King, 2020; Ranft & Lord, 2000), and managers (Krug, Wright, & Kroll, 2014). Still, the influence of suppliers, as well as different types of investors (e.g., institutional, short-sellers), needs to be considered by researchers (Shi, King, & Connelly, 2021). Further, I am not aware of a study that examines multiple stakeholders together, and this is a clear research need as the different interests of stakeholders likely conflict.

254 David R. King

Last but not least, the consistent evidence that acquisitions fall short of creating value suggests managerial hubris with respect to acquisitions. Essentially, every acquisition involves some level of hubris, or an expectation that an acquiring firm's manager can better use a target firm's resources. However, the value created from acquisitions often falls short of expectations. Research is needed to identify the primary sources of value leakage or value destruction. For example, average acquisition performance would increase if only "bad" acquisitions were not completed (Moeller, Schlingemann, & Stulz, 2005). Acquisitions paid for with stock (King et al., 2021) or touted as mergers of equals (Zaheer, Schomaker, & Genc, 2003) are consistently poor performers. This suggests that one way to improve acquisition performance is to improve firm governance of corporate restructuring decisions, but this also requires knowing sources of value and how to achieve them.

In closing, I am grateful to have had the good fortune of picking a relevant research topic during my doctoral program that is complex enough that it will not be easily solved. This has enabled a consistent focus for my research. My career has been based on better understanding this phenomenon, and it is bittersweet to realize that my understanding will inevitably remain incomplete as acquisitions and the firms employing them continue to evolve. However, I remain encouraged that others continue to join the study of acquisitions and related topics. To that end, I hope this book provides a worthwhile resource for future study of corporate restructuring.

References

Achtenhagen, L., Brunninge, O., & Melin, L. (2017). Patterns of dynamic growth in medium-sized companies: Beyond the dichotomy of organic versus acquired growth. *Long Range Planning*, 50(4), 457–471.

Barkema, H., & Schijven, M. (2008). Toward unlocking the full potential of acquisitions: The role of organizational restructuring. *Academy of Management Journal*, 51(4), 696–722.

Bauer, F., Schriber, S., Degischer, D., & King, D. (2018). Contextualizing speed and cross-border acquisition performance: Labor market flexibility and efficiency effects. *Journal of World Business*, 53(2), 290–301.

Bansal, A., & King, D. (2020). Communicating change following an acquisition. The *International Journal of Human Resource Management*, 1–30. https://doi.org/10.1080/09585192.2020.1803947

Campbell, J., Sirmon, D., & Schijven, M. (2016). Fuzzy logic and the market: A configurational approach to investor perceptions of acquisition announcements. *Academy of Management Journal*, 59(1), 163–187.

Chakrabarti, A., & Mitchell, W. (2013). The persistent effect of geographic distance in acquisition target selection. *Organization Science*, 24(6), 1805–1826.

Chung, C. & Luo, X. (2008). Institutional logics or agency costs: The influence of corporate governance models on business group restructuring in emerging economies, *Organization Science*, 19(5), 766–784.

Corporate restructuring research   255

Cording, M., Christmann, P., & King, D. (2008). Reducing causal ambiguity in acquisition integration: Intermediate goals as mediators of integration decisions and acquisition performance. *Academy of Management Journal*, 51(4), 744–767.

Ghemawat, P. (2001). Distance still matters. *Harvard Business Review*, 79(8), 137–147.

Heeley, M., King, D., & Covin, J. (2006). Effects of firm R&D investment and environment on acquisition likelihood. *Journal of Management Studies*, 43(7), 1513–1535.

Keil, T., Laamanen, T., & McGrath, R. (2013). Is a counterattack the best defense? Competitive dynamics through acquisitions. *Long Range Planning*, 46(3), 195–215.

King, D., Meglio, O., Gomez-Mejia, L., Bauer, F., & De Massis, A. (2022). Family Business restructuring: A review and research agenda. *Journal of Management Studies*, 59(1), 197–235.

King, D., & Schriber, S. (2016). Addressing competitive responses to acquisitions. *California Management Review*, 58(3), 109124.

King, D., Slotegraaf, R., & Kesner, I. (2008). Performance implications of firm resource interactions in the acquisition of R&D-intensive firms. *Organization Science*, 19(2), 327–340.

King, D., Wang, G., Samimi, M., & Cortes, F. (2021). A meta-analytic integration of acquisition performance prediction. *Journal of Management Studies*, 58(5), 1198–1236.

Krug, J.., Wright, P., & Kroll, M. (2014). Top management turnover following mergers and acquisitions: Solid research to date but still much to be learned. *Academy of Management Perspectives*, 28(2), 147–163.

Meglio, O., & King, D. (2019). Family businesses: Building a merger and acquisition research agenda. In Finkelstein, S., and Cooper, C. (eds), *Advances in mergers and acquisitions*, Vol 18. Bingley: Emerald Publishing, pp. 83–98.

Meglio, O., & Risberg, A. (2010). Mergers and acquisitions—Time for a methodological rejuvenation of the field? *Scandinavian Journal of Management*, 26(1), 87–95.

Moeller, S., Schlingemann, F., & Stulz, R. (2005). Wealth destruction on a massive scale? A study of acquiring-firm returns in the recent merger wave. *Journal of Finance*, 60(2), 757–782.

Porrini, P. (2004). Can a previous alliance between an acquirer and a target affect acquisition performance? *Journal of Management*, 30(4), 545–562.

Ranft, A., & Lord, M. (2000). Acquiring new knowledge: The role of retaining human capital in acquisitions of high-tech firms. *Journal of High Technology Management Research*, 11(2), 295–319.

Reus, T., & Lamont, B. (2009). The double-edged sword of cultural distance in international acquisitions. *Journal of International Business Studies*, 40(8), 1298–1316.

Rogan, M. (2014). Too close for comfort? The effect of embeddedness and competitive overlap on client relationship retention following an acquisition. *Organization Science*, 25(1), 185–203.

Shi, W., King, D., & Connelly, B. (2021). Closing the deal: Managerial response to short sellers following M&A announcement. *Journal of Business Research*, 130, 188–199.

Siegel, D. (2009). Green management matters only if it yields more green: An economic/strategic perspective. *Academy of Management Perspectives*, 23(3), 5–16.

Stahl, G., & Voigt, A. (2008). Do cultural differences matter in mergers and acquisitions? A tentative model and examination. *Organization Science*, 19(1), 160–176.

Zaheer, S., Schomaker, M., & Genc, M. (2003). Identity versus culture in mergers of equals. *European Management Journal*, 21(2), 185–191.

Index

Note: Numbers in **bold** indicate text indexed within tables and Numbers in *Italics* indicate text indexed within figures

absorption 2–3, 117–18
acculturation **160**, 230–31, 232–33
acquirer 1–5, 14, 54–62, 80, 85, 90, **101**, 104–05, 112–115, 117–18, 119–21, 128–129, 130–135, 135–140, 141–147, **142–43**, **144–45**, **146**, 147–148, 150, 154, 158–159, 161–63, 165–167, **175**, 185, 188, **196**, **197–201**, 219, 234, 235–37
acquiring firm 4, 49, 57–59, 60–61, 62, 63, 66, 68, 82, 83, 107–08, 120, 133, 136–37, **143**, 147, 177, **195–96**, 203, 218, 226, 233–34, 254
acquisition 1–6, 9–10, 13–16, 16–18, 18–21, **19**, **20**, 21–22, 26–27, 28, 30, 35, 37–40, 48–69, **51**, **52–53**, **55**, 113–14, 128–135, 136–40, 141–49, **142–43**, **144–45**, 177–78, 203, 208, 211, 215–17, 218–19, 219–21, 226–34, 239–42, 251–54; cross-border acquisition (CBA) 9–10, 76–97, **87**, **91**, **101**, 157–68, 178, 183, **195**, 226, 232–40; *see also* merger
acquisition activity/propensity 13–14, 15–17, 18, 21–22, 60, 129, 221, 225, 233; acquisition context 178, 203–08
acquisition experience 3–4, 18, **20**, 85, 93, **101**, 112, 159, 167, **195**, **197**, **199**, 253; acquisition friendliness **111**, 114–15, 115–16
acquisition integration 2–4, *2*, 9, 56–58, 60–62, 66–67, 108–09, 113–15, 116–118, 118–20, **200–01**, 225, 230, 233–34, 236–37, 242

acquisition performance 1–5, 56, 62, 65, 68, 103–05, 111–13, 128–31, 135, 141, **142**, 149, 157–59, 175, 177, 179–90, **195–201**, 220, 225–26
acquisition process 2, 4, 9, 103, 107–12, 119–22, 179, 203, 231–34, 238
acquisition program 54, **111**, 112–13, 183
acquisition paymen 3, 5, 65, 68, 115–16, 220
acquisition premium 3–4, 15, 35, 64, 141, **142**, **145**, 149, 208; prior acquisition 18, 55, **142**, **144**, **197**; related 1–4, 28, 30, 32, 36–37, 56–58, 67, 80, 105, 114, 118, 129, 131–32, 134, 138–39, 141, **142**, **144–46**, 147–48, 159, 179, 187, **196**, 203
acquisition size 4, 18, **19**, **20**, 32, **143**, **145**
acquisition speed 118–19, 179, **196**, 231
Adidas 57
Aerospatiale Matra 237
Airbnb 187
AirFrance-KLM 65
Aleris 60
Alitalia 65
alliance 1–5, 9, 13–22, **19**, **20**, 50, 57–59, 68, 120, **142**, **144**, 251–53
AT&T 60

behavioral 28, 31, 202, 213, 236

258 *Index*

capability 9–10, 13, 30, 35, 50, **51**, 61–62, 103–04, 107–22, 128–150, **142–43**, **144–45**, **199**, 253
carve-out 26, 62–64
CASA 237
causal inference 49–50, 84, 89–90, 202–04, 206, 211–13, 215, 219–20, 221
Chief Executive Officer (CEO) 26, 29–30, 34, 38, 58, 149, 167, **197–98**, 206, 210, 236
change 3–4, 31–33, 48, 49, **51**, **53**, 54–58, 61, 62–64, 78–79, 89, 103–04, 107, 109–10, 115, 117–21, 129, 136–38, **142**, 147, 178, 181–83, 207, 214–17, 225, 230–35, 237–242
chief executive officer (CEO) *see* top management team
Cisco 68
civil law 163, **175**
collider 204–05, 218–20
common law 163, 166–67, **175**
complement 3, 10, 16, 26, 35, 39, 48, 54, 67, 76–80, 94–95, 97, 113, **196**, 227
completion 1–2, 50–54
confound 36, **104**, 180, 189, 202–09, 218–221
construct (measurement, clarity, definition) 18, 27, 76–78, 83–85, 89–90, 92–93, 103, 129, 148, 157, 159–60, **160**, 161–63, 180–83, 185–90, 228–29, 242, 252–53
constructionist 227
corporate restructuring 1, 5–6, 10, 26–28, 33, 36–40, 48–54, **51–53**, 66, 68–69, 251–54
cross-border acquisition (CBA) *see* acquisition
culture 3–4, 64, 77, 105, 107–08, 116, 157–63, 165–68, **175**, 178, **195–96**, **200**, 225–42, **239**, 252–53

DASA 237
defier 215
Dell 60
DirecTV 60
Diversification 4, 26, 29–30, 32, 36, 48, 61, 65, 129, 131, **142**
Divestiture 1–2, 5, 9–10, 26–40, *28*, 48–69, **51–53**, **55**, 188, **198–99**,

251–53 *see also* carve out, sell-off, spin-off, and sequence
divestment *see* divestiture
due diligence 3, 5, 189, 235, 237

EADS 236–38
Electrolux 56
Embraco 62
Endogeneity 10, 78, 96, 158, 178, 202–21
Environment 10, 26, 28, 28–29, 31, 35–36, 38, 48, **51**, **53**, 58, 60, 62–63, 104–05, 107–12, 114–21, 126–30, 132–35, 136–37, 139–40, **143**, 147–49, 155–56, 159, 188–89, 207, 233, 236
event window (CAR) *see* stock market reaction
evolutionary 50, **51**, 109
exclusion restriction 203, 205, 214, 216, 221
exogeneity 78, 96, 207, 212, 214, 216, 221
experience *see* acquisition
exploitation 14–15, 21–22
exploration 13–16, 18, **19**, **20**, 21–22

failure 9, 13, 14–15, 18, 21–22, 32, 49, 56–58, 63–64, 66, 68, 115, 179, 229
family firm 10, 29, 37, 186, 188, 252
FedEx 59
Foreign direct investment 9, 38, 76, 78, 80–81, 82–85, 96–97, **101**, 251–52

General Electric (GE) 26
General Motors (GM) 26
Geographic distance **142**, **145**, 159; *see also* culture
greenfield investment 10, 58, 76–82, 83–89, **87**, 90–97, **91**, **101**
growth 18, *28*, 28–29, 36, 38, 48, 56, 60, 65–67, 85, **87**, **91**, 93, **101**, **175**, 251

Hachette 61–62
home country 36–37, 105, 158, 161–68, **162**, *164*, **174**, **175–76**, **200**, 228, 236 *see also* institution
host (target) country 10, 76–77, 79–82, 94–96, 105, 158, 161–163, **162**, 163–165, *164*, 166–68, **175–76**, **200**, 228, 237

Index 259

industry 4, 22, 28–29, 32, 48, 63, 82–86, **87–88**, 88–93, **91–92**, 101, 121, 129–31, 137–40, **143**, 145–46, 147, **195**, **198**, 226, 252 *see also* institution
information asymmetry 28, 30, 32, 34, 36, 61, **104**, **197**
Ingenico 59–60
Ingram 61
initial public offering (IPO) 63
innovation 3, *28*, 36, 38, 48, 56, 62, 64, 103, **104**, 120, 128–29, **160**, **162**, 180–81
institution 5, 28–29, 34, 59, 77, 80, 109, 118, 130, 132, 158–59, 165–68, **174**, **176**, 185, **200–01**, 236
instrumental variable 207–08, 213–17, 218, 220–21
integration *see* acquisition, absorption, preservation and symbiosis

learning 3–4, 14, *28*, 35, 38–39, 50, **51**, 54, 66, 85, 109–10, 158, 163, **174**, 238

marketing 116
mediator **199**, 204, 220
Merck 56
Merger 3–4, 10, 78–84, 86, **87**, 89–90, **91**, 92–96
merger and acquisition (M&A) *see* acquisition
meta-analysis 3–5, 157, 167–68, 220
moderator 35, 39, 129
motive 4, 13, 15, 22, 39, 57, 65, 68, 77, 80, 103, 129, 252

NDS 68
Network 4–5, 13, 39, **51**, 59
Nidec 62
Nike 57
Novelis 60

OECD 136–37, 155, 159, **162**, 163–65, *164*, **174**, 175
omitted variable 78, 89, 203–05, 207–08, 218–19
Opel 26
operations (firm) 29–32, 34, 36–37, 56, 58, 63, 67–68, 76, 81–82, 96, 104, 128–35, 149
organizational learning *see* learning

patent 17–18, **19**, **20**, **104**, 107, 116, 128, 133, 136–37, 139–40, **142**, 150, 155, **160**, 180–81
payment *see* acquisition
performance *see* acquisition
Permira 68
Perseus 61–62
policy *see* merger
pollution 104–05, 128–35, 136–40, 141–148, **144**, 150
portfolio 9–10, 13, *28*, 31–33, 38, 48–50, 54, 60–61, 66–69, 76, 135
predictive modeling 105, 157, 163–66, **164**, 168
premium *see* acquisition
preservation 2, 117–18
process *see* acquisition and sequence
program *see* acquisition

Qualtrics 65, 68

realist 227, 231, **239**, 240
Reebok 57
related *see* acquisition
research and development (R&D) 14–16, 16–17, 18, 36, 58, 61, 85, **88**, 92, **101**, **104**, 133, 139, 210
resources 3–5, 9, 13–16, 18, **19–20**, 21–22, *28*, 29–31, 35, 39, 48–50, **51–53**, 55, 59–62, 65, 66–68, 81, 90, 103–04, 107, 109–10, 113–114, 115, 116–20, 128–30, 133–35, 141, 147–50, 158, **174**, 185, 254
return on assets (ROA) **143**, **145**, **160**

sample 16, 22, 27, 83, 135–37, 158–59, 161, 163, 183, 206; bias 218–19; matching 209–11; rebalancing 208; weighting 211–12
SAP 65
selection 1, *2*, 5, 9, 32, **51**, 208, 213, 218–19; research method 159
sell-off 26–27, 32–33, 39, 54, 62–63
sequence *28*, 48–50, **51–52**, 54–55, 55, 59–62, 64, 66–69
shareholder 4, 30, 32, 34, 37, 54, 66, 114, 148–49, 166, 177, 184–85, 188–89, **195**, **197**, **201**, 220
size (relative size) *see* acquisition
speed *see* acquisition
spin-off 26–27, 30, 32–36, 54, 60, 62–63, 65, 68

260 *Index*

stakeholder 4, 128, 130, 132, 149, 177, 185, 188–89, **196**, 253
stock market reaction (CAR) 3, 138, 143, **144**, **146**, 147, 154, **160**, **162**, *164*, 165, 180, 184–86, **196–98**, 203, 218
strategy: acquisition 10, 237; corporate 3, 5, 9, 49, 54, 56, 202, 251, 253
substitute 10, 77–80, 82, 94–97, 251–52
Suez 60
survey 5, 103, **104**, 160–62, **162**, 165, 167, 183, 253
sustainability 128–29, 149
symbiosis 2, 117–18
synergy 48, 59, 119, 133–34, **199**, 228

target firm 2–3, 15, 35, 50, 55–66, **55**, 66–68, 80–81, 83, 85, 90, 93–94, **101**, 104–05, 113–17, 128–31, 132–35, 136–39, 140–43, **142–43**, **144–46**, 147–50, 159, 161, 175, 185–86, 188, **197**, **201**, 234, 236–37, 254 *see also* host (target) country
Telefonica 63
Terra 63
Tobin's Q 38, **104**, **160**, 184, **201**
top management team (TMT) 38, 115, 185, 188, 233; CEO 26, 29–30, 34, 38, 58, 149, 167, **197–98**, 206, 210, 236
training 237–38
transaction cost economics (TCE) 9, 13–14, 18, 21–22, 28, 29, 35–36, 50, **52**, 81, 158, **174**

Uber 187

Veolia 60
VMware 60

Withings 64
Worldline 59

Printed in the United States
by Baker & Taylor Publisher Services